www.nakedguides.co.uk

Tel: 01225 463983

Publishers: Steve Faragher, Richard Jones
Additional research, editing and writing: Richard Jones
Design/cover artwork: Joe Burt
Maps/street art: Trevor Wyatt
Production editor: Anne Smith

ISBN: 0-9544177-6-3

2nd Edition
Copyright Tangent Books Ltd 2006
All rights reserved

The first moral right of the authors has been asserted

First published in Great Britain in 2004 by
Naked Guides Ltd.
Naked Guides is an imprint of Tangent Books Ltd,
3 Monmouth Place, Bath BA1 2AT
www.tangentbooks.com

Printed by Gutenberg Press.

Tangent Books is a member of the Bristol Books and Publishers group
www.bristolpublishers.co.uk

THE NAKED GUIDE TO
BRISTOL

By Gil Gillespie

THANKS TO...

Contributors: Nick Law, Ian Bone, Mark Fletcher, John Hudson, Leonie Campbell-King,
Caitlin Telfer, Mena Telfer, Mike Goldsmith, Will Scott, Gideon Kibblewhite,
Claire Morgan, Steve Faragher, Anne Smith, Joe Burt, Trevor Wyatt, Johnny Ball
Proofing and subbing: Anne Smith
Marketing and sales: Claire Morgan, 01225 463983
Inspiration: Steve Faragher, Gideon Kibblewhite

Photography: Anne Smith. Other pictures by Richard Jones, Joe Burt, Trevor Wyatt,
Maggie Telfer and Kate McDonnell

Picture credits: Arnolfini, p4 (Jamie Woodley); drawing of Medieval Bristol, p81 (courtesy of Memories,
St Nicholas Market); Brunel, p104 (Institute of Civil Engineers); Casualty, p104, p113 (courtesy BBC Press);
David Neilson, p105 (courtesy ITV Press); Teachers, p105 (courtesy C4 Press); Jane Couch, p109 (Nigel
Turner); Roger Cook and Roger Greenaway, p108, p109 (courtesy Charlie Dobson); Adam Hart-Davis,
p110 (Chris Rydlewski/Andy Green); Ian Holloway, p112 (Empics); Precious McKenzie, p115 (courtesy
Precious McKenzie); Wallace & Gromit, p116 (Aardman Animations Ltd/Wallace and Gromit Ltd 1989);
Tony Robinson, p118 (courtesy C4 Press); Babyhead, p1, p152 (Robin Muscat); Full Cycle, p155, DJ Die,
p156, MC Dynamite, p160, Krust, p164 (courtesy Heavyweight Management/Alexis Maryon); Dubrovnik,
p157 (www.sealstudio.com); John Parish, p166 (Ralph Enard); Hazel Winter, p170 (Jacqueline Glynn);
Experimental Pop Band, p170 (Sebastian Mayer); At-Bristol, p183 (courtesy At-Bristol); ss Great Britain,
p192 (ss Great Britain Trust, Mandy Reynolds). Graffiti street art pictures (p123-136): Anne Smith, Jack
(www.bristolgraffiti.com), Sarah Connolly, Ikue Uyama (relaxmax), Cheba, Iyers.

Copyright: Some of the photographs included in *The Naked Guide To Bristol* are from the authors' and
contributors' private collections. We have made every effort to trace the owners of photographs used in
the book. If we have used a photograph without permission, we apologise. Contact us on 01225 463983.

Cover artwork: Joe Burt. Pictures credits for images used on cover: Clifton Suspension Bridge (Anne
Smith), Ian Holloway (Empics), Onallee and Roni Size (courtesy Heavyweight Management/Alexis
Maryon), Massive Attack (Mark Simmons), Gromit (Aardman Animations Ltd/Wallace and Gromit Ltd
1989), Brunel (Institute of Civil Engineers).

Gil Gillespie would like to dedicate this book to the beautiful Lulu and little Mister Joe Mancini Addison
Gillespie, even though he's been absolutely no help whatsoever. Immeasurable gratitude to Mum, Dad,
Meriel, Rhian, Phil Parkinson, Borja, Megan, Morgan and the Pant and Merthyr three. Significant nods also
go out in the direction of Gary Tipp, Dav Ludford and all the never-say-die *Total Football* boys. Additional
thanks to Cris Warren, Dan Slingsby, Borders bookshop and *The Guardian* for being rungs on the ladder
of recognition. Cheers just for being around to Patrick Duff, Dodge Holme, the Martindales, Corrina
Rowell, Moti Gokulsing, Matt and Aime, Devron, and Neil Whitcombe. Along the way I also wouldn't have
made it without Antonio Gramsci, Franco Baresi, Johnny Owen, the Moonlight Mile, Roberto Mancini,
Michael Foot, Fidel Castro, Hugo Chavez, Cutshaw (the astronaut), AC Milan 4 Barcelona 0, Giancarlo
Gallivoti, Gabriel Marcotti, atheists everywhere, Stan Laurel and Oliver Hardy, David Bowie, Bobby
Gillespie, Conor Oburst, LCD Soundsystem, the World Cup winning Azzurri '06 squad and about one
million others whose names I can't remember right now.

Richard Jones would like to thank Maggie, Caitlin and Mena. Leonie and the girls for their contribution
to Children's Bristol, all the contributors for their patience, but most of all Gil for his vision of Bristol.

Also thanks to: Precious McKenzie, Charlie Dobson, John Parish, Steve Symons, Robin Muscat, Catherine
Mason at Broadcast Books, John and Angela Sansom of Redcliffe Press, Carolyn Jones, Charly Paige,
Beast, Kate Pollard, Francine Russell, Dav Ludford and Rono Kahumbu Turner.

WELCOME

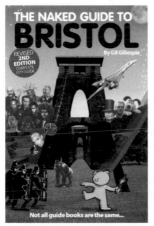

Not all guide books are the same...

Hello and welcome to the second edition of *The Naked Guide To Bristol*. Almost two years have passed since the first book hit the streets and the response, both in terms of feedback and sales, has been overwhelming. Thanks. For this new edition, we have retained the original Naked Guide template and packed in even more straight-talking, off-beat and occasionally off-the-wall observations. We've also added a handful of new features, here and there, just for the hell of it, and updated information where necessary. The music chapter has been extensively re-written to accommodate the recent explosion of genuinely exciting new bands currently perched on the edge of something very significant indeed. And we have, of course, kept an eye on the ever-multiplying number of new bars and restaurants that seem to spring up from nowhere every time you turn a corner. Well, that's just about it. Please turn the page in order to commence the reading process.

Gil Gillespie

CONTRIBUTE TO THE NAKED GUIDE TO BRISTOL

We have done our best to check all addresses, telephone numbers and other contact details, but these details often change. If you would like to update a contact, add your comment to a listing, or tell us about somewhere new, go to **www.nakedguides.co.uk** or call us on **01225 463983**

ABOUT THE AUTHORS

Gil Gillespie first started going out in Bristol when he was 14 and has enjoyed or endured many thousands of evenings in the pubs, bars, restaurants and clubs of the city ever since. Remarkably, he has also found the time to carve out a career as one of the most outstanding and outspoken magazine writers in the country and has sounded off about subjects including music, football, television, movies, technology, politics and culture for magazines such as *Total Football, Venue, Select, Football Italia, Big Issue, .net Directory, Connect, Focus* and *Comedy Review*. He lives in Bishopston with his long-term girlfriend Lucy and their two-year-old son Joe.

Richard Jones first came to the public's attention as the fresh-faced pop page editor of the previously unhappening *Bristol Evening Post*. From here, he introduced the city to exciting new beat combos such as Massive Attack and Smith & Mighty and was one of the first to document the arrival of the so-called Bristol sound. It wasn't long before he was headhunted by Future Publishing and, despite being a lifelong Rovers fan, offered a dream appointment as the editor of *Total Football* magazine. He now runs his own publishing company. His passions include roots reggae (1973-1985) and bemoaning the poor standard of night-time recreational facilities south of the river. He lives in Totterdown with his partner Maggie and their two children Caitlin and Mena.

Area Map

INDEX OF PLACES WITHIN AREAS

CONTENTS

AREA GUIDE P2 From Christmas steps to Picton street, discover the city.

UP CLOSE P80 Go under the skin of Bristol and discover what makes it tick.

LISTINGS P200 Find out where to party, shop, drink and eat.

BS1 The Centre and Old Bristol

Step back in history or step into a theme bar.
The choice is yours in Bristol's Old Town

E arthquakes, floods, riots, slavery, bandits, bombs and the most severe traffic congestion anywhere outside London. The square miles that make up Bristol's heartland have seen it all since their Saxon beginnings. Little pieces of history lurk in every corner...

THE CENTRE

The Centre (so named because it used to be the old tram centre) was once a jumble of concrete and burger bars clustered around the landmark Bristol Hippodrome. The Hippodrome was built by Oswald Stoll in 1912 and is one of the largest stages in England outside of the West End. Cary Grant worked there before he joined a travelling troupe and went to America to seek his fortune. Years ago, the Hippodrome used to have an illuminated board on the roof that displayed messages. So it was traditional to arrange for your Uncle Bill to be on the Centre while 'Happy Birthday Uncle Bill' was displayed on top of the Hippodrome. Oh, for the simple pleasures...

The Centre is now a semi-pedestrianised playground, complete with cobbles, sculptures and a collection of not-very-convincing fountains. Even the Lord Mayor described these dribbling aqueducts as being: 'Like a bunch of old men peeing.' And while we're on the subject of peeing, the notorious cab queue on St Augustine's Parade should be avoided at all costs.

Past Notes

▶ **1140 Building of St Augustine's Abbey, later to become Bristol Cathedral.**

▶ **1239 River Frome diverted to increase trade at the port.**

▶ **1654 Destruction of Bristol Castle by Cromwell.**

▶ **1702 Queen Square built.**

▶ **1831 Riots in Queen Square. Mansion House and Customs House destroyed.**

■ The Bristol Hippodrome, designed by Oswald Stoll in 1912, is now the natural home for big musicals and pantomimes starring Jim Davidson.

■ John Cabot statue outside the Arnolfini. He sailed Bristol ship The Matthew to Newfoundland in 1497.

The Centre, as you see it today, is one of the most controversial developments in Bristol's recent history. Until 1892, the River Frome flowed through the Centre and into the Floating Harbour. It still does, but the Centre was built over it. The City Council decided to redevelop the Centre for the millennium and considered bold plans to re-open the Frome and ban cars. Instead, they opted to redirect traffic around the Centre, making it a car-snarled bottleneck. Several pedestrians were knocked over by cars and buses after the redevelopment because the traffic came from the opposite direction from before and it's not entirely clear where the pedestrian bit ends and the road starts. The fountains, which dribble so unconvincingly, are supposed to provide a cascade of water dancing in coloured lights. Two years after they were installed, the City Council claimed that the constructors had still not provided the software package to create this effect. The large 'ornament' in the middle is symbolic of Bristol's maritime history. Obviously.

The best thing about the Centre is the excellent Falafel King van which is parked up near the Harbourside most evenings and is a favourite snack haunt of clubbers.

Naked Truth

Edmund Blanket
❝The tomb of linen merchant Edmund Blanket, the 'inventor' of the blanket, who died in 1371 lays in St Stephen's Church, St Stephen's Street. The church has Merchant Venturer connections and a good cafe for rolls, soup, tea and cake.❞

QUICK PINT?
Try the **White Lion** on the Centre. Mind the steps to the toilet!

THE HARBOURSIDE

Fountains and dickheads apart, the whole Harbourside has been transformed in recent years as part of the area's massive regeneration programme. The Harbourside is certainly a whole lot better than it used to be – and you'd have a right to expect that because the 11-acre redevelopment will eventually cost more than £450 million. The £97 million At-Bristol showpiece is already the main attraction in the tourist brochures (see Children's Bristol p182). But it wasn't an immediate financial success and had to ask the City Council for a £500,000 sub in 2003, so let's not forget about the other places that have propped up the Harbourside for so long.

Five places...
Top take-aways in BS1

❶ Lamb stew and mash from **Portuguese Taste** stall in St Nicholas Market.

❷ Curry with watercress bhaji from **Spice Up Your Life** in St Nick's Market.

❸ Falafels from **Yorm Adani's Falafel King** van on the Centre.

❹ Fish and chips from **Pellegrino's** at the bottom of Christmas Steps.

❺ Tagine from **Al Madina** in St Nick's Market.

■ Once a working port, the Harbourside in the centre of Bristol now houses pleasure boats and bars.

3

There are those old favourites, the Watershed, Architecture Centre, YHA and the refurbished Arnolfini which are linked by the 'ear-trumpeted' Pero's Bridge. Designed by Irish artist, Eilis O'Connell, the bridge is named after a slave who was brought to Bristol from Nevis Island in the 17th Century. If it's heritage you're after, the ss Great Britain, The Matthew, and the Industrial Museum (closed from Sep 2006 for a £10 million revamp) will plunge you deep into the depths of Bristol's maritime past. If this doesn't satisfy your lust for the sea, try a guided tour offered by the Bristol Ferry Boat Company and Bristol Packet.

BITE TO EAT?

The Watershed has an extensive menu, a well-stocked bar and it's kid friendly. It is still one of the coolest places in town.

■ Pero's Bridge is named after the slave Pero who was the personal servant of John Pinney at his home in Great George Street.

The Harbourside is one of the best things about Bristol, not so much for the corporate regeneration, nor the profusion of theme bars and clubs, but because it's a lovely place to stroll around the water. On warm evenings, drinking outside the Arnolfini is still the venue of choice for Bristol's budding bohemians and artists.

CORN STREET

The rebirth of a city was never going to work on the strength of a few flashy multimedia projects alone. It's the sudden explosion in the centre's nightlife that has really put the spring in its heels. Now dizzy with pseudo-sophisticated style-bars, Corn Street used to be the place where most of the city's business dealings were conducted before the Corn Exchange was built. Transactions were carried out on four flat-topped bronze pillars called the nails. The bronze pillars still stand in Corn Street today and are the origin of the phrase 'to pay on the nail'. Bath, and

■ After a major refit, the Arnolfini is now up and running again. The perfect spot for some summer evening drinking by the water.

Eddie Cochran's death

☀ Eddie Cochran played his last ever show at the Bristol Hippodrome. And when the Ford Consul taxi carrying the rebel rocker slammed into a lamp post at Rowden Hill on 17 April 1960, Chippenham got its one and only rock 'n' roll story.

One of the most defiant young voices of the 1950s, Cochran was famous for anti-establishment classics such as *Summertime Blues, C'mon Everybody* and, most brilliantly,

the snarling proto-punk burn-up *Something Else*. He was in Bristol with Gene Vincent for a week-long rock 'n' roll extravaganza at the Bristol Hippodrome. On the last night of their residence, the two legendary greaseballs and Cochran's squeeze, Sharon Sheeley, made the fatal decision to get a cab up to Heathrow instead of taking the late train. Vincent and Sheeley survived the crash on the A4, but sadly Eddie Cochran died later in a Bath hospital. Chippenham has been etched forever on his soul.

some other towns with nails, also claim ownership of this phrase. Two of the nails on Corn Street are Elizabethan (1594). The others date from 1625 and 1631.

More recent history can be found on Broad Street, home to the Thistle Hotel which has never lived down the day in 1964 when it refused entry to The Rolling Stones because they weren't wearing jackets and ties. 'I realised the young gentleman was something of a celebrity,' said headwaiter Dick Court of Mick Jagger, 'but I would feel compelled to refuse anyone – even a king – if he did not dress correctly'. Mick and the boys probably headed off to King Street, an ancient pub-strewn badlands with many a story to tell.

> ### Naked Truth
> **The Redcliffe Stocks**
> 66 The last use of the public stocks on Redcliffe Hill was in 1826 when two men were put in the stocks for two hours for holding a drunken party in a nearby churchyard. 99

■ The Edward Everard printers in Broad Street: the tiled facade was inspired by William Morris's Arts and Crafts movement.

QUICK PINT?
Horts City Tavern in Broad Street does a nice drop of real ale.

ST NICHOLAS MARKET

St Nick's Market dates back to 1743 and looks even older. It is divided into three parts – Exchange Hall, Glass Arcade and Covered Market. You'll find vegetables, flowers, Beast's Bristol T-shirts, excellent take-away food, vintage clothes, jewellery, second-hand books, crockery, sweets, a milliner, many cafes, old prints, a computer repair unit and a resident psychic. The market is undergoing a resurgence – particularly for food. The Spice Up Your Life curry cafe in All Saints Lane is outstanding, the Moroccan Al Madinha does tasty tagines, and the selection of lamb or pork stew, chicken piri-piri and other delights served up with a helping of mashed potato at the Portuguese Taste stall is one of the best value meals in Bristol.

The market was originally built to get traders off the cluttered streets and has been added to over the years. Its last renovation in 2003 cost more than £300,000.

■ St Nicholas Market off Corn Street has stalls selling delicious Indian, Italian, Portuguese and Caribbean food.

KING STREET

King Street runs parallel to Baldwin Street, next to Queen Square. It's now Bristol's theatreland but once led down to the thriving docks at Welsh Back. The Llandoger Trow pub dates from 1664 and used to be the sort of ★ **Turn to p8**

A TOUR OF OLD BRISTOL

THE MEDIEVAL CITY REVEALED

1. St Nicholas Church, St Nicholas Street
Site of an odd annual ceremony in which school girls pay homage to their 17th Century male benefactor. The pupils from Red Maids School hold a service in front of an effigy of John Whitson in the church's medieval crypt. Whitson, merchant, Mayor and Member of Parliament for Bristol, died in 1629 after falling off his horse. He bequeathed cash for a hospital for '40 poor women children' to be 'apparelled in Red Cloth'.

2. Victoria Fountain, St Nicholas Street
Designed by the Coalbrookdale Iron Company of Shropshire in 1859 to commemorate Queen Victoria's 40th birthday.

3. Veiled Lady, St Nicholas Street
If you face the Elephant pub and look at the shop to the right, you'll spot a row of four figures on the wall. The second from the right appears to have no face. In fact, this is the Veiled Lady. Nobody knows who she is or what she signifies.

4. Corn Exchange and nails, Corn Street
John Woods designed the Palladian-fronted Corn Exchange in 1743, when the corn trade was at its height. The bronze pillars outside are the nails. Traders did business over the nails before the Corn Exchange was built. When the deal was done, the merchants handed over their groats and guineas and literally 'paid on the nail.'

5. Commercial Rooms, Corn St
It was in the Commercial Rooms that the merchants flexed their political muscle. In 1811, John McAdam (who invented Tarmac) became the first president of the Commercial Rooms. The three statues outside represent the City, Commerce and Navigation; the relief over the door shows Britannia with Neptune and Minerva receiving tributes.

6. Lloyds Bank, Corn Street
Opposite the Corn Exchange, the bank was built in 1857 and is based on the Library of St Mark's in Venice. It is the best example in Bristol of the Victorian High Renaissance style. Check out the frieze on the wall. It is believed that the bank was on the site of the Bush Inn as portrayed by Charles Dickens in *The Pickwick Papers*.

7. All Saints Church, Corn Street
One of three churches at the crossroads of the Medieval city. There has been a church here since 1066. The tower and cupular were built between 1712 and 1717. All Saints is now a Diocesan Education and Resource Centre and is not usually open to the public. The church houses a monument to Bristol slave trader Edward Colston, sculpted by Rysbrack, who did the William lll statue in Queen Square.

8. Christ Church, Broad Street
The original Christ Church St Ewan was first mentioned in the 12th Century, but the current one was built in 1790 by William Paty. The church is best known for its clock (Henry Williams, 1883) where two quarterjacks dating from 1728 strike the bells every 15 minutes.

9. High Cross
The site of the original Medieval High Cross. A replica of the High Cross now sits in Berkeley Square, off Park Street (see History, p82).

10. Old Guildhall, Small Street
This was the site of one of Judge Jeffreys' Bloody Assizes, held after the Monmouth rebellion of 1685. Six people were hanged and Judge Jeffreys called the Bristol rebels 'mere sons of dunghills'.

11. Edward Everard Building, Broad Street
The former Edward Everard building is a burst of tiled Art Nouveau colour and oddity. The facade of Carrera marbleware was inspired by the William Morris arts and crafts revival.

A TOUR OF OLD BRISTOL
THE MEDIEVAL CITY REVEALED...

It was built in 1900-1901 to house the works of Edward Everard. Figures on the front are of Gutenburg, who invented a printing process in the 15th Century, and Morris, who in the 19th Century helped to revive fine printing.

12. St John The Baptist, Tower Lane
The church of St John the Baptist or St John on the Wall incorporates the only surviving Medieval gateway on the city walls. The existing church dates back to the 14th Century. Inside, there's an Upper Church and a Crypt. The figures on the outside wall are Brennus and Belinus, legendary founders of Bristol. The church is no longer used for regular services and is part of the Churches Conservation Trust.

13. St John's Conduit, Nelson Street
On the other side of the gate is St John's Conduit, a 14th Century water supply which carried water from Brandon Hill to a Carmelite friary. The parishioners of St John's were allowed to use the overflow from the system. For a short time in World War Two, this was the only water supply for the city centre.

14. St Stephen's Church, St Stephen's Street
The magnificent 152-foot Gothic perpendicular tower dates back to 1470. It has been restored three times following storm damage in 1703, 1914 and 1970. Sadly the view of the tower is obscured by large, modern buildings.

7

place you went to if you were fond of wearing eye patches and carrying parrots on your shoulder. Originally, the pub occupied one of five buildings on the current site and was built on marshland that covered the area between the Centre, Welsh Back and Queen Square.

The pub's odd name comes from Captain Hawkins who retired to run it after sailing a trow – a flat-bottomed sailing barge – between South Wales and Bristol. The Llandoger part comes from Llandogo, a village on the Wye, perhaps Hawkins' home. Robert Louis Stevenson apparently used to drink there and it's also likely that Edward Teach of Redcliffe (aka Blackbeard) may have been a regular when he wasn't pirating. Certainly, Woodes Rogers, the privateer, explorer and colonial governor who lived in Queen Square, popped in for a quick grog. There were a network of tunnels leading to the waterfront that would have been used by smugglers, or by customers fleeing the press gangs. The remains of one tunnel were found but destroyed during refurbishment in 1962. Legend has it that the original pub's ceiling was painted with scantily-clad women but no evidence of this has been found.

BITE TO EAT?

Renato's in King Street is a legendary Italian restaurant much loved by the theatre crowd.

■ From pirates to revellers, King Street has a long history of boozing. And what a spot for it...

King Street is also home to the Theatre Royal and the Bristol Old Vic. The Theatre Royal was opened on 30 May 1766 and survived plans in World War Two to turn it into a fruit warehouse. In 1946, the Old Vic Theatre Company made its home and the entire theatre complex is now known as the Old Vic, encompassing the Theatre Royal and

■ The impressive Queen Square is home to this famous statue of William III.

On the streets of Bristol...

1. **Johnny Ball Lane:** Not, as most people think, a misplaced homage to Zoe's dad. This dodgy looking alleyway near Christmas Steps is actually named after an 18th-Century local character of the same name.

2. **Nelson Street:** Found itself the subject of a campaign by *Venue* magazine who wanted it restored to its original medieval name: Gropecunt Lane.

3. **Pitch and Pay Lane:** Used as a line of segregation between the infected city and the countryside during the Black Plague. Villagers threw their produce over to the townsfolk who threw back their coins in payment.

4. **Wade Street:** Named after an extremely unpopular bloke called Nathaniel Wade who was a conspirator with the Duke of Monmouth in the rebellion of 1685.

5. **There and Back Again Lane:** Appropriately blunt name for the pointless little cul-de-sac opposite Pizza Express just off Park Street. Also the title of a Bristol-based Sarah Records compilation album featuring such luminaries as the Field Mice and the Sea Urchins.

the New Vic Studio. It is the oldest continuously working theatre in England and one of the first theatres to be based on a horseshoe-shaped auditorium.

King Street also has a rich musical heritage. Not only is it home to legendary jazz venue The Old Duke but the old Granary nightclub used to attract names such as Muddy Waters, Thin Lizzy and Led Zeppelin. It also had the worst toilets this side of Glastonbury – dimly lit and wet, with a door that stuck.

While King Street has hardly changed since its ooh-ar-Jim-lad days, Welsh Back now boasts a raft of new hotels, bars and restaurants.

Naked Truth

The Three Kings

❝The Chapel of the Three Kings of Cologne at the top of Christmas Steps is so called because the Three Wise Men of the Bible are said to all be buried at Cologne Cathedral in Germany.❞

Step out of the stylish Brigstow Hotel opposite the Glass Boat restaurant and stroll along the cobbles until you get to Aqua and the Spyglass barbecue and grill. Now take a right turn and walk through the restored and now traffic-free Queen Square. Check out the equestrian bronze statue by Rysbrack of William III, which dates from the 1730s. During World War Two, it was removed for safety to Badminton Park, home of the Duke of Beaufort. It was replaced in the Square after repairs in 1948. Head through the gap in the buildings and you'll come face to face with hip dockside eateries Riverstation, Severnshed and the award-winning Mud Dock Cafe or the still-floating Thekla nightclub. The Thekla has a glorious past. Ki Longfellow-Stanshall and her surrealist performer husband Viv Stanshall (of Bonzo Dog Doo Dah Band and Sir Henry Rawlinson fame) found the German-built boat in a dockyard in Sunderland.

Ki restored her and sailed her round Britain to Bristol with a rookie crew and no insurance. The Thekla (which had been renamed the Old Profanity Showboat) was opened in 1983 as a music venue. In December 1985, the couple staged the English comic opera *Stinkfoot* on board the Thekla. This truly remarkable piece of theatre was described by *Evening Post* theatre critic, the late David Harrison, as: 'a wondrous collection of bizarre characters, eccentric ideas, and at least one top ten contender among

QUICK PINT?
Mr Wolf's in St Stephens Street is a lively bar with music and noodles.

Five places...
To go if you're loaded

❶ **Alfred Chillcott & Co. jewellers,** Park Street.

❷ **Hotel du Vin**, Lewins Mead.

❸ **Guilgert's Handmade Chocolates**, Leonard Lane.

❹ **Crystal Cars** (chauffeur driven), Stillhouse Lane.

❺ **Champagne & Cocktail Bar, Goldbrick House,** Park Street.

■ This is Brennus, allegedly the co-founder of Bristol. His brother Belinus is on the other side of the St John's Arch, the only remaining Medieval gateway to the city.

the songs'. Stanshall's daughter Sydney promoted at the Thekla into the 1990s. Viv Stanshall died in a fire at his London home in 1995 and the rest of the family now live in America. The Thekla remains a cutting-edge music venue.

ST THOMAS

The area on the other side of Bristol Bridge from Baldwin Street has long been a barren collection of half-finished developments, corner shops, billboards and bathroom showrooms. Since the 1990s, the old dockside warehouses have been developed into (even more) posh apartments. The old Courage Brewery that looks over the Floating Harbour to Castle Park now houses 38 apartments and one- and two-bedroom flats – the 'prem lofts' would set you back about £500,000 when they went on the market in 2004, but a one-bed apartment was a mere £170,000. Local CAMRA real ale activists from the *Pints West* publication suggested the site be converted into a museum and visitor centre celebrating the tradition of beer-making in the city. The Council decided flats were a better idea.

> **BITE TO EAT?**
> **Riverstation, Mud Dock** and **Severnshed** in The Grove bring trendy dining to the dockside.

■ St Mary Redcliffe Church looks so good, the city planners decided to build a dual carriageway around it.

There are several decent pubs in St Thomas. The Shakespeare (78 Victoria Street) claims to be one of the oldest (built in 1636) and The Fleece and Firkin (12 St Thomas Street) has been one of Bristol's leading live music venues since the early 1980s. The Seven Stars next door to The Fleece was the setting for a series of hearings held by anti-slaver Thomas Clarkson in 1787 that helped lead to the abolition of slavery. St Thomas is also home to the fantastic Kin Yip Hon Chinese supermarket (16a St Thomas Street) which is next door to the highly-rated Dynasty restaurant (see Listings, p200).

■ The famous Thekla was brought to Bristol in 1983 by Ki Longfellow-Stanshall.

REDCLIFFE

Redcliffe now comprises a towerblock development, St Mary Redcliffe Church, a couple of hotels, three pubs, a school and traffic-snarled dual carriageways. The church was effectively put in the middle of a roundabout, flanked on all sides by major roads, as part of the dreadful outer circuit scheme of the early 1970s (see BS3, p36). In the Middle Ages, Redcliffe was outside the city walls and there was great rivalry with the port of Bristol on the opposite side of the river. The area is steeped in history but sadly, apart from the church, very little remains thanks to a combination of the Luftwaffe and the city planners. The church is still one of the finest sights in Bristol. The present building was founded in 1292 by Simon de Burton, three times Mayor of Bristol, although there was an earlier church on the site. William Canynges Senior completed the building of the church, which was then known as St Mary de Radeclive, back in the late 14th Century.

In 1446, the church was struck by lightning and badly damaged. Canynges' grandson, William, was responsible for funding much of the necessary rebuilding.

> **Naked Truth**
>
> **The Church Cat**
> 66Tom, the St Mary Redcliffe Church cat, who used to sit on the organist's knee while he played, was given a grand funeral in 1927. His grave is on the Bedminster side where he waited to be let in.99

■ This tram rail was thrown over adjacent buildings during a WW2 air raid and remains embedded in the ground at St Mary Redcliffe.

His first celebration of mass at the church in 1468 is still commemorated annually. At this ceremony, called the Rush Service, the church floor is strewn with rushes and rosemary in memory of those ancient times. There is a richly-decorated Canynges tomb where his wife is buried and also a simpler one showing him in his priest's robes. We will resist the temptation to mention the over-used quotation by Queen Elizabeth I about St Mary Redcliffe and instead mention some more recent history. During an air raid in 1941, a bomb threw a tram rail into the air and it became embedded in the churchyard turf. It remains there today, complete with a plaque.

QUICK PINT?
The Fleece and Firkin is the place to go to watch live music while you drink.

■ The Fleece and Firkin has a long history of being one of Bristol's best music venues.

The Georgian House Museum

Seven Great George Street is unlike any of its neighbours' houses. There are no Habitat sofas, no washing machines, not even a dimmer switch. This place remains exactly as it was when it was built in 1790. And if you think this is taking retroism too far, fear not, it's a museum, not a deliberate attempt to live uncomfortably. And like its first resident, Bristol slave trader and sugar merchant John Pinney, you can call in and wander around four of the six storeys from kitchen to bedroom as if you own the place. Austerity dominates throughout but there are a few elegant pieces of furniture and some detailed plasterwork to admire, if you like that sort of thing. The Georgian House was home to Pero, a black slave Pinney brought back to Bristol from the Montravers Plantation on Nevis in the West Indies. The bridge over the Floating Harbour is named after Pero.
■ **Open all year round, Sat-Wed (closed Thurs, Fri), 10am-5pm, admission free.**

BROADMEAD

If all the new buildings around Welsh Back point to a brighter future for the Centre, the dreary 1950s-built Broadmead was an unwelcome stroll down a far less attractive past. At the time of writing, Broadmead was being demolished and the M32 was being rerouted to accommodate the planners' vision for 21st-Century shopping in Bristol. Concrete has crumbled, bridges have been dismantled, carpet showrooms sacrificed, all in the name of the new Broadmead (or the Merchants Quarter, as it was going to be called, until the developers eventually admitted it was a crap name).

■ The statue of Charles Wesley sits in the courtyard of the Methodist New Rooms in the middle of Broadmead.

The new Broadmead is due to open in Autumn 2008. The £500 million makeover will see more than 100 new shops and a state-of-the-art cinema complex built, as well as housing, bars, restaurants and thousands of parking spaces. Harvey Nicks is the flagship store which will nestle under a 17-storey apartment block somewhere near where the Western Star Domino Club used to be.

The Broadmead redevelopment sparked a fierce debate that typifies criticism in some quarters that Bristol City Council has handed the city over to developers at the expense of the interests of long-standing residents. In December 2002, the City Council gave the go-ahead for the regeneration of the area promising a '24-hour living city'. The plan relied on rerouting the bottom of the M32 to allow Broadmead to expand towards St Paul's. The Council would claim that this is an example of visionary inner-city regeneration in partnership with blue-chip developers. In reality, however, it means that people who live in rented homes in St Paul's (the largest concentration of rented

■ The House of Fraser store in Broadmead is designed to resemble an ocean liner.

John Wesley's Chapel

Built in 1739, John Wesley's Chapel is the oldest Methodist building in the world. The building is an oddity in the middle of the concrete surroundings of Broadmead – everything around it was destroyed in the Blitz – and is one of the most interesting places to visit in Bristol. Above the chapel are the rooms where Wesley and his brother Charles lived. Check out the chair carved from tree roots, the graffiti scratched into the glass panes and Wesley's private rooms. Fascinating. Admission is free.
■ The Horsefair ■ Tel: 926 4740
■ www.newroombristol.org.uk

homes in Bristol) will be kicked out to accommodate well-heeled newcomers when the area becomes prime real estate. The population of St Paul's has already seen much of its community destroyed to build the M32. Now the developers seem intent on dismantling still further a well-established community that has been responsible for fostering some of the most creative forces in Bristol.

BUS STATION

If the redeveloped Bristol Bus Station is an indication of what we can anticipate from the rest of the Broadmead redevelopment, expect something functional and characterless where you have to pay 20p to take a leak.

> ### Naked Truth
> **Hole In The Wall, The Grove**
> 66Reputedly, the Spyglass in Treasure Island is based on this pub. It certainly has a spyglass which anxious sailors would peer through to spot approaching press gangs and hen parties.99

■ The view across the water from the Riverstation and Severnshed makes it the pefect spot for a relaxing drink.

Admittedly, the bus station, which was completed early in 2006, now boasts some natural light and doesn't stink of piss. This is a significant improvement on the previous terminus which was built in 1958 and, it is popularly believed, wasn't properly cleaned between 1959 and 2004 when it was probably deemed cheaper to knock it down than to buy enough air fresheners to get rid of the rank urine odour.

QUICK PINT?
The **Mud Dock** on The Grove is a perfect spot for some water-side drinking.

■ The new bus station no longer smells of wee and has numerous clocks so people know just how late the buses are running.

The old bus station, y'see, was probably the most unpleasant first impression of a city anywhere in Europe. The new one is deeply uninspiring, but clean and functional. Its functionality is only marred by the fact that it doesn't have a car park. Don't expect to get a spot in the small lay-by on the side road, head to the NCP instead.

During the rebuilding of the bus station, the City Archaeological Unit uncovered part of the cloister and other original remains of the Benedictine Priory of St James. Founded in 1129 by Robert, Earl of Gloucester (the natural son of Henry I of England), the Priory is almost as old as the city itself and appears in the earliest maps of 'Brigstowe'. When St James' Priory was excavated in 1995, part of the original east end of the church was revealed along with more than 200 human remains from the adjoining burial ground. This site is now covered by an office block on Cannon Street right next to the bus station.

COLLEGE GREEN

College Green at the bottom of Park Street is where the skateboarders congregate after tearing down the hill. It's also a pleasant spot to enjoy a lunchtime sandwich. It's dominated by the Cathedral, Central Library and the Council House ('Counts Louse' in Bristolese) which was commissioned in 1935 when the local authority outgrew its Corn Street base but, because of the war, was not finished until 1956. Check out Brunel House behind the Council House. Originally called the Royal Western Hotel, it was constructed by Brunel as a hotel for passengers disembarking from the Great Western Railway to stay overnight before boarding the ss Great Britain to sail to America. A proposed station near the Cathedral was never built and the hotel eventually became council offices.

There has been a religious building on the site of the Cathedral for more than 1,000 years. The history of the existing cathedral dates back to 1140 when wealthy merchant Robert Fitzhardinge invited monks to set up residence in what was then known as St Augustine's Abbey. Since then, the history of the Cathedral has been one of gradual religious and aesthetic progression. The Cathedral itself was established in 1542 and finished by architect George Edmund Street in 1868.

Just along from the Cathedral sits the Central Library,

BITE TO EAT?

Byzantium in Portwall Lane is a stylish Middle Eastern eaterie with belly dancers, DJs and a 2am licence.

■ The Ostrich has more picnic tables than you've ever seen, and it's right on the water too.

■ College Green is home to the Cathedral, as well as Bristol's skateboarders and students.

Wills Memorial Building

☀ If you've never set foot inside the skyscraper-high building at the top of Park Street, you really should take a detour next time you're walking by. Push open the huge double doors and you will be greeted by a sight so opulent it would make a peacock blush. There are two sweeping stone staircases which drop elegantly from the cavernous ceiling, while the grandest wooden entrance hall you've ever seen stretches out beneath. You don't get this sort of learning environment at Soundwell Tech.

Cigarette tycoon Henry Overton Wills put up £100,000 for the building in 1908 and over the years the Wills family donated the equivalent of £100m to the University. The Wills Memorial Building was opened by King George V and Queen Mary in 1925. The final cost was £501,566 19s 10d. At 215 feet tall, it is twice the height of the Cabot Tower.

The Wills tower, designed by George Herbert Oatley, is constructed from Bath and Clipsham stone. It has been called the last great Gothic building to be constructed in England. The bell inside the tower is called Great George and strikes every hour. It weighs over ten tons and is the fourth largest bell in Britain. The tower, which is covered in grotesque carved heads, was constructed to amplify the sound of the bell striking.

one of the greatest public buildings in the country. The first recorded public library in Bristol was founded in 1613 when a merchant called Robert Redwood gave his home in King Street to the city for conversion into a library. In 1740, a new Library was built on the same site and, in 1906, the Central Library was moved to its current site next to the Cathedral. There is a room at the library called the Bristol Room which is a copy of the old King Street library. It is not open to the public, but you can request a visit.

The library was designed in 1902 by Charles Holden, who later gained fame as the architect of many London Underground stations. The library was funded by a bequest of £50,000 from Vincent Stuckey Lean. Although its influences are Medieval/Tudor, this stunning building is regarded as an example of the early modern movement. The three large windows at the front hold sculptures by Charles Pibworth and depict Chaucer with the Canterbury Pilgrims, The Venerable Bede with Literary Saints and King Alfred.

Inside, the theme is more classical and the most immediately striking feature is the grand staircase which is made of white Sicilian marble from Carrara. The staircase sweeps you up to the reference library, one of the must-visit places in the city. The tunnel-vaulted skylight ceiling filters through a mellow light onto the original teak, leather-topped reading desks and white pillars. The room's design was inspired by the high chambers of the bath buildings of imperial Rome and its most spectacular features are the two great oriel windows at either end of the north wall, ornamented with heraldic panels commemorating figures from Bristol's past.

College Green is also home to the Lord Mayor's Chapel, an ancient house of worship, formally known as St Mark's Church and originally as the Chapel of the Hospital of the Gaunts. It was founded in 1220 by Maurice and Henry de Gaunt, grandsons of Robert Fitzhardinge who, in 1140, built the Abbey of the Black Canons of St Augustine, where

> **Naked Truth**
>
> **The Louisiana Tunnel**
>
> 66There are many ancient tunnels underneath Bristol. One from the Louisiana pub in Wapping Road (the old Sheriff House), is said to have led to the old city jail opposite and was used by the hangman to avoid angry crowds.99

> **QUICK PINT?**
>
> Why not combine pool and beer in the **Elbow Room** on Park Street.

Five things...
....
To keep an eye out for on Park Street
....

❶ Random skateboard freaks bombing down the hill at speeds of 50mph.

❷ Westworld staff doing their best to appear cool and detached at all times. You work in a shop, for Christ sakes!

❸ Saturday parking opportunities.

❹ Brilliant albums at amazingly low prices in Fopp. '1970s Venezuelan Jazz-Funk Odyssey Volume 3 for £5? Got to get it! Bill Nelson Sings the Commodores for only £3? Silly not to!'.

❺ Making sure you don't walk into one of those Christian bookshops by mistake.

the Cathedral now stands. The tower was a later addition in 1487. The building was originally built as a hospital. The nephew of the de Gaunts, Robert de Gournay, also had a hand in its endowment. Visitors should look out for the grotesque carvings that decorate the exterior of the tower and nave.

■ The Red Lodge (box below) was built in 1590 and is home to The Bristol Savages.

PARK STREET

BITE TO EAT?

Cafe Amore in Nelson Street is a bustling eaterie with big mirrors and lots of wood panelling.

It may have lost some of its appeal since the compact formula multinational convenience stores decided to move in, but Park Street is still one of the most elegant places to shop in the land – and one of the steepest. Standing at the top, looking down, you can't help but be impressed. We might take these things for granted, but this is one of the reasons so many visitors fall in love with Bristol. To the right, as you descend Park Street, is Brandon Hill and on top of that is Cabot Tower. It's hard to believe it now, but both have had their moments of controversy. A century ago, the breathtakingly landscaped hill was criticised by a local councillor as being 'a resort of lazy, idle, loafing persons' while the 105-foot tall monument to the explorer was described as 'a complete waste of money'. With this in mind, every visitor should climb up the spiral staircase and take a look at the most spectacular view Bristol has to offer. (Do not attempt this on very windy days or when drunk.) As inspiring as this sounds, however, it's not the reason the crowds flock to Park Street every Saturday. Unlike the Mall and Broadmead, many of the shops here are still independent and variety is still an option. DNA, The Boot Room, Uncle Sam's, the 50:50 skate shop, BS8, Khoi and Bristol Guild all operate, to varying degrees, outside the mainstream. In under

■ Park Street has got to be one of the steepest shopping streets in the country.

The Red Lodge

※ If you thought the Georgian House was ancient, you won't believe the state of this place. Built in 1590, this Elizabethan home was originally a Tudor lodge and home to a number of families over the years. Fortunately, the last people to live here seem to have gone in a hurry and left their furniture exactly as it was. As you tiptoe around, you half expect them to come bursting through the door at any minute demanding to know what you are doing in their house. A paternalistic group of artists, musicians and writers called The Bristol Savages (formed in 1894) hold their club nights in the gardens of the Red Lodge in a building called The Wigwam.

■ Park Row ■ Tel: 921 1360

half an hour, you could sign up for a water divining talk at the Folk House, buy an 'Enjoy Milk' baby top at Khoi, replace your cutlery at Bristol Guild and invest in a pair of dainty embroidered girlie shoes from The Boot Room. It's also worth mentioning that a more leftfield shopping experience can be unearthed on Park Row. To go from the glassy-eyed optimism of the Crystal Shop at the top of Lodge Street to the full metal hardware of Militaria on Lower Park Row takes only a handful of paces but is certainly one hell of a cultural leap. (See Shopping Listings, p232).

If you take another small detour off Park Street onto Great George Street, you will find the popular venue of St George's (see Nights Out Listings, p258).

Naked Truth

Quakers Friars
❝The city registry at Quakers Friars, Broadmead, is on the site of a Quaker meeting house that was built in 1667 on land that was the garden of the old Dominican Friary. Hence the name.❞

Five ancient...

City centre alehouses

❶ **The Hatchet**
Frogmore Street, 1606.

❷ **Ye Shakespeare**
Victoria Street, 1636.

❸ **Llandoger Trow**
King Street, 1664.

❹ **Kings Head**
Victoria Street, 1660.

❺ **Naval Volunteer**
King Street, 1673.

QUICK PINT?
The Bunch of Grapes in Denmark Street is a long-time fave!

CHRISTMAS STEPS

There is a plaque at the top of Christmas Steps that reads 'This streete was steppered done in 1669' but anyone using it back in those days took their life in their hands. Old public records tell of a dangerously steep and muddy path that sent pedestrians hurtling down towards the Centre at breakneck speeds.

And if the conditions underfoot didn't get you, the dagger-wielding muggers would. It used to be known as Knifesmith Street, though this was because the city's knife makers worked here. It was also referred to as Cutellare (cutlery) Street in records dating back to 1389, but by the end of the 16th Century, it had become Christmas Street and Christmas Steps when the steps were built in 1669. Condemned prisoners were taken up the 49 steps from Bristol gaol to be hanged on St Michael's Hill.

■ Christmas Steps was the final walk for prisoners from Bristol gaol before they were taken to St Michael's Hill to be hanged or burned.

MAP
BS1

INDEX OF PLACES

1 Pero's Bridge
2 Industrial Museum
3 At-Bristol
4 College Green
5 Cabot Tower
6 Queen Square
7 Lloyds Building
8 Hippodrome
9 Neptune and Fountains
10 Wills Memorial Tower
11 50:50 Skate Shop
12 The Galleries, Broadmead
13 Arnolfini
14 Youth Hostel
15 St Nicholas Market
16 Watershed

BS2 **Montpelier to Temple Meads**

If Easton is the new Montpelier, where does that leave St Paul's and Old Market?

Only an estate agent would describe Montpelier as Bristol's Notting Hill but this is where the city's leafier crowd hang out. Don't be fooled by the five-storey Regency terraced houses, Montpelier is full of what we used to call Jitters. Linking this counter-culture enclave to the world outside is Picton Street.

■ 'The people down on Picton Street already are superstar,' sang local boy Patrick Duff on the Strangelove track Superstar.

Past Notes

▶ **1873** Residents complain about the filthy state of Richmond Road. One talks of 'a muddy ditch, impassable for pedestrians.'

▶ **1874** The Cheltenham Road Viaduct, better known as The Arches, is built.

▶ **1882** The Montpelier Hotel begins its 100 year lifespan.

▶ **1993** Dozens of 'Picton Street Against The War' posters fail to prevent the invasion of Iraq.

MONTPELIER

It's fitting that Montpelier's main artery is a Georgian raggle-taggle, car-unfriendly lane where it's easier to buy a 'Say No To Esso' T-shirt than a top-up card for your mobile phone. The following organisations are, or have been, located in Picton Street: the British Association of Fair Trade Shops, Eco-Logic Books, Worldly Goods, Bristol Friends of the Earth, Community Recycling Network and Apple Day Resources, a pressure group that champions the rights of apples and orchards. Luckily, there are a few wonderful places to eat and drink too: Bell's Diner (1-3 York Road) is one of Bristol's most inspirational restaurants, the One Stop Thali Cafe (12 York Road) is renowned for its veggie Indian street food, Mela (19 York Road) is an excellent Indian take-away, Licata (36 Picton Street) is an authentic Sicilian deli, Herbert's Bakery (Wellington Avenue) is one of Bristol's finest bread-makers, Radford Mill Farm Shop (41 Picton Street) is a top organic and community wholefood shop while the Wai Yee Hong

■ Bell's Diner is hidden away on the end of York Road. It's well worth searching it out.

Supermarket (4 Station Road) is a warehouse full of unusual delights from the Far East.

If you want a drink stop, why not savour the friendly local atmosphere of the Star and Garter or The Beaufort. For a livelier time, then head up the unassuming Richmond Road until you come to the legendary Cadbury House. Until 2003, when the New Prince of Wales on Gloucester Road took the honours, *Venue* magazine readers voted the Cadbury House the best pub in Bristol for something like the previous ten years running. And it's easy to see why. It's one of just a handful of unique local landmarks that give underground Bristol its identity. You won't find anywhere like it in any other city.

Naked Truth

Andy Goldsworthy
❝Internationally renowned outdoor sculptor/artist Andy Goldsworthy has a house in Montpelier. He's the bloke who goes out into the wilderness and arranges bits of nature into man-made shapes.❞

Four old...
• •
Places in Stokes Croft
• •

❶ **Lifestyle Foodstore:** High-price, no-nonsense convenience store.

❷ **Citi Centa Sauna:** Does anyone actually ever go in?

❸ **Discount Heating Supplies:** Hardcore grates and radiators. Not for shoplifters.

❹ **Fred Baker Cycles:** They have sold bikes since 1935!

QUICK PINT?
The Bell in Jamaica Street is a Butcome pub with DJs most nights.

STOKES CROFT

The long, skinny stretch of tarmac that runs from The Arches down to The Bearpit might have the highest percentage of drink-related broken limb hobblers in the city but this hasn't prevented Stokes Croft from significantly re-inventing itself. Even those terrible toilets next to the Chinese herbal remedies shop, whose owners can't spell, have been sold as a desirable residence. It's easy to see the appeal. Within pissing distance for the new owners are the Comedy Club, Allsorts junk emporium, chic grown-up bar One30, the Bristol Taxi Company, Rita's still essential late-nite take-away, the Blue Mountain club and the already universally-loved Pieminister. Crusts, it seems, have replaced crusties.

At least anyone fortunate, or gullible, enough to buy into the leisure lifestyle development at the bottom of Stokes Croft has something to do other than staring out of the window watching drunks drifting around The Bearpit.

More symbolic of this new-found vibrancy is the re-vamped and re-named Pipe & Slippers. Okay, it's not half as cool as it wants to be but hands up how many of you went in here when it was called The Berkeley Castle? DJs, decent food and an over-riding sense of being involved in a post-modern pub concept leave you feeling slightly

■ You can't miss Herbert's Bakery, – if you don't spot the graffiti the size of a house, just follow your nose. Quite possibly the finest bakery in Bristol.

more fuzzy about what has always been the frayed end of Gloucester Road. Some questions, however, remain. Firstly, what the hell are peticoes? Secondly, just how do sofas riot? And lastly, why are so many blokes falling down the steps of the Magic Box?

But Stokes Croft isn't all about these bold nouveau enterprises, y'know. Some things have been around since the first alarm clock went off on the morning of the dawn of time. Take the heroically-named Everest Secretarial Services, for example. If you need a dissertation, CV, business proposal, manuscript or shopping list typed then look no further. Founded by Mrs Everest, yes really, it is a beacon of traditionalism where typists sit in a pool and quite possibly still buy their nylons off the black market. And their shoes in KBK.

■ **The Bristolian on Picton Street: where the counter-culture meets for breakfast.**

BITE TO EAT?

Mela in York Road is an excellent Indian take-away with loads of options for vegetarians.

One site of historical importance is the building opposite the Here shop at the top of Picton Street. In the early 1980s, this was the legendary Demolition Diner, an anarcho-punk, peace-crazies squat and a centre for unruly

St Paul's Riots, 2 April 1980

The riots that broke out on Grosvenor Road 'Front Line' in 1980 were the most serious in modern British history and the precursors of the summer riots that swept through Britain's inner cities in 1981. A lot has been written about the social causes for the disturbances and certainly the riots had a lot to do with the black and the white community of St Paul's expressing its anger at heavy-handed policing, unemployment and poor housing. And yet the immediate cause of the riots, according to Bristol urban legend, was all to do with a ripped pair of trousers.

The riots started at the Black and White Cafe in Grosvenor Road. The Black and White was run by Stephen Wilks and his partner Shirley Andow. Wilks was a Jamaican national who came to Britain in the early 1960s, settled in Oxford and then moved to Bristol where he took over the Black and White in 1971. The cafe was well known as a haven for drug dealers. Some would say that it was fairly

harmless – a few people indulging in small-time marijuana dealing. But others claimed it was actually the base for one of Britain's most serious drug operations.

What is beyond doubt is that the Black and White was a significant centre for a section of the black community. Detectives raided it on 2 April 1980, but had failed to warn either local uniform police or community leaders. Police met such violent resistance that they were forced to withdraw entirely for several hours and 19 officers were wounded. However, according to the rumours in the following weeks, in the process of searching for drugs, police ripped one of the customer's trousers. He demanded immediate compensation, the police refused, a scuffle followed that spilled out onto Grosvenor Road and... Bingo! Within hours, several thousand people were fighting a pitch battle with police. There were further riots in St Paul's in January 1982.

The Black and White Cafe was closed in 2003 and replaced with housing.

music and even unrulier politics. The night when it was first squatted, police took dogs onto the roof to try and oust the new residents by entering via a skylight. But the dogs got scared and couldn't get down. After some hard bargaining, the police and their dogs were escorted through the skylight and allowed to leave via the front door.

ST PAUL'S

Early in 2003, St Paul's resembled a bit of a war zone. The police helicopter was an almost permanent fixture, as were police vans and road blocks and armed police patrolled the streets.

> ### Naked Truth
> **Faggot anyone?**
> ❝St Paul's was the centre of Bristol's faggot industry. The company that became Brains, formed by A Smith in 1906, had a factory and shop in Upper York Street. Herbert Hill Brain took over in 1927.❞

Just another chapter in the life and often bad times of an inner-city ghetto? No, this is different. Where the Grosvenor Road riots of 1980 were rooted in the punches of Thatcher's poverty plan and sparked by heavy-handed police hassle, today's problems come out of what goes in to one end of a crack pipe.

QUICK PINT?
Join Dutty Ken at **The Star and Garter** in Brook Road for a late night drink.

Was a yardie-fuelled crack epidemic taking over the streets? If so, then community meetings called by the police were too little, too late. But isn't this always the way when it comes to St Paul's? For an area that has given Bristol more than any other in terms of music and character, they don't seem to get a lot in return. The Western Star Domino Club? Closed. Ajax Blues Bar? Shut down. And what happened to the club nights at the Malcolm X Centre? Early in 2004, the community was attempting to make the Black and White cafe (see St Paul's Riots, opposite) the centre of a regeneration programme. Steve Wilks, owner of the Black and White, told a public inquiry that closing the cafe wouldn't solve the St Paul's drug problems. Wilks, 34, whose father opened the Black and White in 1971 said: 'We want the cafe to stay. We want it to be part of the rejuvenation programme for St Paul's'. However, the cafe was closed in 2003 and has now been demolished and replaced with low-cost homes.

In the early 1990s, St Paul's was beginning to buzz again. Anyone looking for after-hours activity of the

Five new...
Places in Stokes Croft

❶ **Pieminister:** Delicious pies from this local success story.

❷ **Sofa Riot:** Designer sofa's at affordable prices.

❸ **One30:** A lesson in what a bistro bar should be.

❹ **Here:** A little shop with some very big ideas.

❺ **Niche Frames:** Blimey, they take framing very seriously in here.

◼ The Black and White cafe in Grosvenor Road was closed down early in 2003 and demolished.

alcoholic kind would head down to the Jamaican Good Food after midnight and choose from the vast array of Red Stripe on offer. Or you could get a late one in the Criterion on Badminton Road. And just around the corner from there is the defiantly original Star and Garter, still shaking its floorboards after all these years. There is a spirit that not even the most destructive drug on the planet can destroy.

■ The Farm pub in St Werburghs offers a country pub setting in the city.

BITE TO EAT?

Cafe Kino on Ninetree Hill is a vegan gaff with a load of cosy extra seating downstairs.

ST WERBURGHS

Narroways Hill, the area of steep wasteland that separates St Werburghs from Ashley Hill, has a history that far exceeds its humble appearance. In the early part of the last century, for example, it was the scene of a terrible murder of a woman called Ada James by her boyfriend Ted Palmer. Once carved into pieces by railway tracks, its junction was a target for Nazi bombs during the war. More recently, British Rail put the land up for sale and local residents decided to raise the money to buy it. Finally, Avon Wildlife Trust registered the

St Paul's Carnival

☀ Bristol's biggest street party is usually held on the first Saturday in July. It aims to promote and celebrate the culture and community of St Paul's – home to much of the city's African-Caribbean population.

The Carnival started in 1968 and has been held every year since, apart from 2002 and 2006. In 2002, it was cancelled following pressure from the police who were concerned about crack gangs looking for revenge for some non-fatal shootings after the 2001 event. There were certainly problems after the 2001 event, but in many quarters it was considered a disgrace that one of Bristol's longest-established, most vibrant and creative community-based cultural events was banned at the height of Bristol's bid to become European City of Culture in 2008. In 2006, it took a year off to undergo a major revamp.

St Paul's Carnival attracts thousands of people to Grosvenor Road and the surrounding streets. Everybody in Bristol who likes partying turns up and increasingly those from much further afield make the trip.

During the day Red Stripe, jerk chicken, fried fish and goat curry abound; after dark the music party moves up a few notches. Cultural events throughout June lead up to the Saturday event at which you'll find costume processions by local schools, community groups and anyone else with access to a float, as well as DJs, sound systems and bands, all blasting out reggae, hip-hop and dub.

For kids, there are two parks (St Agnes and St Paul's Adventure Playground) where they can see puppet shows, do face painting, listen to story-telling, join in drumming workshops and jump up and down on bouncy castles. Carnival has changed very little over the years. It's got bigger, but essentially the form on Carnival day remains the same: watch the procession, eat, drink, listen to music and walk up and down Grosvenor Road until it's time to go home.

St Paul's Carnival is one massive party for all ages and consequently gets very busy, so not one for claustrophobics.

■ **St Paul's Carnival runs from 1pm to 2am and is usually held on the first Saturday in July. Tel: 944 4176** land as a nature conservation site. This is in keeping with the character of the people of St Werburghs; why else would the suburb have been chosen as the site for the St Werburghs City Farm? The Farm pub is a welcoming place with good food and hip-hop and beats DJs on Friday and Saturday nights and occasional sets from the legendary ska spinner DJ Derek. The Victoria (40 James Street), where the pub sign is of Victoria Beckham rather than the usual Queen Vic, has gained a formidable reputation for its Sunday lunches while the Miners' Arms in Mina Road is the favoured watering hole of middle-aged musos. The other

Naked Truth

The Gin Palace

❝The Palace Hotel (Gin Palace) in Old Market was built as a plush hotel in the 1860s by speculators. They were convinced Bristol's main railway station would be built in Old Market, not Temple Meads.❞

■ The Victoria in St Werburghs has a pub sign featuring the other famous Victoria... Beckham, that is.

St Werburghs pubs resemble hostels for mostly drunk but mostly amiable old fellas. St Werburghs has a strong sense of community and the arrival of the uber-organic Better Food Company at the bottom of Ashley Down Road coupled with a retail revamp on Mina Road have added interest to the area. That said, there isn't all that much to get excited about. St Werburghs is Montpelier with a motorway running past it really.

QUICK PINT?

The Punch Bowl in Old Market has a large garden at the back.

OLD MARKET

I first went to Old Market aged 15 in 1979 to see two-tone band The Selector at Trinity Hall. The mod revival was fresh in its sta-press and the air was full of tension and excitement. As soon as Pauline Black and her speedy ska band plugged in, the place exploded. By the end of their set, the stage was bouncing with 15 or 20 uninvited mods. Stuff started to get broken, then someone threw a pint glass across the room; it smacked into the side of mod god Kev Rogers' head and almost took his ear right off. Although a river of blood was ruining his white Fred Perry, Rogers said he was fine, it was an accident, an in-house mod thing.

The Trinity wanted us all out as soon as possible but there seemed to be a universal reluctance to go home. Everyone began loitering outside. Then some of the notorious Barton Hill mod squad began spotting non-

■ You can't miss the Duke of York in St Werburghs – it is covered with graffiti on all sides.

mods and the fists and brogues started to fly. This wasn't playground fighting, this was ultra-violence. It had a cause and there was no bottling out. Yeah, scary. Really scary. As you may know, Trinity Church is opposite one of Bristol's largest police stations and it didn't take long before they noticed what was going on. They stepped outside and charged. Most of us legged it, others picked up bricks. There might have been a riot going on out there but we still had to get home. For what seemed like hours, we ducked in and out of the shop doorways all the way down West Street trying to avoid arrest. And ever since then, I have always had a fear of ever going back to Old Market again. Not least because it has always had a seedy feel to it at night. Blame the sex shop, nearby Stapleton Road and the constant stream of traffic from the busy Barton Hill roundabout.

BITE TO EAT?

The **Whole-Baked Cafe** in Lawford Street, Old Market is a good lunch option, but is only open weekdays.

■ Punch Bowl beer garden: it may be concrete but it is still a garden – a haven in Old Market.

Is it any wonder that the attempt to turn the area into Bristol's 'gay village' never got off the ground? Gay club Castro's (72-73 Old Market Street) has added some all-night hi-energy, even on a Sunday. The closure of the well-known Gin Palace during the Broadmead redevelopment meant that Old Market lost a famous old institution. Old Market, once the main shopping centre for Bristol, is still a dark edge of town.

TEMPLE QUAY

What was traditionally one of the city centre's most miserable areas is now a modern office development and the site of continuous building. Granted, it is still impossible to ignore the Old Market roundabout end-of-the-world concrete underpass and its broken-elevator, cold-bridge, back-of-the-NCP multi-storey brutality, but as you approach the roundabout where the Redcliffe flyover used to be, the new buildings of the £300 million Temple Quay development look pretty impressive. Naturally, this being Bristol, Temple Quay is an entirely corporate office environment that piles thousands more cars onto the already gridlocked roads. The planners also resisted the opportunity to introduce low-cost housing, or build a community in the heart of the city, so, after 6pm, the streets and plazas of Temple Quay are windswept and

■ The Temple Quay development may be impressive but where is the low-cost housing?

SMITH & MIGHTY

THE STORY BEHIND BRISTOL'S MOST INFLUENTIAL AND RESPECTED DANCE DUO FROM ST PAUL'S

■ Rob Smith and Ray Mighty in Bristol in 1988, the year their label Three Stripe Records was born.

Rob Smith and Ray Mighty are the masters of the Bristol Beat, the street sound of St Paul's. They've also been hailed as the originators of drum 'n' bass. Rob and Ray are from radical funk and roots reggae backgrounds; they became Smith & Mighty after meeting up in a funk outfit called Sweat in 1986. They built a studio above a Blues Club just off Ashley Road and, by 1988 (when the picture above was taken), Three Stripe Records had been born.

After a brief collaboration with Mark Stewart from The Pop Group, Smith & Mighty released their sublime broken beats version of Burt Bacharach and Hal David's Dionne Warwick classic *Anyone Who Had a Heart*. This was followed in 1988 by the excellent ultra-mellow, bass-bubbling Jackie Jackson version of *Walk On By*.

They then teamed up with singer Carlton and the people who were to become Massive Attack when they remixed The Wild Bunch's cover of the Bacharach classic *Any Love* – a hauntingly minimalist counter to the richness of their Three Stripe work. Rob and Ray were gods of the nascent dance scene, their *Steppers' Delight* 12-inch is credited as being the birth of Jungle. They teamed up with Fresh Four for the Knowle West outfit's Top

10 version of *Wishing on a Star* (see BS3, p30). Although this track is their only commercial success to date, it's hardly representative of the depth and diversity of their outstanding work. The major labels were on the prowl for Smith & Mighty. Virgin got short shrift when Ray Mighty said of Richard Branson: 'We just don't like his style and the way Margaret Thatcher portrayed him as the ideal business mogul. Maybe it's got something to do with the fact that we used to be punks.'

Smith and Mighty eventually signed to ffrr (London Records) in 1990 but then hardly released a beat for five years. Sadly their legendary *Bass is Maternal* album was never released in its original form; it remains one of Bristol's lost musical treasures. Outtakes from those sessions revealed a work of sparsely interwoven beats, dub, soul and space (silence). A dub reggae version of the album was eventually released, but not until several years later.

After sitting out their contract and then parting company with London, Smith and Mighty added Peter D Rose as a third member and introduced the world to their More Rockers project. Their first album in this new formation was *Dub Plate Selection Volume 1* which is an uplifting gathering of dub and drum 'n' bass. More Rockers went further down the dub reggae path in their work with Henry and Louis (lovely stuff) and continued to record and tour in their own right. After the disappointment of the London deal, Smith & Mighty regrouped around the More Rockers posse and in 2003 were working again with Suv and Krust (originally from Fresh Four) on the outer fringes of hip-hop.

Rob Smith released his first solo album, *Up on the Downs*, towards the end of 2003. This was a heavyweight drum 'n' bass performance which showed a great deal of depth. This fantastic album also retains the accessibility and hooks that have come to be Rob Smith's most well-known and well-respected trademark.

deserted, and the only company is the scores of CCTV cameras. Bizarrely, the first new shops to service the hundreds of office workers in Temple Quay were a Lloyds Chemist, a mini-market and a Starbucks. Presumably these cater for every need of the 21st-Century office drone.

Work on the next stage of this business centre development, the £200 million Temple Quay 2, started in the spring of 2003 to the north of the Floating Harbour and a new concert arena is planned on the Bath Road side of Temple Meads. The developers claim Temple Quay 2 will include affordable homes in the area of Bristol called the Dings. This was once Bristol's working-class heartland – one theory about the name is that it comes from the railway sidings – but has remained a semi-derelict home to industrial estates and car breakers since World War Two. The definition of 'affordable housing' remains to be seen.

■ Temple Meads linked London to Bristol and the ss Great Britain to America.

TEMPLE MEADS

On the other side of Temple Way from Temple Quay is the City Inn, which has a good restaurant, and right in the middle of all this growth, is Brunel's stylish and underrated Temple Meads railway station. It's just a shame that nobody will ever be able to wave anyone goodbye from the platform ever again because First Great Western has installed ticket barriers – don't get us started on those ticket barriers. Suffice to say that if you crave a definition of the words 'feeble-minded' and 'management', just spend 10 minutes watching the barriers in 'operation'. The British Empire and Commonwealth Museum at Temple Meads has 16 permanent galleries, and offers a changing series of special exhibitions, events for families, lectures and seminars. If your train is cancelled and you fancy a drink, the obvious choices are the station bar or the Reckless Engineer opposite the main entrance. Both of these are much improved with the Reckless Engineer offering a selection of real ales. The Bell and Ship in Redcliffe are just too far away for a quick pint, so you're probably better off not having a drink but getting a take-away from the highly-rated Dashi Sushi in the station subway instead.

■ The British Empire and Commonwealth Museum at Temple Meads Station.

MAP
BS2

BS3/BS4 Arnos Vale to Southville

They've been trying to posh up South Bristol for years. So far, it hasn't worked

W e've lumped BS3 and BS4 together because we'll only cover a little bit of BS4. This is the South Bristol chapter. If you're feeling adventurous enough to cross the river, read on…

THE SOUTH BRISTOL STORY

It could all have been so different… If, in 1835, John Miller, Vice-President of the Society of Florists, had gone ahead with his plan to build Bristol Zoo on land at Arnos Vale, then Totterdown and Knowle could now be affluent, sophisticated, leafy suburbs with the zoo and its magnificent gardens at their centre. A bit like Clifton perhaps. It seemed certain that the zoo would be built on the site that Arnos Vale Cemetery now occupies: in March 1835, *The Bristol Journal* reported that 'the planting of the Zoological Gardens,

Past Notes

▶ **1080** Bedminster is listed as a royal manor in the Domesday Book.

▶ **1748** An angry agricultural mob stomp northwards to smash the new Totterdown toll gate.

▶ **1900** First section of the Totterdown YMCA is opened. The Village People's great grandfathers rumoured to be 'delighted'.

▶ **1988** Someone calls Southville 'Lower Clifton' in an attempt to make the area more appealing.

■ The mural at South Street School, Southville reinforces the area's 'Lower Clifton' references much loved by estate agents.

eight acres in extent on Pylle Hill near this city has just been commenced by Mr John Miller.' But the Zoo was built on its current site at Summer Trenmoor near Clifton Down. It now seems an obvious location for such a major project, but back in 1835, Arnos Vale was a pleasant and unspoilt area of open countryside, whereas the Downs were populated by vagabonds and highwaymen swinging in the wind from gibbets. South Bristol lost out. In fact, South Bristol always seems to lose out. One suspects that

■ A bust of Raisa Gorbachev gives Glasnost in Totterdown a very distinctive entrance.

when the Romans arrived in Bristol, they decided to make Knowle West and Hartcliffe the leisure capital of their European empire. The first stone was probably about to be laid when a breathless centurion jogged up Hartcliffe Way and gasped: 'Hang on a minute, I've found this place called Aquae Sulis down the road. You should have a look there first.' Successive attempts to make South Bristol trendy have failed. One theory for the lack of anything much happening in South Bristol is that the secondary schools perform badly in the league tables, so parents who can afford it move to different catchment areas where the schools are better when their children reach Year Six, leaving behind those families who aren't in a position to evacuate the area.

And yet… along with Easton and St Paul's, South Bristol has one of the strongest and friendliest communities in the city.

Naked Truth

Vale Street

❝Vale Street in Totterdown is one of the steepest residential streets in Britain. Local residents hold an egg-rolling competition there on Easter Sunday.❞

QUICK PINT?

The Shakespeare in Henry Street is the best boozer in Totterdown.

TOTTERDOWN

Totterdown is split in two by the Wells Road. On the left going out of Bristol is Arnos Vale; on the right is the area most Bristolians would call Totterdown. The Arnos Vale side is residential. There aren't any pubs, shops or restaurants, though there is a bohemian element to the community which blends in with the established South Bristol chilled-out vibe.

The other side of Wells Road is a far livelier proposition and features one of Bristol's best pubs The Shakespeare (1 Henry Street), the excellent Glasnost restaurant (1 William Street) and the old Lloyd's bank/YMCA building which houses the Banco Lounge (107 Wells Road). There's also a mosque on this side of Totterdown: the Bristol Jamia Mosque in Green Street.

In the 1980s and 1990s, The Shakespeare was run by Mad Ern (Vernon Somers) and his wife Sane Joan. Ern was one of Bristol's greatest characters and The Shakespeare exuded his extravagant personality. The walls and ceiling were completely covered with postcards, posters, witticisms and house rules. You never needed to take anything to read: you could just work your way around

Five phrases…

You might hear in BS3

❶ Thazza grey tide eel (That's a great idea).

❷ Oim goin ter Asdur in Bumster (I'm going to Asda in Bedminster).

❸ Soider oi up lanlawd (Can I have a pint of cider please).

❹ Awrite me babber. Ain't sinew frages (Long time no see).

❺ Surely, the secondary schools can't be that bad (Skoolz roundyear are gert crap).

■ The Shakepeare is one of the nicest pubs south of the river, not that there's a great deal of competition, of course.

WILD WESTERNERS

THE LOW DOWN ON THE BRISTOL FACES WHO HAIL FROM THE DEPTHS OF KNOWLE WEST

■ Lizz E and famous Knowle Westerners Fresh Four: Suv Krust, Judge and Flynn.

You have to climb a hill from anywhere in Bristol to get to Knowle West. High above Victorian Bedminster on the southern fringes of the city, where the wind draughts in from the Dundry Beacon, it's always one or two degrees colder than the rest of town. The irony is that the families who were transplanted to Knowle West in the 1920s were brought from the slums behind Bristol Temple Meads railway station, which were built so close together that the area was always several degrees warmer than its surroundings.

They built Knowle West like a spider's web. Or so it appears from the map, and so it appears from the road. Every street and avenue looks the same and they're all littered with speed bumps. This is where BMX meets joyriding. Certainly, the natives seldom venture out of the estate for any length of time, except to go to Weymouth for their annual Courage Best and Ambre Solaire shandy – or to make it cautiously into the town centre for a little light pillaging, for the crime rate here is high.

At the middle of the web lies Filwood Broadway. Shut-down shops and boarded-up windows face a prevailing wind so strong you can hardly walk against it. Downtown Beirut it's called. Tricky grew up here, as did Julian Dicks. They say the reason Tricky never lifts his head from his microphone is a childhood fear of having his hat blown off. Then there's the graffiti: Sharon-4-Chris, Steve+Tracey4Ever, PIGS (defiantly), and Bruno. He gets everywhere does Bruno. If it's flat, Bruno has signed it. With spray paint and some jumbo markers.

At the edge of the web are the ex-council houses bought by Thatcher's property-owning democrats. All have storm porches. Some have stone cladding. A few have stone-clad storm porches. Here they have trees, and shelter. And hedges. And double-glazing. Elsewhere they have poverty and drugs, and stripped down Capris in the garden. And utter, utter hopelessness. I don't know where Julian Dicks would have gone to learn how to play football around here. In the street? On the rare patches of green? Or in the park at the end of Broadway? There's not much in the way of leisure facilities for the young in Knowle West.

But Filwood is on the up. The developers are moving in and parts are looking better. The double-glazing is on its way – new flats, new community spirit, rumours of a supermarket to replace the derelict shell at the end of the road, and new shop fronts. New flat surfaces. Bruno will like that.

Don Robbin

Four Famous Westerners
1) **Tricky**
2) **Julian Dicks**
3) **DJ Krust**
4) **Suv (Full Cycle)**

This piece first appeared in Total Football magazine as part of a profile of the footballer Julian Dicks who is from Knowle West.

the walls and ceiling. In the midst of this chaos, Ern built himself a DJ den from where he and his mates would treat customers to an eclectic mix of tunes. Ern left in 2000 and a pub full of tat left with him. But under the stewardship of Warwick and Emma, The Shakespeare has maintained its slightly eccentric character. There's a good range of beers, lovely organic Sunday roasts (booking essential), and DJs (in Ern's booth).

The other Totterdown pubs are The Oxford (notorious rough pub), the New Found Out (decent alternative if The Shakespeare is rammed) and The 'is it about to close' Cumberland

Naked Truth

Knowle West's Royal visit
❝King Edward VIII visited a council house in Lurgan Walk, Knowle West on 26 November 1934, when he was the Prince of Wales. He met unemployed labourer William Bailey, his wife and eight children.❞

■ Totterdown people love a party: in fact, they do it in the street.

which used to have a good music club upstairs run by much-respected local muso Dave McDonald. PJ Harvey played there once when she used to live in Totterdown. It is rumoured that Polly enjoyed her 'creative liaison' with Nick Cave in a house in St Stephen's Crescent. Totterdown is now making a national name for itself for its Front Room Art Trail which began in 2000 and, by 2006, featured about 100 artists, 30 houses, three pubs and attracted around 4,000 visitors to Totterdown over two days in November. Basically, artists display their work in houses and members of the public wander in, admire, buy and go for a pint in The Shakespeare. It's a great event – up there with St Paul's Carnival and the Ashton Court Festival in terms of a weekend to make sure you're in town.

QUICK PINT?
Head to the **New Found Out** on Green Street if **The Shakey** is packed.

■ Totterdown is very hilly, much like the rest of Bristol.

KNOWLE WEST

There's absolutely no reason to visit Knowle West. It's a rough South Bristol council estate with enough drug and crime problems to rival anywhere else in Britain. And yet Knowle West has produced three of Bristol's best-known characters: footballer Julian Dicks, hip-hop maniac Tricky (Adrian Thaws) and drum 'n' bass supremo Krust (Keith Thompson). Knowle West was also home to the band that achieved the highest ever chart position by a pre-Massive Attack Bristol outfit when Fresh Four reached number 10 in 1989 with *Wishing on a Star*.

There's certainly a link between Dicks and Tricky: they're both hard bastards. Dicks (whose nickname is the Terminator) was the most feared left-back of his generation at Birmingham City, Liverpool and, most famously, West Ham United; while Tricky was responsible for the most hard-edged, dysfunctional, alienated sounds of the 1990s. Krust too shows glimpses of the urban chaos that surrounded him in Knowle West in his breathtaking *Coded Language* album.

Tricky was christened 'the YTS Kid' by Massive Attack when he worked on their classic *Blue Lines* debut album because he was on a retainer of £25 a week. He was a feature at all the parties in town in the early 1990s and was known to one and all as 'the stoned kiddie from Knowle West'. Tricky's mother Maxine Quaye (after whom his 1995 debut album was named) died when he was four. His father had already left, so Tricky spent his childhood living with relatives around Bristol. He worked briefly with Krust in Fresh Four before moving into a squat with ex-Pop Group main man Mark Stewart, who at the time was working with On-U-Sounds producer Adrian Sherwood and Barton Hill hard case Gary Clail on a series of heavyweight dub reggae projects. In an interview with *Venue* magazine to promote his album *Never Trust a Hippy*, Sherwood claims that Tricky lived in a cupboard under the stairs in Stewart's squat. It may be coincidence, but Kat Day, guitarist with Bristol's finest guitar band of the early 1990s, the Seers, is also from Knowle West. Like Tricky, he sometimes wore a dress on stage. A trend that didn't catch on, luckily.

Fresh Four comprised Knowle Westerners Judge, Suv (now part of Roni Size's Full Cycle crew), his brother Flynn

■ The water maze in Victoria Park marks the site of one of Bristol's original water supplies.

■ The only two places you will find sheep in South Bristol are the Windmill Hill City Farm and on this house overlooking Victoria Park.

The Smythes

☀ John Smythe bought the Ashton Court Estate and large areas of South Bristol in the 16th Century. He is usually referred to as 'a successful Bristol merchant'. However, there is some evidence that he was actually a smuggler. The Smythes commissioned a survey to see if there were coal deposits in Bedminster. There were, and the first pit opened in South Liberty Lane in 1744. By 1830, there were 18 pits in Bedminster, the biggest of which was in Dean Lane. This can still be seen in Dame Emily Park (named after Sir Greville Smythe's wife), where a set of railings (and formerly a bandstand) marks the covered top of the area's biggest pit. The last Bedminster pit closed in 1924.

(of Flynn and Flora) and Krust. Their singer was Lizz E, a Bristol teacher. Tricky was in the same class as Flynn at Knowle Juniors and Merrywood Boys' School. Although *Wishing on a Star* propelled them into the top 10, the follow-up *Release Yourself* disappeared without trace, and so did Fresh Four. (See Bristol Beat, p140).

VICTORIA PARK

Victoria Park lies between Totterdown and Windmill Hill and boasts fine views over the city. The park may lack a central feature, such as a lake but is being increasingly used by the local

Naked Truth

Dame Clara Butt
"Bedminster Town Hall in Cannon Street (now demolished) was the venue for the first ever performance by Dame Clara Butt, Britain's greatest ever contralto, who studied in Bristol."

community for fun days, sponsored cycle rides and dog shows. There's an active Wildlife Group which has created a butterfly and wildlife garden near the bowling green and has initiated various conservation schemes. The park is home to St Mary Redcliffe Primary School and a water maze. The maze, near the playground on the Totterdown side of the park, is on the original course of the St Mary Redcliffe pipe, which supplied the citizens of Bristol with clean water in the 12th Century. Since 1984, the water has flowed from Knowle into the maze, which is built in brick as a replica of a medieval roof boss in St Mary Redcliffe Church.

QUICK PINT?
Grab a pint of organic lager at **The Windmill** on Windmill Hill, Bedminster.

WINDMILL HILL

Like Totterdown, Windmill Hill was a semi-rural area until the railway line from Bristol to Weston-super-Mare and beyond was built in the mid 19th Century. Windmill Hill takes its name from the fact that there was a windmill there – another one faced it across the valley in Totterdown, probably on School Road. Historically, Windmill Hill housed railway and tobacco workers. The Hill is a curious area. It has got a trendy element, yet none of the pubs were particularly interesting until the refit of The Windmill in 2006. There aren't any restaurants and the only nightlife is provided by Fiddlers in Willway Street. But Windmill Hill has a strong identity and is ★ **Turn to page 38**

Five things...
Not to do in S Bristol

❶ Go into Wedlocks in Ashton in a Rovers shirt.

❷ Leave a car unlocked in Filwood Broadway.

❸ Try to make new friends in The Friendship in Knowle West.

❹ Go for a romantic evening in Bedminster.

❺ Ask for 20 Capstan Full Strength gaspers at the Tobacco Factory.

■ **Watch the pigs at Windmill Hill City Farm eat and play football.**

THE OUTER CIRCUIT ROAD

BRISTOL'S ROAD 'REGENERATION' IN THE 1970S

Devastating town planning

Residents of many English cities claim that what the Luftwaffe didn't destroy in the 1940s, the town planners blitzed with far less imagination in the 1960s and 1970s. This is certainly the case with Totterdown.

It's difficult to imagine now that the famous Three Lamps signpost (one of the best examples of early 19th Century signs in Britain, pictured above) at the junction of the Bath and Wells Road once marked the gateway to a vibrant inner city community lining the Wells Road and the Bath Road.

The Three Lamps sign is still there, but that's all that remains of that part of Totterdown. It all went horribly wrong for the area in the 1960s when Britain was obsessed with bulldozing cities to make room for new roads. On 15 December 1966, the Ministry of Transport approved a Bristol City Council plan for a £30 million outer ring road, or urban motorway. The brainwave of the Planning Committee and its chairman Alderman Wally Jenkins (or 'Mr Traffic', as the *Western Daily Press* dubbed him), the plans were truly devastating. Essentially, the planners wanted to drive a dual carriageway-cum-motorway from what is now Junction 3 of the M32 through Easton and St Philip's, over the Feeder behind Temple Meads, across the

Three Lamps Junction, through Totterdown, across Victoria Park and through Bedminster.

Totterdown demolished

It got worse. The motorway would then head across the Floating Harbour, skirting the Cathedral and heading through Jacobs Wells to the Victoria Rooms. The precise route of this section is unclear: certainly there were proposals to turn Park Street into a dual carriageway and there were alternative plans for a flyover to Brandon Hill and a tunnel underneath the Cabot Tower.

From the Victoria Rooms this monster road would demolish Cotham on its way to Montpelier, where it would stop for breath before bulldozing St Paul's and rejoining the M32 (or Parkway as it was then called) at Junction 3. The plans also included surrounding St Mary Redcliffe Church with dual carriageways and driving a main road straight through the middle of Queen Square. In a word: it was madness.

But to the everlasting shame of the City Council, the area of Totterdown above the Three Lamps between the Bath and Wells Road was demolished in 1972 to make way for a four-level spaghetti-junction motorway on stilts. Between Three Lamps and Temple Meads, would be a giant interchange centre about the size of Broadmead where happy motorists would jump on fleets of buses to complete their journey into what was left of the city. Communities, shops and pubs were flattened to realise this nightmare. A total of 500 homes and 40 shops and pubs were demolished. Places like the Lahore Cafe and Club, the Three Lamps Canine and Feline Beauty Centre, the Maypole Dairy, the Bristol Co-operative Society, the Prince Rupert, the Totterdown Hotel and the Phoenix were lost.

Thankfully, the full awfulness of that road scheme was never realised; North Bristol was spared, Totterdown was destroyed but the road was never built. Easton suffered terribly. Ironically, new flats and houses were built on the Totterdown site in the 1990s, but the community has been lost for ever.

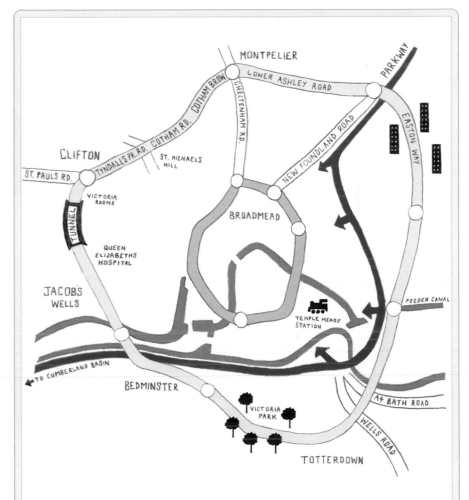

THE ROAD TO RUIN

This map of the proposed route of the outer circuit road is based on an illustration that appeared in the *Bristol Evening Post* on Friday 15 October 1971. The black line shows the route proposed by *Evening Post* reader Paul Chadd, which would have taken the traffic through the largely derelict area of St Philip's.

The grey line is the route preferred by the City Council which was to join the M32 at Junction 3. Much of Easton was demolished to build the first section of the outer circuit road and the lower part of Totterdown was bulldozed in 1972 to make way for it.

It is worth noting the tunnel which would appear to go either under Brandon Hill near the Cabot Tower or under the area of Clifton opposite QEH School on Jacobs Wells Road before emerging near the Victoria Rooms and ploughing straight through Cotham.

a close community within easy striking distance of town. The Off Centre Gallery in Cotswold Road holds occasional exhibitions and is well worth the trek south.

BEDMINSTER

■ Zone A is a small area of land on Wells Road that has been designated as for community use.

Bedminster is older than Bristol and probably takes its name from a monastery or church founded by the monk Beda, or from the old English word 'bedydd', which means baptism. In the 15th Century, this is where the lepers came to live. Bedminster is separated from the rest of the city by the Cut. This was dug (probably by French prisoners from the Napoleonic War) between 1804 and 1809, when the Floating Harbour was built to carry the River Avon around the Harbour. It runs from Hotwells to Totterdown. When the Cut was built, Bedminster was part of Somerset; it was included in the Bristol boundaries in 1897, by which time it was an important industrial area with a coalfield, engineering works, tanneries, tobacco factories, paint and glue works. The population of Bedminster grew from around 3,000 in 1801 to 78,000 in 1884.

> **BITE TO EAT?**
> The **Magnet Fish Bar** on Dean Lane, opposite South Bristol Baths, once won an award for the best chippy in Bristol.

Bedminster was an important area in the very early years of Bristol. The church of St John the Baptist (destroyed in World War Two, but not demolished until 1962) dated from 1003, and it was the mother church to St Mary Redcliffe, which was officially a chapel-of-ease to Bedminster until 1852.

■ Artwork from Bedminster Station in Fraser Street, Windmill Hill. Take a look, these guys are real good.

Nowadays, Bedminster is a run-down, rough-and-ready part of town with a lot of character (and characters) but not much else going for it. It has steadfastly resisted

---

Poet's Corner, North Street

☀ If you look up at the wall of the house on the junction of Merrywood Road and North Street, you'll notice a weathered and crumbling bust and the words 'Poets Corner'. Thomas Chatterton is Bristol's most famous poet, but this memorial commemorates one of the city's worst: Alfred Daw Collard, the poet/butcher of Bedminster.

The Collards were a well known South Bristol family and provided four generations of butchers. There's still the front of a closed Collards' butchers farther up North Street. Collard was famous in the late 19th Century for his dreadful music hall-style poetry, copies of which he sold for a penny to raise money for Bristol General Hospital.

One of his works, *The Redcliffe and Bedminster Christmas Meat Show of 1885*, named the 26 butcher's shops between North Street and Redcliffe Hill. Collard's brother ran a butcher's shop on the site of Poets Corner and erected the memorial as a joke.

attempts to smarten it up and, despite forming a heartland of Labour support in the city, has been overlooked by the Labour Party when it has control of Bristol City Council and, like much of South Bristol, has seen significant inroads by the Lib Dems and Green Party. The housing development on the junction of Bedminster Parade and York Road has been heralded as opening 'the Gateway to South Bristol' and has certainly set the tone for rampant home building in Bedminster. But will such developments smooth the rough edges of East Street? History suggests not.

■ The old police station in Bedminster High Street is now an Italian restaurant.

> **Naked Truth**
>
> **Ashton Court Festival**
> ❝Ashton Court Festival was masterminded from a small room above The Albert Inn in Bedminster for several years in the late 1980s. Landlord Ian Storrer gave the organisers the room for free.❞

Heading over Bedminster Bridge, Nelson Parade becomes Bedminster Parade, which turns into East Street, the main road through Bedminster, which supposedly follows the route of a Roman Road used to carry minerals from the Mendips to the Roman Port at Sea Mills. Just off Bedminster Parade in Stillhouse Lane is the old Bedminster Bridge School, a Grade II listed building designed by WV Gough and built in 1895. Equally impressive is the police and fire station on the right. This grand castle-like building was opened in 1882 by Mr ES Robinson of the paper-bag and printing company. The tower is there for practical rather than aesthetic reasons: it was a watch tower to spot fires. The original police and fire station that once stood here was one of the three built by an Act of Parliament in 1834; the other two were at Brandon Hill and St Philip's. In 1850, Bedminster had only one street light and one flushing toilet: both were at the police station. Shamefully, the building had been left in disrepair for more than 20 years. After the City Council sold the police station to property developers, the buildings around it have now been developed into (yep, you guessed it) flats and a library. Where villains once did time, diners can now do thyme in Bottelinos Italian restaurant which has moved into the police station.

On the left is Philip Street and Windmill Hill City Farm (see Children's Bristol, p182) and one of Bristol's

> **QUICK PINT?**
> **The Ropewalk** in Bedminster Parade is your best bet for a pint in Bemmie.

■ This Grade II listed building was built in 1895 and used to be Bedminster Bridge School.

last real cider houses, the Apple Tree, which has taken to operating a 'regulars only' policy. Fiddler's club is in Willway Street off Philip Street. Opposite Philip Street is the Asda supermarket that was built on the site of the former Wills tobacco factory after that was demolished in 1986. In the 18th Century, the site of the current Asda car park was called the Paddock and was a meeting place for Bedminster's active Methodist community – John Wesley is known to have preached there at least four times. The shops next to Asda are in an original Wills building. Before the arrival of Asda, the lower part of East Street was home to several small greengrocers, a fishmongers and other high-street stores; these were unable to compete with the supermarket and closed down leaving the Bristol end of East Street in a somewhat shabby state. There's little of note as you walk through the pedestrianised part of East Street. The site of St John's Church is about half way up on the left in a small park off Church Road.

> **BITE TO EAT?**
>
> **Taveira** on Cannon Street, Bedminster do a mean Lebanese take-away at good-value prices.

Emerging from East Street, Cameron Balloons was housed in the old red-brick Robinson paper bag factory which has been redeveloped as even more flats. The gabled London Inn, (which has a beer garden), is just to your right. Another famous Bedminster pub was The Albert which sadly closed in 2005. Its landlord Ian Storrer was one of the city's good guys, though you wouldn't

■ The Apple Tree in Bedminster is a cider pub through and through.

■ Gaol Ferry Bridge, Southville.

Billy Butlin of Bedminster

Billy Butlin launched his multi-million pound holiday camp empire with the takings from a hoop-la stall in Bedminster.

Having moved from South Africa to Bedminster and then Canada, after World War One, Billy Butlin worked his passage from Newfoundland to Liverpool. He arrived in England with £5 and headed for Bedminster to find his mother's fairground family. Butlin walked and hitch-hiked the entire way from Liverpool to Bristol. He was given the job of painting and re-fitting rides owned by the family and eventually his uncles set him up a small hoop-la stall at a cost of 30/- (£1.50), with prizes loaned to him by his kinsfolk. His first fair was at Axebridge, where business was very good: Billy made £10 clear profit, far more than the more experienced stall holders.

Butlin had a different outlook to the other stallholders, who made it difficult to win prizes by making the blocks too wide for the hoops to easily fit over. Bill made his blocks smaller so that the hoops went over more easily. He therefore got rid of all his prizes and made a very nice profit. He re-invested his profits and quickly moved from hoop-la stalls to amusement parks. By 1936, he had made enough money to open his first holiday camp in Skegness. His business philosophy goes all the way back to the success of his Bedminster hoop-la stall: give the punters a fair deal and they'll keep on coming back.

necessarily guess it from his sometimes gruff disposition. Apart from serving good food, having a well-kept selection of beer, cider and lager, and boasting a great juke box, The Albert was Bristol's best jazz venue. The lounge walls were covered with Reid Miles' superb artwork for the Old Blue Note covers, and the bar was plastered with covers from *Wire* magazine. Bristol's brilliant jazz saxophonist Andy Sheppard started out at The Albert and all of the city's jazz luminaries have played there. In the mid 1980s and early 1990s, Ian gave the Ashton Court Festival free use of a room for meetings. Bristol owes a lot to Ian Storrer.

> ### Naked Truth
> **Bristol firestarters**
> ❝The first record of a bonfire night celebration in Britain is in Bristol on 5 November 1607. Two years after the Gunpowder Plot. Bristol Corporation paid for a giant bonfire at the High Cross in Broad Street.❞

■ The Coronation is one of the most popular pubs south of the river. It is best known for its Hop Back beer and quiz nights.

Past the London Inn is Bar Salt, a clean-cut bar with beer garden and pool tables at the back. The pub dates back to the 18th Century when it was called The Bull. Around 1900, it was changed to the Star, became a Florikan and Firkin in the 1990s and then the Aurora before opting for the Bar Salt moniker. In 1827, when it was The Bull, Mr Martin, the publican, bought a tiger and put it on show inside a cage in the pub. He paid a man, Joseph Kiddle, to get inside the cage with it. The tiger mauled Mr Kiddle to death.

> **QUICK PINT?**
> **The Coronation** in Dean Lane does take-away jugs of its lovely Hop Back Beer.

Turn right at the mini-roundabout outside Bar Salt into Dean Lane and opposite Bristol South Swimming Baths, you'll find the Magnet Chip Shop. This was voted the best chippy in Bristol in the mid 1990s. The Argus in North Street is also famous for its fish and chips. Keep following Dean Lane past the bendy bit of road to The Coronation which, along with The Shakespeare, can lay claim to being one of South Bristol's best pubs. This friendly, lively local has a good quiz night and does a good range of pizzas. It is also the only Hop Back Brewery house in Bristol, so the beer is excellent. Just before Dean Lane joins Coronation Road, there's a Blue Plaque on the house where the ivory tinkler Russ Conway lived. Strangely, the house just a few doors down where Bear Hackenbush, Skate Muties, the Bugs 'n' Drugs crew and Chaos UK used to live has been afforded no such recognition.

■ Quba Ice on North Street, Southville used to be the worst-stocked greengrocers ever.

SOUTHVILLE

Southville is the residential area between Bedminster and Ashton. It's the poshest part of South Bristol and estate agents periodically try to rename it Lower Clifton or Clifton View in an attempt to push house prices even higher. Southville was largely built on tobacco money from the Wills family, who were teetotal. It is for this reason that there isn't a single pub in Southville, but there are many on the boundaries including the Hen & Chicken, which became Bristol's first theatre pub in 1989 when it was home to the Show of Strength theatre company.

■ The Tobacco Factory has helped make North Street the trendiest place in town.

North Street is the main shopping street in Southville. It has always been a busy high street but in recent years, it has helped Southville become Bristol's coolest neighbourhood. The impetus for Southville becoming so trendy is the Tobacco Factory project. The Tobacco Factory is housed in the last remaining part of the 1906 Old Wills Number 3 factory site on Raleigh Road. It contains a bar, Teoh's restaurant, a theatre complex (Show of Strength's current home) and various media-related enterprises. The building was saved from demolition by architect George Ferguson and is the centre of a movement for urban regeneration inspired by the Manchester Independents Campaign. The campaign philosophy is to encourage independent outlets and businesses and support local character and enterprise.

■ Bob Wherlock's is one of the best butchers south of the river. The huge queue out the door on a Saturday morning proves it.

It certainly seems to be working in North Street: since the Tobacco Factory opened, the area has attracted a good delicatessen, the chilled-out Lounge bar, Caribbean restaurant Quba Ice, Havana Coffee and others while retaining its greengrocer, tobacconist, two butcher's shops, bakeries and the mighty Lions hardware store. Sadly, there has been one loss in the midst of the über-trendiness. The Metro cafe, who made one of Bristol's best fried breakfasts, has been replaced by the Mediterranean-style Cafe Ceiturica. Where students and builders once tucked into fried Saturday morning feasts, middle-class parents now scold their children for fiddling with their falafel. Please observe a few moments silence before you order.

If you follow North Street down towards Ashton Park, where it becomes Ashton Road, you'll find Al's Tikka Grill. This is a cafe by day and BYO curry bistro and take-away by night, and is regarded as one of Bristol's best curry houses.

PAINTWORKS

The land on the left of the Bath Road as you head out of town is home to one of the city's truly innovative developments. The area already houses Endemol West (see Media Listings, p252) and Bookbarn. The remainder of the old paint works site is being developed as Bristol's 'Creative Quarter.' Bocabar was the first business to move in. What follows is a mix of workshops and loft spaces. A new community is being created with a focus on attracting creative businesses to this derelict riverside site.

■ The Bocabar at Paintworks gives South Bristol the kind of bar it was crying out for.

On the other side of the river in St Philips is Bristol Fruit Market, the biggest wholesale outlet to the fruit, veg and flower trade in the South West. On Sundays, there's a 'cheap cuts, CDs and clothes market' on the site. You'll also find Charles Saunders, the city's main fresh and frozen fish wholesaler, down this way too. Underneath the bridge from Bath Road to St Philips behind the old Esso Garage site is a wall loved by the city's graffiti artists.

QUICK PINT?
The Tobacco Factory has led to a food and drink revolution in South Bristol.

WD & HO Wills, Bristol

☀ There were already several other tobacco manufacturers in Bristol when Henry Overton Wills arrived in the city from Salisbury in 1786 and went into partnership with Samuel Watkins. Their first shop was in Castle Street but by 1791, the firm had moved to 112 Redcliffe Street.

The company quickly established a reputation for integrity and quality. The firm made steady progress and in 1871 entered the cigarette market with the original Bristol brand. This was followed in 1874 by Passing Clouds, in 1878 by Three Castles and in 1888 by one of the most famous cigarette brands in the UK, Woodbines, at a price of five for 1d.

In 1886, the firm moved to Bedminster and expanded its operation throughout South Bristol with sites in Southville, Ashton and Hartcliffe. In 1901, the Imperial Tobacco Company was formed to resist an attempt by a powerful association of American tobacco manufacturers to capture the British market; WD & HO Wills took a leading part in its formation. The tobacco industry dominated South Bristol for much of the 20th Century.

In 1969, the Wills' Redcliffe Street premises were demolished and in 1974 production started at the new Hartcliffe Factory. Production was gradually phased out on the East Street and Southville sites and the whole operation was moved to Hartcliffe. In 1986, the original factory buildings at the bottom of East Street were demolished and an Asda supermarket was built on the site.

In 1989, the Hartcliffe head office building was vacated and in 1990 the Hartcliffe factory ceased production. All Imperial Tobacco cigarette production moved to Nottingham, though cigar production stayed in Bristol until the Hartcliffe factory was demolished in 1999.

ARNOS VALE CEMETERY

THIS 45-ACRE SANCTUARY IS BEING RESTORED WITH A £4.8M HERITAGE LOTTERY FUND GRANT

■ Morbid as it may seem, a visit to Bristol's most famous cemetery is an interesting and educational experience.

Save Arnos Vale campaign

Arnos Vale Cemetery is one of the most fascinating historical sites in Bristol, and yet for almost 25 years, it was left in a state of utter neglect. All that has changed since 2003 when the cemetery was runner-up in the BBC's *Restoration* TV series. In 2005, Arnos Vale was handed a £4.8 million grant by the Heritage Lottery Fund. Work started immediately on clearing and renovating the cemetery, setting up a visitor centre and introducing educational, wildlife and conservation programmes.

The cemetery was owned by Anthony Towner, head of the Bristol General Cemetery Company. In 1987, faced with falling revenue, Mr Towner announced that he wanted to sell a large part of the cemetery for residential development. A public meeting was arranged and, with the help of hundreds of protesters, the Campaign to Save Arnos Vale Cemetery was formed. Within weeks 20,000 people had signed a petition against the proposed development plans.

In 1998, the City Council refused Mr Towner a cremation licence because the crematorium failed to meet the regulations of the Environmental Protection Act 1990. So the crematorium ceased to operate and Mr Towner threatened to lock the gates. An angry crowd besieged Mr Towner in his office at the cemetery; the gates remained open and since 1998, the Friends of Arnos Vale have unlocked and locked them every day and done what they can to look after the cemetery and stop the area becoming completely overgrown.

High Court appeal

Bristol City Council was granted a Compulsory Purchase Order for the cemetery in April 2001 and a public inquiry was held in May 2002 to hear the evidence in connection with Mr Towner's objections. The inquiry ended early when the company withdrew its objections. The Council bought the cemetery under the CPO and handed it over to The Friends of Arnos Vale Cemetery.

The cemetery was founded in 1837 when a private Act of Parliament established the Bristol General Cemetery Company. It was planned as a Greek-style Necropolis and was landscaped using trees and plants noted in classical legend. Its Grade II listed Arcadian Garden contains four buildings designed by the architect Charles Underwood: two neo-Greek Doric entrance lodges (both are Grade II listed buildings), an Anglican Mortuary Chapel and a Non-Conformist Chapel.

Arnos Vale is the final resting place of several Lord Mayors of Bristol, an American consul, members of the Wills and Robinson families, George Muller and possibly Mary 'Princess Caraboo' Baker, who managed to persuade the Squire of Almondsbury that she was an Eastern Princess. Further down the Victorian social scale, you'll find the unmarked mounds of the common graves of the poor and the flat markers of the guinea graves of those whose relations had managed to collect 21 shillings (£1.05) to avoid a pauper's burial.

Murdered in donkey dispute

The grave of Mary Carpenter, the Victorian pioneer of juvenile care, was lost in the undergrowth until it was discovered when part of the graveyard was being cleared of brambles. At least two survivors of the Charge of the Light Brigade are buried at Arnos Vale, as is a police officer who was murdered in Old Market whilst trying to intervene in a fight over the ill-treatment of a donkey.

Arnos Vale also contains a considerable number of individual war graves, a small military cemetery with a Cross of Sacrifice, and a World War One memorial classical stone arcade built into the hillside close to the main entrance. Approximately 250,000 burials have taken place in 50,000 graves and 750,000 cremations have also been carried out, with most of the cremated remains scattered in the Arnos Vale Gardens of Rest.

■ Arnos Vale Cemetery needs help to return it to its former glory. Visit the website to find out how to donate.

Raja Rammohun Roy

The most famous resident of Arnos Vale Cemetery is Raja Rammohun Roy, the great Bengali social reformer who died from meningitis on 27 September 1833 while he was staying with friends at Beech House in Stapleton (later to become Purdown Hospital and now a residential development).

Rammohun Roy was a scholar fluent in many languages including Greek, Hebrew and Latin. He wrote books on grammar, geography and geometry and published newspapers and is especially remembered for his campaign to end the Hindu custom of 'sati', the burning of a widow on her husband's funeral pyre. As head of the Atmiya Sabha he spearheaded reform on all fronts: he was against polygamy and the caste system and was a supporter of education for women. The 19th-Century Indian social reformer Ranade called him the 'father of modern India' and Indian academic Professor Brajendraneth Shil described him as 'the pioneer internationalist'. There's now a statue of him outside the Central Library on College Green.

On his death, the Raja was buried in the garden of Beech House. Ten years later, in 1843, his body was moved to a permanent burial site at Arnos Vale so that the public might have access to it. The canopy over the tomb was styled by a Calcutta designer and there are plans for it to be restored to its original glory.

■ The Arnos Vale Cemetery Trust is continuing to raise money through its Guardian Angel scheme.
■ Arnos Vale Cemetery Trust, West Lodge, Bath Road
■ Tel: 971 9117
■ www.arnosvale.org.uk

■ The tomb of Raja Rammohun Roy – Arnos Vale Cemetery's most famous resident.

MAP
BS3&BS4

INDEX OF PLACES

BS5 **Easton to St George**

Home to Bristol's radicals from Ben Tillet to Tony Benn and the Bristol anarchists...

At face value, there may seem little to recommend a visit to the East Bristol inner-city areas bordered by the M32 and the A420. But here you'll find one of Bristol's most pleasant walks (along the banks of the Frome at Snuff Mills), a fantastic shopping street (St Mark's Road), a dub reggae paradise (the Black Swan), loads of good curry houses and some of the city's best street art. Easton is also home to Bristol's active radical element. But be warned: crime is an issue in the area, particularly near the bridge across the M32 and around the underpass at Lawrence Hill.

Past Notes

▶ **1793** First Easton coal mine opens.

▶ **1881** Cricketing legend and ZZ Top beard originator WG Grace becomes Easton's local doctor.

▶ **1886** Eight die in the notorious Easton pit disaster.

▶ **1990** Easton Leisure Centre opens on Stapleton Road.

■ It is unlikely that Tory party activists ask if they can count on Kebele's vote at election time.

EASTON

There is little evidence of it now, but Easton was built on coal. The earliest mining area in Bristol was further east at Kingswood where coal was produced from the 17th Century to fuel the soap-making, glass, brewing and pottery industries. The first Easton mines were developed in the late 18th Century and the industry boomed in the 19th Century.

Today Easton is a buzzing, run-down inner-city area alongside Stapleton Road and home to the city's largest ethnic population. It has a history of political activism dating back to the Weavers' Riots in 1728; there were miners' strikes in the 18th and 19th Centuries and it was the birthplace of Ben Tillett, one of the founders of the Labour movement and the creator of the first unions for unskilled workers. It is currently a base for the Kebele

■ The Sugar Loaf on St Mark's Road has a great beer garden out the back.

Kulture Projekt anarchist centre in Robertson Road (see Underground and Radical Bristol, p98). It's where the anti-car lobby park their bicycles and is the area of choice for a sizeable gay (particularly lesbian) community.

Every visitor to Bristol should take a stroll down St Mark's Road, where you'll find Moroccan cafes, a Bangladeshi restaurant, an African-Caribbean clothes store, a sari shop, the veggie cafe Maitreya and the mighty Bristol Sweet Mart. The Sugar Loaf on St Mark's Road is a well-known and busy pub that merited an entry in the 2002 Good Beer Guide. It's a good spot to sit outside and watch the Easton world go by – there's regular live music in the evenings. The Chelsea on Chelsea Road is the venue of choice for Easton's radical community. The Black Swan near the junction of St Mark's Road and Stapleton Road was the headquarters of Bristol Rovers FC between 1897 and 1910. The original building is thought to date back to 1640, although it was rebuilt in the 19th Century. It's now one of the city's leading dub reggae venues, regularly hosting leading sound systems – a must for bass addicts.

> **Naked Truth**
>
> **Ben Tillet**
>
> 66One of the founders of the Labour Party and the Trade Union Movement, Ben Tillett, was born in 1860 in the now demolished John Street off Felix Road in Easton. He died in 1943.99

> **QUICK PINT?**
>
> You can sit outside **The Sugarloaf** in St Mark's Road at the front or back.

EASTVILLE PARK

Eastville Park was created as a result of public pressure to tackle the problems of overcrowding and poor health in the parish of St Philip's. After much lobbying, 70 acres of land were purchased in 1889 for £30,000 on estate land owned by Heath House and Ridgeway House. At the time the land was on the outskirts of the growing city and many people were against the idea of a park at Eastville because they thought the area was too remote.

Some mature trees already growing there were kept, the existing boundary walls were repaired and paths were laid out with 100 seats and several small wooden shelters. Walks were created by planting an avenue of lime trees (now partly replaced by horse chestnuts) and London planes. The grass was managed with both sheep-grazing

Five things...
To buy on Stapleton Rd

❶ Fresh red snapper and frozen frogs' legs, **Toveys fishmongers.**

❷ Goat curry, rice and peas, **Caribbean take-away.**

❸ Downbeat the Ruler, Killer Instrumentals, Best of Studio One, **Genesis Musik and Clothing.**

❹ Bones for your dog, from **R Jenkins Butchers** (bones free, but make a donation to Cadbury Heath FC Under-13s).

❺ Halal chicken and chips, **Lick 'n' Chicken.**

■ The Bristol Sweet Mart is a legend in Bristol and beyond.

and mowing. The outdoor swimming pool followed in 1905, the bowling greens in 1907, and finally the lake in 1908 to 1909.

The lake is one of the best public park lakes in England; it is designed in a serpentine shape so that wherever you stand you cannot see how big it is. It is bordered by lawns, specimen trees and a hanging wood.

■ Cafe Maitreya is St Mark's Road's award-winning cafe.

BITE TO EAT?

Cafe Maitreya in St Mark's Road has won national awards for its outstanding veggie food.

The park has now lost most of its original features; the bandstand and little kiosks had gone by 1950; only the plinth and footings of the octagonal drinking fountain by the Fishponds Road entrance still survive, with a stand pipe which no longer supplies water.

The Crimean War cannon which stood on a plinth near the bowling green was removed during World War Two to be melted down to make weapons. Almost all the grand entrances to the park have been lost to road-building. The widening of Fishponds Road in 1909 involved cutting back the Park for nearly the whole of its edge by the road. The M32 took away the lower entrance, with its walls, gates and drinking fountain, back in the 1960s. The best entrance is the original one up in the north-west corner, right under the remains of a clump of London plane trees. The pennant wall and gateway are both listed buildings.

You can join the 20km Frome Valley Walkway to Old Sodbury at Eastville Park.

■ Try Toveys on Stapleton Road for Bristol's freshest fish.

Easton Colliery, Felix Road

The Easton Colliery in Felix Road was opened in 1830 and closed in 1911 and was at its peak production in 1870. In common with mines everywhere, conditions were terrible. Children and women worked in the mines because they were able to squeeze through the narrow passageway. At the coalface, miners worked with pickaxes and spades in a choking atmosphere.

The underground workings spread for miles. The Easton Pit was linked to Whitehall pit by an underground railway two miles long.

In his memoirs, Ben Tillett recalls how he was persuaded not to become a miner:

'One of my relatives cured me of my plan to go down the pit. He took me down into the seemingly bottomless pit and terrified me. I saw awesome blackness: spluttering candles on greasy caps, dirt and mud, pools of filthy water, stifling heat, the rush and tempest of everyone pushing, bawling, shouting and cursing.'

On 19 February 1886, eight Easton colliers died in an explosion at the pit. A relief fund was set up and each widow received £5 towards the funeral and 5 shillings (25p) a week for herself and one child under 13, and a further 2/6d (12.5p) if there were other children. The inquest into the disaster was held at Lebeq's Tavern on Stapleton Road.

EASTVILLE

Eastville used to be home to Bristol Rovers Football Club (it is now IKEA) but now people only go to Eastville (or Eastgate as it's been renamed) to shop at Tesco and IKEA, which was built despite a vociferous campaign by locals who objected to the increase in traffic (among other things) that the store would bring. Their arguments were dismissed by the planners, but guess what? Yep, the M32 to IKEA is solid with cars every single weekend. Distressingly for Bristol Rovers fans, the IKEA store is almost exactly the dimensions of the old Eastville pitch. This is because the old Eastville site was developed piecemeal and the pitch was the last bit to go. Bizarrely, a floodlight from the Muller Road end of the old ground was left standing in the Tesco's car park as a memorial to Rovers' home. It stayed there until 2003 when it was removed because it was becoming unstable. As is the way with these things, the lights were auctioned to grateful supporters. Rovers, strangely, plunged into the darkness of the bottom division of the football league for the first time in their history just about the same time as the floodlight was taken down. Now, what does that tell you?

The arrival of IKEA meant the loss of a Bristol institution, Eastville Market, which used to be held in the old Rovers' car park. To be honest, other than shopping at IKEA, there's not a great deal going on in Eastville. The area sits between Easton and Fishponds and marks the transition from inner city to suburban Bristol. Recently, this residential area has seen a drift of prostitution and street crime from the inner city. The police have clamped down on sex workers in the soon-to-be-gentrified St Paul's area, so the women have been forced over the M32 into Easton and Eastville. Nadine Hill, a 25-year-old sex worker, was murdered in Eastville Park in October 2003, increasing calls to establish a regulated red light area in the city.

Naked Truth

Emma Jane Holden

❝International opera star, Emma Jane Holden, was born at 7 Brooklyn Terrace in 1890. She died in 1938. The house was demolished in the mid 1960s to build Easton Way.❞

QUICK PINT?

The Plough in Easton is home to the Easton Cowboys football radicals.

Five famous
Rovers games at Eastville

**❶ Bristol Rovers 15
Weymouth 1**
17 November 1900, FA Cup (played at Stapleton Road). Rovers' record scoreline.

**❷ Bristol Rovers 4
Manchester United 0**
7 January 1956, FA Cup. Busby Babes demolished.

**❸ Bristol Rovers 3
Preston North End 3**
30 January 1960, FA Cup. Record attendance of 38,472.

**❹ Bristol Rovers 4
Bristol City 0**
14 December 1963, Division 3. Biggest post-war win over City.

**❺ Bristol Rovers 0
Sheffield United 0**
(Rovers won 7-6 on penalties). 5 Aug 1973, Watney Cup Final. Rovers' only Cup Final win.

STAPLETON

Stapleton has a village feel about it, despite being right next to the M32 and on the main road from Eastville to Frenchay. The peculiar impression of being time-warped from IKEA into rural England is strongest if you stroll down Colston Hill between Holy Trinity Church and Colston's School. The lane takes you down to the Frome Valley and Snuff Mills, a riverside walk that is one of the unspoilt gems of Bristol.

BITE TO EAT?
Why not stop off at **Bristol Sweet Mart** and sample one of their delicious samosas.

The impressive Stapleton parish church, Holy Trinity, is a particularly fine building. The first record of a church on this site goes back to 1438, but this one was built by Bristol architect John Norton in 1857 – the only other surviving example of Norton's religious architecture in the city is St Mary's in Stoke Bishop. Holy Trinity is built in the Victorian Gothic style with an elaborately carved door and a huge 170-foot tower. It is usually floodlit at night, so it is one of the first buildings you see when you enter Bristol via the M32 after dark. The square font, which now sits in the west porch, has been dated to about 1000AD. It was sold to a bishop's butler at one point in its history; the butler went on to become landlord of The Bell pub opposite the church and took the font with him to use as a geranium pot. It was later discovered and returned to the church sometime in the late 19th century. Colston's School, next to Holy Trinity, is for stripy-blazer posh kids. The nearby Masons Arms has a pleasant garden which offers fine views over the Frome Valley. And that, my friends, is Stapleton.

■ The Holy Trinity in Stapleton is built in the Victorian Gothic style.

■ The Bell opposite Holy Trinity once housed the church's old font. It was used as a flower pot.

Snuff Mills

☀ According to the annoying BBC consumer programme *Watchdog*, Snuff Mills has the worst public toilets in Britain (see p176), so don't go there just for the ablution facilities. However, if you want to discover a riverside walk near the centre of town, do head down to Snuff Mills. Take a picnic, or, even better, a dog. You can also go fishing down there too. Snuff Mills is the area between Blackberry Hill and Eastville

Park and, as far as anyone has been able to ascertain, there has never actually been a mill there that ground snuff.

The mill that used to stand on the Frome here in the 19th Century was called Whitwood Mill but there's evidence of a mill on this site from 1297. It's thought that Snuff Mills got its name from a local character called Snuffy Jack who worked in a snuff mill further upstream and whose smock was always covered in snuff. He may also have worked in or lived near Whitwood Mill.

WHITEHALL TO ST GEORGE

Bob Hope (yes, that Bob Hope) lived at 326 Whitehall Road when he was a nipper. Like most fortunate people, Bob (or Leslie as he was called then) passed through Whitehall on his way to somewhere better. St George's Park, which has a lake and skateboard park, lies between Whitehall and St George, where Tony Benn used to have his Labour Party office on Church Road. The monument on the 'fountain' junction of Church Road, Clouds Hill Road and Summerhill Road is the Don John Cross, which is more than 400 years old and once marked the beginning of the Kingswood Forest. It's said to have taken its name from when the funeral bier bearing the body of a Spanish nobleman rested at the cross for a while before resuming its journey. It's probably not called after the grubby little boozer of the same name just down the road past the Fountain Cafe.

Naked Truth

Famous faces
❝Frances Milton, the mother of writer Anthony Trollope was born in Stapleton back in 1780. Sarah Young, the mother of poet Thomas Chatterton was also born in Stapleton.❞

QUICK PINT?

Eastern Taste in St Mark's Road is a well-established BYO. The fish curry is fab.

■ The Fountain Cafe is the best place for a bacon butty and a cuppa in St George.

■ The Don John Cross is more than 400 years old.

Area Guide

54

MAP
BS5

FISHPONDS RD

CYCLE PATH

GREENBANK VIEW

ROYATE HILL

BANK RD

GORDON RD

BROOK RD

RD

LYPPIAT RD

CHURCH RD

9

10

11

BS6 **Cotham to Westbury Park**

Despite being full of bedsits and students, there's a
leafy calm around the Redland area

T he area to the left as you go up Gloucester Road is
sandwiched between the multi-cultural alternative
vibe of Montpelier and St Paul's and the glaring
commercial bright lights of the Whiteladies Road Strip. But
rather than mixing these two distinct flavours, BS6 has a
character all of its own…

■ Havana Cafe on Cotham Hill is
the perfect spot from which to
watch the world go by.

Past Notes

▶ **1230** Redland is
namechecked in history
books under the names
'Rubea Terra' or 'la Rede
Londe' because of its
ruddy soil.

▶ **1737** The Montague
Tavern on Montague Hill in
Kingsdown is built. Its turtle
soup becomes famous in the
gastronomic world.

▶ **1849** An outbreak of
cholera kills 444 people.

▶ **1940** Redland Church is
all but destroyed by that
Hitler fellow.

COTHAM

Cotham can be confusing
to the first-time visitor. It's a
compact, bohemian kind of
district and yet Cotham Brow
has one of the longest zebra
crossings you've ever seen.
It's full of students, but a one-
bedroom flat around here will
set you back a tidy wedge.
The first recorded resident
of this area, then known as
Codd Down, was a careless
snuffmaker called William
Hulme. Why careless? Well, he
only decided to live in a windmill – not the most sensible
thing to do with all that snuff lying around. Needless to
say, his business was blown away and he was declared
bankrupt soon afterwards.

Cotham is dominated by elegant old houses and
occasional speciality shops, pubs and restaurants. Cotham
Hill, the road that runs off Whiteladies Road at Clifton
Down, is easily the most vibrant area. By day it buzzes with
the coffee bar crowd who kill time and sip espresso in the
very continental Havana Cafe, take coffee on the pavement

■ The healthy alternative – sit
outside bluejuice on Cotham Hill
and enjoy a lovely juice.

French style at Bohéme, or top up their vitamin intake at bluejuice. There are also a few half-decent charity shops, an antiques shop and a shop devoted entirely to kites.

By night, Cotham picks up some of the spillage from the always overcrowded Whiteladies Strip but has a very distinct neighbourhood quality of its own. It's packed with loads of restaurants from right across the global spectrum. The Deco Lounge is the Cotham branch of the Bristol bar group and has more of a wine bar or restaurant atmosphere than its more bar-ish cousins south of the river or on Gloucester Road. Diners with a traditional English palate should set their wallets on stun and head for Juniper on Cotham Road, one of the finest contemporary diners in the whole of the South West where you'll find the likes of slow braised shanks of lamb on the menu with rhubarb crumble with stem ginger custard for pudding.

Naked Truth

Slave Trader's Almshouses
66Slave trader Edward Colston built the almshouses and chapel on St Michael's Hill in 1691. It's possible that the ships' timbers panelling in the chapel is from Colston's slave ships.99

QUICK PINT?

The Hare on the Hill in Kingsdown is a cosy Bath Ales pub with great bar food.

Five things...
To buy on Cotham Hill

❶ Full English breakfast and a mug of tea, **The Friary.**

❷ Calypso 125GX stunt kite, **Kitestore.**

❸ A Flu-Fighter from **bluejuice.**

❹ Stifado with rice, salad and a bottle of Demestica, **Zorbas Taverna.**

❺ A *Step-by-Step Guide to Yoga* at **Books at 58.**

■ **The Friary on Cotham Hill** has been serving top quality breakfasts (and a lot else) since way back in 1979.

KINGSDOWN

According to a Civic Society report published in the 1980s, of all the architectural crimes that were committed in Bristol in the 1960s, 'the destruction of Bristol's most important Georgian suburb' was the most despicable. If you want to see what they mean, take a look up at Kingsdown from the city centre. Interrupting the elegantly distressed original houses are the harsh, slab-like faces of some grim multi-storey council blocks. Equally irritating is the way Bristol City Council has effectively isolated Kingsdown by blocking off the handful of roads that gave vehicles access from Cheltenham Road.

Despite the best efforts of the town planners, Kingsdown has actually been getting more popular in recent years with drinkers looking to escape the nightmare of the naff pub experience. The Highbury Vaults at the top of St Michael's Hill is one of Bristol's best-known pubs thanks to its popularity with students. According to the *Observer Food Magazine* 2004 Awards, it's the Best Place to Drink in the South West, which certainly raised a few eyebrows in the South West. The garden at the Vaults seems to get bigger every year and has a forest of outdoor heaters to keep the regulars warm as they tuck into their pints of Brains SA. They have been known to offer a nice pheasant roast dinner on a Sunday too. Over the road, The White Bear has had some interesting promotions over the years, including a gameshow-style happy-hour wheeze where you could hit a button to determine the price of your drinks from free to full price. More recently, the former coaching inn joined forces with the Rajpoot Express restaurant who have moved in upstairs, so curry is big on the menu alongside the more traditional pub grub.

BITE TO EAT?

The **Deco Lounge** on the popular Cotham Hill is a relaxed diner which boasts a great menu.

■ **Generations of Bristol students have passed through the doors of the Highbury Vaults.**

Cutting through the houses behind St Michael's Hill, you'll find The Bell in Alfred Place and loitering just above the A-road traffic of Stokes Croft are three excellent pubs: the Hillgrove in Dove Street South, the nearby Hare on the Hill in Thomas Street North and The Bell in Hillgrove Street. The Bell is a local institution where you can find the likes of Dope on Plastic's John Stapleton and the Blow Pop DJs delving into their back catalogue in a low key kinda way. Because of The Bell's consistent popularity, people have been hiking up Nine Tree Hill to the Hillgrove, Bath Ales' Hare on the Hill and the other Bell lately. They are all relaxed, back-street boozers, perfect if you want to get away from the busy centre, but be careful of choosing the back table in the Hillgrove: the real fire gets real hot.

■ **La Bohème brings a European feel to Cotham Hill.**

The Kingsdown story

Wealthy merchants began moving to new homes in Kingsdown early in the 19th Century. Their aim was to escape the horrible grime of the city and the overwhelming stench of the foul-smelling Avon and Frome rivers.

Much of the Kingsdown area was owned by a man called Giles Greville. The open fields were known as the Montagues and Greville divided them into plots and then built the Montague Tavern. His plan was to attract Bristol's businessmen to set up home in Kingsdown. The tavern's turtle soup, said to be based on a recipe that had been created by a Lord Mayor of Bristol from the 13th Century, was once the talk of the turtle-supping world.

Civic banquets were held at the Montague Hotel – it has changed is name from Tavern at some point during the 18th Century – and boys from Colston School were taken there for their annual swig of grog. The fields around the Montague Hotel became the site for dawn duels and this continued well into the 19th Century. Even though the areas escaped any serious bomb damage in World War Two, sadly many of Kingsdown's finest houses and landmarks were lost in a wave of post-war redevelopment tantamount to civic vandalism.

REDLAND

If Clifton is Bristol's Chelsea and Montpelier its Notting Hill, then Redland is its Hampstead. There are probably more slightly distressed-looking bay window shutters here than anywhere else in the West Country. It has one of the highest levels of houses in multiple occupancy in the city. Yep, Redland is home to a vast army of students, former students, dope heads, media heads, musicians, teachers and some jaded beatniks who got in before the rents went mad and have managed to stay here ever since. However,

> ### Naked Truth
>
> **Portland Street Chapel**
> ❝One of the most important buildings lost when the bulldozers moved into Kingsdown was Portland Street Chapel where Thomas Webb was buried. Webb introduced Methodism to America.❞

■ The Temple Meads to Avonmouth line was opened in 1885; Redland Station opened in 1897.

not many of these folk can remember what happened last week, let alone when the district was called Rubea Terra in the 13th Century.

QUICK PINT?
The Scotchman and his Pack on St Michael's Hill has a roof terrace.

Geographically, Redland stretches from Redland Green at the top of Redland Road to Cotham Park at the bottom. On either side, Chandos Road and Zetland Road are where its heart beats fastest. Chandos is a deeply cosmopolitan road that has the look and feel of a provincial European back street. The number of new restaurants that have opened here over recent years is bewildering. Culinaria and Moreish are just some of the names now sharing space with more established haunts, such as Ahmed's Curry Cafe. Sadly long-time resident Old Possums Wine Bar closed in 2006.

■ Ahmed's Curry Cafe offers top-quality curry and knock-down prices. And they have happy hour.

A short walk via the Kensington Arms will take you past Redland Station and onto Zetland Road. There you will find Casa Mexicana which brings a Central American flavour to Redland's varied eating out options. For those who prefer their food in liquid form, the area has three pubs, The Shakespeare, The Kensington and The Clyde. Of these, only the Kenny has ever been anything other than a quiet place to have a drink.

WESTBURY PARK

Westbury Park has always been culturally split down the middle. Half the residents have an affinity with Redland; the other half side with half-witted Henleaze. Tellingly, the most interesting thing to ever happen in Westbury Park is the famous episode of the White Tree on the Downs.

According to local legend, there are a number of suspects in the frame for painting the bottom half of the tree trunk with white emulsion. All the stories date from the 1850s. The warm-hearted version has it pinned on a bloke called George Ames who lived at the nearby Cote House and did it as an act of kindness in order to stop his children's German tutor from getting lost at night when he was on his way over to teach them. The funny version blames a Mr Woodward, who did it in a last-ditch attempt to help his regularly inebriated coachman find his way home after another night on the booze. Whoever it was and whatever they meant by it, the original was dug up in the 1950s to make way for a new roundabout. The current incarnation, number three, was planted in 1974.

Westbury Park's main street, Coldharbour Road, is a little underwhelming to say the least. A restaurant, one pub, a fish and chip shop and a couple of pine furniture stores doesn't encourage many people to stop on the way through. North View is more compact and more lively. Once dominated by the cavernous AutoSpeed tyre fitting garage, the road is packed with little specialist shops such as the independent and slightly grumpy vacuum retailer called Homevac Electrics. Sadly a few places have now closed down, such as the weird shrunken Victoriana of the Gillian Richards' Dollshouse Shop. However, Cheung Kong Chinese Restaurant and La Terrazza, with its al fresco dining lend some glow after dark.

■ The Kensington was once the centre for Bristol's thriving Pinball League in the mid 1980s.

■ The house that smells – the most curious landmark in Redland is this sculpted nose on the side of resident Jane Tarr's house in Kensington Road.

Mother Pugsley's Well

☀ Some historians say that Mother Pugsley's Well (aka The Virgin's Well) stood near the junction of Nugent Hill and Arley Hill. Others say that the site is in Hillgrove Street, near the current site of The Bell. It obviously makes more sense for a well with curative powers to be on the site of one of Bristol's finest boozers, so Hillgrove Street it is. The story goes that Pugsley was killed on the day of his marriage when Cromwell's troops stormed Prior's Hill (Kingsdown). Pugsley's wife vowed to remain faithful to his memory and visited the grave on the spot where Pugsley had fallen every day for the rest of her life. Two springs of water appeared next to the grave, one of which flowed into the well. When she died, Old Mother Pugsley was buried in her wedding dress, flowers were strewn in front of the cortege and St Nicholas Church played a joyful peal of wedding bells to celebrate her being reunited with her beloved husband.

MAP
BS6

BS7 Ashley Down to Cheltenham Road

Welcome to Gloucester Road. It may be a bit shabby, but it has got a certain chic quality as well

I f you're not rich enough to live in Clifton, and don't like the idea of being south of the river, BS7 is the place for you. The A38 Gloucester Road is the main artery that connects the more sedate parts of the area to the fleshpots of the town centre. It's an odd mixture of the chic and the shambolic; parts of it are in decay, other bits are bursting with energy. But beware of heading too far out of town on the A38, Patchway beckons…

■ The Arches on Gloucester Road are one of Bristol's best known landmarks. It is also useful for carrying trains over the road.

Past Notes

▶ **1750** Two mounds of earth used for archery practice are christened 'Horfield Butts'.

▶ **1880** Horfield Road is renamed Gloucester Road.

▶ **1921** Postmaster General FG Kellaway lends his name to the Kellaway bit of Kellaway Avenue.

▶ **1990** Despite 16,664 local objections, a Tesco store is built on Golden Hill.

ASHLEY DOWN

Set between Gloucester Road, St Paul's, St Andrew's and St Werburghs, Ashley Down is one of those places you walk through on the way to somewhere else. It wasn't always this way. A couple of centuries ago, a spring in Ashley Down provided most of Bristol with its water supply. And the ludicrously steep allotments on Ashley Hill are a reminder of the days when the area was nothing but farmland. It wasn't until the 18th Century that houses began to be built here, when a number of well-heeled gentlemen chose the site because of its panoramic views over the city. But the most significant resident was a German immigrant called George Müller. Indeed Müller could be called the Patron Saint of Ashley Down. During his lifetime, he educated more than 120,000 children at his orphanage, which is now part of the City of Bristol College. At his funeral in 1898, thousands of people lined

■ After two makeovers, Robin Hood's Retreat is a right nice boozer with great food.

the streets in silent tribute. Today, Ashley Down hums with trainee electricians and beauticians from the College on a weekday, and Rovers and Bristol Rugby fans on alternate Saturdays and Sundays. The Foresters and the Ashley Arms are packed accordingly.

BISHOPSTON

The Nobel Prize winner of 1933, Paul Dirac, began unravelling the mysteries of quantum physics from 15 Monk Road, Bishopston, but even he'd struggle to calculate the rise in house prices around here in the last few years. According to a BBC property programme, Bishopston is one of the UK's 'golden miles': one of the county's hottest areas, where average prices have more than doubled since the previous century shot its bows. It's stupid, it benefits no-one except the banks, but it's easy to see why Bishopston has become so appealing.

> **Naked Truth**
>
> **Massive Attack's schooling**
> ❝Robert Del Naja (aka 3D or Delge) of Massive Attack was kicked out of the sixth form at Monks Park School, Horfield, for repeatedly turning up with his hair dyed different colours. The last time it was blue.❞

QUICK PINT?
The Robin Hood's Retreat has real ale and an impressive menu.

Close enough to the Gloucester Road to pop out for a drink at half past ten on a Tuesday night, but far enough away to ensure you don't step in any Miss Millie's Fried Chicken carcasses as you walk through your front door, Bishopston gives its residents the best of both worlds.

As well as all the shops, cafes and restaurants, it can also claim to be the home of Bristolian sport. Both the Memorial Stadium, where Bristol Rovers and Bristol Rugby Club play, and Gloucestershire County Cricket Ground are located within walking distance. The city's oldest public swimming pool, Bristol North Baths, had been right at its centre. The baths are now closed, but not without a fight from local protestors.

GLOUCESTER ROAD

One of Bristol's longest and most interesting streets, Gloucester Road is an extraordinary mish-mash of trendy bars, spit 'n' sawdust pubs, chic restaurants and cheap cafes. It also has more charity shops per square metre

Five things...
To buy near Gloucester Rd

1 A wooden giraffe and a brightly-coloured shirt from **La Maison du Zigou Dam, African shop**, 336 Gloucester Road.

2 A bag of 100 singles from **Plastic Wax Records**, 222 Cheltenham Road.

3 A Smeg fridge from **Nailsea Electrical**, 171 Gloucester Road.

4 An onion-coated salami and some Y Fenni Welsh cheese from **T & P A Murray** butchers and delicatessen, 153 Gloucester Road.

5 A nice fairtrade, organic cotton shirt from the **Bishopston Trading Company**, 193 Gloucester Road.

than anywhere else in the South West. Cancer Research, St Peter's Hospice, Sue Ryder, Tenovus… you name them, they're all selling terrible jumpers from the 1980s.

Daytime browsers should be prepared to lose hours and sacrifice the soles of their feet in order to fully explore Glossy Road's multitude of nook-and-cranny stores. The best place to begin is around the junction with Ashley Down Road where the Tinto Lounge shares pavement space with the Antiques Warehouse. As you tread southwards, you'll stumble across a vintage Sicilian delicatessen (Licata's), several 1950s-style Italian barbers, hundreds of unwanted Spandau Ballet LPs, thousands of dusty Penguin novels, enough vintage furniture to decorate a castle, an entire shop devoted to the footwear of a certain Dr Marten and an ever growing range of 'gert lush' Bristol dialect T-shirts from Beast.

BITE TO EAT?

Cafe Unlimited is a friendly fairtrade outfit which has sofas and a children's play area. Oh, and great drinks and cakes too.

If you get hungry along the way, the choices are just as varied; from deep-fried chicken in a bucket to award-winning curry, pavement-fried hot-dogs to authentic pizza houses. Gloucester Road is alive with a dizzy melody of aromas from all over the world, especially after dark. New flavours such as the Mediterranean-influenced Bistro La Barrique and the Turkish eaterie Ezo now sit alongside old favourites such as the Sheesh Mahal, the Ganges and the Taste of Morocco and an ever-increasing number of

■ The Prince of Wales on Gloucester Road offers excellent food which is almost all organic.

■ The latest breaks and beats from Rooted Records.

Three strangest shops

Romantica

A peculiar cross between a Liberace museum and the bedroom of the least cultured stalker in England. From sickeningly twee cuddly toys to sickeningly awful posters of semi-naked girls near motorbikes, Romantica is where the tasteless go to celebrate their lack of culture.
■ 139 Gloucester Road ■ Tel: 949 3303

Help The Animals

Beware. You may find yourself drawn into this place, such is the bizarre nature of the frontage. With its original 1960s sign lettering, this is the charity shop that time forgot on a road that boasts some of Bristol's least

bijou charity dens. The window displays are notoriously bleak. The design team drape, say, a yellow cardigan next to a snakes-and-ladders game and lean a broken tennis racket against a naked, one-eyed doll.
■ 7 Gloucester Road ■ Tel: 942 7822

Brewer's Droop

Fermentation vessels, thermometers, hydrometers, yeasts, sterilisation equipment, dried hops, empty bottles and bizarre corking devices aplenty live in this musty and decidedly bearded cathedral of home brewing. If you've ever had the urge to make beer that tastes like old socks, this is the place to come for advice.
■ 36a Gloucester Road ■ Tel: 942 7923

take-aways for the inebriated to stumble into after closing time. Typically, these places are of the strip-lit, no-frills, get-it-down-yer-neck variety. The reason there are so many late-night temples of grease is the number of pubs on Gloucester Road these days. Some are mysterious, net-curtained affairs that haven't changed since the 1960s. But the stylish refurbishments of familiar haunts such as the New Prince of Wales and the Prom Wine Bar and the arrival of the 'shabby-chic' likes of the One30 bar and the Pipe & Slippers on Cheltenham Road suggest that the area is shaking off its reputation as a bit of a rough place to drink on a Saturday night.

> ### Naked Truth
>
> **Jack Board**
> 66 Jack Board, the Gloucestershire and England wicketkeeper in the early 1900s, lived at 22 Manor Road in Bishopston. He died in 1924 on board ship returning to Bristol from South Africa. 99

■ Second-hand clothes emporium RePsycho is also home to the Prime Cuts record store.

> **QUICK PINT?**
> **The Prince of Wales** on Gloucester Rd has organic food and a beer garden.

But what really gives Gloucester Road its 'there and back again' charm is the mixture of old-established businesses and curious newcomers attracted by the cosmopolitan vibe. Butchers Stutt & Son has been trading on Gloucester Road since 1919, Pawsons the greengrocers first opened its doors in 1958 while the Bizarre second-hand furniture shop and Bishop Antiques have been there since the 1970s. It may be long, mainly straight and often scruffy, but Gloucester Road has got deep roots.

■ Cary Grant was born in Hughendon Road, Horfield, and went to Bishop Road School in Bishopston.

HORFIELD

When Buffalo Bill and his Wild West extravaganza came to town in September 1891, he headed for Horfield Common where a 15,000 seat stadium had been built for his twice-daily performances. It was the biggest show ever staged in Bristol: four trainloads of animals, performers and equipment arrived at Temple Meads; the parade up Gloucester Road to Horfield was a mile long. Buffalo Bill (real name Colonel William Cody) staged 12 performances over six days to a combined audience of more than 100,000 people who all paid a shilling each to attend this huge spectacle.

Horfield could attract the stars in those days, although, even 100 years ago, the residents of Horfield were so badly behaved that the area was considered a no-go zone for travellers. All manner of nasty vagrants and thieves liked to lurk in the large wood near the common and records show that one commentator believed the area was 'lawless… worse even than Filton'. Maybe it's appropriate that Bristol's main prison was dumped here.

By the 1930s, Horfield had grown into one of those solidly working-class communities where people left the doors open and no-one ever got burgled. These days the recycling bins of the two-up-two-down terraced streets are full of *Guardians* and *Observers*.

Conversely, the shops remain cheap and not very cheerful. Just so you know, everything in the Pound Store is a quid, so don't make the mistake of asking the assistant how much something is, as someone not a million miles away from the keyboard that is typing these words once did.

The Tinto Lounge, one of a chain of Lounge bars around the city, has brought a touch of sophistication over the road from the John Cabot pub. The Cabot has got the biggest beer garden in Horfield, you know.

BITE TO EAT?

Pop in to **Oh! Calcutta** on Gloucester Road and sample their modern slant on traditional Indian cuisine.

■ Tinto Lounge on Gloucester Road is just one of the locally-owned chain of bars to hit Bristol.

Bristol's last execution

Russell Pascoe, a 23-year-old Bristolian, was the last person to be executed in Bristol. He was hanged at Horfield Prison at 8am on Tuesday 17 December 1963 for his part in the murder of a Cornish farmer. Dennis Whitty, convicted with him, was hanged at the same time in Winchester.

The execution was one of the last to be carried out in Britain before the abolition of capital punishment in 1965. About 70 protesters held a silent vigil outside the prison gates. The Bishop of Bristol, the Rt Rev Oliver Tomkins, who had earlier protested at the death sentence, visited Pascoe in his cell shortly before the hanging. According to the newspaper reports of the time, he emerged pale-faced and weary at the prison gates.

The Bishop asked the 70 people keeping the silent vigil to pray for the condemned man. But when he asked for 'a kind thought for the men who hate having to carry out this unpleasant task', a man shouted: 'They don't have to do it!' The Bishop replied: 'They do.' The demonstrators had kept up a day-and-night protest vigil since the previous Saturday and were joined by Bristol South East MP Tony Benn the night before the execution. Pascoe and Whitty, who had been living with three women in a caravan near Truro, were sentenced to death at Cornwall Assizes for the murder of 64-year-old farmer William Rowe during a robbery. Their appeals were dismissed and on the Saturday before their execution the Home Office said that the Home Secretary had found no grounds for a reprieve. The demonstrators at Horfield included university students, lecturers and a contingent from Cornwall. The *Bristol Evening Post* reported that as the demonstrators dispersed shortly after 8am, one man shouted: 'Sickening! The people of Bristol should have torn the gates down instead of just standing around!' The Bishop of Bristol issued a statement in which he said Pascoe's execution: 'no more justifies hanging than the fact that war may evoke heroism is a justification of war'.
Horfield Prison, 17 December 1963

ST ANDREW'S

This area is clustered around the charming, softly rolling features of St Andrew's Park. Most people laugh when they drive along Effingham Road because it's as close to swearing as a street name can get without someone alerting the authorities. But it's possible that only a handful of people who live outside this most underrated of BS7 areas have ever laid eyes on the very unexpected Sefton Park Post Office and Shop on Surrey Road. This is retailing as a fish out of water; one lone money-making mirage right in the middle of a completely unspectacular

■ Venue magazine is produced from an office on North Road.

Naked Truth

The Memorial Stadium
66Bristol Rugby Club moved to the Filton Avenue Ground in 1921. It was dedicated as a memorial to local rugby players who died in World War One. Bristol defeated Cardiff 19-3 in the opening match. The Rugby Club now shares the ground with Bristol Rovers.99

QUICK PINT?
The Wellington on Horfield Common is a Bath Ales boozer and handy for the football.

residential street. It might be just around the corner from the County Ground but this shop belongs to a more gentle commercial age. Please try to visit. But, a word of advice: think of something to buy before you go in.

Apart from its undiscovered shop, St Andrew's is probably best known as the place where Bristol's *Venue* magazine is put together. Keep an eye out for highly-stressed journos chain-smoking cigarettes on North Road.

■ St Andrew's Park is a large green haven just off the busy Gloucester Road.

MAP
BS7

INDEX OF PLACES

1 Arches	10 Horfield Prison	19 Texaco Garage
2 Bishopston Trading Co.	11 Sportsman Pub	20 RePsycho
3 Cafe Unlimited	12 St Andrews Park	21 Grecian Kebab House
4 Oh! Calcutta	13 Polish Church	22 Bread Basket
5 Antiques Warehouse	14 Venue Magazine	23 Chinese Supermarket
6 Licata's	15 Prince Of Wales	24 Montpelier Station
7 Prom Wine Bar	16 Beast	25 Memorial Stadium
8 One30	17 Tinto Lounge	26 Country Ground
9 Pipe & Slippers	18 Rooted Records	

BS8 Clifton to Blackboy Hill

The Merchant Venturers built much of Clifton, and quite a few of them still live there

It wasn't that long ago that the only places to get a pint on Whiteladies Road were in the intimate surroundings of the Vittoria and the less hospitable environs of the Dug and Duck next to the ABC Whiteladies Cinema. Now the Strip, as it has become known, is a theme-bar, student playground awash with alcopops and cocktails. Clifton hasn't changed that much though…

Past Notes

▶ **350BC** An Iron Age camp appears on Observatory Hill, just above the Suspension Bridge.

▶ **1080** Clifton is described in the Domesday Book as a settlement of around 30 agricultural folk.

▶ **1130** The area falls into the aristocratic hands of a certain William de Clifton.

▶ **1791** Building begins on Royal York Crescent. It takes almost 30 years to complete.

CLIFTON

Bristol's most affluent area sits high above the rest of the city on top of the Avon Gorge. Clifton has got it all: it has an observatory, a camera obscura, the second oldest zoo in Britain – even its very own 'designer' suspension bridge. There's more. Clifton is quiet without being boring, lively without being rowdy; it has more than its fair share

■ **Clifton Arcade on Boyces Avenue is just the ticket for jeans, vinyl, pet portraits and urns.**

■ **The Albion is tucked away down the end of Boyces Avenue. The food is expensive pub grub but the cocktails are worth the visit.**

of pubs and places to eat, but take-aways are few and far between. No matter where you are in Clifton, you're only a brisk stroll away from Park Street, Whiteladies Road and the City Centre. And then there's Durdham Downs, Clifton's unofficial back garden; not to mention Ashton Court and Leigh Woods about a mile over the bridge. And it's not just geographically and aesthetically superior; Clifton has the edge historically too. The fact that it is mentioned in the Domesday Book means Clifton is older than Bristol itself.

There are remains of an iron-age camp near Clifton Suspension Bridge that date back to 350BC. But this being Clifton, it wasn't long before those primitive ways made way for a more refined design for living. From the late 18th Century onwards, the area became a magnet for artistic types and the wealthy. Cricketing legend WG Grace bought a house in Victoria Square, Charles Dickens and Oscar Wilde paid a visit and then the bizarre camera obscura was built.

Clifton stood for culture. And even as recently as the giddy days of post-punk, Clifton was a hotbed of creative activity. In the daytime, the long-gone Focus Cafe was full of dangerous-looking people with long coats and connections to

Naked Truth

Camera Obscura
❝William West may have been one of the first ever conceptual photo-artists. Why else would he lease an old windmill on the Downs and turn it into an observatory, complete with a telescope and a camera obscura?❞

The Pop Group. In the evening, in the back bar of The Lion in Cliftonwood, bands were formed and the record labels Heartbeat and Fried Egg were born. From this whirr of DIY energy came The Cortinas, Social Security, The Europeans, Maximum Joy, the Spics, Jimmy Galvin, Pigbag and more. In 1979, Clifton was the only place to be.

QUICK PINT?
The terrace of the **Avon Gorge Hotel** has fantastic views over the bridge and gorge.

But by the end of the 1980s, the Albion was full of tosspots and their cling-on girlfriends. They thought they were Ben from Curiosity Killed The Cat but they looked more like Huey Lewis from the News. These tragic Jeremys and Nigellas used to be known as 'sloanes'. And they're still hanging around the village now. Sure, they've swapped the rugger-shirts and Barbours for jeeps and beats but the accents and manners are unmistakable. 'An evening at Bar Ha! Ha! and then onto Po Na Nas.' Useless. Boring. Ignore them. But whatever you do, don't ignore Clifton. It might have lost most of its jagged bohemian edges but at least the activity in Christchurch Studios which is run by the Bristol Old Vic Theatre School and whose clients include Massive Attack and Andy Sheppard means it's not an entirely dry zone. And there's plenty of life too at the Amoeba cafe-bar and gallery, the Clifton Arcade, the York Cafe, the Corrie Tap and The Lansdown. But who put that skanky Somerfield supermarket right in the middle of Princess Victoria Street?

Five unusual...
BS8 landmarks

❶ **Blackboy Hill Victorian urinal**: needs must and all that.

❷ **Queens Court**: the art-deco flats on St Paul's Road.

❸ **Toilets** near the water tower on the Downs: Victoria Hughes cared for sex workers when she worked here as a lavatory attendant from 1929 to 1962.

❹ **The Trim Trail** on the Downs: bizarre pre-gym outdoor training option.

❺ **BUPA hospital**, top of Blackboy Hill: once Tiffany's, Bristol's leading plastic-palm-tree disco.

CLIFTON SUSPENSION BRIDGE

One of the most famous landmarks in the world and the most obvious reminder of Isambard Kingdom Brunel's engineering genius, the Clifton Suspension Bridge story goes back to 1753. This was when Bristol wine merchant William Vick left a legacy to build a bridge over the Avon Gorge. In 1829, the Merchant Venturers appointed a bridge committee which announced a bridge design competition with a first prize of 100 guineas. Brunel was 23 and recuperating in Clifton from the injuries he had received when the Thames Tunnel (on which he was working with his father, Marc Brunel) had flooded. He submitted four plans for the competition. His favourite design involved a 91-metre tunnel which emerged from the side of the gorge and ran into another tunnel on the Leigh Woods side. In all, 22 plans were submitted. The elderly Thomas Telford, one of the best engineers of his day, dismissed all the designs, including Brunel's, and instead offered one of his own that involved two mammoth pillars being built from the foot of the gorge. The Venturers rejected this too and in 1831 Brunel's design was accepted. However, big business was reluctant to invest in Bristol following the Queen Square riots of 1831 and it was five years before work began.

In 1836, an iron bar 305 metres long was hauled across the gorge and a basket to transport men and materials slung from it. Brunel himself made the first crossing and the basket stuck at the lowest point 60 metres above the

■ The legendary Primrose Cafe is cafe by day and cosy restaurant by night.

■ Clifton Suspension Bridge was designed in 1831 for horsedrawn traffic, but now carries four million cars each year.

BITE TO EAT?

The York Cafe in York Place is famous for waving a greasy spoon at Clifton's more refined eateries.

Clifton open air swimming pool

Is nothing sacred? Quite apart from the fact that the Clifton Pool in Oakfield Grove behind the Victoria Rooms is a Grade II listed building and of genuine architectural significance, it was one of those out-of-the-ordinary places that people really enjoyed using. In the 1930s, it became the first electrically-heated pool in the UK. It was closed in 1990 after springing a leak. In 1997, Sovereign Homes told the City Council they wanted to demolish the 150 year-old Egyptian-themed heritage site and build some flats. 'No problem,' said the cash-blind suits at the College Green. But then the Glass Boat Company (the people behind innovative eateries Glass Boat and Spyglass) bought the site and put forward ambitious plans to renovate the pool, introduce sauna, spa and massage rooms and create a restaurant and cafe. At the time of writing, the plans were still being shuffled around the planning department at Brunel House where, it seems, anything that doesn't involve building flats gets put to the bottom of the pile.

river. Brunel climbed out of the basket, up the rope and released the cable from the jammed pulley. By 1843, the two towers were completed but funds were exhausted. To save money, the committee reduced the height of the towers and scrapped the decorative sphinxes on them. Brunel died in 1859 aged 53, through overwork and 40 cigars a day, without seeing the completion of his bridge, which he referred to in his diary as: 'My first love, my darling.' The opening ceremony for the bridge was on 8 December 1864.

HOTWELLS

As part of the extensive research carried out on your behalf for the

QUICK PINT?
Enjoy the **Merchants Arms,** a peaceful Bath Ales pub on Merchants Road.

Naked Truth

Flying under the bridge
❝The first plane to fly under Clifton Suspension Bridge was piloted by Frenchman M Tetard in 1911. The practice was banned but in 1957 a pilot from 501 Sqn, Filton flew a Vampire jet underneath the bridge at a speed of 450mph. He crashed into the side of the gorge and was killed instantly.❞

■ Royal York Crescent is one of the longest terraces of its type in Europe. There is no number 13.

purpose of writing this book, the entire publishing team, plus one hitch-hiker on crutches, descended on Hotwells to see what, if anything, had changed. And the one single most significant thing we can report about the area is that it is really, really noisy. Standing on the pavement trying to cross four lanes of traffic on Hotwell Road, the peaceful drink or two we had planned down by the Harbourside felt as if it was in another dimension. Still, it's not as if there's a shortage of ale houses around here. From the Adam & Eve on Hope Chapel Hill to the Bag O'Nails at the bottom of Jacobs Wells Road, Hotwells has more great pubs than its status as Lower Clifton deserves.

■ The terrace of the White Lion at the Avon Gorge Hotel offers a great view of the Clifton Suspension Bridge.

Until 1934, there used to be an almost perpendicular railway at the foot of the gorge that could take passengers up to Clifton in 40 seconds. You can still see the facade of the Clifton Rocks funicular railway on Hotwell Road near the suspension bridge. The station at the top was next to the current Avon Gorge Hotel. There also used to be a spring that gushed out of St Vincent's Rock that drew tourists from miles around (see p75). But back to our walk around the pubs of Hotwell Road. What places like The Bear Inn (261 Hotwell Road) offer is something a little off the cultural beaten track. Every Friday night, for example, The Bear turns into the Bebop Club, a live jazz happening for purists. But for this gang of fume-choked investigators, it's the places that sit on the docks that beckon. Timbers well and truly shivered, we sail into the Nova Scotia (1 Nova Scotia Place), one of the city's last great 19th-Century maritime haunts. It's cosy inside; cold outside. We sit down by the water and freeze. After that we hit the Pump House (Merchants Road), just on the other side of the water. It's more of a restaurant than a bar, but a good place to sit outside in the summer. Next up there is the impossibly pink Rose of Denmark (6 Dowry Place) which offers a friendly welcome and excellent food downstairs in the old cellar. Then on to the Merchants Arms (5 Merchants Road), a Bath Ales pub with an excellent selection of fine beers and the snuggest of wood-panelled snug bars. Back on the main road, the La Demi Lune Bistro (118 Hotwell Road) used to be the Spring Gardens gastro pub but is now a full-on restaurant. The Mardyke (126 Hotwell Road) isn't best known for its food, (although there's the Mardyke Cafe next door), but rather as Bristol's premier bikers' pub. On the day of our visit it was biker-free – and very empty. The Plume of Feathers (135 Hotwell Road) on the opposite side of the four lanes of traffic used to be a lively, if cramped, music venue; now it seems to have reverted back to being a quiet local.

The Hope and Anchor on Jacobs Wells Road has a lovely large Victorian walled garden, a good selection of real ale, a lively atmosphere and a wide range of excellent food. Our last stop is on the outskirts of Hotwells at the very compact Bag 'O Nails (141 St Georges Road), a real ale favourite that used to be called the American Eagle. A rickety old wooden floor, gas lighting and a solid choice of beers made this the regional CAMRA Pub of the Year in 2000. Eccy Thumper, Three Blind Mice and Stout Coffin are just three of the names to conjure with on draught. Duvel, Erdinger Dunkel and Polish import Zywiec line up in the crowded Euro-flavoured bottled department. Top beer and all that, but surely they could have come up with a better name – from a noble bird of prey to a something that your dad keeps in his shed. It would be a little unfair to say that described Hotwells.

■ The entrance to Clifton Rocks funicular railway can still be seen on the Portway. The railway closed in 1934.

■ The Merchants Arms in Hotwells is one of the growing number of Bath Ales pubs in the city.

HOTWELLS SPA
HOW BRISTOL BECAME A TOP BRITISH SPA TOWN

Hot hot hot

The Hotwells area of Bristol takes its name from the hot well or spring that once made Bristol one of the most important spa towns in Britain. The spring is still there, it runs into the Avon below Hotwell Road, just south of the Suspension Bridge. The gassy water emerges at 76 degrees Fahrenheit (23C). According to an analysis carried out in 1912, the water is 170 times more radioactive than the public water supply. Hardly surprising then, that those who have taken the water say it produces a similar sensation to being drunk. The spring was once at the centre of an impressive spa and leisure complex, but today very few Bristolians would even know where to find it. The problem was that the spring was beneath the water level of the River Avon for all but one and a half hours a day.

Bristol's worldwide fame

There is some evidence that the waters were being taken as far back as the 15th Century when sailors used it as a cure for scurvey and other skin conditions. Certainly, it was attracting enough publicity by 1676 for the Merchant Venturers to buy the land, along with most of Clifton. The water was held in a brick reservoir (or well) to prevent contamination from the river. By the end of the 17th Century, bottled Bristol spa water was being sent all over the world.

In 1695, the Venturers leased the spring to Charles Jones and Thomas Callow for £5 a year, on condition that they spent £500 on developing the area. By 1723, a pump room and assembly room had been built and high society flocked to Hotwells to take the waters, attend lavish balls and take river cruises on the Avon. The restorative powers of the water attracted the medical profession to Hotwells and by the mid 18th Century, Dowry Square had become Bristol's Harley Street. In 1729, a playhouse was built at Jacobs Wells then another spring was discovered in the Avon Gorge. Another pumphouse and more lodging houses were built as the Hotwells boom continued. But the second spa

had closed by the end of the 18th Century because access was difficult. The original hot well continued to draw worldwide visitors to take the waters and enjoy this lively resort.

Fallen from grace

A second assembly room was built and the Colonnade was constructed to house expensive shops; it's a private house now on the side of the Portway, but the distinctive columns are still standing. Then the boom economy went bust almost overnight. Samuel Powell, who took over the lease in 1790, more than doubled spa prices; at around the same time a Dr Beddoes in Dowry Square publicly questioned the healing powers of the water and the rumours began to spread that the spring was no longer effective. The boarding houses became known as Death Row with only those desperate for a cure coming to Hotwells. The Avon was highly polluted and the area rapidly fell into decay. It's not a pretty picture: incurable consumptives, run-down houses and a river full of turds. Unsurprisingly, polite society preferred the attractions of Bath or the Continental spa towns.

Various attempts were made to revive the spa and to pump the water up to Clifton to avoid the increasing stench from the Avon. The last serious effort to reestablish Bristol as a spa town was in 1890 when the Merchant Venturers granted permission to George Newnes to build the Clifton Rocks funicular railway on condition that he pumped water to Clifton and built a spa next to the station at the top of the Gorge. In 1894, Newnes opened the Grand Pump Room; four years later he completed work on the Grand Spa Hotel next to it (now the Avon Gorge Hotel). But the spa was closed on health grounds in 1913. By 1920, the Grand Pump Room had become a cinema and, in the 1950s, it became one of Bristol's premier rock 'n' roll dancehalls. It's difficult to imagine that the area around the Portway was once one of the most fashionable resorts in the country, or that the hot spring that brought that wealth to Bristol still pours into the Avon.

WHITELADIES ROAD

It's wrongly assumed by some newcomers to the city that the origin of the Whiteladies Road and Blackboy Hill names are a tasteless reminder of the city's shameful slave past. But it was never the case that white ladies would go up the hill to buy black boys. There was no significant domestic slave trade in Bristol, the slavers unloaded their human cargo in the Americas and brought back sugar, tobacco and cotton so there were relatively few black slaves in service in Bristol.

The name Blackboy is more likely to refer to the tar-painted faces of criminals who were hanged on the gallows on the Downs. Or it could be that the Blackboy Hill takes its name from the Blackboy Tavern, or Blackamoor's Head, a name popularised at the time of the Crusades when it was used as a description of North African Muslims – many inns were given this name complete with a suitably illustrated sign. It's also possible that the name is a reference to Charles II who was known as the Black Boy because of his swarthy complexion. Whiteladies Road is also probably called after an inn.

Up until a few years ago, the long, straight stretch of road that heads down from the top of Blackboy Hill and comes to an end when it reaches the Victoria Rooms was little more than somewhere you'd pass through on your way to Park Street. But as consensus politics got comfy at the end of the 1990s, so an invasion of super-bars arrived to suck up all the affluence. Suddenly, the street was packed full of swish new drinking dens with names, such as Boom, Bar Humbug, Henry J Beans and the Fine Line and the more established haunts, such as the Vittoria, looked like an oddity from a last orders that time forgot.

Someone, somewhere in marketing, nicknamed the whole thing 'The Strip' and it has been Bristol's most sellable night-time leisure mile ever since. Yes, it's as bad as that. When the weekend comes around, thousands of call centre operatives dress up like *Blind Date* contestants so they can stand and shiver in queues just to get in. And what is it they crave so desperately? Five-deep scrums at

BITE TO EAT?

Fishworks on Whiteladies Road is the city's leading seafood restaurant. Great for lunch or dinner.

■ The Vittoria used to be one of the few places to get a pint on Whiteladies Road.

■ Birdcage Walk in Clifton once led to the 12th-Century St Andrew's Church. The church was destroyed in a bombing raid in 1941.

every bar, gormless Ministry of Sound re-mixes chugging away on maximum volume and a wall of bottled alcopops that taste like piss. Those in the know go elsewhere. Thankfully, it is still possible to spend a great evening on Whiteladies Road without bumping into somebody who reads *Heat* magazine every week. Planet Pizza (83 Whiteladies Road) does easy eating; Deasons (43 Whiteladies Road) does it with a bit more class; Quartier Vert (85 Whiteladies Road) was named best restaurant in Bristol in a poll in 2001 for its rustic style of Mediterranean influences, while the Edwardian-themed supper parties at Colleys Supper Rooms (153 Whiteladies Road) has won it many admirers. Kitsch but swish bar Stark (168 Whiteladies Road) is surely worth at least one visit and Alibi (96 Whiteladies Road) almost threatens to be cool. And if all else fails you can always prop up the bar in the old Blackboy Inn (171 Whiteladies Road). 'Pint of Mild is it?'

■ **This doorway round the back of the Avon Gorge Hotel is one of the few remaining clues that the Pump Room used to be here.**

Naked Truth

Pembroke Road

66Until the last century, Pembroke Road in Clifton was known as Gallows Acre Lane, a reference to the gallows that stood on the edge of the Downs.99

QUICK PINT?

The Quinton House in Park Place has a good selection of real ales.

MAP
BS8

INDEX OF PLACES

A brief history of Bristol

Everything you need to know about Bristol history from 978 to now...

Bristol was originally a Saxon settlement called Brigstow or Bricgstoc (the place of the bridge) which was formed where the River Frome met the River Avon near the present-day site of Bristol Bridge. The Frome was later diverted and now joins the Floating Harbour in the Centre. The original settlement was on the site of Castle Park (handy for Broadmead) while the Medieval city expanded into the area surrounding Corn Street and St Nicholas Market.

There is little evidence of major Roman influence in Bristol – they seem to have preferred Bath and (unusually) Keynsham, although a Roman Villa was discovered at Kings Weston during the construction of Lawrence Weston housing estate in 1947. Perhaps Bristol is jealous of Bath's Roman heritage, because since the Middle Ages various historians have fabricated a Roman past to help enhance the city's reputation. It's an equally dubious story with Bristol's founders Brennus and Belinus, whose statues are on St John's Gate (the last remaining section of the city wall) at the bottom of Broad Street.

According to *A History of Bristol* by John Corry, printed in 1810 and based on earlier works, Malmutius (c.483BC) – King of Cornwall, and later Monarch of Britain – and Queen Corwenna had two sons, called Brennus and Belinus. It is said that they reigned jointly as Kings of Britain following their father's death and founded a major settlement at Bristol. Many stories are heard about Brennus and Belinus, but there is no evidence that they actually existed, or even that Bristol was founded earlier than Saxon times. Saying that, some records report that the Romans referred to Bristol as *Caer Bren*, or City of Brennus. However, despite allegedly founding Bristol long before Christ was born,

■ **Queen Elizabeth I entered through St John's Gate when she visited the city in 1584. It is not recorded whether she popped into Horts for a goblet of Youngs.**

Thomas Clarkson
1760–1846

Stayed here in 1787 to research the condition of slaves being transported

■ **The plaque at the Seven Stars pub in St Thomas which commemorates the site of Clarkson's investigations which led to the slave trade being abolished.**

the statues of Brennus and Belinus on St John's Gate show them with crucifixes. Which is slightly odd.

In Welsh legend, Brennus and Belinus were the sons of Dyfnwal Moelmyd, who became King of Britain and built four great roads across the Kingdom, one of which ran alongside a wide gorge at a city known as *Caer Odor*, or The Castle at the Gap. The only remaining reference to Caer Odor appears in the name of the Bristol Welsh Society: *Cymdeithas Cymry Caerodor*.

Even further back in time, the Avon Gorge was said to have been hewn from the rock by two giants, the brothers Vincent and Goram. Goram, who was an idle giant, fell asleep and was tragically killed when Vincent threw a pickaxe to him and it accidentally split his skull in half. This left Vincent distraught and he subsequently left Bristol and headed to Somerset to build Stonehenge. Following this, Vincent swam across to Ireland so that he could construct the Giant's Causeway in what is now County Antrim. He then returned to Bristol and lived by the side of the Avon Gorge, which is why the area is known as Vincent Rocks.

■ Belinus sits alongside his brother Brennus on St John's Arch.

■ A sketch of Bristol believed to date from 1640. It is certainly before 1664 because that is when Cromwell ordered Bristol Castle to be destroyed. Note the shops and houses on Bristol Bridge and St Peter's Church which still stands on Castle Green.

THE BRISTOL HIGH CROSS

A BIT OF MEDIEVAL HISTORY IN BERKELEY SQUARE

One of the few remaining links with Medieval Bristol is tucked away in the corner of a small park in Berkeley Square, off Park Street. It's a replica of the Bristol High Cross, a fine piece of craftsmanship that stood at the centre of the Medieval town. If you imagine that the junction of Corn Street, Broad Street, Wine Street and High Street once formed a town square, that's where the new High Cross was erected to commemorate the granting of Bristol's Charter in 1373. It replaced the previous High Cross, of which there are no remaining records.

The High Cross had four niches containing the statues of King John, Henry III, Edward III and Edward IV, all of whom had contributed to Bristol's expansion by conferring important charters. The whole Cross was gilded and coloured. In 1633, the Cross was repaired and altered to include the figures of Henry VI, Elizabeth I, James I and Charles I, who had further endowed privileges on the city. The Cross was later painted vermilion, blue and gold. By the beginning of the 18th Century, the large Cross, surrounded by steps and an iron fence, was becoming an obstruction in the increasingly busy streets. In 1733, the deputy chamberlain, Mr Vaughan, who lived at the corner of High Street and Wine Street, claimed his life and house were in danger from it every time the wind blew. A petition for its removal described the Cross as 'a superstitious relick' and 'a public nuisance'. Magistrates ordered the Cross to be put away in the Guildhall.

After protests, the High Cross was re-erected on College Green. However, in 1763, the fashionable set, who walked eight or ten abreast on the Green, complained that it impeded their promenading. It was taken down again and stored in a corner of the Cathedral. In 1765, it was given away by the Dean of Bristol to his friend Henry Hoare of Stourhead to use as an estate ornament. The High Cross is still at Stourhead and, in 1973, the Lord Mayor of Bristol unveiled a plaque there as part of the celebrations for the 600th anniversary of the granting of the city's

■ **This hidden gem can be found in the corner of Berkeley Square, just off Park Street.**

charter. In 1848, a replica High Cross was built and erected on College Green. That, too, was demolished because of vandalism; it is the top part of this replica that survives in Berkeley Square. One of the missing statues from the replica is said to be in a private garden in Bedminster, South Bristol.

Occasionally there are campaigns to re-site the High Cross near the top of Corn Street, but they are usually greeted with remarkable indifference. However, the plans announced in 2006 to redevelop the St Mary le Port site opposite St Nick's Church by Bristol Bridge caused such public outrage, that the future of this area and perhaps of the High Cross could well come to the fore. There was another medieval High Cross on Gallows Hill (St Michael's Hill) that marked the city boundary, but there is no record of what happened to it.

A BLUFFER'S GUIDE TO BRISTOL HISTORY

55BC The Romans invade Britain. The Dobunni tribe who live in the Bristol area defend themselves at Blaise, Leigh Woods and Clifton Down. There is no Roman Bristol, though there is a fort and port at Sea Mills.

C10th **978** Two silver coins minted in Bristol at the beginning of the reign of Ethelred II (978-1016) are the first evidence of Saxon Bristol as a centre of commerce and proof that it has its own mint. They carry the stamp of the coin maker 'Aelfward on Bric'.

C11th **1066** Population of Bristol thought to be somewhere between 4,000 and 5,000.

1067 Bristol surrenders to William The Conqueror without a fight. Then King Harold's sons launch an unsuccessful attack on the town from Ireland in an attempt to unseat the Normans. They are beaten back from the city gates and pillage Somerset instead.

1086 The Domesday Book records that Bristol is part of the Manor of Barton. The name Barton survives in the Barton Hill (pronounced 'Bart Nil') area of Bristol, famous for its multi-coloured tower blocks and the Rhubarb public house. By now Bristol is an established port trading with Dublin. There is some evidence of a white slave trade between Bristol and Ireland.

1088 First record of the original Bristol Castle near Bristol Bridge.

C12th **1115** First church built on the present site of St Mary Redcliffe.

1120 Robert, Earl of Gloucester, begins strengthening Bristol Castle. The Castle is built of Caen stone and has a large dungeon. The foundation walls of the keep are reputed to have been 25 foot thick.

1140 Robert Fitzhardinge, Bristol's richest citizen, begins work on St Augustine's Abbey, later to become Bristol Cathedral.

1155 Bristol is granted its first Royal Charter confirming certain rights of the townspeople. No record of this charter survives.

1171 After the English conquer Ireland, Henry II gives Dublin to the people of Bristol as a colony. Many Bristolians settle there.

1188 Date of the earliest surviving Royal Charter. King John's Charter reveals that Bristol is by now a thriving merchant town with a penchant for protectionism – a tradition carried on to this day by the Society of Merchant Venturers (see Underground & Radical Bristol, p98). According to the Royal Charter, non-Bristolians could not buy leather, corn or wool from 'foreigners', only from Bristol merchants.

C13th **1203-41** Princess Eleanor of Brittany is imprisoned in Bristol Castle for all of her life in order to prevent her producing an heir to the throne to rival the Plantagenets: King John and his son Henry III.

1216 The first Mayor of Bristol is appointed.

1220 Foundation of Gaunt's Hospital, later to become the Lord Mayor's Chapel.

1239-47 River Frome is diverted, using just spades and wheelbarrows, to provide more quays to cater for the increase in trade at the port. The work costs £5,000 and the river now provides a soft muddy bottom for boats to rest on when the tide is out. The diverted Frome is 2,400 foot long, 18 foot deep and 120 foot wide. It is one of the most remarkable feats of civic engineering of its time. It was so remarkable that future town planners concrete over it years later.

1247 First record of a High Cross at the junction of High Street and Corn Street.

C14 th **1312** The Bristol Tax Riots: the earliest recorded riots in Bristol and the beginning of a tradition of civil disobedience that saw its most recent expression in St Paul's in 1980. Bristolians rise up in anger when Edward II introduces another tax on shipping. The Mayor, William Randolph, takes over control of collecting the taxes and the ship money from Bristol. Rioting starts soon after; Edward II appoints the Constable of the Castle with powers to overrule the corporation. Thomas de Berkeley is appointed to stop the riots. Twenty men are killed and the King's officers are driven into the castle by the rioters. They remain under siege until the barons call in the army. After four days, the city surrenders. Edward II pardons the rioters but fines them.

1327 Edward II is imprisoned at Bristol Castle. He is then moved to Berkeley Castle in Gloucestershire where he is murdered by having a red-hot poker shoved up his bum.

1371 Bristol linen merchant Edward Blanket, the (ahem) inventor of the blanket, dies. His tomb is in St Stephen's Church, just off the Centre. Blanket lived in Tucker Street and was MP for Bristol in 1362.

1373 Edward III grants Bristol a charter on 8 April making the city the first provincial borough to be a county in its own right. Bristol pays 600 marks for the charter. Edward needs the money to fund the war against France. The first Sheriff of Bristol is appointed; a new High Cross is erected at the junction of Broad Street, Wine Street, Corn Street and High Street to commemorate the event.

1390 Work begins on Temple Church, Bristol's equivalent to the Leaning Tower of Pisa. Work on the church stops when the tower begins to lean and starts again in 1460. The sloping is partially corrected thanks to some heavy stone laying. But by the time it is hit in the Blitz, it has been tilting again for some years and isn't going to stand up straight for that Hitler fella.

C15 th **1446** With rebuilding work almost complete at St Mary Redcliffe Church, the roof is struck by lightning during a violent electric storm and destroyed. The repair work is funded by merchant William Canynges who was Mayor of Bristol five times and the city's Member of Parliament twice.

1497 John Cabot sets sail from Bristol in The Matthew and discovers North America. Born Giovanni Caboto in Genoa around 1451, Cabot is thought to have arrived in Bristol in about 1480 with an ambition to look for Hy-Brasil, an island somewhere in the Atlantic, according to Celtic legend. Cabot leaves Bristol on 20 May 1497 on board The Matthew with a crew of 18. He lands on the East Coast of America on 24 June 1497. On his return to Bristol, Cabot is rewarded for his discovery with a pension of £20 a year. In 1498, he sets off for America again, this time with five ships, and is never heard of again. Cabot's new-found land is named America after the Bristol merchant Richard Amerike.

C16 th **1532** Foundation of Bristol Grammar School by Robert and Nicholas Thorne.

1542 Diocese of Bristol created by Henry VIII.

1552 Society of Merchant Venturers formed.

1555-57 Several martyrs are burned at the stake on St Michael's Hill during the reign of Bloody Queen Mary. The prisoners were led to their deaths from the gaol up the muddy hill that is now Christmas Steps.

1574 Queen Elizabeth visits Bristol and describes St Mary Redcliffe Church as 'The goodliest, fairest and most famous parish church in England'. This is the most overused quote in the history of Bristol and will not appear in this book again.

1586 Foundation of Queen Elizabeth's Hospital School by John Carr. You may see QEH borders around Park Street; they wear traditional Bluecoat uniforms: dark cloaks with white neckbands, knee-length breeches and yellow stockings. Do not be alarmed.

C17 th **1610** Bristol merchant John Guy becomes the first governor of Newfoundland.

1634 Foundation of Red Maids' School. John

Whitson, merchant, Mayor and Member of Parliament for Bristol, dies in 1629, bequeathing monies for a hospital for '40 poor women children' to be 'apparelled in red cloth'. The Red Maids School is originally in Denmark Street next to the present-day Hippodrome, but moved to Westbury-on-Trym in 1930. Girls from the school still celebrate Founder's Day.

1636 Slave trader Edward Colston is born in Bristol. Colston funds the development of much of modern Bristol with money from the slave trade and bequeaths a fortune to the city.

1642 Outbreak of the Civil War. Bristol joins the Parliament side.

1643 Bristol is captured by Royalist forces.

1645 Bristol surrenders to Cromwell's Parliament forces.

1654 The destruction of Bristol Castle by Oliver Cromwell.

1655 First Quaker meeting is held in Bristol at a private house in Frenchay.

1660 Bristol apprentices revolt, demanding a free Parliament and the restoration of the Monarchy. On 5 March 1660, the bellman of Bristol makes the usual Puritan proclamation banning cock-throwing and dog-tossing. The rowdy apprentices attack him and the next day (Shrove Tuesday) squail a goose and toss cats and dogs into the air outside the Mayor's Mansion House. To squail a goose is to throw sticks, weighted with lead at one end, at it. The object is to maim the bird without killing it. The authorities are able to quickly bring the apprentices under control and halt all tossing and squailing.

1674 Ralph Ollive becomes Mayor of Bristol on an anti-Quaker ticket. Major persecution of the Society of Friends continues.

1680 Edward Teach (aka Blackbeard the Pirate) is born in Bristol. Blackbeard is believed to be the inspiration for Robert Louis Stevenson's Long John Silver in *Treasure Island*.

1681 William Penn of Bristol establishes a Quaker community in Pennsylvania.

1694 Society of Merchant Venturers organises protests against the Royal African Company's London monopoly of the slave trade.

1695 William Bonny sets up Bristol's first printing press.

1698 The slave trade begins in Bristol when the London monopoly of the Royal African Company is broken.

C18th **1700** The population of Bristol is estimated to have risen to around 25,000.

1702 Work begins on building Queen Square to celebrate a visit to Bristol by Queen Anne.

1702 Bristol's first newspaper, the *Bristol Postboy*, is founded. The 91st issue, published in August 1704, is the earliest surviving copy of a provincial newspaper in the world and is now at the Central Reference Library. It was produced weekly as a single sheet.

1709 Food riots sweep the city. 200 coal miners from Kingswood, always a rowdy bunch, march into the city and riot against a big increase in the cost of food – a bushel of wheat had doubled in price to eight shillings. The miners disperse after being promised a reduction in the price of a bushel to five shillings and sixpence.

1710 Colston School is founded.

1714 Celebrations for the Coronation of George 1 turn into a riot and two people are killed in the violence.

1727-49 The introduction of tollgates on 26 June 1727 sparks off far more serious riots than those of 1709 or 1714. Two days after they are installed, the turnpikes are destroyed. Wherever they appear, the tollgates are wrecked. For a time in 1734, not a single tollgate is left standing between Bristol and Gloucester. This continues for 21 years, the length of time that the law that allows the tollgates is in force.

1728-33 Riots by Easton and Kingswood weavers, impoverished by the industrialisation of their industry, results in a ★ *Turn to page 89*

COLSTON & THE SLAVE TRADE

THE HISTORY OF THE SLAVE TRADE IN BRISTOL FROM 1698 TO ITS ABOLITION IN 1807

BUILT ON SLAVERY

It has been suggested that Bristol should perhaps be the site for a permanent national exhibition about the African slave trade. Perhaps it will take a gesture of that magnitude to make the city finally confront the demons of its past – there's no getting away from the fact that the wealth of modern Bristol is built on slavery.

At the height of the slave trade, in the mid 18th Century, the Bristol economy and the Society of Merchant Venturers thrived on slavery. For example, sugar was returned to the port from the plantations where the slaves were sold, so refineries were built in the city; the refineries needed power, which was provided by the coal mines of Kingswood. The rapid growth of the city and its growing prosperity in the 18th Century and beyond was significantly based on the brutality and immorality of slavery.

Many of the families and institutions that still prosper and hold considerable influence in the city made their money from slavery. The legacy of Edward Colston dominates Bristol. A statue of the MP and slave trader stands in the Centre near the Colston Hall, (opposite the Colston Tower), there are at least a dozen streets named after him and, of course, there's Colston's Schools. There's even a Colston Bun.

COLSTON'S SECRET

Edward Colston was born in Bristol in 1636, the son of a wealthy merchant. He made his money initially by trading with Spain and other Mediterranean countries. However, although he went to great lengths to keep it a secret, Colston became a member of the Royal African Company in 1680 and took an active part in the planning and financing of slaving ventures to Africa, his name appearing in the company records for 11 years.

The African slave trade began in Bristol in 1698 when the London-based Royal African Company lost its monopoly on English trade with West Africa. Between 1698 and the

■ Edward Colston donated much of his fortune from slavery to set up schools and other institutions in Bristol.

abolition of the slave trade in 1807, more than 2,000 ships set sail from Bristol in search of slaves on the West African coast. It's estimated that 500,000 slaves were carried on Bristol vessels out of a total trade of 2.8 million (*The Bristol Slave Traders: A Collective Portrait,* David Richardson), although other researchers put the figure as high as 8 million (*A Shocking History of Bristol*, Derek Robinson). As many as a quarter of the slaves died or were murdered at sea. So it's possible that around two million bodies of slaves were thrown overboard from slave ships.

Liverpool and London were the other two major slave ports, but it is estimated that half of the slave ships that left England for Africa in 1730 sailed from Bristol. The city's share of the slave trade had fallen to 25% by the 1750s as Liverpool became the dominant slave port and, by the time of abolition in 1807, Bristol had just a 2% market share.

WEST AFRICAN TRADERS

The slave trade worked on the triangular model, making a profit on each stage of the voyage. Ships left Bristol with a cargo of cotton, brass, copper, gin or muskets, which were bartered for slaves with the West African traders. The ships then embarked on the Middle Passage to the West Indies or America where the surviving slaves were sold at a profit, often to plantation owners originally from Bristol. The ships then returned home with a cargo of sugar or tobacco which was again sold for profit. During the 18th Century, 32 of the city's leading slave traders became members of the Society of Merchant Venturers and 16 went on to become Master.

Naturally, the Africans fought the traders sent to capture them and many committed suicide when they were captured; thousands more were killed in mutinies or died due to the dreadful conditions at sea. Perhaps most shocking of all, there is a body of evidence which suggests that Bristol captains drowned their entire cargo of diseased slaves so that the loss could be claimed on the owners' insurance as 'legal jettison'.

WOMEN AND CHILDREN

Slave ships were specially converted so they could carry the maximum number of bodies. Typically, a ship would have a hold about five foot high, so the owners built two six-foot wide platforms either side of the hold to create two decks. Slaves were driven into the hold and forced to lie on the bottom in rows until it was covered. Then another layer of people were forced onto the platforms.

On some of the larger ships a second platform was added, giving a headroom of about 20 inches for the three layers of people. The tallest slaves were put amidships; the smaller ones and children were wedged into the stern. The space per person was very restricted. A male slave was allowed a space six foot by 16 inches; a woman was allowed five foot by 16 inches; a boy five foot by 14 inches and a girl four foot by 12 inches. They lived, and died, in these conditions on the passage from Africa to the West Indies and America. They were often seasick and had no alternative but to foul themselves.

The Africans were supposed to be brought on deck every morning to be fed and cleaned, but some captains left them in the holds for the entire journey (between six weeks and three months). Bristol merchants, sea captains and crews were responsible for the most appalling and degrading treatment of human beings. This was a crime as great as the Holocaust.

In June 1787, the Rev Thomas Clarkson arrived in Bristol to begin his fact-finding tour of the slaving ports that was to lead to the abolition of the slave trade some 20 years later. However, it was not just the suffering of the Africans that began to change public opinion, but the poor treatment of the Bristol slave crews.

Naturally, the Society of Merchant Venturers did everything possible to halt Clarkson's investigations, but he persevered. He interviewed 20,000 sailors and collected equipment used on the slave ships, such as iron handcuffs, leg shackles, thumbscrews, instruments for forcing open slaves' jaws, and branding irons. Clarkson set himself up in the Seven Stars pub (which is still there, next to the Fleece and Firkin on Thomas Lane) whose owner was sympathetic to William Wilberforce's anti-slavery movement. Pub landlords played a key role in recruiting crews for the slaving ships, and the landlord of the Seven Stars explained to Clarkson the way the business worked and introduced him to the slaving underworld that inhabited Bristol's dockside taverns. He pieced together a picture of the reality of the business and discovered that crews were recruited in three ways:

Lying: men were lured from the drinking dens of Marsh Street with promises of high wages and an exotic life at sea.

Doping: pub landlords were bribed to spike sailors' drinks and they were abducted.

Blackmail: the landlords encouraged men to borrow money for drink and then threatened them with jail unless they joined a slaving crew.

Once on board, the crew was forced to sign ship's articles legalising their poor pay. Often the crew were paid in virtually worthless foreign currencies.

Clarkson managed to gain access to the Merchant Venturers' records. From their own Muster Rolls, he found that the mortality rates of Bristol slave ship crews were very heavy in comparison to those of other cities involved in the triangular trade. His interviews revealed that the crews were treated appallingly by slaving captains. Some men were murdered; sometimes a quarter of the crew died at sea from disease, ill treatment and torture. Obviously, their suffering was nothing compared to the African people, but Clarkson's revelations began to get the attentions of the Bristol public. Not surprisingly, these revelations started to disturb people.

PUBLIC OUTRAGE

Clarkson managed to take the murder of two seamen on board a slaver to trial, despite two slave traders sitting on the bench at the initial hearing. His witnesses all mysteriously disappeared by the time the case was due to be heard, but finally the word was out and the Bristol public were shocked by what they heard about the treatment of their local sailors. It seems they cared little for the suffering of the slaves, although there was an anti-slavery movement in the city led by Quakers and Methodists. In fact, Bristol was the first city outside London to set up a committee for the abolition of the slave trade; some 800 people volunteered to sign the first Bristol petition against the slave trade in 1788.

The Yorkshire MP William Wilberforce, the public face of the abolition campaign, came to Bristol in 1791 to encourage the local campaign. The poets Robert Southey, William Wordsworth, Hannah More, Anne Yearsley and Samuel Coleridge all wrote against the trade. John Wesley, who founded the Methodist Church, wrote against slavery and preached against the trade in the New Rooms in Broadmead. This was one of the first political campaigns in which women played

an active part and, in 1787, Hannah More was instrumental in organising a boycott of West Indian slave sugar in Bristol.

Parliament first debated a motion calling for the abolition of the slave trade in 1788. The Society of Merchant Venturers and other business interests in Bristol lobbied strongly against Wilberforce and the abolitionists, claiming it would be 'ruinous in the extreme to the petitioners engaged in the manufacture, but the mischief would extend most widely throwing hundreds of common labouring people wholly out of employment'. The slave business won the day and Parliament merely passed an Act aimed at improving conditions on slave ships by limiting the numbers carried. The Bristol Corporation ordered church bells across the city to be rung in celebration.

The Society of Merchant Venturers fought against abolition to the last, even though Bristol's share of the trade was fairly insignificant by comparison at the end of the 18th Century. The merchants could make handsome profits by trading directly with the plantation owners, many of whom were from the city, rather than undertaking the far more risky triangular voyages. The abolition movement suffered a setback in 1793 when Britain went to war with France. The slave trade was seen as the 'nursery of seamen' and abolition of the trade was postponed. Eventually, in 1807, the slave trade in the British colonies was abolished and it became illegal to carry slaves on British ships.

■ **The Slave Trail leaflet is available from museums and tourist offices.**

■ **For further information, please contact the City Museum & Art Gallery, Queens Road, Bristol BS8 1RL. Tel: 922 3571**

■ A diagram from the 18th Century showing how slaves were packed onto the lower deck of a Bristol vessel.

mill owner shooting dead eight protesters. Two of the Easton weavers' leaders are executed.

1737 Bristol Royal Infirmary opens.

1739 John Wesley invents Methodism. On 2 April, Wesley gives his first open-air sermon in St Philip's. The New Room in the Horsefair is established as the world's first Methodist chapel later in the year.

1743 The Exchange in Corn Street is built by John Wood The Elder.

1745 The original glass-roofed St Nicholas Market is built.

1749 John Wesley's brother Charles, the greatest ever hymn writer, moves to Bristol and lives in a house at 4 Charles Street, opposite the present site of the bus station.

1750 Population of Bristol about 50,000: the city has doubled in size in just 50 years.

1752 The poet Thomas Chatterton is born into an impoverished Bristol family in Redcliffe.

1753 Very bad harvests in 1752 are the cause of food riots in 1753. Despite shortages, Bristol merchants are still exporting grain for huge profits. On 21 May 1753, Kingswood miners lead a march into the city and ransack a ship, The Lamb, that was preparing to sail with 70 tons of wheat to Dublin. On 25 May, a crowd of 900, made up mostly of colliers and weavers, break into the Bridewell and release prisoners. Four rioters are killed, around 50 injured and 30 are captured.

1766 The Theatre Royal is opened.

1774 The future Poet Laureate Robert Southey is born the son of a linen draper at 9 Wine Street on 12 August.

1780 The development of Upper Clifton begins.

1786 Tobacco company WD & HO Wills is founded by Henry Overton Wills when he moves from Salisbury to Bristol and goes into partnership with Samuel Watkins. They start with their first shop in Castle Street but, by

1791, the firm has expanded and moved to 112 Redcliffe Street.

1799 Humphry Davy administers nitrous oxide to visitors to the Pneumatic Institute in Dowry Square, Hotwells. After watching the effects on people who inhale it, Davy coins the term 'laughing gas'.

C19th **1800** Humphry Davy works with Thomas Beddoes at his clinic in Dowry Square, Hotwells. Davy publishes the book *Researches, Chemical and Philosophical: Chiefly Concerning Nitrous Oxide* in which he describes inhaling nitrous oxide (laughing gas) and obtaining a degree of analgesia from a painful condition he was suffering. Davy's research into anaesthetic effect are not tested and utilised for another 45 years; instead, the primary use of nitrous oxide is for recreational enjoyment and public shows. So-called 'nitrous oxide capers' took place in travelling medicine shows and carnivals, where the public paid a small price to inhale a minute's worth of gas. Many dignitaries and famous individuals come to inhale Davy's purified nitrous oxide for recreational purposes, including the poets Coleridge and Southey, the potter Josiah (later Sir Josiah) Wedgwood, and Roget of Roget's Thesaurus. 'I am sure the air in heaven must be this wonder working gas of delight,' wrote Southey after a swift inhalation in Dowry Square.

1801 Population of Bristol is around 68,000.

1803 An Act of Parliament is passed to allow the construction of the Cut, a new course for the River Avon to enable the Floating Harbour to be created.

1806 Isambard Kingdom Brunel is born at Portsea, near Portsmouth, on 9 April. His mother is English; his father is the great French engineer Sir Marc Isambard Brunel.

1823 The Bristol Chamber of Commerce is established.

1823 A Bristol inventor takes his Charvolant, or Flying Car, to Ascot Races to demonstrate it to George IV. This magnificent contraption, which was tested on Durdham Downs, is the brainchild of Clifton schoolmaster George

Pocock, an eccentric boffin who had already built an automatic caning machine to deal with his wayward pupils. The Charvolant is made up of a carriage for four people that is powered by two giant kites. On a good day, it can reach speeds of 25mph. After displaying his machine to the public, Pocock begins using the Charvolant as a family vehicle, tearing through towns and villages outside Bristol at speeds that scared the living daylights out of the locals. While he might have seemed a complete maniac at the time, in hindsight he looks like an Eco travel pioneer. Albeit an eccentric one.

1831 Riots in Queen Square. The Mansion House, Customs House and other buildings in the Square are destroyed.

1831 Brunel begins work on the Clifton Suspension Bridge. Building stops in 1836 and the project is abandoned in 1853. Work restarts in 1862 and the bridge is eventually opened on 8 December 1864. The final cost of the project is £100,000, about £45,000 over budget. Brunel does not live to see the completion of this wonderful bridge, he died in 1859, aged just 53.

1831 Bones belonging to the Bristol Dinosaur (Thecodontosaurus Antiquus, to give it its proper name) are discovered in a quarry on Durdham Downs. The dinosaur is similar in size and table manners to the Diplodocus and is thought to be one of the oldest of all the giant plant-eating reptiles dating back some 210 million years. Now scientists have even been able to pinpoint the exact spot that the big beast called home. In 1881, local geologist Charles Moore identifies the dinosaur's stomping ground as being in the Belgrave Terrace area off Blackboy Hill, just a rock's throw from the Downs. The area has now been built on, so no more evidence can be found, not that any more fossils are needed. In 1975, five tonnes of Thecodontosaurus bones were found in a quarry near Bristol and the whole lot was taken to the University for further study. It took 25 years for the Bristol Dinosaur Project to secure the funding they needed to start work. In 1999, a team of palaeontologists began the laborious process of separating rock from bone. Needless to say, they're still at it.

1836 Bristol Zoological Gardens opens.

1837 Brunel's Great Western steamship is launched in Bristol.

1841 The opening of Brunel's Great Western Railway between Bristol and London.

1843 Prince Albert visits the Great Western Dockyard in Bristol and names Brunel's new ship the Great Britain.

1848 Hirsute cricket legend WG Grace is born on 18 July in Clematis House, North Street, Downend, though the family lived a few doors away in Downend House.

1861 The Durdham Downs in Clifton are secured as public open spaces.

1862 Clifton College opens. Its most famous old boys are Douglas Haig, the Commander in Chief of the British Army in France in World War One and John Cleese of *Monty Python* and *Fawlty Towers* fame.

1864 On 8 December, the ceremonial opening of Clifton Suspension Bridge takes place – five years after the death of Isambard Kingdom Brunel. A long procession sets off from the city centre, including soldiers, sailors and groups with banners representing various trades, plus organisations and friendly societies of the city. At least 16 bands take part, flags fly, field gun salutes are fired and church bells are rung. After the ceremony at midday there is a banquet for invited guests in the Victoria Rooms and at night the bridge is illuminated for the first time. In 1753, Bristol wine merchant William Vick left a legacy for a bridge to be built over the Avon Gorge. After 110 years of uncertainty, Vick's vision is finally realised.

1870 Gloucestershire Cricket Club is founded.

1876 University of Bristol is founded.

1881 Population of Bristol is 266,000.

1883 Bristol Rovers Football Club is founded as the Black Arabs FC at a meeting at Collins Restaurant on Stapleton Road.

1880s The tradition of a Jack-in-the-Green is resurrected in Victorian Bristol. Jack is nine foot tall, covered from head to toe in flowers and dances like a demented Morris dancer with a firework up his trousers. On the first Saturday in May, Bristol's Jack-in-the-Green still makes his way from the Arnolfini all the way to Horfield Common followed by a colourful procession of flute-blowing vegetation. Why does he do this? In order to release the spirit of summer, of course. Isn't it obvious! This bizarre Victorian tradition probably has its roots in ancient pagan rituals and has only recently been resurrected in Bristol. Crowds are encouraged to follow Jack through the streets and on to his final destination, where he eventually curls up and dies. This is one spectacle that's guaranteed to frighten the life out of any children unlucky enough to be watching.

1881 Robert Louis Stephenson writes *Treasure Island*. The Spyglass Inn in the book is based on the Llandoger Trow pub in King Street. It is still there to this day.

1888 Bristol Rugby Football Club is founded.

1894 Bristol City Football Club is founded as Bristol South End.

1896 On a cold and rainy night on 18 September 1896, a bankrupt grocer called Charles Brown took his two daughters, Ruby and Elsie, up to the Clifton Suspension Bridge and threw them into the muddy water below. Luckily, there was a high tide that night and as the girls plunged into the water, the crew of a passing pilot boat spotted them and dragged them away to safety. Ruby suffered injuries to her spine while Elsie had only minor leg injuries. Both girls had recovered within a couple of weeks. Charles Brown was subsequently arrested and brought to trial. 'Father caught hold of me and I began to scream,' said Ruby while giving evidence in court. 'He lifted me up on the side of the bridge and put me over.' Unsurprisingly, the judge concluded that the poor girls' old man was utterly insane and should spend a considerable amount of time in an asylum.

1897 Bristol Rovers' Eastville Stadium is officially opened on 5 April with the visit of League Champions and FA Cup holders Aston Villa. Rovers lose 5-0 to set the tone for the next 89 years at Eastville.

C20th 1901 Population of Bristol rises to an estimated 330,000.

1904 Hollywood actor Cary Grant is born at 15 Hughenden Road, Horfield on 18 January. He was christened Archibald Alexander Leach.

1908 Edward VII opens the Royal Edward Dock in Avonmouth.

1911 Bristol miners strike for three months over pay and loss of jobs.

1911 Bristol Aeroplane Works opens in Filton.

1914-18 About 55,000 men from the Bristol area enlist for World War One. More than 7,000 men from the Bristol area died.

1917 Avonmouth becomes the centre of the British chemical warfare manufacturing drive. The plant makes 20 tons of mustard gas a day. In December 1918, the plant Medical Officer reports that in the six months it has been operational, there are 1,400 illnesses reported by its 1,100 workers – all attributable to their work. There are 160 accidents and over 1,000 burns. Three people die in accidents and another four die as a result of their illnesses. There are 30 resident patients in the factory hospital tended by a doctor and eight nurses. The gas produced at the Avonmouth plant doesn't arrive in France until September 1918, two months before the Armistice.

1920 On Sunday 11 July 1920, Charlie Stephens, a barber from Bedminster, tries to shoot Niagara Falls in an oak barrel. Sadly, Charlie's barrel is way too heavy and he crashes straight onto the jagged rocks at the bottom. The following morning, an arm is rescued from the water bearing a tattoo that reads, 'Forget me not, Annie.' Charlie has previous: when he was five years old he was pronounced dead and laid in a coffin before springing back to life; at 16 he was almost run over by a coal wagon. Then he spent three years in the trenches of World War One and came home without a scratch. As well as running a busy barber's shop and bringing up 11 children with his wife Annie, Charlie fancied himself as a bit of a stuntman. First, he began performing daring tricks in a lions' den; then he parachuted from a balloon;

then he dived off the Forth Bridge head first. Niagara should have been Charlie's finest hour. Instead, Bedminster's answer to Houdini had tried his luck once too often.

1925 King George V and Queen Mary open the new University buildings.

1926 Opening of the Portway between Bristol and Avonmouth.

1930 Official opening in May of Bristol Airport at Whitchurch by Prince George. Whitchurch is only the third civil airport in the country.

1940 Hitler claims Bristol has been completely destroyed following a night of intensive bombing on 2 November in which 5,000 incendiary and 10,000 high explosive bombs are dropped on the centre of the old city. On 24 November, the entire area that is now Castle Park is destroyed in a bombing raid. During World War Two 1,299 people in Bristol are killed by German bombing. About 3,000 buildings are destroyed and 90,000 are damaged.

1941 The infamous Good Friday air raids on Bristol see more destruction in the centre of the city plus major damage to Knowle, Hotwells and Filton. The last air raid on Bristol is on 25 April 1941, when Brislington, Bedminster and Knowle are badly hit. Prime Minister Winston Churchill visits the devastated city on 12 April 1941 and is booed by crowds amid rumours that the city's air defences are not being properly managed.

1945 Prime Minister Winston Churchill, Chancellor of Bristol University, receives the freedom of the city.

1947 Some Bristolians begin to complain about an odd buzzing noise and the Bristol Hum is born. According to the 5% of people who can hear it, the hum sounds like the dull drone of a distant aircraft. It varies in intensity from a soft background noise to an overpowering onslaught and causes headaches, nausea, dizziness and even muscle spasms.

1949 The Bristol Brabazon, the world's largest passenger airliner, makes its maiden flight from Filton on 5 September.

1952 Following the failure of the Brabazon project, the Bristol Britannia makes its maiden flight from Filton. It goes on to become the first plane to carry 100 passengers non-stop across the Atlantic.

1956 Queen Elizabeth II opens the new Council House on College Green.

1957 The Duchess of Kent opens Bristol Airport at Lulsgate.

1958 On 5 December, Queen Elizabeth II makes the first trunk dialling call in Britain from Bristol Central Telephone Exchange. Trunk dialling is making a long-distance call without the aid of an operator. She calls the Lord Provost of Edinburgh. Her call lasts two minutes five seconds and costs 10d (4p).

1959 Bristol's first curry restaurant opens. The Taj Mahal in Stokes Croft is run by Mr Ahmed, a Bengali. It is the first Indian restaurant in the West Country. Writing in *Muktodhara, Bengalis In Bristol*, Mr Ahmed says: 'I put a poster in the window saying "Indian Restaurant Opening Shortly". People used to come in, push the door and say "When are you opening, I can't wait for a curry!" My second restaurant was in the Centre by the Hippodrome Theatre, called Koh-I-Noor. Every night there was a fight. We used to sell curry for 3/6d. They used to eat and then run without paying. And we used to catch up with them!'

1961 The Arnolfini is established by Jeremy and Annabel Rees above a bookshop on the Triangle, Clifton.

1963 Paul Stephenson leads anti-racist protests against Bristol Omnibus Company following the company's refusal to consider black people for jobs.

1965 The Race Discrimination Act is passed by Parliament after Bristol South East MP Tony Benn takes up the campaign started by Paul Stephenson.

1965 The Cumberland Basin road and bridge scheme opens.

BRISTOL RIOTS OF 1831

THREE DAYS OF RIOTING IN QUEEN SQUARE

The Queen Square riots began on 31 October 1831 and remain one of the most serious outbreaks of civil disobedience in the history of England. The disturbance is thought to be connected to uprisings across the country sparked by the rejection by the Lords of the Reform Act. However, there is evidence that the fighting was a local uprising in protest at a corrupt City Corporation: it was more of a revolution than a riot.

It all kicked off thanks to the arrival in town of the Recorder of Bristol, Sir Charles Wetherell, a committed opponent of reform Sir Charles pitched up on 29 October to preside over the Court of Assizes. Two days later, the centre of Bristol was in flames. The fires could be seen in Newport and Sir Charles was forced to escape from the Mansion House in disguise by clambering over rooftops.

The Bristol Riots lasted for three days and were centred on Queen Square. The Mansion House, Excise Office and Custom House were torched and the Toll House destroyed. Prisoners were released and the prisons set on fire at Bridewell, New Gaol and Gloucester County Gaol. Private houses on two sides of

Queen Square were destroyed. A watercolour of the riots by TLS Rowbotham (on show at the City Museum and Art Gallery in Queen's Road) shows the mob being attacked by soldiers from the 14th Light Dragoons, or the Bloody Blues, as they were known. The 3rd Dragoon Guards, who were based in the city, were thought to be sympathetic to the cause, which could explain why Bristol was controlled by the rioters for three days.

The arrival of Sir Charles Wetherell may have sparked the Queen Square riots, but it's likely he was the catalyst for the uprising against a 'rotten' Corporation. The Corporation had become secretive, out of touch with the city and, by 1831, was as unpopular with the Tories as it was with the masses.

In 1833, a Royal Commission on Municipal Corporations investigated the Bristol Corporation and reported that: 'The ruling principle of the Corporation appears to have been, at all times, the desire of power, the watchful jealousy that nothing should be undertaken within the limits of the city over which they cannot, at pleasure, exercise their control.'

■ TLS Rowbotham recorded the scenes at the Queen Square riots in this watercolour. It shows the protesters being attacked by solidiers from the 14th Light Dragoons, or the Bloody Blues, as they became known.

Up Close

1966 The Queen opens the £10 million Severn Bridge on 8 September.

1966 On the 19 May, a leisure complex on Frogmore Street is opened. The venue has been an entertainment centre ever since. The Academy is the latest arrival to move in.

1967 Steve Marriot writes the Small Faces hit *Itchycoo Park* while staying at the Grand Hotel.

1968 The first St Paul's Carnival is held with the procession trouping past the Lord Mayor of Bristol.

1969 In April, Brian Trubshaw pilots Concorde 002 on her British maiden flight from Filton to RAF Fairford in Gloucestershire. On emerging from the cockpit he says: 'It was wizard! A cool, calm and collected operation!'

1970 On 12 April, more than 100,000 people line the banks of the River Avon to watch the ss Great Britain being towed home on the last leg of her journey from the Falkland Islands.

1971 Christine Preece becomes Bristol's first woman bus driver.

1972 Theatre Royal and Coopers' Hall restored and re-opened.

1974 A bomb goes off in Park Street on 18 December. 15 people are injured but amazingly there are no fatalities.

1974 Royce Creasey organises the first Ashton Court Festival, a series of four Sunday events at Ashton Court. Fred Wedlock plays one of the days, as does a band called Pussy Spasm.

1975 The Arnolfini moves from the Triangle to its current site, Bush House, a former tea warehouse on Narrow Quay.

1977 Royal Portbury Dock opens at Avonmouth.

1978 Bristol Industrial Museum opens.

1978 Louise Joy Brown, the world's first test-tube baby is born on 25 July to Lesley and John Brown of Hassell Drive, Easton.

1980 Rioting breaks out in St Paul's following a police raid on the Black and White cafe in Grosvenor Road. It is the first of the inner city riots of the early 1980s.

1982 The Watershed, Britain's first 'media centre', opens across the water from the Arnolfini. To this day, nobody in Bristol is quite sure what makes two cinemas, a bar and a gallery a 'media centre'.

1982 Bristol City FC goes bust and is reformed as Bristol City (1982). Eight of the club's highest earners from the Division One days agree to tear up their contracts so the club can survive. They become known as the Ashton Gate Eight.

1986 The Dug Out club closes following a campaign by police that culminates with police solicitor Richard Crowley telling the City Council's Public Protection Committee that the club is like a 'Fagin's kitchen'.

1986 On 26 April, Bristol Rovers play their last ever game at their spiritual home, Eastville. It's a 1-1 draw with Chesterfield.

1991 *Blue Lines*, the first Massive Attack album is released on 6 January.

1991 New shopping centre the Galleries opens in Broadmead. It's a 'totally enclosed mall with three levels of shopping and eateries and a 950-space car park' and replaces the old concrete monstrosity, Fairfax House with a new brick monstrosity. Hurrah!

1995 Portishead win the Mercury Music Prize with their debut album *Dummy*.

1996 The second Severn crossing opens. It cost about £300 million.

1997 Roni Size wins the Mercury Music Prize with his album *New Forms*.

1999 Pero's Bridge opens linking the Watershed with the Arnolfini. Designed by Irish artist Eilis O'Connell and named after a slave brought back to Bristol by John Pinney, the bridge is generally regarded as one of the better things to have been built in Bristol in recent years.

1999 The new-look City Centre opens to the public on Millennium Eve.

C21st **2000** The £97 million At-Bristol project opens, comprising Explore, Wildwalk and the Imax cinema (see Children's Bristol. p182). The project is the first stage of a £450 million urban rejuvenation scheme, covering 11 acres of Bristol's Harbourside.

2001 The population of Bristol is 380,000.

2001 Prime Minister Tony Blair is hit by a tomato during a protest against sanctions against Iraq when he visits Bristol to open the City of Bristol College.

2001 PJ Harvey wins the Mercury Music Prize with her album *Stories From The City, Stories From The Sea*.

2002 In October, Bristol is short-listed as a candidate for European City of Culture 2008.

2002 Downing Street insists there was nothing wrong in Cherie Blair's purchase of two Bristol flats with the help of a convicted fraudster. She faced much criticism in December after confirming Peter Foster had helped her, despite earlier denials from the Number 10 press office. The flats are in the Old AA building opposite the nice Victorian toilets on Park Row.

2003 The Labour Party is swept from power in the May local elections after the best part of 30 years in power. No party has an overall majority and it takes the local politicians a couple of weeks to come to agreement about how to share power. Strangely, the city seems to run itself perfectly efficiently without anybody being in control.

2003 Liverpool is chosen ahead of Bristol as European City of Culture for 2008. According to the judging panel, Bristol was the most European of the nominated cities, but its road system counted against it. The judges felt that the districts were 'divided by motorways'.

2003 Massive Attack make a triumphant homecoming in August with a huge gig in Queen Square. 'Keep Bristol music progressive!'

is Robert Del Naja's message to his hometown crowd. He dedicates *Teardrop* from the *Mezzanine* album to Bristol.

2003 Tens of thousands of people stare into the Bristol skies on 27 November as Concorde returns to the city for the last time. For many, it's an emotional moment as the beak-nosed supersonic jet appears out of the clouds and zooms over the Clifton Suspension Bridge.

2005 Bristol is awarded Fairtrade City status in a ceremony at the ss Great Britain during Fairtrade Fortnight in March.

2005 On the same weekend in October that Aardman Animation celebrate *Curse of the Were-Rabbit* breaking box office records, a fire destroys the company's warehouse in St Philip's. The blaze destroys the entire collection of Wallace and Gromit props and models plus many other artefacts from the last 30 years.

2006 At the Oscar ceremony in March Aardman's *Curse of the Were-Rabbit* wins the gong for the Best Animated Feature. Aardman mainman Nick Park says: 'This is a great day for Aardman and most importantly recognition for the 200-plus dedicated crew that gave up over two years of their lives to work on the film.'

2006 Labour take a predicted battering in the May local elections. The Lib Dems don't have an overall majority but take control of Bristol City Council. Charlie Bolton becomes the city's first Green Party Councillor after winning Southville from Labour by seven votes.

2006 Work is halted on the huge Broadmead redevelopment and Bristol is gridlocked after a suspected Second World War bomb is discovered under the demolished Allied Carpets shop. It turns out not to be a bomb. Art Squatters who took over a building at Temple Meads to stage an exhibition celebrate because police trying to evict them are called away to deal with the 'bomb'.

2006 In July, Louise Brown announces she is pregnant. Bristol girl Louise who lives in Knowle became the world's first test-tube baby in 1978.

2007 The 200th anniversary of the passing of the Abolition of Slavery Act.

SORELY MISSED

GIL GILLESPIE PAYS A PERSONAL TRIBUTE TO SOME OF BRISTOL'S ABSENT FRIENDS

1. The Dugout, Park Row
It didn't seem seminal at the time; you shuffled along the corridor, you shoved your quid under the glass, you wandered about for a few hours with your shoes sticking to the floor and then you went home. And yet the Dugout is a hugely significant landmark in the history of the city of Bristol. This is the place where all our musical boundaries were shifted. We saw our first multi-million pound pop videos here, upstairs on the giant screen. This is where we were when Live Aid happened, when the St Paul's riots kicked off, when trousers began to get really baggy. Almost always trouble-free, its closure was at the hands of a bunch of misguided Park Street shopkeepers worried about their windows.

2. The Kings Arms pub on Whiteladies Road
Another social landmark that was sent to an early grave. In its heyday, the Kings Arms (now Babushka) at the top of Whiteladies Road was one of the city's most popular meeting places. Its lighthouse location and sheer size made it impossible to miss. And with wheeler-dealer Crystal Palace fan Terry at the helm, the place was rocking every night of the week. We'd often spend all day and night there; you could never be too drunk to be in the Kings. 'Is it all right to cash another cheque, Tel?'

3. Wendy the Elephant, Clifton
Ask anyone who knows me and they'll tell you that I am the least animal-sentimental person they know. But something very strange happened to me on both occasions I have visited Bristol Zoo. When I laid eyes on Wendy the Elephant, I began to cry, yes cry, right in front of all the other 'human browsers'. When I returned in 2002, the same thing. Why? Maybe it was something to do with dignity and small cages not mixing. I might set up a charity called Complete Freedom for All Medium to Large Animals Except Lions and Tigers, in honour of my now-departed elephant friend.

4. Six Fox Launderette, Zetland Road
Back in the days before 'I can't believe it's not butter' branding became the language of choice for signs, almost anything could have a really good name. Zetland Road's Six Fox Launderette was one such place. But what in the name of half a dozen Basil Brushes did the name mean? As far as I know, foxes have absolutely no link with the business of washing clothes, whatsoever. Truly, the Six Fox was a legend in its own spin cycle.

5. Revolver Records, The Triangle
My mate Rick worked at Revolver in the days before I knew him. Rick is damn cool. He ran Planet Records. He was in Flying Saucer Attack. Anyway, one day I went into Revolver and asked if they had two Beck albums I'd heard about that were only available on import. 'You mean *One Foot In The Grave* and *Stereopathetic Soul Manure*?' sneered Rick with the cynicism of someone who had bought them ages ago. 'You were a right snotty twat,' I told him a year later and we both laughed at the notion that working in Revolver was a one-way ticket to taste fascism. The shop's motto could have been 'you're not really going to buy that are you?'

6. ABC Cinema, Whiteladies Road
In the early 1980s, me and my mate Kerry Turner wandered into the ABC Cinema in the middle of a weekday afternoon just for something to do. Kerry was the best punk in Bristol at the time, a Bambi-faced pretty boy with giant glue-sharpened spikes exploding from his head and the word 'discharge' painted across the back of his thousand-stud leather jacket. Anyway, we went to see *Arthur* – there was nothing else on. We were the only ones in the whole auditorium, so we put our feet up on the velvet seats in front of us and laughed our heads off. A couple of years later Kerry got a nasty type of schizophrenia and was carted off to a mental institution

somewhere in Wales. All he needed was a couple of hours with Dudley Moore in the ABC on Whiteladies Road.

7. The Cellar Bar, Stokes Croft

For a few decadent months at the end of the 1990s, Stokes Croft had an after-hours underground bar that felt like the centre of the universe to anyone who went there. Like all cool clubs, the hidden basement of this little cafe was always packed way beyond its capacity: a heaving, sweating, choking mass of beer-deprived early Herbie Hancock aficionados and a slow-motion barman. Yeah, it was great: the Stooges, Credence Clearwater, Chairmen Of The Board, DJ Shadow… hey, it was only rock 'n' roll and we liked it.

8. The Montpelier Hotel, Montpelier

The Mont was like the Cadbury with tattoos and a cocaine problem. It was not a place to take your parents. Whatever happened at the Mont did so upstairs in the pool room. It was a bit rough around the edges, a bit lairy, full of discreet hand-to-hand exchanges and shifty-eyed blokes looking well scary. You never heard anyone say, 'oh we met some lovely people in the Mont last night'.

9. The Redcliffe Flyover

As with most non-permanent things, the Redcliffe Flyer had more than an element of irresponsibility about it. It was an eyesore in an eyesore part of town but it gave bored drivers the opportunity to have the occasional Scalectrix moment in a lifetime of gridlocked traffic. It is for this reason that we must salute it. Apparently, a bloke called Bill Spring was the first and last person to drive over it.

10. Paradise Garage

For the nervous 14-year-old looking to jump on the punk bandwagon, Paradise Garage was a terrifying but empowering shopping experience. Stashed away at the end of a concrete tunnel off the Broadmead Bearpit, it was the coolest shop in the universe, a hangout for Bristol's punk elite. They sold bondage trousers, Sid Vicious's cowboy T-shirts, and shock-coloured mohair jumpers. Some kids had to go there with their mum, which must still rank as the most humiliating

experience of many people's lives. They sold me my four-inch-heeled electric blue Chelsea boots, a Clash T-shirt, a shiny two-tone suit and several silver-buttoned cowboy shirts. By the time it closed down, I got to know the shop's owner Rich and we would sneer and laugh at a whole new generation of terrified 14-year-old kids. According to Massive Attack legend, it was in Paradise Garage that Daddy G met Milo Johnson and they went on to form The Wild Bunch.

11. Western Star Domino Club, St Paul's

When a work colleague told my friend Simon that the Western Star had been pulled down to widen the junction of the M32 with Broadmead, he cried in front of the whole office. 'It was brilliant,' recalls Simon. By day, the place was an actual domino club, with its tables packed full of old West Indian guys who made the game look as exciting as ice hockey. And by night, it was a great music venue, attracting bands such The Cortinas and the Blue Aeroplanes. Occasionally, it would also attract trouble and one night someone was killed at a Crazy Trains gig. But despite this, the place oozed with first-generation West Indian street spirit and friendliness. Without it, the M32 is now only a long, straight road to nowhere in particular.

12. Dreadlocked Ex-Bank Manager Tramp

He looked like Santa Claus after 200 years of heavy drinking and for the best part of a decade he lumbered all over Bristol as the undisputed king of the down-and-outs. People used to say, 'he used to be a bank manager, you know', as if being a bank manager was better than being a tramp. Nobody knew the real story of his life and it was perhaps fitting that he left without saying goodbye. I wonder what happened to him? Let's hope he's all right and hasn't fallen back into banking.

13. The AA Building, Park Row

Okay, so it was a characterless concrete lump of a building with a few yellow signs. But the former home of the Automobile Association was preferable to what we have now. The Blairs bought a flat for their student son Ewan in the new building.

Underground & Radical Bristol

Ian Bone decries the inept political establishment in Bristol and applauds those who are undermining it

B
ristol's going Green. Slowly. Probably. The city that has tons of lycra-clad cyclists battling the smog-hazed traffic every morning, that hosts more vegan, veggie and organic food fayres than any other, that's home to the Soil Association, Sustrans and more sustainable eco-friendly, self-build initiatives than you can shake a teepee at, might become the first city in Britain to go Green politically. But it'll take ten years. At least.

The Green Party won its breakthrough seat on the City Council in May 2006 with the election of Charlie Bolton with a majority of seven votes, but positioned itself in a healthy second place in six more seats showing to Bristol's already Greenish voters that a Green Party vote was not a wasted vote. They may well go on to pick up a couple more seats at every local election. The problem is that we have a ludicrous system where only one third of council seats are up for election every year so it may well take another decade before they get the whiff of power in their nostrils. But political inertia and gradualism somehow matches the modern mood of the city.

The evenly matched – but mutually deeply loathing – Lib Dems and Labour muddle through at proving equally inept at managing the city. In truth, the City Council has had most of its powers passed on to unelected quangos like the South West Regional Development Agency but, even so, the Council is enmeshed in a soggy, swampy mire of management speak and unfulfilled promises that fuels cynicism and undermines belief in the possibility of any real change. There are no discernible political differences between Labour and Lib Dems, no identifiable left or right wings of either party, no discernible ideas on anything except management by muddle and fudge. For

■ Banksy's monkey stencils: you can still spot some if you look hard enough.

■ The Spark is a curious organ that has been going since 1993.

election night fun, you have only the Filwood ward where the candidates' loathing of one another teeters on the possibility of outright and physical warfare!

Filwood is the heartland of Paymaster General Dawn Primarolo's South Bristol constituency. 'Dimarolo' – as christened by *Private Eye* – has presided over fiasco upon fiasco from child tax credits to flogging off the Inland Revenue's offices to an offshore tax avoidance company. However, not only does she appear immune from the sack, but her loyalty to Gordon Brown has her even being touted as Deputy Prime Minister. The saints preserve us!

Her loyal constituents in Hartcliffe are rewarded with a burnt out shopping centre in Symes Avenue worthy of downtown Baghdad and a housing office fortress worthy of an American outpost in Falujah – well worth a tourist trip to check out the benefits of the city's regeneration initiatives. These have attracted an army of 'poverty chasers' who chase government money round the city

Top five...

Bristol riots

❶ Bristol Bridge Riot (1793):
Second only to the Gordon Riots in terms of those killed and injured in the 17th Century.

❷ Queen Square Riot (1831):
The Biggie: 20,000 rioters over three days, 500 killed, three executed. The most violent riot in British history.

❸ Poll Tax Riot (1990):
A feisty little rucker – right outside the Council House. We won!

❹ St Paul's Riot (1980):
People outside the city were shocked to realise there were black people living in Bristol. It set the tone for 1981's summer of countrywide rioting.

❺ Hartcliffe Riot (1992):
Two local lads were killed in a police car chase, feelings erupted and the cops took a battering on Symes Avenue. Part of 1992's wave of council estate riots.

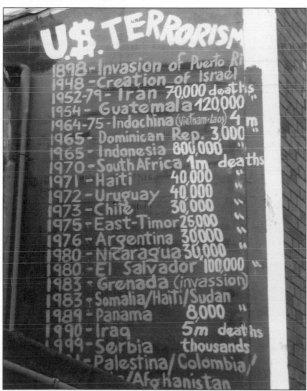

■ You're left in no doubt what the Kebele Kulture Projekt thinks of America's 'peacekeeping' role.

BRISTOL'S FIGHTING HEROES

RADICAL PAST AND PRESENT

Past

1. Dorothy Hazzard
Early Baptist dissenter who, with 200 women, defended the Frome Gate from Prince Rupert in the Civil War. Commemorated in a painting in the city's registry officez. A lotta bottle.

2. James Nayler
Model Army Leveller whose Quaker radicalism was disliked by the authorities who prosecuted him for blasphemy after he rode up Corn Street on a donkey in 1656 claiming he was Jesus Christ. His barbaric torture and humility suggest they may have been right!

3. Thomas Clarkson
Came to Bristol to expose the slave trade – a risky business given the balance of power in the city. From his base in the Seven Stars, Clarkson dug out the crucial eye witness reports. Bristolians turned against the trade because of the high mortality rates of the slave ship crews!

4. Kingswood Colliers
Lawless bunch who'd march on the city to wreak havoc and mayhem. Commemorated by a Wetherspoons on Kingswood High Street. Not to be confused with that equally lawless desperado crew the Cock Road Gang from Hanham. Just don't mention 'the Cainses' in Hanham High Street. Still crazy.

5. Blackbeard & Long John Silver
Blackbeard was born in Redcliffe and Long John Silver came to life in Bristol boozer, the Llandoger Trow in King Street. Shamefuly there's no plaque to either but there are plans for a Long John statue. Radical? Long John was. Pirate crews were very democratic electing their leaders and sharing booty. Who stood against Blackbeard for Captain? Er, well, um... no secret ballot, so no one fancied it.

6. The Black Hand Gang
A gang of leftie Bemmy toughs from the 1920s – sworn enemies of The Monkey Town Mob from The Dings. Again no plaque. I can't think why not!

Present

1. Tony Benn
He is not strictly a Bristolian cos he don't live here no more, but this ex-MP was first elected to represent Bristol South East in 1950. He was eventually 'got rid of' with the help of the boundary changes in 1983. Benn was a hugely committed local MP who still has strong links with the city he served for almost 25 years and can still pack out the Colston Hall.

2. Julie Burchill
Well, yes, she don't live here neither and by the time you read this she may have reverted back to her 1980s Thatcher adoration. She is currently as acerbic a proletarian socialist columnist as there is and it all comes straight out of her years growing up in Fishponds and Barton Hill.

3. Jo Wilding
Feminist, human rights activist, smuggler of banned Iraqi dates, sanctions buster, tomato thrower at Mr Tony Blair. Wilding also travelled to Iraq to defy Bush's bombs. This lady certainly has guts!

4. Dr Margaret Jones
A veritable Bristol institution as the city's most arrested activist. Veteran of road and anti-war protests who regularly takes a toothbrush to Magistrates Court hearings. She once blocked Bristol University/UWE boat race with her own boat protesting for the Gandalf Three. No? You'd better ask her!

5. Massive Attack
They bottled it when their name changed to 'Massive' in the Bush production Gulf War One. However, for the Bush Jnr production Gulf War Two, Massive Attack were fully on the anti-war campaign. This local band have consistently refused to play at the city's Colston Hall because of the fact it is named after the notorious Bristol slave trader Edward Colston. Throughout the Gulf War, the official Massive Attack website automatically redirected thousands of its visitors through to the CND website.

from St Paul's to Barton Hill hoovering up millions in the process and leaving the locals unaware they have had their capacities built and been empowered and regenerated.

A similar cabaal of culture wallahs and wonks hovers between the Arnolfini, At-Bristol and the ss Great Britain risibly touting Brunel as a great Bristolian – and ignoring fearsome Bristol-born natives like the mighty, terrible Blackbeard – and now looking to explore an even more ludicrous Charles Darwin connection to keep their snouts in the trough for another three years!

■ Street art stencil on a wall at the steps at the bottom of Park Street.

But it's the slave trade question that has Bristol collectively on the psychiatrist's couch – which is lucky because Bristol has more counsellors per head than any other city in Europe. But even this army of dreamcatchers and rebirthers can't beat the class divide on this vexed issue. The guilt-ridden middle classes want to apologise for the slave trade whereas the feckless proletarians don't see why they should. The black community remains largely indifferent. There's probably a strong case to be made for the Society of Merchant Venturers to apologise since they initiated the trade and still dominate the economic life of the city. However, expecting an organisation that still worships arch slave trader Edward Colston's fingernail annually to apologise is not a likely winner. Tellingly, no vestiges of political activism from the 1960s and 1970s remain in the city's black community.

Indeed, very few signs of any radical political activism at all remain and those that do play only to an in-house

■ The Yellow Pages billboard by the Three Lamps junction is a subvertising hotspot.

ghetto of the usual suspects. Greenleaf, the city's long-running radical bookshop, closed in 2005 unable to withstand the pincer movement of Waterstones and Borders. The muckraking scandal sheet *The Bristolian* ceased publishing shortly before being nominated for the Paul Foot Award for investigative journalism. The Centre hosts the daily Peace Vigil opposite the Hippodrome – staffed by heroic octogenarians, it is now the world's longest running peace vigil. But it is perhaps more of a threat to the Guinness Book of Records than the continuation of the Iraq war.

■ The famous Greenleaf radical bookshop was closed in 2005.

You can't really begin to understand political Bristol without appreciating the role of the sinisterly-named Society of Merchant Venturers which is headed by 'the one they call the master'.

Historically, the SOMV has dominated the economic and commercial life of Bristol for 450 years, profiting greatly from the slave trade. Today, it has eased up on the Masonic secret password, roll-your-trouser-leg-up connections, and puts more emphasis on its charitable work. In reality, it still functions as a clique of powerful businessmen who dominate the commercial life of Bristol in a way not found, or tolerated, in any other city in Britain. Edward VI granted letters patent on 18 December 1552 to form a body to protect merchants from those 'not brought up in the merchants' art'. Only those admitted to the Society of Merchant Venturers were allowed to trade by sea from Bristol. In the 16th Century, the SOMV moved into property and still owns and controls the development of large swathes of Bristol.

■ The Bristolian Party's attempt to sweep to power on a wave of popular disaffection didn't quite work out.

■ *Ian Bone arranges political walking tours of central Bristol. For further details, please contact him via email: localnews4us@yahoo.co.uk.*

THOSE IN THE KNOW

A WHO'S WHO OF BRISTOL POLITICS

■ The Kebele Kulture Projekt is a cafe/shop and anarchist collective in Easton.

The Cube

The Cube building has a history of radical entertainment dating back to the 1950s when an am-dram group built the wooden theatre. In the 1970s, it was Bristol Arts Centre, home to the radical Avon Touring Company and where earnest young men read Orwell and Marx in the bar. Nowadays, The Cube screens local films before the main features and holds an astounding diverse set of gigs and events.
■ **4 Princess Row, Kingsdown**
■ **Tel: 907 4190** ■ **www.cubecinema.com**

The Spark

The now venerable *Spark* magazine underwent a stylish revamp in 2006 while maintaining its position as the fount of all wisdom on all things green with a comprehensive listing of the city's alternative therapy practicioners. Quarterly. Free.
■ **86 Colston Street** ■ **Tel: 914 3434**
■ **www.thespark.co.uk**

Kebele Kulture Projekt

Easton-based cafe/shop and anarchist collective, Kebele came into being as a squat collective in the mid 1990s. It now runs a weekly (Sunday) vegan cafe and bike workshop. There is a radical library and internet access and it hosts film nights, exhibitions and more.
■ **14 Robertson Road, Easton** ■ **Tel: 939 9469**
■ **www.kebele.org (archive only)**

Bristol Indymedia

Web-based volunteer run alternative news service linked to Indymedia worldwide and providing a vital source of news distinct from the local Northcliffe media monopoly. This hard-working and resilient collective has survived police seizures and endless whinging from the moaners of the Left and spamming by local nutters. A good first point of call for a what's on guide to local radicalism.
■ **Box 7, Booty, 82 Colston Street**
■ **www.bristol.indymedia.org**

Easton Cowboys

A whole social network of football, cricket and netball teams with a vivacious group of can-can dancers now added to their roster. Close links with the Zapatistas in Mexico through regular trips to Chiapas. They even played cricket in Compton, Los Angeles. Gigs, meetings, local campaigning – usually found in their spiritual home, The Plough in Easton.
■ **www.eastoncowboys.org.uk**

Subvertisers

At least two long established crews of subvertisers are out radically altering the messages of advertisements most weeks. Playful and funny with a hard edge – the best traditions of situationalism. Offshoots have moved on to chopping down intrusive billboards altogether. Check out the excellent *Graphic Attack* book which was produced by *Bristle* and features 500 subvertising pictures.
■ **www.graphicattack.org.uk**

Bristle

The quarterly *Bristle* is your anti-globalisation, think-global, act-local, direct-action magazine with good listings of local campaigning groups. (See Media Listings, p252).
■ **c/o Kebele, 14 Robertson Road, Easton**
■ **Tel: 939 9469** ■ **www.bristle.org.uk**

Who's Who of Bristol Celebrities

Nipper, Cary Grant, Bananarama, Julie Burchill, WG Grace, Jane Couch: all made in Bristol

For a long time, Bristol had a celebrity count as low as a rattlesnake's belly. In the 1970s and 1980s, even if famous people lived in Bristol, they didn't seem to want to admit to it. With no big sports teams and no music celebrities, Bristol didn't feature on the cool map of the world. Sure, it was an exciting place to live – particularly the late 1970s with the vibrant fusion of punk and rasta culture based around the Dugout club on Park Row. But Bristol simply didn't have the heritage that football and The Beatles brought to Liverpool, or Two-Tone gave to Coventry. Sheffield had Joe Cocker, the Human League and the Leadmill; Hull had the Housemartins; Oxford and Cambridge had their universities; and is there anyone in the world who hasn't heard of Manchester United? Even Shrewsbury was associated with T'Pau. And Basingstoke had John Arlott. But if you'd asked the Great British public to name a famous Bristolian, they would probably have said Brunel. And he was from Portsmouth.

■ OK, he's from Portsmouth, but nobody has done more to distinguish Bristol than Brunel.

But now, all that has changed. The BBC series *Casualty* did what *Shoestring* never quite achieved in terms of raising the city's profile, and then came Massive Attack (see Bristol Beat, pg140). Robert Del Naja, Grant Marshall, Mushroom and their collaborators propelled Bristol from its status as an inland port where people talk 'gert funny' to being the coolest place in the universe. And suddenly we discovered that Bristol is full of famous people and has a long tradition of producing major talents in the arts and sciences, from Thomas Chatterton and Humphry Davy to Paul Dirac and Cary Grant.

We bring you a comprehensive list of Bristol's finest talents from way back when, right up until the present day. Who knows, you may even be surprised!

■ Charlie off of the BBC's *Casualty*. See if you can spot the Bristol backgrounds next time you're watching.

Celebrities

A Sophie Anderton

Famously spoilt former Redland High School pupil who found fame and fortune by modelling underwear and dating, amongst others, Marc Bosnich. Sophie is originally a Henleaze girl. 'Her astonishing beauty only became apparent after she was hit by a car,' reckons one of her ex-school chums.

B Edward Hodges Bailey

Sculptor born in Bristol in 1788 who is best known for the statue of Nelson in Trafalgar Square. The frieze over the Freemasons' Hall in Park Street is one of the few examples of his work in his native city.

Bananarama

Two-thirds of Bananarama (the most successful British girl group ever) were born in Bristol and the other one married Dave Stewart. Keren Woodward and Sarah Dallin from Mangotsfield certainly had their moments, *It Ain't What You Do...*, *Really Saying Something,* and *Cruel Summer* being the most memorable.

■ David Neilson used to commute from Bristol to Coronation Street where he became Roy Cropper.

Cathy Barry

Living, silicone-enhanced proof that erotica and the Kingswood accent do not mix. Despite having tits the size of Jordan's and heels higher than her IQ, Cathy Barry remains Britain's most accidental and most unlikely porn star. But her video sales tell a completely different story. We can only assume that the nation's biggest wankers aren't put off by a girl who seems only mildly interested in shagging and sounds like a dinner lady. It's too good to be true, but yes, Cath does come from Cock Road in Kingswood.

■ Kurt (Navin Chowdry) from the tele programme Teachers, which is filmed at the old Merrywood School in Knowle West.

Ernest Bevin

A founder member of the Transport and General Workers' Union, Bevin became the Union's first Secretary in 1921. He was born in Winford near Bristol and then lived at 39 Saxon Road, St Werburghs, where there's a blue plaque in his honour. In World War Two, Churchill made Bevin Minister of Labour and National Service. He is best known for introducing a scheme for young conscripts to work in coal mines rather than join the forces – hence the term Bevin Boys. He was Foreign Secretary from 1945 to 1951.

Elizabeth Blackwell

The first woman doctor, Elizabeth Blackwell was born in Counterslip, St Thomas in 1821 and also lived in Wilson Street St Paul's. She emigrated to America with her family where she qualified as a doctor. On eventually returning to England, she became the first woman to be enrolled on the British Medical Register and was an ardent campaigner for the reform of the medical profession.

Norman Bowler

Regular viewers of *Emmerdale,* after it lost the Farm bit of its title will remember this fella as the craggy-featured down-on-his-luck

BANKSY

AN INSIGHT INTO BRISTOL'S MAN OF MYSTERY

You've got to admire his ambition. From humble beginnings in the back alleys of Bristol's mean streets, Banksy has now sprayed walls all over the world without ever revealing his identity to the authorities. Not bad going for a kid who was expelled from school at 14.

'I started off painting graffiti in the classic New York style... but I was never good at it,' he revealed in one of his rare interviews. Not long after, he cut his first stencil. 'The ruthlessness and efficiency of it is to start revolutions and to stop wars,' he says of his weapon of choice, 'they look political just through the style'.

Easton, Bedminster, Windmill Hill and St Paul's became his canvas as images such as Michael Douglas from *Falling Down*, *The Mild Mild West* and his modified Van Gogh and Mona Lisa started appearing all around town. Now he is something of an international man of mystery. London, New York, the Israeli/Palestine security wall. He also sabotaged The Turner Prize, designed the cover of Blur's *Think Tank* album, has been commissioned by several multi-national companies including MTV and released a number of books.

And this, and a rumour about a £40,000 deal with Puma, has led some people to accuse Banksy of selling out. Has the lionised faceless subversive of the art world become part of the capitalist machine he once raged about? Not really, no.

Firstly, he has consistently turned down huge sums of cash from Nike because he believes they are an unethical company. It is ludicrous of anyone to expect Banksy to spend the rest of his life as a penniless hero. Why shouldn't he make some money?

Secondly, and more importantly, his work was never all that revolutionary in the first place. Images like the two coppers kissing, the *Pulp Fiction* killers firing bananas, the teddy bear throwing the petrol bomb, the give-peace-a-chance daubings in the Middle East are playful comedic observations rather than militant hollerings. His urban décor hardly spits as angrily as the rapid spray-paint sloganeering of ETA or the Sandinistas. He is no André Breton.

And yet he still has an overwhelming need to subvert his environment, as do the thousands of other kids he has inspired. In an age when they are bombarded with the clinically-selected bits-and-pieces of a popular culture that they aren't necessarily into, graffiti is a way of stamping their mark back on the world in which they live. What makes Banksy radical is not the form of his work but the process. It is hazardous, easy to get caught and takes place in the dead of the night. His most impressive stunt in the name of art to date was in London Zoo where messages were left in the animals' cages saying things like 'I'm bored, I want to go home'.

Banksy's work has slowly been disappearing from Bristol walls, but his best known work remains the *Mild Mild West* at the bottom of Stokes Croft which has pretty much become an unofficial 'Welcome to Bristol' sign. Apparently Banksy and 3D from Massive Attack beg to differ on the merits of the work. His shortest lived contribution to Bristol street art was a diver emerging from the Floating Harbour onto the stanchion of Pero's Bridge. Banksy worked through the night from a rowing boat to complete the diver by dawn. Bristol City Coucil had removed it by 10am.

'It's all about retribution really,' Banksy told *The Guardian*. 'If you don't own a train company then you go and paint on one instead. It comes from school when you had to have name tags in something – that makes it belong to you. You can own half the city by scribbling your name over it.'

For his relentless pursuit of the things he believes in the face of clear and present danger, we should salute him.

Find out more about Bristol street artists:
www.bristolgraffiti.com – a website that is dedicated to the streets of Bristol.
www.woostercollective.com – worldwide street artists, many from Bristol.
www.ekosystem.org – an influential street art site, which features Bristol's best.
www.12ozprophet.com – graffiti magazine and forums.

squire grizzler Frank Tate. Frank, y'see, had everything – beautiful wife, beautiful house, beautiful horses – but he ended up losing it all in a relentlessly soapy cyclone of heavy alcohol, double-crossing and sexually confused offspring. Frank had a heart attack and nearly died. Then his conniving, unfaithful wife Kim cheated on him, died in a car accident, came back to life and gave him the fright of his life. Or his death, to be more accurate. Bowler later revealed that he had based his alco-acting on the behaviour of his one time drinking partner Jeffery Bernard.

■ As well as famously surviving five days trapped on a boat, Tony Bullimore also used to co-own The Granary rock club.

Derren Brown

Britain's answer to David Blaine is one of those people who came to Bristol to study and liked it so much he stayed. The genuinely spooky mind-controller has said he enjoys dining out in the city alone, so anyone who starts feeling queasy in a restaurant should take a look at the table behind them.

Isambard Kingdom Brunel

The great engineer's legacy to Bristol is Temple Meads railway station, the ss Great Britain and Clifton Suspension Bridge, plus various bridges and bits of railway. Strangely, there is only one monument to Brunel in Bristol: a fairly anonymous affair tucked out in the Temple Quay redevelopment.

Tony Bullimore

Sailor who famously capsized 1,500 miles south west of Australia and spent five days trapped in an air pocket in the upturned hull of his yacht. He was once the co-owner of The Granary rock club.

■ The Death of Chatterton: the boy poet from Redcliffe was one of our greatest ever writers.

Julie Burchill

The only original thinker in the British press had her rough edges sharpened by a childhood in Bristol. 'The dog whimpers in its sleep,' she once wrote. 'It's having a bad dream. So am I. It's called living in Bristol.'

John Cabot

John Cabot set sail from Bristol in 1497 in a small ship, The Matthew, in search of the Far East. Instead, he discovered North America. Anyone who tells you that Columbus was the first European to land on the continent don't know Jack Shit. A replica of The Matthew is now moored alongside the ss Great Britain in Hotwells. The Cabot Tower on Brandon Hill (see Children's Bristol, p182) is the best public monument in Bristol.

Princess Caraboo

Mary Willcocks, a cobbler's daughter, fooled Bristol for three months in 1817 as Caraboo, Princess of Javasu. She turned up at a cottage in Almondsbury speaking in a strange tongue. Many people tried to identify her language until a Portuguese sailor, claiming comprehension, announced that she was from an island in the East Indies. He said she was brought to Bristol against her will and was a person of rank. She maintained the ruse, never

Up Close

lapsing from her peculiar tongue and even managed enough consistency for a dictionary to be created. Her beautiful manners and peculiar habits captivated everyone, but publicity finally led to her discovery and a generous benefactress quietly shipped her to America.

Mary Carpenter

The 19th-Century social reformer was the daughter of the Minister of the Unitarian Church in Lewins Mead. Moved by the plight of homeless children in Bristol, she opened the Red Lodge reform school for girls in 1854 on a site which is now covered by the Colston Hall.

Glenn Catley

It may surprise you to hear that the WBC super middleweight world champion lives and trains right here in Bristol. The former electrician is a product of the Empire Club and a bit of a hero south of the river.

■ Roger Greenaway: half of one of the most successful songwriting partnerships ever.

Thomas Chatterton

He was either the Nick Drake of the 16th Century or the Dom Jolly of ecumenical prose. The story of Bristol's doomed boy poet is the stuff of rock and roll mythology. Born next door to St Mary Redcliffe Church in 1752, the teenage Chatterton was clearly one of life's more reflective souls. With time to ponder, he became obsessed with odd bits of Medieval manuscript that he found stored away in Redcliffe Church. Eventually, he began writing poetry in the name of an imaginary 15th Century monk called Thomas Rowley. Rowley's challenging 'work' was at first authenticated and then universally applauded and Chatterton set off for London to pursue his own literary career. Sadly, all his attempts were greeted with indifference. Apparently crushed by the criticism, Chatterton swallowed a bottle of arsenic and was found dead at his home on 24 August 1770. This gifted, rebellious youth later became a hero to the romantic and pre-Raphaelite poets, several of whom, notably Keats and Coleridge, wrote poems about him. He became regarded as the first Romantic poet. A statue of Chatterton used to stand outside St Mary Redcliffe Church, but fell into disrepair and was removed. The house that Chatterton grew up in is on the other side of the dual carriageway from St Mary Redcliffe. Sadly, it is not open to the public; it is occupied by one of the City Museum staff, but if you're lucky, he might let you look round.

■ Roger Cook: the other half of one of the most successful songwriting partnerships ever.

John Cleese

Although born in Weston-super-Mare, the *Monty Python's Flying Circus* founder member and one of Britain's favourite comedians John Cleese was a pupil at Clifton College in Bristol. Rumour has it that it was at the College where he first developed a penchant for silly walks. Allegedly, Cleese practised his silly walks on the cricket pitch to annoy teachers and impress fellow pupils. A match report from the 1950s refers to 'many Cleesian glides'.

Stephanie Cole

Just as she did when she played Diana Trent in *Waiting For God*, Stephanie Cole isn't afraid to speak her mind. In an interview with the *Evening Post*, she once launched a savage attack accusing the toothless local media of going out of their way to damage arts in the area. Would it be so difficult for *HTV News* and *Points West* to include a five-minute arts feature occasionally, she asked. Unfortunately, Steph, they do like to devote themselves to mediocrity on a full-time basis.

Justin Lee Collins

You know the bloke. Scruffy, shoulder-length, strawberry ginger hair, shouts a lot and gets over-excited in a broad Bristolian accent about nothing in particular on pointless late night Channel 4 programmes commissioned by overpaid half-wits who clearly didn't understand *Nathan Barley*. Yeah, the irritating one. Well, he's a Southmead boy, so he reckons. And, apparently, when he's not fronting terrible telly such as *10 Things You Didn't Know About...* and the even more unnecessary *Strictly Come Dancing* BBC 3 update, he is a half-decent stand-up comedian. Don Ward from the *Comedy Store* even described Justin as 'the most original comic I've seen since Harry Hill'. Are you sure about that?

■ Cook and Greenway as David and Jonathan in their George Martin days.

Russ Conway

Born in Bedminster (there's a blue plaque on the wall of his home in Dean Lane), Trevor Stanford changed his name to Russ Conway and rose to stardom in the late 1950s. He went on to have more than 20 hit records. In fact, he spent a total of 168 weeks in the charts and remains the biggest selling pianist in UK pop history. Unless you count Elton John.

Cook and Greenaway

One of the most successful songwriting partnerships ever, Roger Cook and Roger Greenaway were born in Bristol in 1940 and 1938 respectively. Cook lived at 8 Forest Road, Fishponds; Greenaway was brought up at 98 Spring Hill, Kingswood. After knocking about with various Bristol bands (such as the Kestrels), they were discovered in 1965 by Beatles producer George Martin. Martin's wife, Judy, suggested they record under the name David and Jonathan and they reached number 11 in the charts with Lennon and McCartney's *Michelle* in 1966. A string of other singles followed, but it is as songwriters that Cook and Greenaway made a huge impact. They've written for artists including Gene Pitney (*Something's Gotten Hold Of My Heart*), Cilla Black, Cliff Richard, Kathy Kirby, Hank Marvin, Deep Purple and the Sweet, to name but a few. Cook joined Blue Mink in 1969 and recorded Cook and Greenaway's anti-racism classic *Melting Pot*. But it's as the writers of the 1970 Coca-Cola jingle *I'd Like To Buy The World A Coke*, that Cook and Greenaway reached an audience of millions around the globe. This was recorded as *I'd Like To Teach The World To Sing* by the New Seekers and released in December 1971. It brought Cook and Greenaway their first number one in January

■ Jane Couch: you try telling her boxing is just for blokes. Go on then!

1972. In that month, three of the top four chart songs were Cook and Greenaway creations: at number two was *Softly Whispering I Love You* (The Congregation) and Cilla was at number four with *Something Tells Me Something's Gonna Happen Tonight*. They were only prevented from a straight top three run by the number two sound of Benny Hill with *Ernie: The Fastest Milkman In The West*. Cook and Greenaway have always been mighty proud of their Bristol roots and have returned to the city regularly over the years. We think they rival Massive Attack as Bristol's most successful musical export.

■ **Adam Hart-Davis relaxes in the garden of his Bishopston home.**

Jane Couch

After years of hard living, Jane Couch has done more for women's boxing than anyone before her. Her motto, 'man or woman, if you take me on, you're history', has more than a ring of truth to it. She even left the British Boxing Board of Control on the canvas. That's feminism. The world welterweight champion trains with Tex Woodward at the Spanorium Gym in Compton Greenfield. Couch burst onto the world boxing scene in May 1996 when she out-pointed French star Sandra Geiger in Copenhagen to win the WIBF welterweight title. The 10-round fight was watched by a European TV audience of 3.5 million. Couch said after this fight: 'My cheekbone was busted, my eye was out to here and I was a mess of bumps and bruises'.

Robin Cousins MBE

Ice skating's very own Alan Partridge won gold at the 1980 Winter Olympics and had a sports centre named after him in his home area of Shirehampton. Cousins is set to return in an 'ice extravaganza' up on the Downs'. No change there then.

David and Jonathan

See Cook and Greenaway.

■ **Sapphire: has been a famous face of Bristol for as long as anyone can remember.**

D Sir Humphry Davy

Born in Penzance in 1778, Davy pursued his scientific career from a laboratory in Dowry Square, Hotwells. He discovered laughing gas and invented the miners' safety lamp.

Adam Hart-Davis

The eccentric historian and TV boffin lives in Bishopston. Adam is, among other things, a companion of the Institution of Lighting Engineers, a Fellow of the Royal Society of Arts and a member of the British Toilet Association, a pressure group that campaigns for 'better public toilets for all'.

E Lee Evans

You begin to understand just why Lee Evans is so nervously hyperactive when you discover that he was born in Avonmouth, the home of petro-chemical spillages. The supple-limbed comedian couldn't wait to live somewhere else and has now settled in Southend.

LOCAL HEROES & ECCENTRICS
PEOPLE TO SPOT IN YOUR AREA

Cider Jim

'Cider' lurches around Redland/Clifton like some sort of Ziggy-fixated Quaker, frightening the life out of new students and anyone with a nervous disposition. The stories about his antics are legendary. He can usually be spotted swaying through Clifton Village shouting: 'In the 1960s I took cannabis, in the 1970s heroin, in the 1980s cocaine and in the '1990s... cider! cider! cider!'

Sapphire

If you've been handed a club flyer in Bristol in the last 20 years, chances are you already know this absurdly flamboyant transvestite firework on legs. Sapphire (pictured left) has been around for as long as anyone can remember. Who is he? He's Ru Paul from the street, Grace Jones with added self-belief, Sugar Plum Mary with God and the DHSS on her side. A BBC documentary broadcast to commemorate his 50th birthday did little to dent his outrageous public persona.

Leather Jockstrap Caveman

You know you're going to see him striding nowhere in particular at the Ashton Court Festival. But if you're lucky you might get to see him going about his daily business, at the top of Park Street, by the big post office on Queen Square, or heading off in the direction of the bus station. Whatever the day, whatever the weather, you can be sure he'll be wearing nothing except that old leather jockstrap he loves so much. A beautiful sight.

The Singing Lady on the Stoke Bishop bus

The Singing Lady looks just like any other pensioner. This is why nobody is afraid of sitting next to her. Old dear, what harm can she possibly do? But as soon as the bus pulls away, she bursts into song: a high-pitched, high-volume and completely unashamed medley of pre-Elvis chandelier-shakers leaving you in the most uncomfortable seat. Do you grit your teeth and stay on the bus, or bottle out at the next stop?

Andy Sloan and Matt Holyfield

In the spring of 2002, two Bristol students set off on the adventure of a lifetime with a 141lb table football as their luggage. Sloan and Holyfield spent £10,000 and played matches in 41 countries, crossing Europe, India, Thailand and the Middle East before reaching their final destination of South Korea in time for the start of the World Cup. Along the way, they played table football in the Olympic Stadiums of Rome and Munich and had a game with FIFA president Sepp Blatter at his offices in Zurich.

Clint

Unless you misspent a large part of your youth hanging around in Westbury-on-Trym village, chances are you won't know who Clint is. If you did, you'd swear Clint had based his daily performances on Groucho Marx. He'd throw funny one-liners at anyone who looked as though they were taking themselves too seriously. I once saw him standing in the chemists holding a glass of water. He looked around shiftily and whispered, 'I'm only here for the water,' out of the corner of his mouth. A living genius in Bristol BS9.

Bill Spring

As claims to fame go, Bill Spring's is one of the most pointless and most unusual to make the record books. Bill, you see, was the first and last person to cross the Redcliffe flyover, the now deceased temporary road bridge that once made driving in the Temple Meads area a bit like being in loop-the-loop Scalextric

Late Bus Woman

Described by one witness as being 'terrifying, absolutely bloody terrifying,' this elderly lady from Westbury-on-Trym has got a problem with buses being late. If the bus is so much as a minute behind schedule, Late Bus Woman attacks the driver with a painful torrent of expletive-riddled abuse and doesn't stop until she gets off half an hour later down the route. As a sideline, she also shouts at girls who wear Dr Martens boots.

F George Ferguson

The 'Red Trousered Philanthropist' is doing more to shape a creative vision of Bristol than any number of planners and developers with their mind-numbing plans for the new Broadmead or absurd justifications for building a concert arena with no car park. George, who is famed for wearing red trousers and being on Channel 4's *Demolition* programme, is one of the country's leading architects and is a passionate believer in building sustainable communities by reclaiming land and buildings. He has also been a Merchant Venturer, but we'll forgive him that. He has been in Bristol since his student days in the 1960s and has been the creative force behind many leading initiatives. George's vision is best realised in his Tobacco Factory and Bristol Beer Factory projects in Southville which paved the way for the boom of independent businesses migrating to North Street. The Tobacco Factory was originally part of a much grander scheme under which George would have created an 'urban village' on the sites of all the former tobacco industry buildings in Southville. George was President of the Royal Institute of British Architects from 2003 to 2005 and has won numerous awards for his work.

■ Cary Grant: the most famous old boy of Bishop Road Primary school and Fairfield School.

Keith Floyd

Legendary snorter of claret and one of the first TV celebrity chefs, the bon viveur's bon viveur used to have his very own restaurant on Chandos Road, in Redland.

G WG Grace

Cricket's first ever superstar was an extremely bearded and notoriously fierce fella who annihilated bowlers and intimidated batsman for Gloucestershire and England. William Gilbert Grace was born in Downend in 1848; he played 22 times for England between 1880 and 1899, scoring 1,038 runs. He was a GP in Bristol with a surgery in Stapleton Road, Easton from 1881 to 1895.

■ Ian Holloway, who was born in Kingswood and played for Bristol Rovers, has a way with words.

Cary Grant

Bristol's golden boy. (See profile, p120).

H Anthony Head

This Bristol-based actor was once known only as 'that prat off the Gold Blend ads' but a leading role in *Buffy The Vampire Slayer* changed all that. He claims his 19th-Century house in Bristol is haunted by the ghost of a young girl. 'She is not frightening at all,' added the demon destroyer.

Damien Hirst

Of all the 'enfant terribles' of the over-hyped late 20th-Century Brit Art uprising, this Bristol-born originator remains the most convincing. Sharks, cows and sheep have been preserved in formaldehyde, flies have been given life and promptly killed again and medicine bottles have been used as the theme for a restaurant. And yet, somehow, pretentiousness has never been an issue… Damien was born in the city in 1965, the son of a car salesman. His family moved to Leeds when he was a nipper, but those vital formative crayoning years were spent in Bristol.

Ian Holloway

Iconic Bristol Rovers player and manager who hails from Kingswood. Ollie gained national celebrity for the bizarre way in which he expressed himself at press conferences when he became manager at Queens Park Rangers. There's an excellent collection of his best quotes called *Let's Have Coffee: The Tao of Ian Holloway* (Toilet Books, £4.50, www.letshavecoffee.com) which contains such gems as 'Every dog has its day and today is woof day! I just want to bark!'

Bob Hope

Yes, that Bob Hope. The legendary Hollywood entertainer spent his early years at 326 Whitehall Road. Hope returned to Bristol in 1943 and met his former next-door neighbour Annie Pugh. Asked if he remembered her, Hope replied: 'Remember her? Oh sure: I was four at the time and we were going steady.'

■ The house in Whitehall Road where entertainer Bob Hope spent his childhood.

Wayne Hussey

It's a little known fact that the goth superstar from the Sisters of Mercy and the Mission spent his formative years as a pupil at the Ridings High School in Winterbourne, just outside Bristol.

K Nik Kershaw

Nicholas David Kershaw was born on 1 March 1958 in Bristol. His mother was an opera singer; his father a flautist. Nik is best remembered as one of the most forgettable singer/ songwriters of the 1980s; the man responsible for the turgid *I Won't Let The Sun Go Down On Me* and the Cluedo-like *The Riddle*. He moved to Ipswich with his family when he was a nipper.

■ Kwame Kwei-Armah (second left) not only stars in Casualty, he is also an ambassador for Christian Aid.

Kwame Kwei-Armah

Anyone who knows Kwame only as paramedic Finlay Newton in *Casualty* is only dipping their toe in the shallowest end of a reasonably deep ocean. As well as charging about the familiar *Holby City* area in an all-in-one green jumpsuit, the London- and Bristol-based father of three has written two plays, *Blues Brothers, Soul Sisters* and *A Bitter Herb*, plus a musical called *Hold On*. He showed off his vocal talents on BBC dirgefest *Fame Academy* and acquitted himself more than adequately as a cultural critic on *Late Review*. He's also an ambassador for Christian Aid and a keen supporter of fairtrade. 'I can honestly say that *Casualty* is the best,' he enthused once. No it isn't. ER is.

L David 'Syd' Lawrence

Dangerously inconsistent Gloucestershire and England fast bowler turned high-profile restaurateur. The man who gave us Boom on Whiteladies Road is the most visible BMW owner around town.

ON LOCATION
THE VERY BEST OF TV FILMED IN BRISTOL

■ **The famous Batman and Robin scene from Only Fools and Horses was filmed in Knowle, South Bristol.**

Casualty
The BBC's flagship hospital drama has been filmed in Bristol for so long that most locals don't take any notice of speeding ambulances any more. 'Bloody *Casualty*,' drivers mutter, as another 'emergency' brings traffic to a halt.

Shoestring
For most TV viewers, Eddie Shoestring was a beige radio phone-in host/private eye who seemed to solve even the most complex of West Country crimes through a series of half-arsed shrugs. For Bristolians, however, it was a weekly opportunity to spot places you knew on the telly. 'Oh look darling, there's the post box at the end of Coldharbour Lane.'

The Young Ones
Once considered seminal, now thought of as pretty crap, the madcap student sitcom that launched a dozen comedy careers was filmed in and around Redland. The most memorable Bristol scene took place in Henleaze's bizarre circular drinking den, the Cock O' The North, which was renamed the Kebab & Calculator for the occasion.

Teachers
The former Merrywood school was turned into Summerdown Comprehensive for Channel 4's gutsy and eventually hilarious drama starring teachers who smoke, drink, use expletives and one who rides his bike into school every morning giving the director

an opportunity to show off some excellent panoramic views of the lovely Bristol.

Animal Magic
Johnny Morris was fortunate that none of the animals he got into conversations with at Bristol Zoo in *Animal Magic* were actually born and raised in Bristol. Can you imagine a camel with a Hartcliffe accent? *Animal Magic* ran for 21 years and more than 400 editions. Morris, who was from Newport, adopted the persona of a keeper at Bristol Zoo and created a startling range of voices for each of the zoo's animals. The show was dropped in 1984 when it was felt to be too old fashioned. Johnny Morris died in 1999.

House of Eliot
This very crap and very prim-and-proper period drama about needlework was shot on location in some poncy guest house in Clifton Village. According to Mrs Fotheringham-Herefordshire from the Keep-The-Unemployed-Out-Of-Clifton Society, you can still hear the sound of hems being stitched as you walk past the filming site.

Paper Mask
The presence of Paul McGann, the I from *Withnail & I*, doubled the local interest. A Bristol-based movie starring a Bristol-based actor. In a chilling precursor to the Bristol Royal Infirmary heart scandal, this half-decent medical thriller told the tale of a fake doctor administering pin-the-tail-on-the-donkey science to the city's ever-dwindling population. Much scarier than *Casualty*.

Only Fools and Horses
Not so much 'stick a pony in your pocket' as 'whack a dirty gurt twenny in thur me babs'. It's true! Nelson Mandela House was actually Whitemead House in Duckmore Road, Bristol. The BBC switched filming to Bristol from an estate in Acton, London. The Nag's Head was a Bristol boozer (among others) and the famous Batman and Robin scene was filmed in the Broadwalk shopping precinct in Knowle.

Celebrities

The Mabbutts

The nearest thing that Bristol has to a football dynasty. Ray Mabbutt played almost 400 League games for Bristol Rovers between 1957 and 1969. Younger son Gary overcame diabetes to follow Ray into the Rovers first team and he played 122 League games between 1978 and 1982. He then moved to Spurs and went on to win 16 England caps. He was awarded an MBE for his services to football, but most fans will remember him as the bloke with the squeaky Bristol accent. The elder brother, Kevin, was regarded as having more potential than Gary and played for Bristol City between 1977 and 1981 before joining Crystal Palace where his career was cut short by injury. He moved to America where he owns an exclusive restaurant in Santa Fe, California.

Paul McGann

He will be forever remembered as the I from *Withnail & I*. McGann lives in Clifton and tries to avoid blokes in pubs who shout 'we've come on holiday by mistake' at him. He was special guest at the opening of the Katmandu restaurant in the Colston Tower after being a regular at the take-away in Easton for 16 years.

Precious McKenzie MBE

The little fella with the big dumbells was born in Durban, South Africa. He is the only Bristol celebrity whose father was killed while hunting crocodiles. McKenzie became a top weightlifter in South Africa, but wasn't allowed to compete because he is black. He moved to England, made Bristol his base and went on to become British and World Champion and represent Britain in three Olympic Games between 1968 and 1976. McKenzie was a hugely popular local character who worked tirelessly to promote sport, especially with youngsters. He lived in Leighton Road, Southville, trained at the Empire Gym in St Paul's and worked at an Ashton tannery. Legend has it that the Queen was late for an official engagement because she was so determined to see Precious McKenzie win his third Commonwealth weightlifting gold medal. The 4ft 11in tall McKenzie was nicknamed the 'Pocket Rocket'. Although he now lives in New Zealand, Precious is fondly remembered as one of Bristol's finest adopted sons.

Steve Merchant

Former *Venue* magazine work-experience hack turned award-winning comedy writer and Ricky Gervais' lanky other half added some unmistakable touches of Bristolian weirdness to the BBC 2 sitcom *The Office*.

Sean Moore

The Manic Street Preachers' drummer is rumoured to be living in deepest, darkest Emerson's Green, Mangotsfield, with his girlfriend. 'It's a good place… and it's far enough away that my mother doesn't visit me every day,' he says of his adopted home.

■ World weightlifting champion Precious McKenzie with the world heavyweight champion Muhammad Ali.

■ Precious McKenzie: more than 30 British and world titles and four consecutive Commonwealth gold medals. What a guy!

Up Close

Nipper the HMV dog

The Bristol-born dog (part bull terrier with a trace of fox terrier) was bought as a pup in 1884 by flamboyant local artist Mark Barraud. Fame beckoned after Mark's death when his brother Francis painted an oil painting in 1895 of Nipper listening to an old phonograph which was chosen to be 'the loyal mutt' for the His Master's Voice advertising trademark.

David Neilson

Aka Roy Cropper from Coronation Street. As Mike Baldwin once put it: 'He's a bit of a nutter, but harmless enough.' The actor responsible for Corrie's nervy, transsexual-marrying anorak loves Bristol so much, he commutes to Weatherfield every week. Or he used to until the traffic got so bad that he moved to Spain and commuted from there instead.

■ Nipper: this statue of the most famous dog in the world is at the junction of Woodland Road and Park Row.

Nick Park

The Oscar-collecting Aardman Animations (see Media section, p252) main man with an ill-advised love of revolving bow ties. Park acknowledges the debt Wallace & Gromit owe to the city: 'I think a lot of the humour has come from being rooted in the Bristol area,' admits the patient Plasticine botherer.

Jonathan Pearce

Every nation gets the punditry its football deserves. In England, Bristol-born Jonathan Pearce is now the voice you hear more often than any other. Radio 5 Live, Channel 5, Saturday afternoon, every week night, he was even on *Robot Wars*… The shouty Pearce is a Bristol City fan who attended Queen Elizabeth's Hospital School at about the same time as Hugo Weaving (see p118).

Colin Pillinger

The son of a Bristol gas-fitter, the world's only inter-planetary Wurzel admits he was: 'rubbish at chemistry at school and dreamt only of playing for Bristol Rovers'. Despite getting Damien Hirst and Alex James from Blur to work on the art and sound, the Mars Express orbiter and its Beagle 2 probe still haven't sent so much as a postcard.

■ Wallace & Gromit were created by Aardman Animations main man Nick Park.

Samuel Plimsoll

Born at 9 Colston Parade, Redcliffe in 1824, Plimsoll came up with the idea of putting a line on a ship's hull which would fall beneath the waterline if the vessel was overloaded. This led to the Merchant Shipping Act of 1876, which made it law for all boats to carry a Plimsoll Line. He died in 1898. There's a bust of him on the Portway in Hotwells.

Vicky Pollard

Matt Lucas and David Walliams based the character of Vicky Pollard in *Little Britain* on their observations of working-class Bristolian teenage girls while they were drama students at Bristol University in the mid 1990s. Stroll down Filwood Broadway in Knowle West and you will be surrounded by Vicky Pollards. It would be bold to claim that their presence is an ironic gesture, but it really is like that out Knowle West.

Harry Potter
See JK Rowling.

Dave Prowse
Originally a weightlifter, Prowse was not only the original Green Cross Code Man, but the body of Darth Vader. Why only the body? Can you imagine hearing: 'May the force be with you, me babber' in a deep Bristolian accent? He once worked as a bouncer at Romeo and Juliet's on Nelson Street.

■ Dave Prowse as Darth Vader: the most evil man in the universe used to be a bouncer down at Romeo and Juliet's in town.

R Sir Michael Redgrave CBE
Actor, author, director, producer, great grandfather of thespianism and one half of the couple that gave us Vanessa and Lynn Redgrave and Natasha and Joley Richardson. Born the son of a silent film actor in Bristol in 1908, this giant of stage and screen made his first professional appearance at the Liverpool Playhouse in 1934 and went on to star in movies such as Hitchcock's *The Lady Vanishes, Kipps, The Dam Busters* and *Mourning Becomes Electra*, which earned him an Oscar nomination. He is most fondly remembered for his towering Shakespearean performances and lived long enough to open Clifton College's very own theatre named in his honour. (See Culture Listings, p246).

Tony Robinson
Once upon a time, he was Baldrick in *Blackadder* and everybody loved him. Now he gets paid to spend two weeks digging up tiny fragments of iron-age flint in Channel 4's remarkably tedious *Time Team*. Live archaeology? Whatever next?

Isaac Rosenberg
Arguably the greatest of the First World War poets, Rosenberg was born in Bristol in November 1890 of Russian Jewish immigrant parents. The Peugeot garage diagonally opposite Temple Meads stands on the site of his birthplace.

■ And here is Dave Prowse again. This time he is the Green Cross Code Man.

JK Rowling
Joanne Kathleen Rowling was born in Chipping Sodbury near Bristol to an apprentice engineer and a French/Scottish mother. She also lived in Yate and then Winterbourne. If you'd bumped into a young JK, you would have found her (in her own words): 'A shy, snotty, swotty little kid and very insecure'. Hermione Granger is supposed to be based on her. While living in the Bristol area, she wrote her first book, *Rabbit*, at the age of six.

S Richard Scudamore
The flappy-eared Premier League chief executive is originally from Soundwell, Kingswood. He went to St Stephen's Primary school, where he no doubt shaped his views on supporting Bristol

City, the offside rule and making football more inclusive for the community. If he still lived in Soundwell, you'd probably find him in the Jolly Cobbler reading the Green 'Un of a Saturday evening.

Adrian Stone

Former light-middleweight world boxing champion nicknamed The Predator. He was brought up in Horfield and went to Monks Park School. Stone is now based in America, but is still managed by Bristol promoter Chris Saniger.

Randolph Sutton

The music hall performer who popularised *On Mother Kelly's Doorstep* was born in Anglesea Place, Clifton in 1888. Sutton was able to pack in his job as an accounts clerk at Robinson's packaging in Bedminster when he won a talent contest while on holiday at Burnham-on-Sea. His trademark stage outfits were pink or mauve suits and he quickly became one of Britain's most popular comedians before the Second World War. He was offered *On Mother Kelly's Doorstep* by a London coalman called George Stevens who was inspired to write the song by the sight of two ragged children sitting on a doorstep. Stevens sold the song for five shillings on condition that it was performed by Randolph Sutton. A few years before he died in 1969, Sutton recorded a nostalgic trip around Bristol for television with his old friend Sir John Betjeman.

■ Tony Robinson inspects his change from the pie stand at Ashton Gate where he is a keen Bristol City fan.

T Dave Thompson

Although he's a stand-up comedian and a celebrated television gag writer, Dave Thompson is best known for being sacked from the role of Tinky Winky out of the *Teletubbies*. 'I was never stoned in front of the camera,' he retaliated as the tabloids hurled accusations. 'The weirdest dude on the face of the earth,' concluded *Time Out* magazine.

Michelle Thorne

Local girl who made a name for herself as a singer, particularly by entertaining fans at Bristol City and Rovers games at half time. This encouraged Michelle to enter the *X-Factor* where she was knocked out in the third round. The classically-trained vocalist then opted for a career in the porn industry where she specialises in lesbian hardcore, sometimes working with Bristolian Cathy Barry (p105).

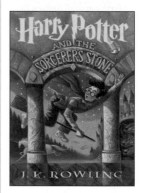

■ JK Rowling, the author of Harry Potter, was born in Chipping Sodbury, just outside Bristol.

W Hugo Weaving

Better known as Elrond in *The Lord of the Rings* films, or Agent Smith in *The Matrix*, Hugo went to Queen Elizabeth's Hospital School on Jacobs Wells Road. The school was notable for not having a drama department then, and for making pupils wear moleskin britches and yellow stockings in public.

Fred Wedlock

Irritating straw-haired yokel who continues to reap the benefits of his one solo hit record, *The Oldest Swinger In Town*, and as a

JOHNNY BALL

KIDS' PRESENTER SHARES HIS BRISTOL MEMORIES

■ **The nation's favourite children's presenter relives some stories from his early life in Kingswood**

I was born at the Royal Infirmary on 23 May 1938, the only child of Daniel and Martha Ann Ball. I was christened Graham Thalben Ball after the organist and religious composer, Dr G Thalben-Ball (my parents didn't know that the G stood for George).

The infirmary is only a few hundred yards from Johnny Ball Lane, but I wasn't called Johnny until about 1953. That was the year of the Matthews Cup Final when Blackpool beat Bolton Wanderers, 3-2. The right-back for Bolton was Johnny Ball and my Bolton schoolmates started calling me Johnny Ball and it stuck – I have not used Graham since.

My parents lived in a cottage on Warmley Hill, but we soon moved to 111 New Cheltenham Road – the fourth house up from the shops, on the right. I add that, because I remember the Kingswood Cubs was also the 111th Bristol so I wonder if my memory has tricked me here?

I went to Kingswood Primary School from five-years-old and took and passed my eleven plus there, before we moved to Bolton in 1949. The Head was Mr Benson and it may have been he who instilled in me a love of maths. However, my parents were also a help there, as we always played dominoes, cards or a complex bagatelle game in which I learnt to handle numbers well from an early age.

Dad worked at the Magnal in Warmley, moulding aluminium aircraft parts and worked nights almost all the way through the war. Mum worked at Pratt's Boot factory making Burma Boots for the Far East. On air raid nights, we used next door's (Mrs Church's) air-raid shelter once, sat under the stairs a couple of times, under the table a couple of times and then ignored the raids. Mum and I would just play 20 Questions.

My mother talked of being machine-gunned in Kingswood High Street, by returning German aircraft. She tried to get into Woolworths doorway but it was already crowded and they would not let her and myself in the pram, get in. I wonder if anyone else remembers this incident?

I never missed the Odeon Saturday morning show. There was also a cinema across the road, which I think was called the Regent. My parents loved to walk (miles) to pubs in the area. Mangotsfield and Syston Common were summer weekend destinations and especially Frenchay Common – Dad loved cricket. Their favourite pub was the Queens Head at Hanham – I popped in there last year and said I had been in before. 'When?' they asked. 'Oh around 1948!' I said.

There was a very tall man called Albert at the Queen's Head, who would charm warts. If you had warts, you went home, stripped off, counted them and wrote the total on a piece of paper. You brought it to Albert. He secretly looked at the number, threw the paper in the fire and a few day's later, your warts were gone. If it failed, he made you count your warts again, as the right number was essential. He had a large smooth bump on his forehead and everyone said that was where the warts ended up.

He once came from the garden into the Children's Room with a huge garden snail. As we kids watched mesmerised, he placed the snail on his tongue. It slowly crawled further and further down his throat until his mouth closed with a 'crunch' and that was that.

CARY GRANT

THE BEGINNINGS OF OUR MOST FAMOUS STAR

✳ Unlikely as it may seem, Hollywood's smoothest ever leading man was born to Elias and Elsie Leach in Hughenden Road, Horfield. The small terraced house bears a blue plaque outside which reads, 'Archibald Alec Leach, better known as Cary Grant, was born here on 18 January 1904.'

After attending Bishop Road School in Bishopston, he won a scholarship to Fairfield Grammar School in Montpelier, where there is a plaque commemorating the school's most famous pupil. It doesn't mention that Grant was expelled. The exact reason for the expulsion is unclear, but on one occasion Grant said it was because he was found in the girls' lavatory.

Grant had a confused and unhappy childhood. His father was a womaniser who had a son by another relationship. When Cary Grant was 10, he left home to go to Boy Scouts one evening and on his return found his mother had disappeared. In fact, she had been placed in the Fishponds Country Home for Mental Defectives by his father. His father never told Grant what had happened to his mother, but in 1935, he learned that she was still alive in an institution.

By the time he found out his mother was still alive, Grant was already on his way to becoming one of Hollywood's greatest

ever leading men. He was introduced to the theatre at the Bristol Hippodrome where he worked as a caller and, in 1920, he headed for the USA along with a troupe of acrobats from the Hippodrome.

Archie Leach became Cary Grant in 1932 when Paramount purchased his contract. Part of that contract stipulated that he change his name. Paramount gave him a list of Anglo-Saxon sounding surnames, and the man known as Archie Leach became Cary Grant.

Grant established himself in a series of screwball comedies such as *The Awful Truth* with Irene Dunne, *Bringing Up Baby* with Katharine Hepburn, *Girl Friday* with Rosalind Russell and *Arsenic and Old Lace* with Priscilla Lane. Alfred Hitchcock was a great admirer of Grant's smooth, charming, yet complex screen persona and once described him as: 'The only actor I ever loved in my whole life'. Grant appeared in such Hitchcock classics as *Suspicion, Notorious, To Catch a Thief* and *North by Northwest*.

Apart from being a great actor, it transpired that Grant was also a famous adventurer with LSD. During the filming of the movie *Operation Petticoat* with Tony Curtis, he told astonished reporters that his relaxed condition was due to the insights he had achieved using the then experimental mind drug on about 60 occasions. 'I have been born again,' Grant said. 'I have been through a psychiatric experience which has completely changed me.'

Grant was a proud Bristolian and returned to the city many times to visit his mother. Sometimes hundreds of fans would turn out to welcome him 'home' when they knew he was arriving in town. He continued to visit Bristol regularly, even after her death.

Cary Grant died just hours before he was due on stage for *A Conversation With Cary Grant* in Iowa on 29 November 1986. A bronze statue was unveiled in Millennium Square in December 2001. Perhaps the many dilemmas in his life are best summed up by Archibald Leach himself who said: 'Everyone wants to be Cary Grant. Even I want to be Cary Grant.'

presenter for terrible HTV programmes about car boot sales. Truth is, Wedlock is worse than The Wurzels.

Naomi Wilkinson

The face of *Milkshake!*, Channel Five's morning show for kids, Naomi no doubt perfected the Milkshake Shake in the playgrounds of Henleaze Infant and Junior School where she was a pupil. The North Bristol stunner went on to attend Colston's Girls' School where her celebrity credentials were confirmed by a virtuoso solo performance of the first verse of *Once In Royal David's City* at the school carol service at Bristol Cathedral. She was a regular competitor at the Bristol Dance Eisteddfod from the age of four and once played glockenspiel at a performance of Carmina Burana at the Colston Hall. With star credentials like that, a glittering television career clearly beckons. Naomi is also a keen fairtrade supporter. Good on her!

■ Hugo Weaving: the Queen Elizabeth's Hospital School old boy went on to become Agent Smith in The Matrix and Elrond in The Lord of the Rings.

Robert Wyatt

He might have been co-founder of experimental jazz-rockers the Soft Machine and one of the only wheelchair-bound artists in pop history, but Robert Wyatt is probably best remembered for his cover of Elvis Costello's anti-Falklands war song *Shipbuilding*.

BRISTOL
STREET ART

> Bristol's graffiti tradition stretches back to
> the 1980s when it was heavily influenced by
the New York hip-hop and street art crews. Street
artists from the Big Apple who visited St Paul's
and Barton Hill left a legacy that has been passed
on from 3D, Nick Walker and Die in the 1980s to
Inky and Banksy in the 1990s and on to the likes
of Cheba, Sickboy, Sums and Ghostboy. Here we
trace Bristol street art from that first 3D image
of two policemen (the first example of graffiti
in Britain?) through to the latest offerings from
Bristol's dedicated army of taggers, stencillers
and sprayers...

History of the Bristol Beat

From the Pop Group to Massive Attack with a detour via the Moonflowers and Strangelove

I f there was any kind of music scene in Bristol before 1977, his name was Russ Conway and he liked to play the piano. It wasn't until the jagged edges of new wave began to cut the shock tactics out of the punk movement that the first serious local bands began to emerge from their Clifton and Redland hideaways. So we'll make 1977 our starting point for a tour of the Bristol music scene.

First out of the blocks were The Cortinas, four sneering teenagers in torn blazers not long out of grammar school sixth form. Fittingly, their feisty and dangerously energetic double-A-sided single *Fascist Dictator/Television Families* set the standard that others would have to follow. And sure enough, by the middle of 1979, hundreds of nervy young punk bands were popping up all over town. A fanzine called *Loaded* sprang up in support like a regional *Sniffin' Glue*. Suddenly, there were six or seven live venues. Then Heartbeat Records released the *Social Security* EP which featured four irreverent dum-dum bullets, including the immortal *I'm Addicted To Cider*.

Bristol was up and running as a music town. The fledgling label followed their debut release with another excellent single, *The Europeans*, by the Europeans. The Europeans became the first but certainly not the last Bristol band to be linked with a major record deal that never quite came off. The likes of the Pigs, the X-Certs, Joe Public and The Numbers all followed. Aggressive, confrontational upstarts all.

But from here on in, the sound of young Bristol splintered in several different directions. There was wheel-spinning R&B in the shape of 14-year-old rebel-rousers The Untouchables. There were experimental types, such as the Art Objects, Glaxo Babies and Essential Bop. Black Roots

■ Nick Cave called The Pop Group 'the best band in Britain'. This sleeve design is by Rich Beale who later joined ex-Pop Group conspirator Gareth Sager in Head.

■ The Cortinas appeared on the Bristol music scene in 1977 as 16-year-old grammar school boys.

140

introduced the dub influence while Shoes For Industry volunteered to be ringmaster for weird circus rock and confirmed their status by getting the lead singer to wear an inside-out brain on his head. And, most controversially of all, Melanie, the daughter of Bristol City manager 'Alan-Alan-Alan' Dicks did a pouty Wendy James type of thing for a band called Double Vision. Ashton Court Festival became a canvas for the city's eclectic range of characters. The Wurzels were not welcome.

But lording it over this newly-built sonic kingdom were the mightiest of all the pre-1990s Bristolian hollerers, The Pop Group. How good were The Pop Group? Well, when Nick Cave and his growling Birthday Party entourage first landed on these shores in 1980, they spent every night going to gigs all over the capital but were shocked and disappointed by the limp, bloodless bands they found. 'It was like being gang-banged by a pack of marshmallows,' commented Cave, savagely. Then one night he saw The Pop Group. The experience changed his life. As part of Channel 4's *Music of the Millennium* series, Cave chose *We Are All Prostitutes* as his favourite piece of music of all time. 'The beginning of the record is the greatest start of any record, ever,' claims the awesome Aussie. And you wouldn't want to disagree with him.

This is why it's The Pop Group who are cited as being one of the biggest influences on what became known as

Five great...
Bristol beat albums

1 Massive Attack, Blue Lines: As startling now as it was in 1991. One of the greatest albums ever made.

2 Portishead, Dummy: Monumental achievement: timeless, faultless and utterly unique.

3 Tricky, Maxinquaye: Brooding with sexuality and ghetto intent. Inspired and uncomfortable.

4 Roni Size and Reprazent, New Forms: Drum 'n' bass and urban noise engineering at its most precise.

5 Alpha, Come From Heaven: An LP of impossible beauty and poise that should have sold millions.

■ Bristol dub kings Black Roots were produced by the Mad Professor who remixed Massive Attack's Protection album.

the Bristol sound. Even if it's not all that easy to see why, or how, they laid the foundations for Massive Attack. The Pop Group, y'see, made a fearsome, chaotic noise that was always experimental and sometimes plain unlistenable. Their first single, *She Is Beyond Good And Evil*, might have been as infectious as it was deeply disturbing, but much of the *Y* album sounded like a load of out-of-time clanging and primeval hollering, interrupted by the occasional blast of raucous feedback. These elements burned on a fire already white hot with punk, funk and thunderous dub to make a protest music completely out on its own.

■ Social Security announced their arrival with a crashing guitar sound on their debut EP.

So what does all this have to do with the birth of The Wild Bunch and everything that followed them? Crucially, Mark Stewart's unholy Pop Group crew were the first to assimilate the city's black, or more accurately Rasta, counter-culture into their social life, their worldview, and ultimately their sound. Back then, music allowed you to define your enemies more clearly. 'With the roots worldview… the feeling of spiritual uplift was undeniable,' says singer Stewart of his dub days. As if this wasn't significant enough, the band also spent their youth going to clubs and listening to dance beats. 'We were like the Bristol funk army,' recalls Stewart. 'We'd go to clubs and dance to records by T-Connection, BT Express, Fatback Band, all this heavy bassline funk.'

■ How good were Talisman? Good enough to support The Rolling Stones at Ashton Gate in 1982.

And this is how The Pop Group invented the politics of dancing. Their dance was a warped, out-of-shape boogie, but a boogie none the less. 'They even used to dance in the most peculiar way,' remembers one fan. Sadly, by the time they'd made their third album, titled *For How Much Longer Do We Tolerate Mass Murder?*, all the incendiary radicalism had got a bit out of control. Maybe it's best to let the band explain their style of music. 'We were creating a wall of noise for the lyrics to fight against,' sighs drummer Dan Katsis. 'We were challenging the production process, disrespecting the machines.'

■ Barton Hill bass terrorist Gary Clail. A Clail and Tackhead Sound System gig at the Western Star Domino Club was so loud that the queue to get out was as long as the one to get in.

Something inevitably had to give, and the six members went their separate ways. Gareth Sager formed the distinctly patchy Rip Rig & Panic, bassist Simon Underwood sought relief in the happy honking of jazz-funkers Pigbag and had a top 20 hit, and Mark Stewart sank still deeper into the well of nihilistic creativity in which he had always prospered.

ALMOST FAMOUS
FIVE BRISTOL BANDS THAT DIDN'T QUITE MAKE IT

1. The Seers
Spider and his punky charges welded Beatles melodies onto Pistols energy a decade before those Gallagher brothers thought of the idea. Mouth-almighty manager David Darling whipped up controversy too. The single *Lightning Strikes*, about the Hungerford massacre, caused outrage in the tabloids and catapulted the band to a national level. The Seers were a formidable live act, but never found a producer capable of capturing their energy in the studio. Sadly, a European tour supporting Iggy Pop and a series of dates with their spiritual backing band, The Ramones, was as close as they got.

2. Monk & Canatella
Monk & Canatella started out as a feint Strangelove copy and went on to become one of the most incendiary hip-hop acts the UK has ever seen. Jim Johnston and Simon Russell would have made Limp Biskit and Co fill their shorts. A deal with Telstar, representation from Vision Management and a ferocious album should have put them straight on the cover of *Kerrang!* But the Jerry Lee Lewis-like Johnston chose to go to the pub instead.

■ The Seers are an excellent live band although they didn't quite make it to the big time.

3. Moorhaven
According to local industry gossip, Martin Barnard and Angelo Bruschini's acoustic rockers had a deal from a major label on the table but told them where they could shove it. They still failed to put pen to paper after playing in front of most of London's A&R army at The Fleece (see Nights Out Listings, p256). The momentum wilted and the arguments intensified and Moorhaven split. Martin Barnard went on to work with Alpha, Hazel Winter went solo and former Blue Aeroplane Angelo Bruschini got signed up by Massive Attack to work on their *Mezzanine* album.

4. High Coin
The premature demise of High Coin is one of the most distressing Bristol music tales of recent years. Everyone who knew them were convinced that they could and should have

gone further. Fusing elements of Jimmy Webb, Big Star and Gram Parsons, High Coin had the poise and grace of a band on the verge of greatness. 1997's *Raise A Smile* saw them really hit their stride but soon afterwards Geoff Cook and Jeff Green fell out big time. We were left with a couple of great singles and a case of what might have been.

5. The Cortinas
They burst onto the punk scene as disaffected 16-year-old grammar school boys in 1977 with the unstoppable and promising double-A-sided Step Forward single *Fascist Dictator/ Television Families*. Then they signed to CBS and completely lost their way. Guitarist Nick Sheppard later joined the last incarnation of The Clash to replace Mick Jones and resurfaced briefly to hook up with Gareth Sager, Rich Beale and Will Ng in Bristol sleaze-rockers Head.

They were only around for two years or so but The Pop Group cast one hell of a long shadow. There were a lot of bands who found themselves permanently stuck in the shade. Performance art, free-festival politics, second-hand clothes, a vibrant live scene and copious amounts of cheap drugs all played their part in a shift towards an artier and more off-beat order. If you can track down copies of the compilation albums *Avon Calling, Fried Egg – Bristol 1979-1981, Wavelength/Bristol Recorder 1979-1980*, or *Western Stars Vol 1 – The Bands That Built Bristol* (now on Sugar Shack – www.sugarshackrecords.co.uk) you can hear for yourself. It's from this increasingly bohemian atmosphere that Gerard Langley's first band Art Objects sprang.

What we didn't know then is that Bristol was about to rewind to a second year zero. It began down among the funk jams and scratched beats of the St Paul's cafe sound system scene. With the fragments of post-punk scattered all over the place and pulsing electronic dub everywhere, something truly remarkable emerged. The Slits made an unlikely union with Dennis Bovell, The Clash raised swords with Mikey Dread, and The Specials united black and white to fight against anyone who wanted to make something of it. Bristol had reggae collectives Talisman, Black Roots and Restriction. At the Dugout on Park Row, DJs were lining up Chaka Khan against Superfly Soul as the first blasts of urban hip-hop began to filter across the Atlantic.

■ The Wild Bunch: from left 3D, Milo, Nellee, Mushroom. Smith & Mighty produced The Look of Love on the B-side of this ultra-rare Friends and Countrymen EP.

■ The Wild Bunch crew, circa 1985 outside Special K's (now gone) on Park Row. From left: Daddy G, 3D, Claude (aka Willie Wee), Nellee Hooper, Milo Johnson.

Meanwhile, somewhere around town, Robert Del Naja was getting arrested for decorating walls with a spraycan. Soon, he joined Nellee Hooper, Daddy G and Milo in a hip-hop collective called The Wild Bunch. That same year, St Paul's Carnival played host to a number of heavily-amped crews such as 3 Stripe Posse, 2Bad, City Rockers, UD4 and FBI Crew. But bigger and bolder than the rest were The Wild Bunch, who blocked off Campbell Street with their colossal, towering bass bins. The band's reputation spread by word of mouth and they were invited to play at London's Titanic Club. Then they set up residency on Wednesday nights at the Dugout, spinning 12-inches, rapping over the top, heads nodding eerily in time. 1986 saw Smith and Mighty produce The Wild Bunch's cover of Hal David's and Burt Bacharach's *The Look of Love*.

Hindsight has given The Wild Bunch a legendary status in modern music folklore. But Milo's retrospective album, *Story of a Soundsystem*, suggested this is as much myth as reality. It's party music, full of sax burps, cheesy disco jangles and it's very much of its time. Robert Del Naja puts his own perspective on it. 'People always ask us about The Wild Bunch,' he says. 'But the truth, is it's just history to us now. I don't know why people go on about it so much.'

No, the first truly staggering thing The Wild Bunch ever did was to become Massive Attack. And the first thing Massive Attack ever did was to take a giant leap ahead of anything that had come before. *Daydreaming* is one of the most original and self-assured debut singles ever made. Even now it sounds as fresh and as relevant as it did back in the early 1990s. And there was so much more to come.

From its majestic opening line – *'Midnight rockers, city slickers, gun men and maniacs'* – it was obvious the *Blue Lines* album was going to be a classic. Three hit singles – *Daydreaming, Safe From Harm* and *Unfinished Sympathy* – propelled the band right across the globe. At the same time, they redefined what dance music could be. As 3D put it at the time: 'We're not just interested in making something for people to throw their arms and legs about to on a dancefloor.'

Everything had changed. Suddenly, Bristol was being talked about as the 'coolest city on the planet'. Then someone, somewhere in the media, labelled the sound 'trip-hop' – a supposedly softer, near-ambient version of

Five more...
. . . .
Bristol beat albums
. . . .

① **Bass is Maternal, Smith and Mighty:** The original beat gangsters' album is a monument of the Bristol scene.

② **Coded Language, Krust:** This concrete-edged, crash-bang-wallop of a record is merely a warning of darker territory to come.

③ **Emotional Hooligan, Gary Clail:** Dub-heavy polemics in an On-U-Sound stylee.

④ **The Call is Strong, Carlton:** Falsetto, sparse, beautiful. Produced by Daddy G and very rare.

⑤ **Dub Plate Selection Vol 1, More Rockers:** A modern drum 'n' bass-cum-reggae classic rooted in the finest traditions of dub rockmillions.

LOCAL MUSIC MAVERICKS

A WHO'S WHO OF THE BRISTOL SOUND HEROES

1. Mike Crawford
Who is he? One of the longest enduring survivors of the Bristol music scene and easily its most handsome face. Back in 1979, Crawford formed nine-piece soft-soul groovers the Spics before heading across the Atlantic to work with the legendary Booker T. On his return, he started writing songs with ex-Head singer Rich Beale for Apache Dropout. In recent times he has been a guest for acts as diverse as Patrick Duff and drum 'n' bass soldier Krust.
Legend has it... In the 1980s mighty-mouth promoter David Darling secured Crawford a US tour supporting soul icon Geno Washington. But Mike missed his kids and caught a plane straight back home again.
Last seen... Crossing the road on his way to The Bell down by Stokes Croft.

2. The Insects
Who are they? From Massive Attack's *Karma Coma* and *Eurochild* to Alison Moyet's comeback album *Hometime*, from Strangelove's *All Because Of You* to a whole raft of film and television scores, Bob Locke and Tim Norfolk are two of the most respected behind-the-scenes writers and producers in Bristol. And they've got an Emmy award to prove it. They used to be called the Startled Insects and produced soundtracks to wildlife documentaries. Now they are working on their own album, featuring a who's who of a guestlist. It could be another huge moment in the history of the Bristol thing.
Legend has it... The Insects are among Bristol's most hard working musicians. They arrive at Christchurch Studios in Clifton not long after 9am and are usually still there around midnight.
Last seen... Late at night in Christchurch Studios working on a few soundtracks and that long-awaited Insects album.

3. Jimmy Galvin
Who is he? Jimmy Galvin's floppy fringe has been around since floppy fringes were fashionable. Describing himself as 'the missing link between Stravinsky and the Teletubbies', Galvin attaches bits of hip-hop, jazz, soul, punk and folk onto his piano-driven songs. He enlisted the help of Adrian Utley and Roxy Music's Andy Mackay on his 2002 album *Surburbia Kills*.
Legend has it... Galvin is an accomplished fine artist and one of the city's most professional coffee drinkers.
Last seen... Finally getting the recognition he deserves under the banner System Vertigo.

4. Davey Woodward
Who is he? Bristol's very own Edwyn Collins. Woodward is the man behind the Experimental Pop Band whose history goes back as far as the 1980s when he fronted jangly hooligan popsters the Brilliant Corners. His purist's charter may have shifted towards a more post-modern vision over the years, but the generously-lipped veteran of the Bristol scene has never strayed too far from his self-laid path of artistic obscurity. Despite this, you can't help feeling that one day you'll see him on a music show on tele.
Legend has it... Davey's uber-cool persona suggests a childhood spent in BS8, but he actually grew up in the wastelands of Lawrence Weston.
Last seen... Striding purposefully down the Wells Road.

5. Jesse Morning Star
Who is he? One of the founding members of The Moonflowers along with Sonik Ray, Jesse is fondly thought of as one of the Bristol music scene's flakiest flakes. But behind the whacked-out public persona there is a supremely talented multi-instrumentalist and songwriter who has devoted every hour of his adult life to the pursuit of his art. Jesse still has a twinkle in his eye that suggests that his finest hour may be yet to come...
Legend has it... Nobody in Bristol has as many rock 'n' roll rumours about them
Last seen... Fronting the excellent Morning Star and playing guitar with the soon-to-be-huge Jukes.

hip-hop, unique to the South West. Apparently. And within minutes, the city was overrun by gangs of A&R clowns frantically searching for the next Bristol sound sure-things. Not only was the local music mafia not talking, they were also trying to get as far away from the term as possible. 'Who in here likes trip-hop?' asked Tricky at an early live show. When the audience all raised their hands he retorted, 'Well fuck off home, then!'

Surprisingly, no staggeringly, the next giant wave in the West Country sound surf came not from the inner city but from dozy seaside nowhere resort Portishead. Geoff Barrow had been a tape operator for Massive Attack and Neneh Cherry and, with the help of an Enterprise Allowance grant, he recruited jazz head Adrian Utley, drummer/programmer Dave MacDonald and Janis Joplin cover singer Beth Gibbons to form a band named after his home town. Portishead's slow-burning cinematic scores were slow to make an impact but then a press campaign involving hundreds of mannequins placed in various locations around London grabbed the attention of the public and fired the band's third single *Glory Box* straight into the UK charts at number 13. By the end of 1994, Portishead's album *Dummy* had sold more than 1.5 million copies, won the Mercury Music Prize and been voted Album of the Year by *Melody Maker*, *Mixmag*, *ID* and the *Face*. Sales in the US topped 150,000. It was no more than Portishead deserved. *Dummy* is one of the best albums of the 1990s: a faultless and seemingly effortless record to rank alongside *Blue Lines*. And, with *Blue Lines*, it is still the chosen soundtrack for any television programme dealing with crime.

For Massive Attack, meanwhile, making a follow-up to the internationally lauded *Blue Lines* was proving to be a long and difficult affair. 'If a thing's worth doing, it's worth doing slowly,' deadpanned Del Naja. But while 1994's Nellee Hooper-produced *Protection* had its moments, most notably *Karma Coma* and *Eurochild*, it was, in truth, a bit of a disappointment. The choice of Tracey Thorn from Everything But The Girl as vocalist pushed the sound closer to the coffee table and away from the barrier-breaking low temperature hip-hop of *Blue Lines*.

By now the friction between the band members was well documented. Daddy G revealed just how bad it was. 'It's a nightmare, really... we hate each other,' said the mild-

■ Carlton McCarthy's Cool With Nature single. Daddy G produced this release before Massive Attack kicked in.

■ Rob Smith and Ray Mighty's Three Stripes label was based above a Blues Club in St Paul's. The duo were credited with inventing drum 'n' bass.

■ Blue Lines: one of the greatest albums ever made.

mannered bass boomer. Tricky was the first to exit stage left. The only 'kiddie' from Knowle West to ever go out in public wearing a wedding dress, Tricky had always been the unhinged little hooligan of the band. He was the voice of naivety who didn't understand the impact of Thatcher's economic policy. 'Maggie this, Maggie that, Maggie means inflation,' he had observed, incorrectly, on *Daydreaming*. Nobody really expected Massive's equivalent of Sid Vicious to release an album as stunning as *Maxinquaye*. It was a deep, dark and dangerous masterpiece and the third truly great record to come out of Bristol in four years. It seemed Bristol was the coolest city on the planet after all.

■ The Corners started out as psychobillies from Lawrence Weston and ended up as the darlings of Bristol's indie scene.

Predictably, the city's beat-dependent music scene was given fuel by the successes of the 'big three'. Some attempted mimicry and failed; some folk were barking up the wrong tree entirely; others drew a line in the sand and set about pushing back the boundaries even further. And a few brave souls continued to pick up their guitars and play the old-fashioned way. It was an odd time for Strangelove to come along, but on a cold February night at The Underworld in Camden Town, they arrived with the proverbial thump. Containing two Blue Aeroplanes escapees and a singer with charisma to burn, Strangelove instantly broke the city's 'guitar jinx'. The Camden gig got them a life-long fan in *Select* magazine's Dave Cavanagh and a deal with Food Records. Within a year they had become the biggest and best 'indie' band to ever come out of Bristol. Even Radiohead later described themselves as a 'post-Strangelove band'.

■ Despite boasting a Bristol superstar line-up, Head never really captured the popular imagination. A cruelly under-rated act.

But if Bristol was famous for anything in the mid 1990s, it was its love affair with slow, slacker beats. All that was about to change: Smith & Mighty's More Rockers project had already signalled the start of some serious bpm multiplication, but it was Roni Size's 1997 album *New Forms* that really whacked the turntable into overdrive and span off the scale. Drum 'n' bass was thrust into the mainstream and the innovation spotlight shone on Bristol yet again. DJ Krust, DJ Die, DJ Suv and their miniature dreadlocked leader found themselves in the news, in the charts and on stage picking up the Mercury Music Prize. Yet again, journalists wanted to know about the Bristol sound. 'I am from Bristol, and I do make music from Bristol, so I am it and it is me,' said Krust to stun one American reporter

■ Andy Sheppard lived in Southville, played at The Albert in Bedminster and became one of the world's most inventive jazz musicians.

into silence. Roni Size meanwhile, prophesised to anyone who'd listen: 'I'm a junglist and jungle is the future.' Utter nonsense, of course, but at least he said it with conviction.

The activity levels at Full Cycle records might be as frantic as ever, but drum 'n' bass has faded back into the underground again of late. Krust understands this too well: 'Forget drum 'n' bass,' he says. 'This is about endless possibilities, endless configurations, endless structures and restructures – it's infinite.' He is quite right, it is infinite. As are the possibilities. We've barely scraped the surface of electronica and Bristol is sure to be at the forefront of whatever comes next.

Massive Attack may be coming to their natural end, you are far more likely to bump into Tricky in New York than Knowle West and Portishead is again just an estuary town in Somerset, but the Bristol beat made the city the coolest place on the planet for a decade or more. It has left a legacy that a new generation of Bristol soundscapers will surely emulate. 'Some people say that Bristol is the graveyard of ambition,' Robert Del Naja once said. But ambition has now learned to dance to Bristol's tune.

Five great...
Bristol indie LPs

1 **Psych Out, The Seers:** The Ramones meet The Monkees and discover cider and P-funk.

2 **Everything I Ever Wanted, Brilliant Corners:** Lovely stuff. Davey Woodward's lyrical tour de force.

3 **The D Is For Drum, Automatic Dlamini:** Art rock with rhythms.

4 **Siamese Boyfriends, Gerard Langley and Ian Kearey:** Poems and tunes for the missing-a-beat generation from Blue Aeroplanes and Oyster Band frontmen.

5 **Love and Other Demons, Strangelove:** The last great Bristol indie album?

■ The Blue Aeroplanes with Gerard Langley in the foreground.

ART FOR ART'S SAKE

NICK LAW EXPLORES HOW THE BRISTOL MUSIC SCENE DEVELOPED AFTER MASSIVE ATTACK

Beautiful isolation

In the wake of Massive Attack et al, there seemed to be many who agreed with Robert del Naja's theory that Bristol is the graveyard of ambition and considered the city's music dead in the water. A brief signal flare was thrown up by the aforementioned Strangelove, strong and bright but alas it didn't set the world on fire. Emerging from the fog came a raft of bands who exhibited a laudable do-it-yourself ethos which garnered loyal and rabid fanbases, if not critical acclaim and large-scale record sales.

The excellent Chikinki fulfilled their potential by releasing a string of EPs culminating in a major label signing and the *Lick Your Ticket* LP on Island Records, owned by Universal – who promptly dropped them. The suits deciding, apparently, that Chikinki weren't the new Kasabian after all. Idiots. What do they know? Fortunately for all concerned, not least the band, they've emerged unbowed, philosophical and with their big tunes intact. They have now returned to releasing stuff on their own label, Urban Cow, and these former sons of Bristol should hopefully be poised to make their breakthrough. It is true that they have since moved up to London, but we can't begrudge them that surely. Up there in the belly of the beast, hopefully, they will, at last, get the recognition they deserve.

But what of the here and now in this great city of ours? Are we likely to produce anything to rival Leeds, Sheffield or Glasgow – which gave us the Kaiser Chiefs, Arctic Monkeys and Franz Ferdinand – at the present time? Well, the short answer is no. The reason is equally simple: we exist in a strange and beautiful isolation from the rest of the country. Not just in other people's perceptions but in our own attitudes. Hell, we're even our own county. What could be more insular than that?

As a result of this comes a particular sense of pride and loyalty that is to be commended and enjoyed but it must, surely, make it

■ After being ditched by their label, Chikinki are happily releasing stuff on their own label Urban Cow.

difficult for new bands to make their mark on the rest of the populace. Or even get noticed in the first place. Ed East, guitarist in Chikinki, wholeheartedly agrees:

'One of the downsides is that you don't necessarily get taken seriously by the music industry because it is such an isolated community. It's a very artistic kind of community, art for art's sake rather than for industry's sake. London is so focused on itself that it doesn't really take much notice of what's going on in other cities. So it can be difficult for bands in Bristol to break onto the national scene.'

So what to do when 'The Man' doesn't bother coming to the party (as he has to stay in and wash his lank, thinning hair?) Well, the new wave of Bristol bands are making their voices heard and they're doing it by shouting and screaming very loudly indeed into a feedbacked microphone, while blankets of distortion, blurping, bastardised keyboards and the amplified sounds of dolls heads being smashed with a mallet provides the soundtrack to a Sellafield meltdown. With extra guitars.

Passion is the key

The current Bristol beat is an (electro)shock sonic attack on our hammers, anvils and stirrups. A deliberately lo-fi, raucous racket and a vociferous 'fuck you' to ponytailed A&R men everywhere.

It's like trip-hop never happened. Gone are the lush, cinematic soundscapes, loping beats and stoner vocals. Instead, we are assaulted by a brittle and sometimes brutal clamjamfrey of stuff, that blows away any past legacies in a massive attack of *Blitzkrieg Bop*. These new noiseniks have ripped, slashed and burned all copies of the rule book. And then they have written their own, simply stating: there are no rules.

The music is infused with the heady aroma of punk's attitudes and aspirations. Turning its back on the commercial world of pop puppets and management muppets, energy and enthusiasm are held in greater esteem than deft musicianship and even defter marketing. Bristol band 3hostwomexicansandatinofspanners (standard bearers for this kind of antiestablishmentism) say: 'It doesn't matter how "good" a player/singer you are. You've just got to mean it. Do what you like, and then you'll feel passionately about it. Music never changed anything, but the people who listen to it did.'

Probably the most extreme exponents of this style are Bristol/Southampton band Hunting Lodge who sound like a pig(bag) being slaughtered. Halal-style. There is also Geisha: the aural equivalent to having your ears syringed in reverse. Which is a rather pleasant experience as fuzzy, multi-layered rock 'n' noise is squeezed into your canals, but then medical chart mix-up shenanigans ensue as suddenly the doc' comes in and opens your cranium with a circular saw.

Of course, to some, it's unlistenable but as the Japanese noise pioneer Masami Akita,

who records under the name Merzbow, has said: 'If by noise, you mean uncomfortable sound, then pop music is noise to me.'

Acquired tastes, perhaps, but rather like acclimatising your stomach to new food experiences, if you don't fancy trying the 'sautéed kangaroo scrotums served on a bed of wild 'shrooms with an oxblood jus' just yet, you can always fill up on the excellent White Trash Ambition who serve tasty home-grown chunks of punk with lashings of art school squall. This is not your Damon Albarn/Blur kind of institution, mind. This is more your progressive polytechnic that lets you bunk off, go to the pub, get smashed on three pints of Thatcher's then stagger back before the class ends to throw some paint against a sheet of corrugated iron while setting everyone else's drawings on fire, and still get an A-grade at the end it.

One of the admirable qualities of this rebellious gang is that they are exactly that. A gang. A collective. An incestuous congregation who play not just with themselves but each other too. Whether that involves twiddling knobs in a recording studio or popping up in a live show, they lend a helping hand, they muck in and generally contribute to a very vibrant and eclectic community of talented artists and performers. Tracing these complex connections between the various in and out members of some of these groups is a bit like untangling a huge pile of speaker cables after a gig. But then again, this group would probably say 'Why not plug 'em in as they are. We might get some interesting interference.'

Hands in many pies

Whether you regard these bands, their side-projects or others of their ilk as acts of genius or acts of vandalism, they're inescapably exciting. True, their particular brand of 'no-brand' is unlikely to appear at Bristol's controversial enormo-dome anytime in the near future and yes, they may be under the radar and off the map but 'so what?' they would say. Yet you never know. Cartographers of the Middle Ages had gaps in their charts as well and in those dark, unknown corners would be written 'Terra Incognita', meaning undiscovered land. One of those was Australia. And just look how big that turned out to be.

A WHO'S WHO OF BRISTOL MUSIC

■ Babyhead offer an energetic live set with their version of punk, ska and hip-hop.

The Bristol Beat doesn't exist,' said Daddy G in 1990. Well, if there was no discernible shared sound then, there sure as hell isn't one now. Here's our tribute to the people who have influenced the diverse sounds of Bristol in recent years and those who are shaping its promising future…

🅐 Joe Allen

Flexibly-jointed ex-Coltranes, Aeroplanes and Strangelove bassist, last seen zooming up and down his fretboard for Breakbeat Era. Trivia fans may like to know that he used to eat nothing except cold toast. And that he once drunkenly formed a pretend band called Fulham with the author of this book.

Aspects

Influential hip-hop crew with a West Country edge who went their separate ways in 2004. DJ Specify, MCs El-Eye, Bubbaloui and ProbeMantis along with scratch DJ Nu-Balance and engineer 7-Stu-7 were the earliest acts to sign for Bristol's Hombre Records.

The Autos

Ignore the disappointing name and the band's apparent unwillingness to spend a significant amount of time in the spotlight, these drainpipe 'n' daps upstarts are one of the most exciting new-wave bands in the land right now. Mercifully, The Autos influences are The Cars, The Saints, Telephone and the Only Ones – they sound nothing like the bloody Jam.

■ Geoff Barrow and Beth Gibbons put a Somerset commuter town on the international music map.

🅑 Babel

It's difficult to think of any Bristol bands, past or present, who have been as original, as inventive or as shoe-stompingly self-assured as Babel. They are heads and shoulders and violins and tambourines above just about anyone. A swaggering chariot driven by their heroic leader Danny Coughlan.

Babyhead

Full-on fusion of punk, ska and hip-hop with horns. The band has a justifiably impressive live reputation and are capable of delivering a truly stunning stage performance.

Geoff Barrow

A music industry insider once revealed that they had never met anyone as devoted to music as Portishead founder Geoff Barrow. 'His refusal to use backing tapes when playing live keeps him awake at night,' apparently. A bright light in an age full of dim stars.

Rich Beale

There is a rumour going around that Rich Beale has been on the dole since 1975. For this alone, he deserves an award. Add a CV that includes Head, Pregnant and Apache Dropout and you get a true renaissance man of the Bristol underground.

Blackout

Hard-hitting, live drum 'n' bass outfit formed in 2003, Blackout teamed up with ex-Breakbeat Era vocalist Leonie Laws in 2005. Their first single, *Massaka*, was released on Random Audio Records in the summer of 2006. Played a famous house party in Picton Street in July 2006. The windows were still rattling in August.

Beki Bondage

Self-styled Queen of Punk (for a few weeks in 1980 at least), Beki (real name Rebecca Louise Bond) joined Bristol punk outfit Vice Squad at the tender age of 15. The band was never fully accepted in Bristol, but enjoyed success in the States where Beki is still touring as Vice Squad, although she's actually the only original member left.

Matt Booth

Dynamic promoter turned manager, Matt Booth arrived on the scene like a whirlwind sometime in the late 1990s, totally transforming the local live arena with his finger-on-the-pulse booking policy. He then turned his attentions to the Ashton Court Festival and he played a pivotal role in shaping the local shindig that we know and love today.

Five great...
Bristol dub tracks

1 Dole Age, Talisman: Anti-Thatcher dub from the eclectic Talisman.

2 No Protection, Mad Professor: Dub-heavy remix of Massive Attack's highly-rated Protection album.

3 Juvenile Delinquent, Black Roots: Traditional Jah reggae from the St Paul's frontline.

4 Tenth Dub, Henry and Louis: From the excellent Rudiments LP on Smith & Mighty's More Rockers label.

5 Jerusalem, Mark Stewart and The Mafia: Peculiar goings on from Pop Group founder. Find it on On-U-Sound's compilation Pay it all Back album which also features Gary Clail's False Leader track.

■ Chikinki's Experiments with Mother album took them to a new level in the Bristol scene.

Up Close

Dave Brailey
When promoter Dave Brailey came to town in the middle of the 1990s, he gave the local music scene a much-needed kick up the arse. It wasn't long before he graduated to The Fleece. Few people have done more for Bristol's live music culture.

Breakbeat Era
Defunct offshoot of the Full Cycle project featuring Roni Size, DJ Die and singer/songwriter Leonie Laws. The *Ultra-Obscene* album mixed drum 'n' bass with rock influences.

Bronnt Industries Kapital
You can tell by their name that they are in the business of making art noise. Their debut limited-edition EP contained a statistical information sheet, a map and a noose made of electrical flex. With gestures like this, they could well find themselves at the forefront of the UK avant-garde music scene.

■ Kid Carpet uses plastic toy instruments to create his own very unique sound.

Angelo Bruschini
When the former Numbers, Aeroplanes and Moorhaven guitarist got the call from Massive Attack, he can have had little idea just how vital he would become. Proof positive that Ange himself was wrong when he once uttered the immortal line: 'A leopard never changes its stripes.'

ⓒ Kid Carpet
Whacked-out lank who hammers the living crap out of plastic toy instruments to create a squashed and fried hip-hop that he sometimes likes to call 'Kiddie disco punk'. He does gigs at carpet shops and car boot sales too. Brilliant and berserk.

Neneh Cherry
Miles Johnson, founder member of The Wild Bunch, went to Cotham Grammar School with Pop Group drummer Bruce Smith, who married Neneh Cherry, who sang for boho-funk surrealists Rip Rig and Panic, some of whom used to be in The Pop Group, who were fronted by Mark Stewart, who shared his squat with Tricky and worked with Smith and Mighty, who produced a Wild Bunch track. Much of Massive Attack's *Blue Lines* album (featuring Tricky) was originally recorded at Neneh Cherry's London home. Cherry also worked with Mark Stewart and Ari Up of the Slits as the New Age Steppers who recorded on Adrian Sherwood's On-U Sounds label, which later became home to Gary Clail…

■ Neneh Cherry – Massive Attack created their debut Blue Lines album at her home studio.

Chikinki
This is what happens when you throw together a mix of krautrock, squelchbeat, blipfunk and unholy rock and give it a damn good shake. It could also be the future. Ever since the release of their *Experiments With Mother* album, these deeply unhinged art noise upsetters have been the lunatics that seem most likely to take over the asylum. Nobody who has seen them perform live was surprised when they signed to Island Records.

BRISTOL'S RECORD LABELS
THE HEROES BRINGING MUSIC TO YOUR EARS

Full Cycle Records
www.fullcycle.co.uk
Tel: 935 6677
Drum 'n' bass may have shuffled off into the corner but in Bristol, at least, it shows no sign of giving up on its mission. Full Cycle is home to Roni Size, Krust, Die and Clipz and continues to be the hottest melting pot of jungle-related ideas. Check out the Full Cycle radio player on the website.

Blood Red Sounds
www.bloodredsounds.co.uk
parlourmusic@yahoo.com
'Passionate, inventive and uncompromising', says the Blood Red website when describing itself, and it is very hard to disagree. Blood Red is one of those for-the-love-of-it outfits that was born way back in 2004. It is now home to left-fielders new wavers such as Big Joan, Mooz, Geisha and Hunting Lodge.

Sink and Stove Records
www.sinkandstove.co.uk
info@sinkandstove.co.uk
From humble, regional beginnings Stink and Stove have forced the UK's alternative industry heavyweights to sit up and take notice. They have acted as a springboard for the likes of Chikinki and Gravenhurst who went onto sign for Island and Warp respectively. They show no sign of losing their Midas touch either with acts like The Playwrights and The Vibration on their roster.

Label7
www.label7.co.uk
Tel: 07799 745 870
This is a local label but with offices in Manchester and London. Label7 are still relatively small, but with their unstoppable energy and belief in live music, they'll get there, have no doubt. Electronic acts, both bands and DJs, are the focus at Label7. In the summer of 2006, they released the promising debut album from local band Dubrovnik. Keep an eye out for their DJs at Bristol hippest clubs too.

■ Roni Size and the boys from Full Cycle Records

Hope Recordings
www.hoperecordings.com
Tel: 953 5566
Leon Alexander once stayed on my floor in Tufnell Park, London for a few months and he ate nothing except fig rolls. Odd. Thankfully, he has gone onto far bigger and better things, notably Hope Recordings who recently celebrated their 7th birthday. To celebrate the birthday, Hope have released the wonderful *7 Year Itch – A Hope Recordings Retrospective* which features the likes of Timo Maas, Loafer and Filmpalast.

Invada
www.invadarecords.co.uk
fatpaul@blueyonder.co.uk
The Bristol arm of an Aussie label with Geoff Barrow and Fat Paul doing the A&R. Unsurprisingly, they have one battered Converse dap firmly planted in the field furthest to the left and have a fantastic artist roster that includes The Heads, Gonga, Fuzz Against Junk and Amusement Parks on Fire.

Up Close

Gary Clail
Former car salesman turned sound system impresario turned 'emotional hooligan', Clail is usually remembered for his chart-troubling single *Human Nature*, but don't hold that against him.

Sean Cooke
Spiritualised escapee turned Lupine Howl frontman who eats, sleeps and breathes rock 'n' roll with a conviction that goes way beyond the call of duty. Apparently, he never gets up before 4pm as a matter of principle. Respect.

Mike Crawford
Although he has won the Unofficial Best Looking Bloke in Bristol Award for the last 17 consecutive years, Mike Crawford shows no sign of hanging up his cheekbones. He was last seen working with Krust on the *Coded Language* album.

■ Massive Attack's Daddy G has been a hero of the Bristol music scene for a long long time.

Ⓓ Daddy G
After taking time out from the recording of Massive Attack's *100th Window* album released in 2004, Grant has gone back to his roots on the local and national DJ and festival circuit. Grant has towered over the Bristol music scene for as long as anyone can remember. 'Oh yeah, that was cool shit,' he said, commenting on Massive Attack's back catalogue.

Robert Del Naja
3D might be the hippest of hip-hop priests and one of the most underrated vocalists of the last 20 years but Massive's mainman has never forgotten his Bristol roots and has the Bristol City season ticket to prove it.

Mike Derby
Not content with being the owner of Sugar Shack Records and the invisible force behind the staggeringly complete Bristol Music Archive website (www.sugarshackrecords.co.uk), Mike Derby is also the youngest golf club captain in the area.

■ DJ Die: discovered hip-hop at an early age and preferred it to his mum's Big Country albums.

DJ Derek
DJ Derek used to be the old bloke in the cardigan in the corner of The Star and Garter playing a cool set of obscure ska. He went on to become a leading figure in the world of dub, reggae and ska. His trojan collection *DJ Derek Presents Sweet Memory Sounds* was released in the summer of 2006. He used to be an accountant at Fry's but gave it all up to play ska and reggae. Good man!

DJ Die
Brought up in Totterdown, DJ Die discovered the hip-hop, graffiti and skateboarding craze that swept Bristol at a tender age in the mid 1980s. Those roots remain core to his work with Full Cycle and with Krust as I Kamanche. 'We make dark music, but it's still party music,' he says. Die is still an avid skateboarder and one of the biggest musical talents in town.

Conal Dodds

If you've seen an internationally recognised band in Bristol in the last ten years, chances are you've got promoter Conal Dodds to thank for bringing them here. Once took a punt on a band called Oasis – whatever happened to them eh?

Dubrovnik

With origins in the heavy dub depths of Zion Train and Dubmerge, Dubrovnik know how to handle their bass levels. Add some warped beats, brass, and a troupe of exotic dancers and you've got a full-on carnival of dub with lashings of electronica. Dubrovnik's debut album was released in the summer of 2006.

■ Dubrovnik's carnival-style performances include a troupe of exotic dancers.

Ben Dubuisson (100 Strong)

Hundred Strong is the musical project of producer Ben Dubuisson, a leading light on the club scene and one of the main DJs at Native (see Nights Out Listings, p256). There's usually a big slice of soul in Ben's productions. The single *Dream On Delay* (from the 2005 album *Basement Blues*) featuring NYC soul singer Alison Crockett was nominated as a Gilles Peterson's worldwide track of the year.

Patrick Duff

Ex-Strangelove heartthrob, often mistaken for a tortured soul drowning in self-pity. Not true. Yes, Pad is analytical to the point of destruction. But he laughs just as intensely. Songwriter, storyteller, philosopher, comedian and Mervyn Davies fan.

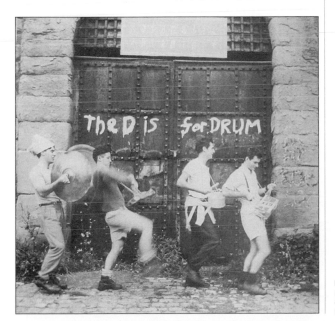

■ Automatic Dlamini's photoshoot for The D Is For Drum album was at the old Bristol prison on Cumberland Road.

THE MOONFLOWERS

THIS LEGENDARY BAND HAVE A SPECIAL PLACE IN THE HEARTS OF BRISTOL'S MUSIC COMMUNITY...

■ The 1998 EP which includes the songs Rock and Roll, My Baby, All or Nothing and Johnny.

1. Accidental party people
In December 1987, Jesse Vernon got a sort of band thing together with the intention of playing a few parties. At the time, there was no wigged-out psychedelic funk scene in Bristol, so The Moonflowers created their own. Daubed in war paint and almost always naked from the waist up, the band began playing impromptu gigs wherever they could and soon had a fanatical following. Their audiences were encouraged to hold hands in an attempt to achieve world peace as the band cavorted wildly around the stage. You could say that they were the first hippies with a sense of humour.

2. The DIY approach to becoming pop gods
Never ones to create too much unnecessary hassle, The Moonflowers' first EP *We Dig Your Earth* had a pressing just large enough to cater for family and close friends. Amazingly, some copies found their way to London and the band's reputation went nationwide. They set up their own label, Pop God Records. And

with backing from hip indie label Heavenly released the magnificent *Get Higher* on 12-inch. It is chosen as *NME* single of the week. The superbly shrugged chorus chant *'Can't get what you want from life, might as well get higher,'* perfectly captures the E-swallowing mood of the day and propels The Moonflowers into the top 40. Trouble is, the 'single' is so long it actually qualifies for the album chart.

3. Exit Planet Earth
The success of their debut album *Hash Smits* left our heroes feeling a little empty. Desperate to throw off the shackles of their new commercial existence, they decided to release a statement declaring that they have left that world and now resided in a creative and spiritual utopia of their own making called Rainbowhemia. To the rest of us, it looked like an old yellow tour bus. It sounds like The Moonflowers had been taking a few hallucinogens.

4. Revolutionaries do the hoovering
1992 saw The Moonflowers really finding their comedy touch. After recording a bizarre, farmyard-animal-noise-assisted version of *Get Higher* for a John Peel Session, they release another EP with the truly inspired title *Tighten Up On The Housework Brothers and Sisters*. The EP's main track was the anthemic *Brothers and Sisters* but also included a well-chosen cover version of the Damned's *I've Just Got To Be A Discoman Today.*

5. Making an impression on A&R
Sooner or later, all this activity attracted the attention of the A&R departments of several major record labels. And, sure enough, The Moonflowers were invited to play a set in front of a collection of top industry spotters at the Marquee Club in London. They set off for the big smoke in an agreeable enough mood but something, quite possibly involving the

consumption of illegal substances, altered their attitude along the way. By the time they hit the North Circular, they had decided that the whole thing was a load of rubbish and was not what they were about as a band in any way. Our heroes arrived, plugged in and proceeded to embark on an impenetrable and unbroken 30-minute jamming session. Needless to say, the sensitive A&R folk walked out half-way through and funnily enough vowed never to go near The Moonflowers ever again.

6. Big in Japan

Naoki and Miwako were running a record shop called Zero and a fanzine called *Grassroots* in their home town of Tokyo when they first heard The Moonflowers and decided to run an interview with the Bristol bohemians. The band saw the interview and duly invited the pair to Gloucester to watch them play live. The enthusiastic Japanese fans took them up on their offer. 'They

■ The Moonflowers were known for their outrageous and outstanding live performances.

welcomed us as friends,' recalls Naoki. 'We really wanted to invite them to Tokyo to play and we managed to get someone to pay for them to come and visit.' And so, with all the wonkiness of a seriously wasted Godzilla, the Moonflowers landed in the Far East. Against all the odds, the tour was a resounding success. In fact, the 'love' vibe was so strong, Naoki and Miwako decided to get married. The happy couple then chose to spend their honeymoon in the lovely St Werburghs.

7. Nous sommes des rock stars

In 1993, The Moonflowers released their second album, the cosmically-entitled *From Wales To Jupiter And Beyond The Stars To Rainbowhemia*. The album captured a jazzier, more relaxed sound, with tracks such as *Smile In The Face Of Evil And Dance* and *There We Will Find The Sun* even hinting at their most commercial edge to date. But anyone anticipating seeing some naked buffoonery on *Top of the Pops* was about to be disappointed. As soon as the album was released, the band upped sticks and moved to a remote farmhouse somewhere out in the sticks in Normandy in France. For the next couple of years, The Moonflowers all lived communally and continued to do their groove thing, but without the audience. When they next surfaced, they did so with a double album, *Colours And Sounds*. Unfortunately, it would be their last.

8. Toby Pascoe: 1970–2002

This is the story of a life less ordinary. When multi-instrumentalist Toby Pascoe joined The Moonflowers in 1990, his skills transformed them from a shambolic party band into the irresistibly funky boogie merchants that we all remember. Toby seemed to have the same effect on everyone he met. He was always out there, unafraid to put himself on the line in the name of art. Bizarre experiments involving a steam-powered drum machine programmed by a roll of paper followed. Then at the end of the 1990s, he joined the breakbeat era and really began pushing his remarkable percussive brilliance to the edge of its limits. When he died, Toby left a daughter Seren and a motto that will live forever in the hearts and minds of all those who heard it: 'Tread lightly,' he could be heard to say, 'and you'll never spill a drop.'

MC Dynamite

Sensational frontman for the live Reprazent experience, MC Dynamite's musical background is in Motown and reggae. Like several of his conspirators in Full Cycle and Reprazent, he was drawn to fledgling hip-hop and house clubs. By the time rave and drum 'n' bass broke, he was already deeply absorbed by the party scene. As an MC, he has the ability to slip into the mix like a third turntable, hyping the crowds with his lyrics and rhymes but never dominating the experience.

E Matt Elliot

He might have a reputation for making soundtracks for a collapsing world but the former Third Eye Foundation bloke has clearly got a well-developed sense of humour. How else would he have come up with wonderfully self-mocking titles like *You Guys Kill Me* and *Borderline Schizophrenic*?

■ After the demise of Strangelove, singer Patrick Duff sat down for a bit before starting his solo work.

Rob Ellis

As the multi-instrumentalist and producer of PJ Harvey's *Dry* and *Stories From The City, Stories From The Sea* albums, Rob Ellis has gained a reputation as being Bristol's equivalent to Nick Cave's right-hand man Mick Harvey.

E Duncan Fleming

Innovative boy wonder behind War Against Sleep who signed to Fire Records in 2003. Fleming's welding of piano, Mini-disc and four-track continues to unsettle and amaze in equal measures with albums, film soundtracks and epic live installations all part of his single-minded vision.

The Flies

Some bands are born with a buzz around them. 'It's about the occasional corruption of men by women and the ease with which men are susceptible to corruption,' says vocalist and former Spiritualized and Lupine Howl frontman Sean Cook of The Flies stunning debut album. With its dark hypnotic jazz beats and brooding, whispered vocals, Cook – and heavyweight Insects cohorts Bob Locke and Tim Norfolk – have sculpted a shadowy soundtrack to a freak-strewn post-midnight netherworld. Think Max Steiner doing electronica, the sharp shuffling feet narrative of a James Ellroy crime scene or William S Burroughs rattling down a sidewalk with a hatful of narcs in his head.

■ MC Dynamite: Reprazent's dynamic frontman has gone solo.

Dave Francolini

The legendary sticksman who leapt into the rock 'n' roll hall of fame by running over a Bristol Grammar School security guard who wouldn't let him into an exam. His drumming was once accurately described as being 'like the first 20 minutes of *Saving Private Ryan*'.

Four Track

Any band with a drummer who is as high profile as Purple Penguin boss Ben Dubuisson has definitely started out on the right foot. Four Track are the latest turntablists to look back to the days before young people started gathering in fields and taking E.

Fuzz Against Junk

At first, they were just rumours. Ian Green, the most enthusiastic and dedicated music collector in all of Bristol, had got a band together. 'No. You're joking?' whispered the sceptical masses. Then it was news. 'Green's band are brilliant,' we said, amazed. FAJ are not just Green but they are as intricately layered and as challenging as expected. But who'd have thought the ultimate fan could pull off a transfer like this. Respect Sir.

Freakeasy

Well-respected hip-hop crew with depth and intelligent lyrics. Freakeasy are great live and played a storming set at the Ashton Court Festival back in 2003.

G Gonga

Hairy, heavy, headbanging. Although the chords may hark back to the days when Black Sabbath were being introduced to the rock world as 'a promising young group from England', the band's sheer unrelenting ferocity takes them way beyond retro. Gonga's debut album *Stratofortress* was released on Geoff Barrow and Fat Paul's Invada label.

Gravenhurst

What's the best way to describe Gravenhurst? There have been the inevitable Nick Drake comparisons but this doesn't even begin to tell the story. Nick Talbot is a fast-fingered virtuoso of the strings and it is this, more than anything else, that separates him from what's come before. A prince of scattered nostalgia.

Ian Green

Mind-bogglingly enthusiastic 13th Floor Elevators fan around town and DJ who once harangued a clearly frightened Hank Marvin for half an hour with an in-depth discussion of the Shadows twanger's Marshall amp.

Alison Goldfrapp

Notoriously sour-faced art house sex kitten who has purred studied perfection all over Goldfrapp's admirably oblique nu-disco flavoured rise up the charts. Has been known to wear a tail. Think Marilyn Monroe meeting Shirley Temple in outer space. Or something like that. Your move Roisin Murphy.

H PJ Harvey

OK, she's from Dorset, but Bristol (Totterdown) was the base from which Polly worked with Automatic Dlamini, John Parish's experimental percussive music project which Polly joined as a slide guitarist, saxophonist and backing singer. She toured extensively with the band before going solo.

New beat...
How to speak the language of sound

1 Crunk: High energy, club-orientated hip hop. Not something you find between your toes after wearing dirty flip-flops.

2 Emo: Abbr. emotional. Form of punk often with angst-laden lyrics and big riffs. Not a character from Sesame Street.

3 Glitch: Electronic music utilising cut up beats and processed sounds. Not an uncomfortable irritation caused by the wearing of thongs.

4 Grindcore: Heavy metal characterised by intense drumming, grinding guitars and vocals like a frog's fart. Not a building aggregate.

5 Scrumpy & Western: Particular brand of comic folk music from the West Country. Not a pint of cloudy and a crap local paper.

ALCOHOL AND OTHER DEMONS

A STORY OF STRANGELOVE ON TOUR

1. Wannabe starting something?
Strangelove's complete lack of muscle didn't stop them from getting in a number fights with other bands on the road. One night at the Colombia Hotel, singer Patrick Duff 'went outside' with the Buzzcocks after calling them 'a load of has-beens'. Shelley and Co. bottled out. Terrorvision, however, were less willing to turn the other cheek when a paralytic Patrick waltzed into their dressing room after a particularly heavy binge and announced to them : 'Remember, you are Wombles'.

2. Premature Glastonbury experience
It seemed like a good idea at the time. You know, getting to Glastonbury early, avoiding the rush. Strangelove decided to head off on Tuesday night and arrived at around 2.30am. For the next three days most of the band continued in full-on party mode and unsurprisingly were in no fit state to do anything by the time the festival began on Friday. Somehow they took to the stage on Sunday and were one of that year's highlights.

3. I will walk a thousand miles…
Singer Patrick Duff went through a stage of going on walks so long they put Ian Botham

to shame. Following a heated 2.30am argument with the author of this book at Rodney Allen's house in Pilton, Pad stormed off in protest and began what was to be a very long stroll back to Stokes Croft. It took him and his co-sufferer Dodge eight terrible hours before they reached Bristol. A few weeks later the pair went even further. Nottingham, to be exact, most of it up the hard shoulder of the motorway armed only with a giant bottle of vodka. They eventually reached Nottingham and went straight down the pub for a rest.

4. Pushing the boat out with Pusherman
If the path of excess does indeed lead to the palace of enlightenment, then Strangelove's tour support Pusherman were some seriously enlightened gentlemen. Armed with a carrier bag full of E and a shoebox of assorted 'extras', the band set out to prove that they, and not lightweights Primal Scream, were the number one rock 'n' roll lifestyle band in Brighton. Strangelove hitched a ride and shared the prescriptions. "I saw Pusherman soundcheck pissed out of their heads one night," recalls Patrick Duff. "It was the most dangerous thing I've ever seen." Every day, for four long weeks, the party raged. Pusherman split afterwards and a few of them died soon after that.

5. Hear the drummer get wasted
It's 1996 and Strangelove are in London to play at the Clapham Grand. It's an important gig for the band with representatives from Food, Parlophone, EMI, Blur and the national music press on the guest list. Strangelove are due on stage at 9.30pm, which would be fine except that it's 6.30pm and drummer John Langley is paralytic. He's so drunk that he walks the length of Kentish Town Road saying, 'I'm John,' to each person who walks past. 'Pleased to meet you.' He's no better by 7.30pm. At 8pm, deep panic sets in. At 9.30pm, against all medical possibilities, Langers sits at his drum kit and plays a blinder. 'He's the best drummer in the world,' says someone afterwards. They're not wrong.

Nellee Hooper

A gang of us called round Nellee Hooper's house once when we were mods but his mum said he was out. A few years later, there he was on *Top of the Pops* with Jazzy B. Nellee, Mushroom, 3D and Milo were The Wild Bunch line up for the *Friends And Countrymen* EP in 1988 and became one of the most sought-after producers in the biz.

Graeme Howell

He might look like a friendly plumber but this is the fella who bought together the London Philarmonia and I Am The Mighty Jungulator. The affable Colston Hall business director is one of the city's prime movers when it comes to experimental music and he somehow finds time outside his day job to act as the director of the Bristol Music Foundation and the chair of the Bristol Music Industry Forum. Sainthood surely waits.

■ Alison Goldfrapp's band are a huge success story having reached platinum status.

Steve Hunt

Steve, or Stem to his friends and about a thousand local bands who have wanted to be his friend over the years. For longer than can possibly be good for the health, Stem has been co-ordinator of the Ashton Court Festival. He is a hero and he deserves your thanks. And your money.

The Insects (Bob Locke and Tim Norfolk)

Aka the Startled Insects. These two Emmy-award winning behind-the-scenes maestros have been responsible for a vast library of film and TV scores, as well as tracks for the likes of Massive Attack, Goldfrapp and Alison Moyet.

I Am The Mighty Jungulator

Ever since Bristol's very own genre-stomping, ultra-sensory, avant-garde virtuoso electronic supergroup picked up the best new electronic act at the Diesel New Music Awards 2004, they've exuded an air of anything's possible. Not content with a sonic canvas that takes in krautrock, drum 'n' bass, speed garage, dream-core and ambient, they invented 'a sonic philosophers stone' in the form of an audio engine. Whatever next? Re-imagining Shostakovic? Why not? An educational, mostly inspirational, always unblinking experimental foot forward.

■ The most inspirational female rock artist of her generation, Polly used to live in Totterdown.

Andy Jenks

One half of Alpha and the only person in Europe to have decorated his living room with a 12-foot billboard of Roy Castle. Jenks' thirst for the perfect sound is unparalleled.

Joe 90

DJ and musical connoisseur of the highest order, Joe 90 is responsible for pushing the freshest jazz, funk, soul and hip-hop sounds to lift Bristol's clubbing scene out of the 1990s. Joe 90 is the promoter of Bristol's highly- acclaimed club night Seen. Described by those who know him as: 'a master of the low-slung bling'.

Simon John

Talented and thoroughly likeable Federation main man and former Roni Size bassist whose free-flowing finger noises were the scaffolding of the Mercury Music Prize-winning *New Forms* album. Now in a band called the Mighty Ging.

Jukes

According to reports, this lot are something very, very special indeed. The sound is a high and happy country soul that resonates with all the melancholic grace of Nielsson or Jimmy Webb. When they finally announce their arrival, they will probably do so in front of a wall of expectant A&R people.

Kosheen

The trio who make up drum 'n' bass adventurers Kosheen are Markee Substance, Darren Decoder and Sian Evans. The band's grounding is in the Bristol Roughneck Ting drum 'n' bass raves and the Breakbeat Culture shop and record label. Their *Hide U* single was voted best single at the 2003 UK Drum 'n' Bass Awards.

■ Simon John played on Roni Size's Mercury Music Prize-winning album New Forms.

Knowledge of Bugs

Live electronica outfit responsible for Bristol label Clean Cut Records. *Venue* magazine said of the *Woodwork* EP: 'a kind of autumnal melancholy that will have you gazing out of the window to watch and see if the leaves are turning brown.'

Krust

Krust (real name Keith Thompson) had a wide-ranging beat education that included acid house, hip-hop, drum 'n' bass and rave. He progressed through Fresh Four and Smith & Mighty to co-found the Full Cycle collective with Roni Size. The solo *Coded Language* album followed along with the *I Kamanche* collaboration with DJ Die and the 2006 *Hidden Knowledge* project.

■ Keith Thompson, aka Krust, has worked with Bristol's finest.

Gerard Langley (Blue Aeroplanes)

One of the most original voices in British art rock of the last 20 years. The Blue Aeroplanes founder and wordsmith hasn't wavered from his poetic mission in all that time and still has the fan base to prove it. The Aeroplanes signed to EMI in 2006.

John Langley

A genuine Bristol rock 'n' roll legend with a thousand stories to tell, most of them involving heavy drinking and broken spectacles. Langers is a drummer and a human being of unparalleled genius. He's also Gerard Langley's brother and used to play drums for Gerard's band the Blue Aeroplanes.

Alex Lee

Ex-Coltranes, Aeroplanes and Strangelove, Lee became Suede's multi-instrumentalist who Brett Anderson calls 'my little virtuoso'. Lee was born with a plectrum in his fingers and everything he has done since has been blessed with easy, unaffected cool.

Ⓜ Madnomad

Maybe they've suffered by being placed in the 'oddball', rather than the 'original' category, but if you wear pig masks on stage what do you expect? The release of the *Tamper Evident* album was met with rapturous local and national reviews and *Venue* was prompted to describe Madnomad founder Rob Parry as: 'truly the most original, confrontational artist Bristol has seen in a long time.'

Moonshot

Hugely entertaining ska band who formed in the skinhead/ska revival the end of the 1980s and still resurface now and again.

Jim Moray

From his makeshift studio in a Bedminster bedroom, Jim Moray has become a genuine phenomenon. Bono's journo pal Neil McCormack called the 24 year-old 'the biggest leap forward in folk for 30 years'. Other writers are saying that he could do for folk music what James Blunt has done for whimpering like a girl. In February 2004, he was presented with the BBC Radio 2 Album Of The Year Award for *Sweet England* as well as the BBC Radio 2 Horizon Award 2004 for best newcomer. His follow-up album, *Jim Moray*, was released in May 2006.

Ⓞ Onslaught

Five lads from the Banjo Island badlands of Cadbury Heath moved from punk to death/thrash/speed metal. Onslaught became big news on the European circuit, signed to London Records and released their heavy metal monster *In Search Of Sanity*. Management fall-outs, sackings and acrimony followed and Onslaught were no more. No Bristol band has come close to taking their heavy metal mantle.

Julian Owen

It takes either a brave or desperate man to set himself up as the target of a thousand crap local band demo tapes every month, but hey, someone's gotta do it. The hugely approachable *Venue* music editor can be pestered at small venues around town most nights of the week.

Ⓟ John Parish

AKA Scott Tracey. John is the founder of Automatic Dlamini who featured Polly Harvey on slide guitar and vocals. Parish went on to be a mainstay of Polly's success. He is now one of the most highly-rated producers in the business and a hugely versatile musician. He produced the 2003 Eels album and has shared studios with loads of local bands, including the Experimental Pop Band and many of Fat Paul's Swarf Finger artists.

Fat Paul

Paul Horlick is the Swarf Finger and Espionage labels main man and money-where-his-mouth-is champion of experimental

Five Great...

Experimental albums

❶ Mirror, Flying Saucer Attack: From their lofty position at the top of the steps in Revolver Records, Dave Pearce and company spent 15 years or so as darlings of the alt. fanzine Underground. Bristol's most challenging band.

❷ You Guys Kill Me, Third Eye Foundation: 'I got a bigger, fatter sampler, the biggest and fattest you can buy. You Guys Kill Me is the result of that,' says soundscaper Matt Elliot.

❸ For How Much Longer Do We Tolerate Mass Murder?, The Pop Group: Nihilistic, tribalistic white boy funk and one of the sit-up-and-listen albums of the post-punk era. An anti-Fascist groove thing.

❹ Teenagers In Trouble vs Fat Paul: Eponymous mini-album of beats and breaks featuring Rick from Planet Records, Fat Paul, Andy and Corin from Alpha and Receiver.

❺ Weep Hippies Weep, Pregnant: Second album from the queasy Beefheartian slouch funksters with Gareth Sager as unsettling and off-the-wall as ever.

noiseniks everywhere. Horlick has spread his wings Down Under and is now one half of the UK arm of Aussie label Invada.

Dave Pearce

Bristol's professor of feedback has been a bit quiet of late but he's still the closest thing Bristol has got to its very own Kevin Shields. Like many before him, he juggled his Flying Saucer Attack duties with a job at Revolver.

The Playwrights

'Have we mentioned that we LOVE The Playwrights?' commented *Rolling Stone* when reviewing The Playwrights *The National Missing Person* album. In just a few short years, Sink & Stove's impeccably literate, often twitchy left-field pop visionaries have become one of the most inventive and thoughtful bands around. Additions such as a xylophone, a theremin, a cornet or a melodica mean they have more in common with the likes of Josef K than one-dimensional tosh like The Editors. A national treasure already.

■ John Parish is one of the most highly-rated musicians in the Bristol scene and beyond.

⑤ Gareth Sager

The legendary Pop Group loon came snaking out of Redland over 20 years ago and can now be thought of as Bristol's uncle avant-garde. Rip Rig and Panic, Head, Pregnant and now the excellent Nectarine No. 9 have kept him busy.

Michele Schillaci

Remember Toto Schillaci, the brilliant bug-eyed Sicilian goal-poacher from the Italia 1990 World Cup? He's Michele's uncle. Michele himself is a veteran of several commercially attractive indie bands. His dad owns the Louisiana.

Andy Sheppard

South Bristol jazz genius always experimenting with new forms. Andy is of the few artists in any genre to constantly set new musical challenges.

■ Mercury Music Prize winner Roni Size is hugely influential in the local music scene.

Nick Sheppard

Original punk and guitarist in Strokes-esque dot-dash new wavers The Cortinas. Sheppard famously went on to replace Mick Jones in The Clash shortly before they took the final curtain. Very much part of the where-are-they-now brigade.

Roni Size

Drum 'n' bass adventurer, Mercury Music Prize winner and sometime shopper at Waitrose in Henleaze, Roni seems to be permanently tuned into some pioneering noise frequency. His impact and influence on the local scene is immense.

Mark Slater

'I like to look at musicians as unique characters', is not the normal spiel you get from music promoters but Mark Slater is no ordinary promoter. Passionate, innovative, open-minded, openly kneeling

BRISTOL'S BEST-EVER GIGS

Roxy Music: Colston Hall, 1973
Unlike those dismal comedy copycats The Darkness, this bunch of intergalactic space lizards did not seek permission to land. But land they did. In 1973, they brought art rock to the West. Eno and all.

The Clash:
Exhibition Centre, 1977
It's bonfire night 1977 and Strummer and co. roll up in their subversive drainpipes and chop out every ferocious gem from their incendiary debut album. Excited Bristol almost has a riot.

The Pop Group:
Hope Chapel, 1979
Troublesome funk meets terrible noise in front of every member of the Clifton Experimental Post-Punk Disco Society. After much howling and hollering, the assembled hipsters go home and plan to start their own bands.

The Specials: Locarno, 1980
'This one's for the Barton Hill mods,' said Terry Hall and over a thousand two-tone-clad ace faces nodded in respect. The Specials bounced, shuffled and moonstomped with an unbelievable energy. Completely exhausting.

Rolling Stones:
Ashton Gate, 1982
From the opening bars of *Under My Thumb*, Mick strutted and snarled for the full 90 minutes. A 'relaxed' Keef produced the noisiest set of guitar feedback ever heard in Bristol.

Blue Aeroplanes:
Victoria Rooms, 1990
The moshpit faithful went so beserk, they went through the floor. Aeroplanes management duo Simon Esplen and Cerne Canning had to form a protective barrier around the hole to prevent anyone from falling in.

Nirvana Bierkeller, 1991
The start of the UK Nevermind tour and the night Kurt met Courtney. Those who went left knowing Nirvana played the most super-charged garage punk since The Stooges. Nothing would be the same again.

PJ Harvey: The Fleece, 1996
Two hot, steamy nights in the company of the coolest chick to ever slouch in a pair of stilettos while strumming a battered guitar. Those lucky enough to get in saw Polly Harvey confirm her place as the most outstanding alt. rock female on the planet.

Portishead: Ashton Court, 1997
A staggering end-of-tour homecoming where the band's fragile, ultra-precise soundscaping seemed to hang like dust in the misty evening air. A truly spellbinding end-of-the-day, end-of-the-tour set; one of the most memorable homecoming gigs of all time.

White Stripes: Louisiana, 2001
The Louis is the best place in town to see up-and-coming Yank schmindie bands plus get yourself a sauna in the bargain. In more recent times, the likes of Interpol, Outhud and Wolf Parade have played blinders but this White Stripes' show is still the yardstick by which all Louis gigs must now be measured. Sweaty, loud and a genuine sense of seeing something very special gaining momentum before your very eyes, this was good enough to make the cover of the next week's *NME*.

Massive Attack:
Queen Square, 2003
Great choice of venue, fantastic support bands, menacing triumph of a mega set, awful catering. But after more than a decade of trying, Bristol's biggest band finally got the homecoming they deserved.

Stephen Malkmus & The Jicks:
Anson Rooms, 2005
'He never does Pavement songs…' So why's he singing *Grounded* then? Yet another example of this city bringing out the best in passing musical trade. In his Pavement guise, Malkmus has played Bristol a fair few times (even playing the Anson Rooms a decade earlier) but rather than the brainy slacker lo-fi of old, here was a relaxed (read sozzled) Brit folk troubadour so happy with his West Coast audience that he decided *Eye of the Tiger* would make a perfect encore. And he was right, it did.

at the alter of greatness and perfection. Slater claims to be just one of an army of volunteers who put everything into the organisational side of the Bristol's independent recording and live scene in order and take something out.

Smith & Mighty

Generally regarded as Bristol's seminal dance music duo, Rob Smith and Ray Mighty were there when the storm broke and are still hugely influential today. They were joined by reggae man Peter D Rose in 1998 and have been the inspiration behind numerous collaborations, including 3 Stripe, Henry and Louis and More Rockers. Rob Smith released his solo album, the excellent *Up On The Downs*, in 2003.

Spider

At well over six foot tall with legs like fireworks, the lead singer of the Seers, Bonesaw and Zoomer must rank as one of the most dangerous stage performers since Arthur 'My Head Is On Fire' Brown. Not many Crowded House fans are as reckless.

John Stapleton

There aren't too many DJs anywhere on the planet who have a vision as wide as John Stapleton's. Dope on Plastic's vinyl flicker supremo can trace the line that links Pere Ubu to Aphex Twin and will survive the club crash because of it.

Mark Stewart

Towering ex-Pop Group lamppost and all-round awkward sod, the consistently difficult Mr Stewart has been wearing the same nihilistic boots that inspired him to make crazy noises in the first place. An English icon.

Stoloff & Hopkinson

Montpelier's Mr Stoloff and Mr Hopkinson are a mysterious pair of electronica gents known for their prankish sense of humour and huge production talents. Their *Trademark* EP was described by one reviewer as: 'a genre-dodging journey through the record collections and video libraries of the eccentric duo'.

▣ Nick Talbot

Drawn to Bristol in the late 1990s by a love of Third Eye Foundation and Flying Saucer Attack, Talbot's solo project *Gravenhurst* is one of the city's most lauded acts. Signed to Warp in 2004, they released the albums *Black Holes in the Sand* and *Fires in Distant Buildings* to universal acclaim.

Team Brick

Its easy to get typecast when you're messing about at the edges of sonic sanity. 'I am not dark noise!' bellows the fantastically whacked-out Team Brick. 'I am not Nazi army jacket! I am happy noise fun!' Improvisation rules his chaotic one-man live shows while clarinet, cheapo keyboards, loops, carrier bags, wood

■ John Stapleton is known for his huge vision.

■ Bristol's Smith & Mighty produced Carlton's (above) Call is Strong album.

and shouting are his tools. From free jazz to slamming metal, weird opera to manic psychedelia, the Brick boy makes the most appropriate modern noise possible.

Martina Topley-Bird
This Bristol schoolgirl was discovered by Tricky when she was having a crafty fag between lessons in Clifton. The voice of Tricky's *Maxinquaye* album, she released her outstanding solo album *Quixotic* in 2003.

Tricky
You've got to admire the single-mindedness of Adrian Thaws Knowle West's most famous son: instead of building on the critical and commercial success of his dysfunctional masterpiece *Maxinquaye*, he moved to New York and headed down a one-way street called Experimental and Obscure Avenue.

■ Tricky aka Adrian Thaws was born in the lovely Knowle West.

Adrian Utley
The supremely talented Portishead bass boss is one of the hardest working men in alternative showbiz. Sparklehorse, Goldfrapp, Patrick Duff, Jimmy Galvin and Beth Gibbons are just a few who have benefited.

Unforscene
You've probably heard their cinematic soundscapes on TV documentaries, however, Unforscene also perform as a kicking live act with guest vocalists. Very much a behind the scenes outfit, with a heavyweight list of collaborations.

Joe Volk
There is, it seems, nowt so cool as folk. As the introspective acoustic movement grows another foot or two of stubble, its participants are beginning to show signs of being less boring than knitwear spods Damian Rice and Jack Johnson. The solo voyage of Gonga roar-maker Joe 'It's German for people' Volk demonstrates this more than most. And it's the reference points that lift it out of the ordinary. In keeping with English songwriting law, Nick Drake has been mentioned by all reviewers. But no one really sounds like Drakey do they? No, Volk is closer in style and spirit to someone like Elliot Smith.

■ Unforscene like to stay behind the scenes, so here's a picture.

War Against Sleep
Another great name, another classy shimmy towards the leftfield. War Against Sleep is actually little more than Duncan Fleming and a keyboard. The resultant noise is startling: it's lip-curling, lovesick and loungey, a darkly comic voyage into an as yet unwritten chapter of rock 'n' roll. Fire Records, home of Pulp, won the signing war, offering the boy wonder a nice three-album deal.

Ben Westbeech
With a list of influences that range from Roy Ayers to Dr Alimontado, Nirvana and DJ Shadow, you won't be surprised that

Up Close

it's not easy to categorise Ben Westbeech. The classically-trained singer, producer and musician was on the fringes of the Full Cycle crew before signing to Gilles Peterson's Brownswood label in 2006.

The Wind Marbles
If anyone needed proof of the genuine diversity of the current local music scene, The Wind Marbles surely provide it. As their soft and gentle name suggests, these bold young adventurers are at the forefront of the new Bristol folk scene. Cool roots?

Hazel Winter
Former Blue Aeroplanes and Moorhaven guitarist whose critically acclaimed John Parish-produced solo album *Put The Sharp Knives Away* drew comparisons with PJ Harvey and Kristin Hersh. If you have heard but not seen Hazel, you could be forgiven for expecting her to look like a cross between a kewpie doll and the girl with the machine gun from the Bader Meinhoff Gang.

■ Hazel Winter: the former Blue Aeroplanes and Moorhaven guitarist who went solo.

Davey Woodward
The perennially groovesome ex-Brilliant Corner and Experimental Pop Band frontman has slowly grown into one of our most warped art pop visionaries over the years. It's a long way from the cheeky chappy sound of the Corners' Brian Rix to the EPB's Tracksuit Triolgy but it's been worth it.

🅨 Yolanda
Top vocalist and MC, Yolanda has worked extensively with doyens of the Bristol club scene Blowpop, Seen and DJ October and is in increasing demand as a guest vocalist for live and studio projects.

You & The Atom Bomb
This lot ooze cool bubblegum punk aesthetics from every pore. There's the name, for a start. Then there's the fact that they've got two vocalists, one called Suzi Gage and the other Jean-Marc De Verteuil. And on top of this, they manage to mix crazy lyrical gymnastics with a breezy 1960s pop sensibility that could well propel them into the charts. Their mini-LP *Shake Shake Hello!?* was in a new wave all of its own.

■ Davey Woodward formed the Brilliant Corners and the Experimental Pop Band and.

🅩 Zen Hussies
Some call it goodtime swingska others label it boogaloo, but whatever the term the Bristol and Bath-based Zen Hussies deliver it with good-humoured, old-time panache. Released *Their Flatfoot Sharpsuit* album in 2004. A second CD, *Absolutely*, is due for release as we write.

Up Close

Rumba Lament
(Rob Smith, guitar, Nellee Hooper, drums)

Restriction
(Rob Smith, guitar, Nellee, sound engineer, Daddy G, DJ)

Sweat
(Rob Smith guitar, Ray Mighty, synths)

Wild Bunch
The original Wild Bunch crew was Nellee Hooper, Daddy G and Milo Johnson

Call Is Strong
Daddy G and Smith & Mighty produce Carlton

Any Love
Massive Attack, Carlton and Smith & Mighty team up for the first MA release

Wild Bunch
3D and Mushroom join and Milo and Nellee leave

Massive Attack
3D, Daddy G, Mushroom and Tricky create the stunning Blue Lines. Much is recorded at Neneh Cherry's home studio

Pigbag
Nellee Hooper meets Simon Underwood in Pigbag

Raw Like Sushi
Massive Attack work on Neneh Cherry's debut solo album

Soul II Soul
Nellee Hooper joins Jazzie B's new project

Pop Group
The original line-up is Mark Stewart, Gareth Sager, Simon Underwood, John Waddington

Rip Rig & Panic
Gareth Sager and Bruce Smith recruit Neneh Cherry for their new band

Head
Gareth Sager forms Head with Nick Sheppard and Rich Beale

1977-1983   1984-1990   1991

The Bristol Beat

THE MUSIC TIMELINE: 1977-2003

Smith and Mighty
Rob Smith and Ray Mighty form S&M and are later joined by Peter D Rose

Mark Stewart
Stewart releases Stronger The Love with Smith & Mighty

Fresh Four
S&M work with Suv, Krust, Flynn, Judge and Lizz E.

More Rockers
Heavy dub offshoot of Smith & Mighty

Mad Professor
Ex Black Roots producer remixes Massive Attack's Protection

Tricky
Stewart's lodger meets Martina Topley-Bird

Full Cycle Roni Size forms Full Cycle from the Basement Project in St Paul's. He is joined by , Krust, Suv, Die, MC Dynamite, Onalee and others

Reprazent
Wins the Mercury prize for Roni Size

Sinead O'Connor
Nellee Hooper produces the Nothing Compares 2 U monster hit. He also works with Madonna, Bjork, Smashing Pumpkins, All Saints, U2 Janet Jackson and others

Gary Clail
Mark Stewart works with Gary Clail at Adrian Sherwood's On-U-Sounds

Tru Funk
Talented youngsters Jody and Sam and their mate Dan (DJ Die) persuade S&M to produce their 4am single

Portishead
Formed by Geoff Barrow, engineer on Blue lines

Massive Attack
100th Window released in 2003. Massive Attack (3D and Grant) play Queen Square

1995   1996-2000   2000+

Unusual Bristol buildings

John Hudson checks out some of the more interesting brickwork dotted around the city

Bristol may lack the architectural impact of its neighbouring city of Bath, but there are still a number of buildings of merit, particularly around Corn Street and up in Clifton. Sadly, many historic sites were destroyed in World War Two, but aside from the obvious architectural big names, such as St Mary Redcliffe and the Victoria Rooms, there are some unusual buildings tucked away among the modern buildings. Here we take you on our tour of some of Bristol's less obvious buildings of merit...

ART DECO

You can look long and hard for decent art deco in Bristol. It is not exactly one of our strong points. There's a pretty good Odeon building in Union Street in Broadmead, opened in 1938, not long before World War Two, but its curved corner tower has not been the same since it lost its canopy and top. Weston-super-Mare is the place to go for a classic Odeon, cinema-organ and all. But at least Bristol's has a ghost: a long-ago projectionist murdered in some steamy sex scandal. Not many people have seen him but there's always something about the layout of these old buildings, with their lonely back corridors and stairs, that makes you expect the unexpected. Not a place to go at night if you get spooked!

The hotspot for 1930s 'modern movement' buildings is in and around the Centre. At the Broadmead end of this huge traffic roundabout that replaced redundant docks is Electricity House, opened in 1938 and designed by Giles Gilbert Scott to look like an ocean liner. You can see its stepped upper decks best from the side angle in Broad Street. It was given a welcome facelift in 1990, but with so

■ Next time you're hurrying towards the Galleries, take a good look at the Odeon. It's art deco, don't you know.

■ The Evening World used to hit the streets from this art deco office on the Centre.

much destroyed by the War, and then the planners, it is still hard to imagine the first shock of its contrast with the medieval city around it.

After the War, a group of architects called for the whole of the Centre to be rebuilt in the same style. Some hope… But at least the ship theme was picked up on by Percy Thomas and Son when they designed the showpiece store for Broadmead in the mid 1950s, on the corner of Haymarket and the Horsefair. It helped pioneer the new shopping centre, and there was much grumbling about it at first – until critics saw that it was a Rolls Royce of a building compared with most of what followed. It's currently occupied by House of Fraser, though a number of chains have come and gone over the years. The cold, commercial fact is that it's not all that big, with that wedge shape hemming it in. But it was refurbished lavishly in the 1990s by the Home Counties group Bentalls, who got their fingers burned mightily for their pains, and it's now even more classy inside than out.

NAKED FACT

The leaning tower of **Temple Church** in St Thomas is approximately 1.5m out of true.

Back around the Centre, swish apartments now occupy the symmetrical, angular offices from which the long-lost *Evening World* once hit the streets. There's something austere and Eastern European-looking about the place, but that's the way inter-war media moguls seemed to like their buildings. Around the corner, the redevelopment of the Colston Hall has meant the loss of the old Bristol Gas Company showrooms of

Five facts…
About Bristol buildings

❶ The **Spike Island Arts Centre** was originally the Brooke Bond tea-packing warehouse. It was converted in 1998.

❷ The distinctive **electric cranes** outside the Industrial Museum were to be scrapped until public outrage decreed otherwise in 1975.

❸ The tower of the **Wills Memorial Building** on Queen's Road is 65.5 metres tall.

❹ The **Paty family** were Bristol's leading architects, builders and craftsmen in the 18th Century.

❺ **Bristol Bridge** was built by Thomas Paty in 1764-67 on the site of the previous 13th-Century bridge.

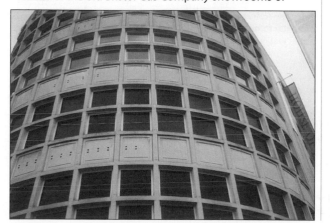

■ House of Fraser dominates the Haymarket side of Broadmead with its ocean-going lines.

BRISTOL LOOS

☀ Bearing in mind all the usual health and safety warnings, you can have an interesting afternoon touring the vintage public loos of Bristol.

Three of them are classic iron pissoirs straight out of the seedier quarters of Paris, and you'll find them on Horfield Common, in Mina Road, St Werburghs and at the top of Blackboy Hill. The first two are listed buildings and the Blackboy one is also protected, being in a conservation area.

A tad more discreet is the ancient convenience on Park Row, which is not officially listed but everyone thinks it should be. Connoisseurs also speak glowingly of the facilities in Prince Street and Cheltenham Road, and the gents' beside the Suspension Bridge on the Clifton side. Sex discrimination is rife in this list, but not all is lost. "The ladies in Stoke Road are a joy to behold," says one who knows.

THE FIVE WORST TOILETS IN BRISTOL

1. Snuff Mills
These were named by the BBC's *Watchdog* programme in March 2003 as the worst public toilets in Britain. Dr Clara Greed, a member of the judging panel on the show said: 'It is pretty dirty and poorly maintained. They have put blue blocks into the urinals, but they are still dirty, chipped and disgusting. And the wash basin obviously hasn't been cleaned in a million years.' *Naked Bristol* visited the toilets in Summer 2006. Our photographer was almost overcome by the stench of stale urine, but still managed to take these snaps (right).

2. Next to Mary Le Port Church on the Centre
Deep, dark and concrete cavern of a convenience. You'd imagine that Siberian toilets at the height of the Cold War were just like this.

3. Temple Meads
They put in that funny low lighting for a while to discourage drug use. No self-respecting junkie would go anywhere near the place.

It's now a bright stainless steel affair with automatic hand-washing facilities. There's plenty of light to skin up in.

4. Blackboy Hill bogs
The funny little Victorian pissoir stranded on the traffic island is supposed to have some architectural merit. Sadly it stinks of piss.

5. Centre on a Saturday night
It must be those fountains that make everybody want to go.

1935 which, it has to be said, were sniffed at by purists as a deco cliché, but had an unusual air of seaside pavilion tattiness about them. Just up the road, Friary House, opened in 1938, is seen by those who know as a more worthy survivor of the modern movement.

Finally, if you're out in the suburbs at posh Sneyd Park, you'll find a clutch of cubist houses from the 1930s, all following Le Corbusier's lead. And in the Ridgeway at Westbury-on-Trym, not too far away, you can see through the trees an art-deco classic of a house, with its style once more hinting at the ocean liners that never did come in to Bristol. It was built in 1934, and while it looks as if it should be basking in the sunshine of Miami Beach or St Tropez, its name is a reminder that it is pretty much one of a kind down in this part of the world. It's known simply as Concrete House.

Five tallest...
Offices in Bristol

❶ Castlemead, Old Market **262ft (80m).**

❷ Froomsgate House, Rupert Street, Broadmead **205ft (62m).**

❸ Colston Centre, Colston Avenue **205ft (62m).**

❹ One Redcliffe Street, Redcliffe **198ft (60m).**

❺ Grey Friars, Lewins Mead **195ft (59m).**

Courtesy of www.skyscrapernews.com

BRISTOL GUILD

NAKED FACT

Plans to create **Park Street** started in 1740. It was laid out in 1758 and work began in 1761.

The Bristol Guild shop in Park Street really can trace its history back to the 'guilds' of the arts and crafts movement. Today it's simply a shop specialising in glass and ceramics, furniture and furnishings, kitchenware and toys, but it's still more willing than most to showcase up-and-coming talent. William Morris' Arts and Crafts Society was founded in 1883. There was a big stir when the London-based Guild of Handicrafts moved to Chipping Campden in 1902, and though the Cockneys in Arcadia experiment was short-lived, the idea of craftspeople banding together for support and marketing opportunities was not.

■ **The Bristol Guild on Park Street can trace its roots back to 1907.**

The Bristol Guild of Handicrafts was opened in Park Street in 1907, the forerunner of the city's Guild of Applied Arts which started in the following year. There had been earlier arts and crafts groups in the area but none with a chance to sell in posh Park Street, 'the Bond Street of the West'. The stained-glass artist Arnold Robinson became its sole owner in 1929 and moved across the road to the present premises four years later, and from then on machine-made goods were accepted, as long as they were 'original, functional and made to the highest standards'. Ceramics by Susie Cooper, Ruskin and Royal Lancastrian were among Robinson's early favourites, as well as Elton

Ware, made just along the road at Clevedon. Today the shop is owned by Bristolian Ken Stradling, who joined the company when he was demobbed from the Royal Corps of Signals in 1948.

PERCIVAL HARTLAND THOMAS

Percival Hartland Thomas was the most off-beat of Bristol's 20th Century architects. He started his career designing arts and crafts houses and ended it with gothic churches, but in the middle years, he hit on a weird style of simplified gothic, redbrick Norman and bauhaus white, which could have added up to something big if he'd been a more influential name and had given it a bit longer. His three key churches are St Oswald's, Bedminster Down (1927), St Mary's, Shirehampton (1929), which is probably his masterpiece and St Cuthbert's, Brislington (1933). Pevsner says Shirehampton Church is neo-gothic, 'but handled with so much freedom and personality and with so much of the spirit of the 20th Century that the compromise remains convincing'. Others say uncompromising is more the word, with its huge square windows and macho-looking rubble walls. He was never as adventurous again, but when it comes to ease on the eye, a lot of his fans like Brislington best. Outside, the Norman-arched brick doorways of St Cuthbert's are undeniably great works of art, while inside Thomas created a huge light space of white illuminated by windows which are gothic in shape if not in fussiness. Hartland Thomas lived on until 1960, but sadly, he was never on this kind of form again.

■ The shell of St Peter's Church is the centrepiece of Castle Park.

■ The carvers who created the choir stalls in Bristol Cathedral had a little fun with their designs.

CATHEDRAL CHARACTERS

The misericords on the choir stalls at Bristol Cathedral date mainly from around 1520 and, being half-hidden, gave their carvers plenty of scope for fun. They include images of Adam and Eve, Samson and the Lion, a mermaid, Reynard the Fox, the bear caught in the oak tree, dancing bears, a pig being killed, the spinster leading apes in hell, a woman taking corn to a windmill and a husband and wife doing battle with broomsticks.

Fast-forward more than 400 years and on the north windows on your left, just after you've entered the cathedral, you will see a memorial to all the Home Front services who helped guard the city and the cathedral in the World War Two. It shows a policeman, firemen, WVS member, air raid warden, nurses, and so on. The windows were unveiled in 1951, replacing earlier ones blown out by bombs, and at a 50th anniversary service in 2001, there were still plenty of old-timers around who'd served in those organisations. One of them even claimed to be the original model for one of the portraits. They're not exactly great art, but there's a nice human touch to them.

OLD MARKET AND CASTLE PARK

You need a huge leap of imagination to take on board the fact that the shopping heart of Bristol once stretched from Old Market up along the river to Bristol Bridge. The inner ring road of Temple Way and Bond Street – did you ever see a less likely looking Bond Street? – now cuts the wide Old Market off from the heart of town, while Castle Park has greened over a network of teeming little streets that had survived from the Middle Ages until the day the Luftwaffe called.

In the middle of them there were always the last traces of the Castle, a scene of Civil War derring-do when it fell to the Roundheads in 1645 but demolished a dozen years later. In fact, at the end of the park near the Marriott Hotel there are still some much-modified remains, but the most striking sight in the park today is the bomb-ruined shell of the 14th-Century St Peter's Church. Its paved areas and terraces have become quite a popular meeting place but, while it's great in a sunny lunch hour, it can be seen as a little seedy at other times. It cost £50,000 to restore it in the 1970s, which was widely derided as a scandalous waste of money then, but wouldn't buy you a garage in Clifton now.

It's more cheerful to imagine Old Market in its heyday, especially on a busy Friday evening, which was the main shopping time for many Bristolians. Most of them would take home 'tea fish' as a special treat – dried and salted and the local answer to the Manx kipper or the Arbroath smokie. You only had to leave it to soak in a pan for two days and it was just the job for Sunday tea.

NAKED FACT

Gardiner Haskins in Broad Plain was originally the Thomas Soap Works.

Five ugliest
Buildings in Bristol
(and the people who designed them)

❶ Student's Union, Queens Road – Alec French and Partners, 1965. *'Perhaps Clifton's most bruising post-war intrusion.'*

❷ New Bristol Centre, Frogmore Street – Gillinson, Barnet & Partners, 1963-1966. *'Brutalises everything around it by scale and texture.'*

❸ Froomsgate House, Rupert Street, Broadmead – Alec French & Partners, 1971. *'The most offensive of the area's gargantuan monliths.'*

❹ Former Norwich Union Building, Castle Park – Wakeford, Jerram & Harris, 1962. *'Deflates one of the city's prime sites.'*

❺ Trenchard Street Car Park, Trenchard Street – Architect unknown, 1967. *'A multi-storey monster.'*

Descriptions from Pevsner Architectural Guide to Bristol. Buildings chosen by Naked Guide to Bristol

STATUESQUE

GIL GILLESPIE'S BRIEF GUIDE TO SOME OF BRISTOL'S INTERESTING MONUMENTAL FIGURES

■ Neptune moved to make way for the fountains on the Centre. He is now opposite the Hippodrome.

1. Neptune

Location: He keeps moving around Bristol, but he is currently in the pedestrianised area on the Centre.

Who's he when he's at home? Well that's just it, he hasn't had a familiar place to hang his ragged cape lately, moving all over town in the name of Harbourside regeneration. The Mer King was first erected in the Temple area, near Bristol Bridge. He then moved to Temple Street and was left on some glebe land until 1872. The statue was then moved to the junction of Temple Street and Victoria Street and was later re-erected at the Quay Head in 1949. He moved to his present site back in 2000.

Was it worth breaking the mould for? The big man of the ocean has been clutching his fork of defiance for longer than he cares to remember. He's always been gnarly, shrivelled

and as stubborn as a limpet and there is no more heroic ocean figure around.

2. Equestrian bronze of William III

Location: Queen Square.

Who's he when he's at home? An unusually heroic-looking member of the aristocracy.

Was it worth breaking the mould for? Dating back to the 1700s, this impressive looking, er, lump, of bronze man-and-his-mount was once so valued it was hidden away during World War Two and only put back again in 1948. 'Has he gone yet?' whispered his caretakers. 'Who?' came the reply. 'That horrible little German fella with the funny moustache.'

3. Edmund Burke

Location: St Augustine's Parade (the Centre).

Who's he when he's at home? MP for Bristol 1774-1780 but sadly no relation to either Solomon or the newsreader turned emergency service expert Michael.

Was it worth breaking the mould for? Two moulds, actually. There is a marble replica in St Stephen's Hall, Westminster. Bristol gets the much cheaper version. "I wish to be a member of parliament, to have my share of doing good and resisting evil," reads the inscription. Looks like he is another berk who underestimated the persuasiveness of Tony Blair then.

4. Rajah Rammohun Roy

Location: Outside the Central Library on College Green.

Who's he when he's at home? Celebrated Indian social reformer whose standing, even after his death, did much to stop the bulldozers threatening to flatten Arnos Vale Cemetery where he is buried inside a mighty impressive tomb.

Was it worth breaking the mould for? Absolutely. When it was unveiled in 1997, this public monument was a long overdue acknowledgement of the closest thing Bristol has to Ghandi – even though he was only visiting the city when he died.

5. Sabrina, Goddess of the Severn
Location: Courtyard of Broad Quay House.
Who's she when she's at home? Naked, watery nymph types in hot lesbo action. Teenagers? Yes. Witches? More like suggestive fairies really.
Was it worth breaking the mould for? Well, artist Gerald Laing calls her: "A metaphor for the triumph of life over death." We think she is nothing of the sort.

6. William Penn
Location: New Millennium Square.
Who's he when he's at home? Quaker son of Bristolian Admiral Sir William Penn and the founder of Pennsylvania. His scroll reads 'Death is but crossing the World as Friends do the seas, they live in one another still'.
Was it worth breaking the mould for? Aren't a million boxes of Quaker oats memorial enough?

7. Small Worlds, a tribute to Bristol-born physicist Paul Dirac
Location: On Anchor Road outside the At-Bristol complex.

■ There is a marble replica of the Burke statue in St Stephens's Hall in Westminster.

Who's he when he's at home?
Stephen Hawking reckons: 'Dirac has done more than anyone, with the exception of Einstein, to advance physics and change our picture of the universe.' He won the Nobel Prize for Quantum Mechanics in 1933.
Was it worth breaking the mould for?
Apparently, the concentric cones of the sculpture represent the theoretical movements of the physicist.

8. Charles Wesley
Location: The courtyard on the Horsefair side of Wesley's chapel in Broadmead.
Who's he when he's at home?
The lesser-known brother of that Methodist preacher bloke, John. Charles was a prolific hymn writer and regarded by some as the hymn writing equivalent of Lennon and McCartney. His biggest 'hit' is *Hark! The Herald Angels Sing*. He lived in Stokes Croft.
Was it worth breaking the mould for?
The most striking thing about this impressive 1939 tribute to one of the founders of Methodism is his extraordinary, and very ill-advised, Yeoman-about-town mullet. In bronze. Could Charles Wesley be sporting the heaviest hairstyle in history?

■ Bristol's most famous statue is the 1730s equestrian bronze of William III by Rysbrack in Queen Square.

The best bits of children's Bristol

The top attractions in town and beyond researched by our enthusiastic team of young adventurers

Bristol is an excellent place for kids: there's probably not another city in Britain with so much to do in a relatively small area, and it's got countryside and seaside within easy striking distance as well. In addition to the obvious attractions, such as Bristol Zoo and At-Bristol, there are also plenty of open spaces and hidden treasures to discover. The *Naked Guide to Bristol* asked 13-year-old Caitlin Telfer, her sister Mena (7) and Caitlin's best-friend Leonie Campbell-King (14) to choose their favourite places in Bristol and to pick the best destinations for a day trip away from the city.

AT-BRISTOL

■ **Harbourside, BS1 5DB**
■ **Tel: 0845 345 1235** ■ **www.at-bristol.org.uk**

The £97 million At-Bristol development is essentially the entire area to the north of the Floating Harbour and includes Wildwalk, Explore, the Imax Cinema and Millennium Square. It was *The Good Britain Guide*'s Family Attraction of the Year in 2001 and has won several other tourism and design awards, even one for its car park which was named as one of the best in the UK by the AA in 2005. At-Bristol did hit financial problems and, in August 2003, it had to ask Bristol City Council for a £500,000 loan to cover running costs. Although it is undoubtedly a major family attraction, there are two things that may dissuade you from visiting: it's expensive; Nestlé are a major partner. If that puts you off, here's what you're missing...

Explore: Science and natural forces are the themes of the two storeys of displays and exhibitions, many of them interactive. Highlights on the ground floor include putting the kids on a treadmill to lift water from one tank to

■ Mena, Caitlin and Leonie (left to right) set out to explore the best children's attractions in Bristol and beyond.

■ The waterpools at Millennium Square are a favourite with kids in the summer.

another, several displays involving magnets and magnetic fields and a particularly visual film about the journey of a sperm. It's all a bit like *Tomorrow's World*, but without the lure of Maggie Philbin or the avuncular presence of Raymond Baxter. Upstairs, visitors get to enjoy a harp that uses lasers instead of strings and a gyroscopic briefcase with a 'mind of it's own'. The virtual beach volleyball court is a hoot once you get the hang of it and visitors can create their own music or play slap pipes. The TV studio is popular as the kids play weather forecasters and newsreaders in front of computer-generated backgrounds. The large silver ball you can see from outside is the planetarium where you can watch the universe go by.

Wildwalk: The natural history area of At-Bristol is great. The illuminated Tree of Life inside the entrance is an imposing introduction and then it's information overload as you're presented with displays about fossils, evolution and the suchlike. Staff are on hand to explain it all to the parents as the kids take it in their stride. Walk through the botanical house of fern, fauna and rainforest with its frog and insect soundtrack to the dimly-lit next floor where there are loads more interactive displays about everything from invertebrates to wild habitats. Then through the botanical house (with the occasional butterfly) to a display about people's impact on the natural environment.

Imax Theatre: A seriously big cinema screen with surround sound, Imax shows 3D movies which are often about dinosaurs.

Open: *daily except Christmas Day. Call for details.*

Five best...
Kids playgrounds

① Hengrove Park, Hengrove Way.

② Blaise Castle, Lawrence Weston.

③ Easton Play Park, Chelsea Road.

④ Oldbury Court, Snuffmills.

⑤ Castle Park, Broadmead.

■ The At-Bristol project is the showpiece for the Harbourside regeneration project.

ALPHABET ZOO CHILDREN'S PLAYCENTRE

■ **Old Bingo Hall, Winterstoke Road, Bedminster, BS3 2NW** ■ **Tel: 966 3366**

Large indoor soft-play area with enclosed aerial walkways, ball pools and slides. Sit down in this old bingo hall and read the papers as the kids run up and down the walls. Separate area for toddlers. Popular for children's parties.

Open: 10am-7pm. Last admission 5pm. Cost: Mon-Fri, under 4-year-olds, £2.75; 4-year-olds and over, £3.40. Weekends, under 4-year-olds, £2.75; 4-year-olds and over, £3.99.

■ Ashton Court is a huge area for kids to run around in. Perfect for bikes, kites and picnics.

ASHTON COURT ESTATE

■ **Two miles from Bristol City Centre. Main entrances are off the A369 Portishead Road at Kennel Lodge Road and at Clifton Lodge**

No gimmicks, no play area; just loads of grass, woods and a deer park. Fly a kite, ride a bike, take a picnic, play cricket. Use your imagination. Check out the sunken garden and pet cemetery behind the mansion house.

Open: 8.00am to dusk. Cost: free (excluding some events).

BLAISE CASTLE HOUSE AND ESTATE

■ **Blaise Castle Estate, Henbury Road, Henbury, BS10 7QS** ■ **Tel: 903 9818 for play area events**

There are three distinct attractions in the grounds of this estate to the north of Bristol: the large children's play area is one of the best in Bristol (but still not as good as Victoria Park in Bath); the house has exhibitions of Victorian domestic furnishings, toys and costumes and there's also a display about Edward Jenner, who discovered vaccination; the grounds surrounding the gothic-style folly castle are a mixture of open grass and woodland.

■ As well as exploring the castle and house, kids can also enjoy the play area at Blaise Castle.

You can walk by the side of the Hazel stream (quite marshy and spooky, even on a bright day) as far as the rocky outcrop where you'll find the 'castle' on the site of an iron age fort. The castle was built in 1766 by Thomas Farr, who in 1771 became Master of the Society of Merchant Venturers and in 1775 became Mayor of Bristol. Farr was declared bankrupt after the American War of independence in 1778.

Open: Sat-Wed, 10am-5pm. Cost: Free.

BRANDON HILL AND THE CABOT TOWER

■ Off Park Street

One of the best things to do as a visitor to Bristol is climb the Cabot Tower: the views from the top are fantastic. You can see virtually the whole city and it's the only place where you'll get such a dramatic impression of Bristol past and present. Kids love huffing and puffing up the narrow spiral stairway and are usually fascinated by the distance finder at the top, which tells you how many miles it is to many of the major cities of the world and various places of local interest.

Brandon Hill Park is Bristol's oldest public space: it was given to the city corporation in 1174. It's an ideal place to take children for a picnic if you've been shopping on Park Street or wandering round the docks. The play area on the Hotwells side of Brandon Hill has equipment for toddlers as well as more adventurous climbing frames for older children. Brandon Hill is full of greedy tame squirrels, so take a bag of nuts along with you.

Open: Brandon Hill Park is open 365 days of the year. Cabot Tower is open from 8am until just before dusk (call Bristol Tourist Information Centre on 0906 711 2191 to check times).

BRISTOL HAWKS GYMNASIUM

■ Roman Road, BS5 6DH ■ Tel: 935 5363

One of the more civilised ways to spend an hour or so on a Saturday morning is to drop the kids off at Bristol Hawks and head to nearby St Mark's Road for a coffee and a mooch around Bristol Sweet Mart (see Shopping Listings, p232). Bristol Hawks is a proper gym with vaulting and bars; it's cheap (about £3, depending on age) and fun. Parents aren't allowed into the classes, but you can watch the kids tumble and vault from a room above the gym. Interesting venue for children's parties.

Open: Phone for details of opening hours and prices.

BRISTOL ICE RINK

■ Frogmore Street, BS1 5NA ■ Tel: 929 2148
■ www.jnll.co.uk

Going 'down the rink' is a Bristol rite of passage. Almost every teenager who has lived in Bristol in the last 30 years

Five best...
Places to skateboard

① Dean Lane Skate Park, Bedminster.

② St George's Park Skate Park, St George.

③ Sk8 & Ride, St Philip's.

④ Hengrove Park.

⑤ Steps at Lloyds, Harbourside.

■ Brandon Hill and Cabot Tower are popular places to take the kids. Make sure the greedy squirels don't steal your lunch.

has slipped and stumbled their way round the ice while trying to look cool and attract members of the opposite sex. The ability to skate backwards helps in the rink courtship ritual, but only if you can do so without flailing your arms about like a windmill in a hurricane. Ice skating is fun, even if the skates can hurt your shins a bit and you might suffer the occasional tumble. There are various family offers and promotions available, or you can push the kids gently onto the ice and proudly watch them glide helplessly across the rink as you retire to the bar.

Open: Family sessions Sun, 10am-1pm, Thurs 8.30pm-10.30pm. **Cost:** *from £4.60 to £5.20, plus £1.30 skate hire. Check with ice rink for details of special offers.*

■ The Bristol Old Vic is kid-friendly. As well as its under-5 shows on Friday mornings, it also offers workshops and festivals.

BRISTOL OLD VIC

■ **King Street, BS1 4ED**
■ **Tel: 987 7877** ■ **www.bristol-old-vic.co.uk**

There are regular children's workshops and festivals at Bristol's main theatre. The programme is challenging and varied. You'll need to call to confirm the details or check the website. There are also shows for under-5s on Friday mornings. Best to book in advance.

BRISTOL ZOO GARDENS

■ **Clifton, BS8 3HA**
■ **Tel: 974 7399** ■ **www.bristolzoo.org.uk**

The zoo's riposte to caged-animal criticism is that it's at the forefront of conservation campaigns. It's a world leader in breeding programmes for endangered species and is active in the campaign to halt the trade in gorilla and chimpanzee bush meat in Cameroon. They might also point out that the Pelican Restaurant doesn't sell cod.

■ Wendy The Elephant was the star of Bristol Zoo. The whole city mourned when she died in September 2002.

If you visited the zoo in the mid 1960s and returned in the mid 1990s, you'd be hard pressed to notice any real change. The polar bear was still pacing up and down and had actually worn a furrow in its concrete enclosure. This sad, demented animal summed up everything that is wrong about zoos. But in recent years, there has been a radical change. Many of the larger animals (bears, giraffes, the grumpy kangaroo and the much-loved Wendy the Elephant) have gone and have been replaced by the excellent Penguin and Seal Coast, Twilight World, Zona Brazil and the Monkey Jungle. The giant tortoise enclosure is a popular attraction for the young 'uns. The gorillas do sometimes look a bit forlorn on their island, although Romina, the female Western Lowland gorilla has perked up since it was discovered that she was virtually blind and had her sight restored by a cataract operation in April 2002.

The zoo has a children's play area for toddlers and older children and the magnificent 12-acre gardens provide a safe and stimulating environment for kids. The progress made by the zoo was recognised in 2000 when it won the Zoo of the Year award. It won the award again in 2004. The zoo is particularly worth visiting out of season; it gets extremely busy in summer when most of the population of South Wales descends upon it. If you're visiting during the summer, try to get there early to avoid the rush. You can easily spend an entire day at the zoo and need a minimum of two hours to take in the highlights.

Open: Daily, 9am-5.30pm in Summer, 5pm in Winter. Last entrance is an hour before closing. Closed Christmas Day.
Cost: Adult £11, child (3-14 years) £7, under 3s free, concessions £9.70. Wheelchair-friendly.

CINEWORLD KIDS CLUB
■ **Cineworld, Hengrove Leisure Park, Hengrove BS14 0LH** ■ **Tel: 0871 2208000**
■ **www.cineworld.co.uk**
Kids pay a quid to go to the flicks on a Saturday morning. There's usually some entertainment, then a choice of three films. Under-5s must be supervised.
Open: Sat, 10am. Cost: £1, under 11-year-olds.

Five best...
Things to do at the zoo

1 Go underwater at the Seal and Penguin Coast.

2 Visit Biggie Smalls, the Giant Galapagos tortoise who was reunited with his mate in August 2003 after a separation of 25 years. Biggie is aged between 75 and 100.

3 Take a picnic and avoid the rush at the Pelican Restaurant.

4 Visit the Animal Encounters sessions and let the kids get up close to something furry or scaley.

5 Buy a season ticket: you'll start saving money after three family visits.

■ **Geoffrey's Marmosets are just one of the many fantastic attractions at Bristol Zoo Gardens.**

CITY MUSEUM AND ART GALLERY

■ **Queen's Road, BS8 1RL**

■ **Tel: 922 3571** ■ **www.bristol-city.gov.uk/museums**

The City Museum combines all the old-fashioned qualities of a civic collection (stuffed animals and bits of flint from Severn Beach) with some excellent contemporary exhibitions and regular events for children. The stuffed animals seem to fascinate kids – especially the dodo and Alfred, the gorilla from Bristol Zoo. As for the wolverine and the tiger, they are just plain scary.

■ The City Museum offers Family Fundays on the first Sunday of each month.

The museum has presence: it's as imposing and impressive inside as its magnificent Venetian Gothic facade would suggest. Hanging in the foyer is a reproduction Bristol Boxkite aeroplane, which featured in the 1963 film *Those Magnificent Men In Their Flying Machines*. It lends the entrance a surreal quality. The Egyptology gallery contains real mummies. The Family Fundays on the first Sunday of every month are popular with kids. Check with the museum for details of these and other children's events. The cafe at the back of the Museum does a special Munchkin Box and children's menu.

Open: Daily, 10am-5pm. Cost: Free.

CITY SIGHTSEEING OPEN TOP BUS TOUR

■ **Tel: 0870 4440654** ■ **www.bristolvisitor.co.uk**

Buy a 24-hour tour ticket and you can hop on and off the red bus as it wends its way past Bristol's attractions. This is an excellent way to see the city and makes an adventure of your trip through town.

Open: Apr-Sep. Cost: Adult £8.50, child £4, OAP/student £7.50. One free child per adult.

■ The stuffed animals at the City Museum: Alfred, the gorilla from Bristol Zoo, will fasinate children of any age.

CLIFTON SUSPENSION BRIDGE

■ **Leigh Woods, BS8 3PA (visitor centre)**

■ **Tel: 974 4664**

■ **www.clifton-suspension-bridge.org.uk**

The two things that everyone should do on a visit to Bristol are climb the Cabot Tower and walk across Clifton Suspension Bridge. Both expeditions are healthy, educational and free. And you'll work up an appetite so

CYCLING

Bristol isn't the best city for cycling: the combination of steep hills and heavy traffic makes it hard work cycling around the city, particularly for kids. But there are several pleasant off-road rides. The Bristol to Bath Cycle Path is 15 miles of flat cycling along the route of an old railway line. The path was built between 1979 and 1985 by Bristol-based sustainable transport group Sustrans and features a sculpture trail by artist Katy Hallett.

You can join the path at a number of clearly-marked points at Temple Meads, Broadmead, Whitehall, Easton and Mangotsfield. Among the best stopping-off points are the Willsbridge Mill nature reserve, Bitton Station which is home to Avon Valley Railway Company which runs steam trains along a short length of track, and the Bird in Hand or Jolly Sailor at Saltford.

The Ashton to Pill Cycle Route heads out of the city under the Suspension Bridge alongside the River Avon. It's a fairly easy five-mile ride to Pill, although the path can get a bit muddy in places after rain. Eventually, the path is supposed to link Bristol to the old Severn Bridge.

For off-roaders, there's an excellent Timberland Trail through the Forest of Avon at Ashton Court. It's an 11km twisty, loopy sort of ride through the Ashton Court estate and the adjoining 50 Acre Wood. There's also a pleasant ride along the banks of the Avon which you can join at the Conham River Park.

For further details of cycling in Bristol and to get hold of maps, try the addresses below or contact Bristol City Council. The Sustrans website has a cycle route directory.

- **LIFE CYCLE UK**
  Tel: 929 0440 www.lifecycleuk.org.uk
- **SUSTRANS**
  Tel: 926 8893 www.sustrans.org.uk
- **TIMBERLAND TRAIL**
  Tel: 953 2141 www.forestofavon.org.uk
- **BRISTOL TRAILS GROUP**
  www.bristoltrailsgroup.com

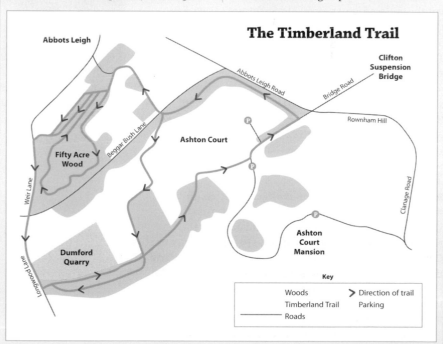

The Timberland Trail

Key

Woods	> Direction of trail
Timberland Trail	Parking
Roads	

you can gorge yourself on burgers and chips at The Mall afterwards. When you cross the bridge, call into the nearby Visitor Centre where you'll find a variety of interesting displays, models and lego for the nippers.

Visitor Centre: Open daily, 10am-5pm. Admission free, donations welcome. Free 45-minute guided tours at 3pm on Sat, Sun and bank holidays from May to Sep. Please call to arrange group tours.

■ Spy on the unsuspecting Bristol public with the camera obscura at the Observatory.

DURDHAM DOWNS, THE OBSERVATORY AND CAVE

■ **Litfield Place, Clifton Down**

■ **Tel: 924 1379**

Spend an afternoon playing football on the Downs and then take a look at one of Bristol's more curious attractions, the camera obscura and observatory near the Suspension Bridge. Originally a snuff mill, the building was partially destroyed during a gale in 1777. Apparently the sails went round so fast in the storm that the machinery caught fire. The old mill was rented to the artist William West in 1828 for use as his studio. He installed the camera obscura and cut the underground passage to St Vincent's Cave. The cave's visiting platform can be seen clearly from the Clifton Suspension Bridge, set within the sheer 250-foot cliff face. The camera obscura projects a panoramic view of the surrounding area onto a white surface inside a darkened room. A box on top of the building contains a lens and sloping mirror. Light is reflected vertically downward onto the table, giving a true (not mirror) image. The technique, which originated in the 16th Century, gives best results on bright days. Odd but fasinating.

■ Hengrove Park offers a range of playground equipment.

FERRY TRIPS

■ **Tel: 927 3416** ■ **www.bristolferryboat.co.uk**

It may be an inland port, thus rendering it useless for shipping, but all that water in the middle of Bristol supports a thriving ferry boat service. The Bristol Ferry Boat Company has been going for more than 25 years now and provides a daily commuter service from Temple Meads to Hotwells and the city centre. A boat trip is an adventure for the kids in its own right and is a great way to see the city from a different angle and get across town.

There are occasional services along the Avon to the

Avon Wildlife Park at Saltford at Easter and bank holidays and trips to Beeses Tea Gardens at Crews Hole, plus Booze Cruises and other events. A family multi-stop ticket for two adults and two children costs £17 for a day and means you can hop on and off the boats as often as you like.

HENGROVE PARK

- **Hengrove Way, next to Cineworld**
- **www.hengrovepark.com**

Skateboard and BMX ramps, a huge octagonal climbing frame plus loads more playground equipment and a separate under-5s area. There's also a good BMX and skate park at Dean Lane in Bedminster.

Open: All year. Cost: Free.

HORSEWORLD

- **Staunton Manor Farm, Staunton Lane, Whitchurch, BS14 0QJ ■ Tel: 01275 540173**
- **www.horseworld.org.uk**

A visit to this charity for rescued horses and donkeys is a must for the equine-obsessed or anybody who fancies a slightly different day out. Situated in listed Mendip Stone Farm buildings off the Wells Road on the outskirts of Bristol, there are (obviously) loads of horses and donkeys plus a video theatre, nature trail, play area, bouncy castle, shop and cafe. Available for children's parties.

Open: Daily, Easter-Sep, 10am-5pm; Oct-Easter, Tues to Sun, 10am-4pm. Cost: Adult £5.75, child (3-15) £4.75, under 3s free, family ticket (2+2) £19.50.

SNUFF MILLS/OLDBURY COURT ESTATE

A lovely wooded riverside walk along the River Frome which you can start from Eastville Park or Oldbury Court in Fishponds. There's a good play area at Oldbury Court.

Open: Daily. Cost: Free.

SS GREAT BRITAIN

- **Great Western Dock, Gas Ferry Road, BS1 6TY**
- **Tel: 929 1843 ■ www.ssgreatbritain.org**

Built in Bristol by Brunel, the ss Great Britain was the world's first iron-hulled, screw propeller-driven, steam-powered passenger liner, and the only surviving 19th-

Five best...
Surprise activities

1 Learn to climb at the Undercover Rock centre in St Werburghs.

2 Go ten pin bowling at the Bowlplex, Longwell Green; Hollywood Bowl, St Philips or Megabowl, Ashton Gate.

3 Go karting at Castle Combe or West County Karting, Winterbourne.

4 Take a dog for a walk from Bristol Dogs' Home, St Philip's.

5 Go horse riding at Kingsweston Stables, Lawrence Weston or Leechpool Riding Stables, Yate.

Century example of its type. It has now been restored and converted into a museum and visitor centre and is also available for hire as a banquet, wedding reception and conference centre. The ticket price includes entrance to the Maritime Heritage Centre (an exhibition on the history of shipbuilding in Bristol) and to The Matthew (a replica of the ship in which John Cabot sailed from Bristol to discover Newfoundland in 1497). The ss Great Britain won the Gulbenkian Prize for Museum of the Year 2006.
Open: Apr-Oct, 10am-5.30pm. Nov-Mar, 10am-4.30pm. Check for Christmas opening times. Cost: Adult £8.95, child £4.95, OAP 6.95, family ticket (2+2) £24.95, under-5s free.

■ Walk along the Harbourside and take a tour of Brunel's ss Great Britain steamship.

ST WERBURGHS CITY FARM
■ **Watercress Road, St Werburghs, BS2 9YJ**
■ **Tel: 942 8241** ■ **www.stwerburghs.org**
Same proposition as Windmill Hill City Farm (see below), but on the other side of town. Apart from the allotments and animals, there's a wildlife pond, adventure playground for the under-8s and a cafe (closed Mon and Tues). St Werburghs has the added attraction being near the highly-recommended Farm pub (see Pubs & Bars Listings, p200).
Open: Daily 9am-5.30. Cost: Free (donations welcome).

WILLSBRIDGE MILL
■ **Avon Wildlife Trust, Willsbridge Hill, South Gloucestershire, BS30 6EX** ■ **Tel: 932 6885**
■ **www.wildlifetrust.org.uk/avon**
Delightful wooded valley on the eastern fringe of Bristol. The 18th-Century mill has been restored and contains a visitor centre with hands-on wildlife and conservation displays. The woodlands are at their best in spring when they are full of flowers and birds. The ponds are important homes for frogs, toads, dragonflies and dippers. If you're lucky, you might even spot a kingfisher near the stream.

■ Blossom the Gloucester Old Spot Pig is one of Windmill Hill City Farm's most senior residents.

WINDMILL HILL CITY FARM
■ **Philip Street, Bedminster, BS3 4EA**
■ **Tel: 963 3252** ■ **www.windmillhillcityfarm.org.uk**
Windmill Hill City Farm is free, it's relaxed and it has a cafe. Admittedly, there's not much else to do in the immediate area – this is, after all, Bedminster – unless your idea of a good time is a trip to Asda. But you're only a few minutes

away by car from the docks and it's a pleasant 20-minute stroll from Bedminster through Redcliffe to Queen Square and the dockside.

The farm was established in 1976 – the first city farm outside London – on a derelict World War Two bombsite. It's a working farm with ducks and some fairly formidable geese wandering around the farmyard, and pens for calves, goats, pigs and sheep. Behind the farmyard there are larger pastures for more goats, sheep and pigs and a small nature reserve with a pond full of newts and frogs.

The rest of the farm is given over to allotments, meeting rooms, computer rooms, conference and community rooms, a nursery, adventure playground and a children's activity centre. There is also a five-a-side football pitch for the kids to play on.

The cafe serves enormous meat and veggie breakfasts as well as a full lunch menu, cakes and snacks. Sunday morning breakfast at the Farm is something of a South Bristol institution. It can get quite busy at the weekends, especially when the weather isn't good enough to make the most of the outside seating area. The cafe is occasionally open in the evenings, check for details. The farm shop was given a makeover in 2006 and the opening hours became less erratic. It sells freshly-laid hen, duck, goose and bantam eggs, frozen and fresh meat, Ecover refills, bread, a small selection of fresh veg, tinned food, dairy products and some kids' toys and trinkets.

Open: Tues-Sun, 10am-4pm. Closed Monday. Entry free, donations encouraged.

Five best...
Places to go for a walk

1 Ashton Court Estate: woods, deer park, gardens, cafe and visitor centre.

2 Blaise Castle Estate: follow the stream through the woods. Can be muddy.

3 Frome Valley Walkway: join the path at Eastville Park and walk to Snuffmills.

4 Leigh Woods: variety of walks, some on hard surfaces. Lovely display of Bluebells in April/May.

5 Kings Weston Wood, Shirehampton: walk through the woods leads to the mansion house and grotto.

■ **St Werburghs City Farm has all you need for a kids day out with the benefit of a pub nearby.**

TOP 10 DAYS OUT FROM BRISTOL

I f you fancy a break from city life, Bristol is perfectly placed to simply hop in the car or on the train and travel to any number of other great places which will help keep the children entertained. Whether you want animals, caves, beaches or countryside walks, we provide all the information you need for a great day out.

1. WESTON-SUPER-MARE

40 MINS

In the height of summer or on bank holidays, Weston can be too busy to enjoy. But out of season, it's a great place to spend a few hours. It offers loads of beach, the Grand Pier, donkey rides, pleasant sea-front walks and plenty of cafes. Weston is proper seaside; the only traditional seaside element it lacks is, er, sea – the water beyond the mud is actually the Bristol Channel.

The Weston experience comes wrapped in an atmosphere of faded elegance and seaside tackiness. OK, Weston is an acquired taste, and if you'd rather not experience the full-on kiss-me-quickness of the resort, try the long, sandy – and far quieter – beach at Brean to the south. Other attractions at Weston include the Aquarium on the Marine Parade seafront (01934 641603, www.sealife.co.uk), the Helicopter Museum on Locking Moor Road (01934 635227, www.helicoptermuseum.co.uk) or the Kidscove indoor adventure centre (01934 417411, www.kidscove.co.uk). The Tourist Information Centre is at Beach Lawns (01934 888800, www.n-somerset.gov.uk/tourism).

■ Just a quick snack before getting stuck into the candyfloss at Weston-super-Mare.

2. WESTONBIRT ARBORETUM

45 MINS

■ **Near Tetbury, off A46, Gloucestershire**
■ **Tel: 01666 880220**
■ **www.forestry.gov.uk/westonbirt**

More than 18,000 trees and shrubs from all over the world in 600 acres of beautifully landscaped countryside. There's a visitor centre, plant sales, a restaurant that does good Sunday lunches, and loads of fresh air. Westonbirt is invigorating in winter, inspiring in spring, beautiful in summer and stunning in autumn. It's also a great place to

■ Amazing what you can do with a tree and a penknife at Westonbirt.

take the kids to see Father Christmas. They make a special effort with the grotto and children are given a Christmas Tree seedling and a present. And the adults get to enjoy their lovely mulled wine while waiting.

Open: Daily, 10am-8pm (or dusk). Cost: Prices vary according to season. Adult £5 to £7.50, child £1, under-5s free.

3. SLIMBRIDGE

■ **The Wildfowl and Wetlands Centre, Slimbridge, Gloucestershire. Off the M5 at Junction 13 or 14**
■ **Tel: 01453 890333**
■ **www.wwt.org.uk/visit/slimbridge**

Formed in 1946 by artist and naturalist Sir Peter Scott (son of Polar explorer Captain Robert Falcon Scott), Slimbridge is a haven for rare waterbirds. You can view them from hides or from high up in the Sloane Observation Tower which provides fantastic views over the River Severn. There's a cinema, a wildlife art gallery and a tropical house where the hummingbirds hum.

■ Scare yourself at the sight of the Witch of Wookey underground at the Cheddar Gorge.

Open: Daily except Christmas Day, 9.30am-5.30pm (5pm in winter). Cost: Adult £6.75, child £4, under-4s free.

4. CHEDDAR CAVES AND GORGE

■ **Cheddar, Somerset, between A38 and A37**
■ **Tel: 01934 742343** ■ **www.visitcheddar.co.uk**

Some of the caves can be tricky to navigate for the very young or the elderly (Gough's Cave has 70 steps), but it's worth making the effort to explore this ancient underground world in the limestone gorge. Above ground, the Gorge offers some fine walks and rather too many scrumpy and cream tea emporiums. Jacob's Ladder is a good climb while Britain's oldest skeleton is on display at the Cheddar Man Museum.

■ Slimbridge Wildfowl and Wetlands Centre is a haven for birds and kids alike.

Open: Jul-Aug, 10am-5.30pm; Sep-Jun 10.30am-5pm. Cost: Explorer Ticket adult £11.50, child 5-15 years £8.50, under-5s free, family ticket £31.50.

5. LONGLEAT

■ **Near Warminster off the A36 between Bath and Salisbury** ■ **Tel: 01985 844400** ■ **www.longleat.co.uk**

Watching the monkeys remove loose bits of car trim and wonky aerials in the Safari Park is great fun. Until it happens to you. Longleat is a big day out. In fact, you need more than a day to see everything. The Passport ticket allows you to come back and see anything you didn't see at a later date during the same season. Apart from the Safari Park with the giraffes, zebras, elephants, lions and tigers, there's also a safari boat trip where you can see hippos and sealions. Other attractions include the Postman Pat Village, butterfly garden, maze, adventure playground, pets' corner and miniature steam railway.

Open: House and gardens open daily, 10am-5.30pm (except Christmas Day); Safari Park open daily, Apr-Nov, 10am-4pm.
Cost: Longleat Passport (includes everything), adults £19, child £15, under-3s free. Contact Longleat for prices of the individual attractions.

■ Feeding the deer at Longleat is a great fun for all the family. Be warned, your car will need a good clean afterwards!

6. AVON VALLEY PARK

15 MINS

■ **Pixash Lane, Bath Road, Keynsham, off the A4**
■ **Tel: 986 4929** ■ **www.avonvalleycountrypark.co.uk**
Adventure playground with death slide and 32-acre farm with pleasant walks along the banks of the Avon. Animals include Shire horses, Shetland ponies, deer, donkeys, llamas, wallabies and many breeds of goat, sheep and cattle. Other attractions are an undercover soft-play area, mini steam train rides, mini quad bikes, boat trips and falconry displays.

Open: Apr-Oct, 10am to 6pm. Closed Mondays except bank holidays. Open daily in school holidays. Cost: Adult £6, child £5.50, OAPs £5.50.

■ Cerne Abbas is best know for its Rude Man. Take a walk up the hill with the kids before checking out the village pubs for lunch.

7. LYME REGIS OR THE GOWER PENINSULA

2 HRS

Though 'proper' seaside is difficult to find near Bristol, these are the two of the best bits of coast within two hours of the city. Lyme Regis is a charming Dorset seaside town. A higgledy-piggledy, steep-sloped town with a small fishing harbour, good beach and the Cobb wall made famous by that Meryl Streep scene in *The French Lieutenant's Woman*. The Gower Peninsula is an Area of Outstanding Natural Beauty and boasts many fine bays and coastal walks. The high-sided Three Cliffs Bay is worth the walk down through the dunes, while the long sands of Llangollen with the Worms Head and Rhosilli at the far end provide one of the most invigorating lengths of coastline in Britain. Don't forget your camera!

8. CERNE ABBAS

2 HRS

■ **Dorset, A352 near Sherborne**

There are many splendid villages and country walks around Bristol, but there's something compelling about the simplicity of a day trip to Cerne Abbas. This is the site of the Cerne fertility giant, or rude man – the 180-foot-high man wielding a large club and erection cut into the chalk hill above the village. There's an excellent walk up to the giant while the village provides a pleasant stroll. The New Inn, Red Lion and Royal Oak all welcome kids and do good food. The Red Lion is a particularly relaxing place to read the Sunday papers and sample the Palmer's beer. The church is fascinating and there's a walk through the ruins of the Benedictine Abbey to the well and up to the giant.

■ The Roman Baths are well worth a trip to Bath for. You might just learn something.

9. A DAY OUT IN BATH

30 MINS

■ **Victoria Park, Roman Baths, American Museum**

There's so much to do in Bristol that there's really no need to travel the 13 miles down the road to Aquae Sulis. But if you do, you'll find that Bath is a very different proposition, with three attractions that can't be found in Bristol. 1) The American Museum with displays of American decorative art from the17th to 19th Centuries plus authentic furnished rooms and lovely terraced gardens. 2) Victoria Park – a fantastic kids adventure play area with big skateboard ramp. 3) The Roman Baths and Pump Room: one of the most remarkable ancient sites in Europe. A living history lesson that's fascinating for adults and kids.
For more information, see The Naked Guide to Bath.

■ Take it easy at Bowood House. There is more than enough to keep the kids busy.

10. BOWOOD HOUSE

1 HR

■ **A4 between Chippenham and Marlborough**
■ **Tel: 01249 812102** ■ **www.bowood-house.co.uk**

Country house and gardens that boasts the best adventure playground in the West for children under 12. Bring a picnic and chill out while the young 'uns wear themselves out. Most of the items, including a superb pirate ship, have been designed by former boat builder Alistair Guy. Among the recent additions are the space dive and curving tubular metal slides entered from a wooden tower.
Open: House and gardens daily, Apr-Oct, 11am-5.30pm.
Cost: Adult £7.50, child 5-15 £5, child 2-4 £3.80, OAPs £6.50.

FREE TRAIL

A FREE DAY OUT FROM WINDMILL HILL CITY FARM TO THE CABOT TOWER

① Windmill Hill City Farm
Start the day with a hearty farm breakfast and a mug of tea.

② St Mary Redcliffe Church
See if the kids can find the Church Cat's grave and the tramline embedded in the grass from a World War Two air raid.

③ City docks
Take a stroll down to the ss Great Britain and The Matthew. An impressive sight, even without having to pay the entrance fee.

④ The Arnolfini
Take the kids round the gallery or just join Cabot outside for a quiet sit overlooking the Harbourside.

⑤ The Millennium Square Fountains
On a warm day, the fountains are full of children splashing around. Remember to bring a towel.

* Bring a bag of nuts

⑥ Cathedral
Time for a snack in the refectory or a sandwich on College Green?

⑦ Georgian House
Call into this 18th-Century house which has been kept just as it was when merchant and slave trader John Pinney lived here.

⑧ Museum
If you follow this trail on the first Sunday of the month, you should find special children's activities laid on.

⑨ Brandon Hill and Cabot Tower
Climb the tower, visit the play area and dig out the bag of nuts you've carried with you all day. It's time to feed the squirrels!

Listings Pubs & Bars

B ristol, like every major British city from Aberdeen to Brighton, has undergone something of a drinking evolution in the last few years. An endless array of bars have been springing up all over the place while the number of independently-owned pubs has gradually been shrinking away.

Unless you like your ale stodgy and your seat splintered, this continental drift does have its upside as well as its downside. The best of the new Bristol bars have added a whole new dimension to the drinking experience. Places such as Severnshed, E Shed, One30 and the Lounge bars are chic, cosmopolitan alternatives to the tired old oak-and-brass Victoriana of the pub. And they've got sofas. Unfortunately, the majority of new bars are more like a cross between the cattle-market and the super-club. Okay, so it's nowhere near as easy to find a scruffy little boozer with a decent jukebox as it used to be. But if you negotiate your way around the backstreets of Clifton or Kingsdown or Montpelier, you'll find that the old-school drinking hole is still very much alive and selling peanuts out of clapped-out machines. Ancient haunts like the Cadbury, the Highbury, the Corrie Tap, The Bell, The Lion and the Hare on the Hill remain popular places for those who don't want to drink in the city centre.

Harbourside and Centre BS1

ARNOLFINI
16 Narrow Quay, Harbourside
Tel: 917 2300
www.arnolfini.org.uk
We expected something radical from the revamped Arnolfini bar when it reopened in October 2005 after being closed for almost two years as part of a massive redevelopment. Instead we got a bar that occupies the same space as before but seems a lot smaller. The Arnolfini bar is no stranger to controversy. The original bar had terrible disabled access and was designed by artist Bruce McLean who once said: 'The only reason to be an artist is to be stupid.' Some observers maintain that McLean has reinforced this statement with his design for the revamped bar. Anyway, the real attraction of the Arnolfini is sitting outside on the Harbourside on balmy summer evenings. The arrival of Bath Ales on draught in 2006 made the 'space' a lot more acceptable.

BSB WATERSIDE
U Shed, Canons Road
Tel: 922 0382
This waterfront bar has a tiled floor that gives it the feel of a Barcelona bar. But at night, the tiles are trampled by hordes of shirt and stiletto locals and it loses its Euro aura.

BRIDGE INN
16 Passage Street, St Thomas
Tel: 949 9967
This is a small pub with a big reputation for the excellent quality of its Bath Ales and guest beers and ciders.

BUNCH OF GRAPES
8 Denmark Street
Tel: 987 0500
www.thebunchofgrapes.co.uk
One of the contributors to *Naked Bristol* was a regular in the Bunch of Grapes 25 years ago and still pops in for an occasional pint today. He reckons the pub has hardly changed, maintaining its slightly boho, music and theatre credibility. The Grapes is renowned for its good beer and dodgy cover bands, and is

opposite the Hippodrome stage door, so there is a whiff of greasepaint in the air.

CORNUBIA
142 Temple Street, St Thomas
Tel: 925 4415
If you ever find yourself doubting that beer is the best drink ever, reaffirm your faith by nipping down the Cornubia for a slice of beer heaven. Despite being wedged round the back of the fire station and some office blocks, it is a must-visit pub for anyone who likes beer. As NG went to press, the Cornubia was changing hands. We are hoping they keep it true to its real ale roots.

MR WOLF'S
133 St Stephen's Street
Tel: 927 32215
www.mrwolfs.com
Offering noodles, live music and a late night bar, this is a hip and vibrant hangout bang in the centre of things. Try out the 'Gas Chamber', a drink which basically involves inhaling hot absinthe fumes and a lot of coughing.

THE OSTRICH
1 Lower Guinea Street
Tel: 927 3774
One of the largest waterside drinking spots in Bristol. Great for a sunny day.

PITCHER & PIANO
V Shed, Canons Road
Tel: 929 9652
www.pitcherandpiano.com
Housed on three floors of a converted warehouse, this self-consciously modern bar overlooking Bristol Docks has got so many sofas it's like a DFS advert. If it's so 'sophisticated', why do they need bouncers?

QUEEN SQUARE DINING ROOM & BAR
63 Queen Square
Tel: 929 0700
www.queen-square.com
Bristol might not have many Post Offices but it has got many new bars. This one is in the old Post Office building on the corner of Queen Square and provides informal dining and wining. The revolutionary mob probably didn't have this (or indeed a Post Office) in mind when they torched Queen Square in 1831. (See History, p80).

5 ESSENTIAL BARS

1. BANCO LOUNGE
Where is it? In the old Lloyds Bank building on Wells Road, Totterdown.
What's it like? Strippped wood floors, art deco lighting. Kids welcome. Very cool.
Upside: Totterdown has been waiting for a place like this for years.
Downside: It's on the busy Wells Road.
Crowd: Totterdown's chattering classes, families, singles who are 'just popping out for a pint of milk from Patcos'.

2. TOBACCO FACTORY
Where is it? On the corner of Raleigh Road and North Street, Southville.
What's it like? Unlike anywhere else in town. Relaxed, spacious, hip.
Upside: It has energised the whole area.
Downside: It's not exactly central.
Crowd: New Southvillians, boho Bemmies.

3. WATERSHED
Where is it? Harbourside.
What's it like? The coolest bar in town. It simply doesn't have to try too hard.
Upside: Location, location, location.
Downside: Stepping out into the middle of Harbourside stag/hen party.
Crowd: Hip people on their way in or out of the cinema, gay men, students.

4. SEVERNSHED
Where is it? The Grove – the more select bit of the Harbourside near the Thekla.
What's it like? Cavernous but lively. One of Bristol's slicker drinking holes.
Upside: Balcony overlooking the water.
Downside: Unisex loos confuse some folk.
Crowd: Lively mix of cocktailers, office workers and foodies.

5. MR WOLF'S
Where is it? Right in the middle of townie territory in St Stephen's Street.
What's it like? Small bar, DJs and live music. Lots of street art and photography.
Upside: Cool clientele attracted by Mr Wolf's attitude rather than its dress code.
Downside: If the music is crap, you'll suffer. At its best as an early or late venue.
Crowd: Skaters, artists, musos.

Listings

RIVER
The Watershed, 1 Canons Road
Tel: 930 0498
www.theriverbristol.com
A few weeks after it first opened its doors to the public, River picked up the Best New Bar in the South of England at the *Theme Magazine* Bar & Restaurant Awards. Owner James Savage has a habit of doing this. Having successfully kept the townies at bay (most of the time anyway), what he offers is a nice spot for some waterside drinking, and the food's not half bad either. If you actually want a seat, this is a good spot for a drink before watching a film at the nearby Watershed.

THE RUMMER
Tel: 0845 004 3206
All Saints Lane, St Nicholas Market
www.therummer.co.uk
This famous old pub is remembered fondly by Bristolians of a certain age for its cellar bar crew and live music. There are records of an inn on this site going back to a joint called the Greene Lattis in 1241 so it could be that Bristol's first pub stood where the Rummer now is. Despite its history and prominent position on the approach to St Nick's Market, the pub fell into shameful disrepair and was closed for years before being reopened in 2006 as an elegant bar and cocktail lounge. It's tastefully decorated and boasts a huge array of spirits including about 40 rums and 20 brands of gin and vodka. At the time of writing, there were plans to re-open the cellar bar.

SEAMUS O'DONNELLS
3 St Nicholas Street
Tel: 925 1283
Cool little Irish bar just opposite St Nicholas Market. A few shots of the Potreen (75% vol. Irish whisky) and you've as good as kissed the Blarney Stone.

SEVERNSHED
The Grove
Tel: 925 1212
www.severnshed.co.uk
Its cocktails are top notch and the three-hour weeknight 'happy hour' allows people of every wallet size to get in on the act. All this with a waterfront balcony. There is great European food on offer. (See Eating Out, p216).

SEVEN STARS
Thomas Lane, St Thomas
www.7stars.co.uk
There's been a pub here since at least 1760 and the Seven Stars is best known as the base for the anti-slavery campaigner Thomas Clarkson who stayed there in 1787. The clientele is traditionally a transient mixture of office workers and pre-Fleece and Firkin gig goers, but it has also built an enthusiastic following of regulars. There are usually a few guest real ales on tap and the picture is completed by dark-stained wood floors, a pool table and jukebox.

WATERSHED
The Watershed, Canons Road
Tel: 925 3845
The relentlessly popular bar of the Watershed media and arts centre is one of the most difficult places to get a table anywhere in Europe. It's no longer the cutting edge radical place it was a decade ago, but is still a cool, lively place on the water serving good food and a wide range of drinks. There are computers with free internet access in the

Five worst bar names
1. BAR HA! HA!
What's so bloody funny? Bar Ha! Ha! has to be the most irritating name ever given to anything in the history of the world. Ever.

2. BAR EXCELLENCE
It's the name your parents would suggest if you told them you were opening a bar.

3. BAR HUMBUG
The owners must have been blind drunk when they agreed to use this cringeworthy Dickensian cliche. Unbelievable.

4. TANTRIC JAZZ CAFE
Manages to combine the twin horrors of twiddly melodic meddling and Sting's favourite sexual technique in one moniker.

5. BAR ROOM BAR
Say that again please? Bar Room Bar, that's what we thought you said. Are those the only words you know or did you get stuck half way?

bar too. Sadly the Watershed does have a tendency to dumb down and do the DJ thing at weekends.

WHITE LION HOTEL
Quay Head, Colston Avenue
Tel: 925 4819
Once the waters of the Frome would have run in front of this quayside pub. Now the White Lion is an oddity – a proper pub in the middle of stiletto and theme-bar land. You can sit and watch the Centre go by. A small, one-bar Wickwar Brewery boozer, the White Lion's spiral staircase provides the most challenging journey to a pub toilet in Bristol.

ZERODEGREES
53 Colston Street
Tel: 925 2706
The concept is fine: giant glass-floored bar built around microbrewery which is spread over two floors, and serves good food and is dedicated to the local and organic ethos. The reality is a little less interesting. If it's quiet, the stark interior seems impersonal and when it gets busy with pre-clubbers, Zerodegrees becomes beer city.

Clifton BS8

ALBION
Boyces Avenue
Tel: 973 3522
www.thealbionclifton.co.uk
Stashed away down a short but sweet cobbled cul-de-sac in Clifton, the Albion is certainly a great find. With not just one but two open kitchens (one dedicated purely to pudding – yum), the focus here is on quality, but quite pricey, food. The jugs of classic cocktails are affordable and go down far too well on a warm summer afternoon sitting in the ample and peaceful outside seating area.

ALMA TAVERN
18 Alma Vale Road
Tel: 973 5171
The Alma has never been a cool pub, but it has always been a busy one. Attracting the more rugby-shirted end of the student market, this huge pub off the beaten track in Clifton boasts three large seating areas and a small garden and yet still manages to look like a scrum, especially at weekends.

AMOEBA
10 Kings Road
Tel: 946 6461
Not so much a bar-cafe as a little explosion of ideas down a street in Clifton Village. This little corner of bohemia is stuffed with off-beat art, crazy kitsch and unsettling seating. Friday and Saturday evenings offer DJs spinning funk, classic soul and beatsy jazz. With 25 continental lagers and work from different local artists.

THE CLIFTON
6 Regent Street
Tel: 974 6321
No longer a dingy dive, this is now all cosy sofas, retro flocked wallpaper and one of the finest Sunday roasts in all of Bristol. They have a whole host of rotating guest ales, such as Bath Ales and Butcombe.

CLIFTON SPORTS BAR
33-37 Gordon Road
Tel: 923 7971
This used to be the Richmond Spring and was famous with generations of students who spent their grant cheques or increased their student loans on the premises. In the World Cup summer of 2006, it rebranded as a big-screen sports bar, though it has maintained much of the character which made it such a popular haunt.

CLIFTON WINE BAR
Richmond Terrace, Queens Road
Tel: 973 2069
A large, cave-like wine bar that oozes cellar appeal. Giant oak vats and loads of nook-and-cranny seating areas add to the authentic atmosphere. Sadly, it has been known to fill up with tosspots at the weekend.

CORONATION TAP
8 Sion Place
Tel: 973 9617
www.thecoronationtap.com
For well over 100 years, committed disciples of the Church of the Fermented Apple Beverage have come here to worship. With a range of ciders wide enough to keep several generations of Wurzels happy, this one-room 19th-Century pub claims to be famous all over the world. That'll be the cider talking probably. Their celebrity drinkers include 3D out of Massive Attack.

GRAPES TAVERN
3 Sion Place
Tel: 946 7123
Small, local pub within touching distance of the Clifton Suspension Bridge, at least for those of you with 200-metre long arms. The emphasis here used to be on tradition, but it was refurbished in 2003.

GREYHOUND
32 Princess Victoria Street
Tel: 973 4187
Anyone who wandered down the corridor into the back room of the Greyhound in the mid 1980s could expect to be greeted by an art-rock army of Edwyn Collins look-a-likes. Sadly, the days when this place was the only place to discuss Belgium import Josef K singles are long gone.

HOPHOUSE
16 Kings Road
Tel: 923 7390
Large pub and cafe in the heart of Clifton village which was converted from the entrance to the arcade that runs behind it. The place has an unashamedly Blair era leisure feel to it, all airy open planning with balcony to go.

JOE PUBLIC'S
3 Queens Avenue
Tel: 973 1249
www.joepublics.com
Live music bar with unusual décor of bits of car and aeroplane. This popular student hangout is literally underground (below Habitat).

LANSDOWN
8 Clifton Road
Tel: 973 4949
The rough-round-the-edges boozer that once lorded it over every other pub in Clifton has seen its reputation fade over the last few years but at least the close proximity of the student halls of residence ensures continuing popularity. Had a bizarre interlude as a classical music bar. Celebrity fact: Buster Bloodvessel used to play pool upstairs when Bad Manners were in town.

LION
19 Church Lane, Cliftonwood
Tel: 926 8492
www.thelion.biz
The Lion has a mythical status – in the 1970s

and 1980s, this place was as trendy as it is hard to find. More Bristol bands were formed here than in any other boozer in Bristol. Now it's a perfectly agreeable local pub. You'd be more than happy to have it at the end of your street, but you wouldn't cross the city to visit it.

MALL
66 The Mall
Tel: 974 5318
Briefly, stupidly, re-named the Footbridge & Firkin, this sizeable corner pub is now defined by soft furnishings both upstairs in the smaller bar and downstairs the sprawling cellar bar. This is a popular meeting place pub for people of all ages and has good food options.

PORTCULLIS
3 Wellington Terrace
Tel: 970 6886
Built into a historic crescent, this is a rarity among Clifton pubs: a pub full of people from Clifton. Upstairs has the feel of a wine bar, downstairs is more like a traditional alehouse. Perfect for escaping all those weekend tourists.

QUADRANT
2 Princess Victoria Street
Tel: 973 6414
Despite its prime position in the middle of Clifton Village, only those in the gang used to dare enter. But now the owners of the Clifton Sausage have transformed it into a light, bright affair upstairs, with good local beer and cider, and a great wine cellar in the basement. Beware the big screens.

QUINTON HOUSE
2 Park Place
Tel: 907 7858
A boozer's boozer. At lunchtime, it fills up with suits grabbing a sandwich and a pint but in the evening this tiny side-street hideaway is packed with local drinkers. A fraternal yet almost cultish experience.

RACKS WINE BAR
St Paul's Road
Tel: 974 1626
www.racks-bristol.co.uk
Despite its pleasant terrace, this a determinedly nondescript restaurant bar with an expensive but unimaginative menu and cheesy piped music. When we went in we also found the service somewhat terse. Oh yes, and

£5.80 for a couple of bottled lagers in 'happy' hour? It's the Clifton equivalent of a mugging.

SOMERSET HOUSE
11 Princess Victoria Street
Tel: 923 7214
When we visited this refurbished Princess Victoria Street pub recently, we were surprised to see a clientele made up almost entirely of the over-60s. A freak occurrence? An OAP coach party refuelling session? We're not entirely sure. Why not send your nan along to find out.

VICTORIA
2 Southleigh Road
Tel: 974 5675
This used to be a tremendously cramped and dowdy boozer chock-full of 1950s rock 'n' roll memorabilia. Now, and in keeping with this evermore-moneyed area of town, it has been bought up by the Dawkins group and tuned into a pubish wine bar. Still feels like a local, despite all the wine.

WHITE LION CAFE BAR
Avon Gorge Hotel, Sion Hill
Tel: 973 8955
This isn't just any old hotel bar, for it is blessed with a sprawling Monte Carlo-esque drinks terrace complete with a spectacular view of the gorge and Suspension Bridge. It offers a better than the average bar menu and a small but well-chosen wine list. Is there a better way to spend a sunny afternoon than enjoying a whole oven-baked Le Pont l'Eveque cheese, freshly baked bread, a lovely bottle of wine and such a spectacular view?

Whiteladies Road
Blackboy Hill, BS8

ALIBI
96 Whiteladies Road
Tel: 973 7225
A combination of comfy sofas, sturdy wooden tables and giant plasma screens place Alibi firmly in the shabby-chic range of Bristol bars. Specialises in cocktails, spirits and has an extensive wine list. Or you can just have a beer under the day-glo pictures of Che Guevara. Open fronted, so good for watching the Whiteladies world go by.

BAR HUMBUG
89 Whiteladies Road
Tel: 904 0061
www.barhumbug.co.uk
A whole lot better than its abomination of a name suggests, Bar Humbug sits right at the heart of the Whiteladies Strip and offers hip-hop, nachos and all manner of bottled bliss to a mostly under-25 audience. Prepare to queue to get in on Fridays and Saturdays.

BEAUFORT ARMS
23 High Street
Tel: 973 5906
You'd never know it these days, but for a brief period in the 1980s, this was the hippest, mostly underage drinking hangout in town. Sadly, the smell of Country Born setting-gel has faded and the Beaufort is now just another quiet backstreet pub again.

BLACKBOY INN
171 Whiteladies Road
Tel: 940 6130
Old school pensioner chic dominates, from the age-sympathetic seating to the air of suspicion that greets anyone under the age of 65. 'I said, would you like a biscuit?'

CHANNINGS HOTEL
20 Pembroke Road
Tel: 973 3970
Come summer, anyone who is anyone in the teenage public school snogging association plays tonsil-tennis here. An absolute must for every Tim, Rick and Harry on the Clifton sixth form social scene.

COACH & HORSES
2 Highland Square
Tel: 974 5176
The largest of the just-off-Blackboy Hill pubs looks out on what optimists would call a square and realists would call a car park. Maybe this is why it used to be a popular biker pub. Traditionalists will love the decor – hundreds of paintings featuring coaches and their all-too-familiar friends, horses.

FINE LINE
59 Whiteladies Road
Tel: 973 7727
www.thefineline.co.uk
Huge, light 'n' airy cafe by day. Huge, light 'n' airy super-bar by night. Fullers' first venue

outside the capital is all polished floors
and moulded curves, but it's the enormous
French windows that really give the place
its identity. There is, however, a fine line
between sophistication and the living rooms
in *Footballer's Wives*.

HENDERSONS CHAMPAGNE BAR
135 Whiteladies Road
Tel: 970 6589
Just when it was about to be called the most
exciting new arrival on Whiteladies Road,
along come the *Daily Mail* with plans to do a
profile. In spite of this early setback and the
tacky 'ladies can drink as much wine as they
like for £7 between 9pm-2am' promotion,
Hendersons is still a great idea. And it is ideally
situated on The Strip.

HENRY AFRICA'S HOTHOUSE
53 Whiteladies Road
Tel: 923 8300
The original Whiteladies Strip super-bar
was busy shaking cocktails before any of its
neighbours had even prepared their olives. It
can get nightmarishly busy at weekends but
there is nowhere better to mix your spirits like
there's no tomorrow.

HENRY J BEANS
93 Whiteladies Road
Tel: 974 3794
www.henryjbeans.co.uk/bristol
As loud and distasteful as you'd expect a place
called Henry J Beans to be. Happy hour and
happy house collide as the dim-witted down
as much alcopop as possible without saying
a word to one another. Possibly the last place
on earth where the phrase 'a slow comfortable
screw against the wall' is still funny.

JERSEY LILY
193 Whiteladies Road
The Jersey Lily was once a cosy, but fiercely
local, pub from which it seemed far too easy
to get ejected, so quickly was the landlord
offended by youthful high spirits. It has now
been reinvented as a bright bar-cum-pub with
a couple of decent real ales, comfy sofas and
benches and a big screen for sport. It's not
quite in the gastro pub premier league but
generous portions of organic meat dishes, a
selection of fish, lite bites and a pudding club
certainly keep it in the first division.

MY BAR
Clifton Down Shopping Centre
At the top of the steps as you leave Clifton
Down station, My Bar offers regular student
discounts and promotions.

PENNY FARTHING
115 Whiteladies Road
Tel: 973 3539
Like the advert says, 'it used to be a bank,
now it's a trendy wine bar'. Or in this case
an abstractly arranged, neither-here-or-
anywhere-else pretend pub. The ultimate irony
is that it used to be a NatWest bank.

PORT OF CALL
3 York Street
Tel: 973 3600
If you can make it up the hill, you'll discover
the ideal alternative to the Whiteladies Strip
and all its associated nonsense. A stranger
to the paintbrush and the post-modern
ornament, traditionalists will love the wobbly
table legs and the below-zero temperature in
the toilets.

RED LION
26 Worrall Road
Tel: 903 0773
After spending decades undiscovered, Clifton's
scabbiest cider house has been made over and
was included in the *2006 CAMRA Good Beer
Guide*. Expect to find new-fangled comforts
such as seats, light-shades and cigarette
extinguishing facilities. A revelation.

ROO BAR
Clifton Down Station, Whiteladies Road
Tel: 923 7204
Large Australian theme pub and sports bar. Big
screen, cheap eats, too much bunting outside.

SLOANES
66 Whiteladies Road
Tel: 946 6366
Not the ultra-posh place you might expect
from the name. Sloanes is a regular kinda
bar which often features appealing drinks
promotions and has a 1am licence.

STARK
168 Whiteladies Road
Tel: 973 9522
The bar formerly known as Babushka is
a multi-level affair that holds 400 people

in kitsch-themed surroundings. Cocktails, burgers, Pieminister pies and free popcorn on movie nights set the tone. It seems impossible that many years ago this place was called the Kings Arms and even more years ago it was the roughest biker boozer in town.

VITTORIA
57 Whiteladies Road
Compact and traditional one-bar local that suffers from an overspill of overspilt builder's bellies come summer. But this is a lovely olde worlde pub from back in the day when brass wall hangings were the only art you could ever possibly need.

Park Street/Triangle
BS1/BS8

ANTIX
44 Park Street
Tel: 925 1139
Bar, cafe and club. In the evening, there is a dance floor area and comfy sofas

BAR HA! HA!
20A Berkeley Square
Tel: 927 7333
www.hahaonline.co.uk
The most irritatingly named of all the Bar Blah Blah venues and with a clientele to match. Posh students, posh chaps, posh totty and loads of other posh tosh dissolve in a hopeless fizz of Champers and hopeless un-cool.

BAROQUE
2 Byron Place
Tel: 929 9322
Formerly the Lord Byron and the Hobgoblin, this is an excitable late-licensed weekender pub full of excitable weekender youngsters bent on getting totally pole-axed and then shagged. The obligatory giant TV screen provides them with something to stare at and the hi-volume shite house takes care of the conversation. Safe.

BERKELEY
15 Queens Road
Tel: 927 9550
This Wetherspoon pub used to be a shopping arcade and still has a window display element for passing Park Street pedestrians. It's an ideal

place to meet before or after shopping but pretty ordinary after dark.

BRISTOL RAM
32 Park Street
Tel: 926 8654
What used to be the overcrowded and deeply uncool Château Wine Bar has been turned in to a relaxed Youngs-owned wood and mirrors pre-club zone. The stench of over-powering Blue Stratos and Impulse have gone. The whiff of Waggledance bitter has taken their place.

ELBOW ROOM
64 Park Street
Tel: 930 0242
www.theelbowroom.co.uk
A feast of double kissing, plants and canons, the Elbow Room is a popular, posh pool joint with a cocktail bar, DJS and nice burgers.

GOLDBRICK HOUSE
69 Park Street
Tel: 945 1950
www.goldbrickhouse.co.uk
Right in the middle of Park Street, finally we find something totally different from all the other bars and restaurants in Bristol. A collaboration between a number of local restaurateurs, the elegantly decorated Goldbrick House is a huge space, offering a cafe-bar downstairs, a Champagne and cocktail bar upstairs and restaurant with a beautifully airy terrace on the third floor. If you want to know about the history, take a look at the blog on the website which has followed the growth of Goldbrick House from its original conception all the way to completion.

MBARGO
38 Triangle West
Tel: 925 3256
Another silly name for a bar. But at least the leather sofas, marble tables, classic cocktails and loads of imported bottled beers make up for it. Students can go in what used to be The Phoenix and be certain of not getting their heads kicked in.

THE PARK
38 Triangle West
Tel: 940 6101
A couple of years ago, *Theme Magazine*, the catering industry's answer to *Wallpaper*, gave The Park a best-new-bar-in-the-West-and-

Wales award and it's not hard to see why. This is everything a modern, city bar should be – you know, distressed wood, deep leather benches, funk, jazz and hip-hop DJs and Polish vodka. It has big windows for summer drinking and it's open until 1am these days.

SQUARE BAR
15 Berkeley Square
Tel: 925 4000
Members-only 'celebrity' hangout where *Casualty* actors and media whores can earn some credibility by rubbing up against a few less-than-impressed local musicians. It's still a fantastic bar mind you. You can have drinks brought to your table all night long – truly an life-changing experience.

THE WOODS
1 Park Street Avenue
Tel: 925 0890
After suffering an avalanche of truly terrible Bristol bar names, at last the place behind the Elbow Room comes up with a funny and original one. Add press adverts showing a collection of threatening trees in silhouette and you have the concept of the year. A courtyard, a 6am weekend licence and a imaginatively-stocked bar should keep the wildlife happy.

Hotwells BS8

ADAM & EVE
9 Hope Chapel Hill
Tel: 929 1508
Upper Hotwells or Lower Clifton? It's neither here nor there. Location hasn't stopped the Adam & Eve from being hugely popular. The perfect place for a quiet sit and a read of their many books on a Saturday afternoon but gets busy later on. Get there early if you want one of their Sunday roasts.

BAG O' NAILS
141 St Georges Road
Tel: 940 6776
www.bagonails.org.uk
It's all about the beer in here. In fact, they are so committed to the stuff, they haven't even got electric lights or carpet. Landlord James Dean – yes, that's really his name – presides over a dozen guest ales and numerous bottled imports. Not a women's pub.

ELDON HOUSE
6 Lower Clifton Hill
Tel: 925 7592
www.eldonhouse.moonfruit.com
After a brief flirtation with the pre-club gay scene when it changed its name to Bar Icon, the Eldon is still popular with the gay crowd but has reverted to being a neighbourhood pub with good food and beer. Although it's not officially a Bath Ales pub, it has strong connections with the brewery and you'll usually find Gem, Spa and Rare Hare alongside well-chosen guest ales and ciders.

HOPE & ANCHOR
38 Jacobs Wells Road
Tel: 929 2987
Half-way down that hill that goes to Hotwells, you'll find the lazily hip Hope & Anchor. This is a real pub with its own identity, where the landlord chooses the sounds from his stack of classic vinyl under the bar. You might get Dexys, you might get Credence Clearwater Revival. Relaxed alternative to the more 'bubbly' Clifton pubs. The steep garden adds another dimension to the place in summer.

MARDYKE
126 Hotwell Road
Tel: 907 7499
If you'd wandered in here a few years ago, you'd have found yourself surrounded by serious bikers including some from Bristol's chapter of Hells Angels. The bikers have mainly gone now, replaced by a pool table, a giant-screen telly and *Blackbird I'll 'Ave 'E* on the jukebox. The beer is a bargain here.

MERCHANTS ARMS
5 Merchants Road
Tel: 907 0037
Mer'chant n: A Bristolian male behaving in an inappropriately lairy manner while dressed in substandard clothing. Examples: scaffolder, XR3-i racer, middle-aged slob who wants a fight. Thankfully, you won't find too many merchants in this Bath Ales pub. There's too much wood panelling and quiet real ale appreciation for yer lads.

NOVA SCOTIA
1 Nova Scotia Place
Tel: 929 7994
Traditional waterside pub that's salty enough to have a Captain's Room and old enough

to remember pirates. If you sit around long enough you might get to hear some tales of life on an ocean wave. If you sit around too long, you'll be the one telling them.

PLUME OF FEATHERS
135 Hotwell Road
Tel: 9298666
www.plumeoffeathers.com
Sitting with its back against the river, this is a no-frills, some-food-but-nothing-fancy kind of pub frequented by an established bunch of friendly locals. Topics of conversation might include the Harbourside redevelopment, the new student flats and Bristol Rovers' weak defensive axis.

PUMP HOUSE
Merchants Road
Tel: 927 9557
Surprisingly enough, this used to be an old pump house. A large, riverside pub that benefits from a south-facing patio area that gets very busy in summer. The food is good but the restaurant area feels a little like a school canteen on a busy day.

ROSE OF DENMARK
6 Dowry Place
Tel: 940 5866
www.theroseofdenmark.com
This wonderfully restored boozer is hidden away under the charmless Cumberland flyover, but is well worth seeking out. Big, bright wooden surfaces, loads of happy locals and friendly bar staff brighten the atmosphere. Upstairs, take a pew at the big tables or settle into an armchair by the massive fireplace. The airy restaurant downstairs does hearty, proper pub food and magic, inventive Sunday roasts usually cooked by the woman responsible for restoring this gem, Jess Spavins. For what is basically a roundabout with houses on, Hotwells doesn't half do well for drinking holes, and this is one of its finest.

THREE TUNS
78 St George's Road
Tel: 926 8434
Although it was sensibly refurbished to coincide with the completion of the student complex next door, the Three Tuns has since reverted into a characterful dockside pub with a quirky streak as wide as the pool table that dominates the one-bar establishment. This is

the only pub in Bristol where the menu boasts such wonders as fish fingers and chips in a basket (£2.70) and Spaghetti on Toast (£2).

Gloucester Road BS7

ANCHOR
323 Gloucester Road
Tel: 924 1769
There must have been a huge number of Australians in the Horfield area because for the last few years this place was known as Bar Oz. Following a paint job but absolutely no injection of soul, it's now the Anchor – big, busy and beered-up at weekends.

BRISTOL FLYER
96 Gloucester Road
Tel: 944 1658
This was formerly the Horfield Inn, then the Bristol Flyer and then the Goose and is now back to the Bristol Flyer again. This huge identity crisis of a pub has always had about as much appeal as one of its fruit machines: full of flashing lights, promising much, but delivering nothing.

CAT & WHEEL
207 Cheltenham Road
Tel: 942 7862
You'd be forgiven for thinking you need a tattoo in order to be allowed entry here. It's the sort of pub Daisy Duke would shoot pool in. If it were made of cloth, it would be denim. Underneath the A38 Arches it may be, but the Cat & Wheel is half-way to Alabama.

GOLDEN LION
244 Gloucester Road
Tel: 924 5006
Now that its former incarnation as Finnegan's Wake has been buried, this pub can get back to being a sizeable space for students and locals to play pool and table football again. A simple, decent boozer. Nearest boozer to the prison and so traditionally the first port of call for the newly-released.

HALO
141 Gloucester Road
Tel: 9442504
www.halobristol.co.uk
This relative newcomer has slipped easily into the Gloucester Road mindset. It's a

Listings

continental-style bar where you can get brunch, lunch or a pre-club drink on your way 'down town'. A good selection of cocktails a nice garden and regular live acoustic acts.

HOBGOBLIN
69 Gloucester Road
Tel: 940 1611
Full of students and *Venue* hacks on weekdays, known to attract gangs of shirts at weekends, the Hobgoblin is still one of the best boozers on Gloucester Road. It's been getting more studenty of late too, maybe because it has colossal ale and a colossal telly for the football.

INN ON THE GREEN
2 Filton Road, Horfield
Tel: 952 1391
A bit of a trek out the top of Gloucester Road but worth the visit. Pub food with a touch of class and a great guest range of real ale and ciders are just two of the reasons why this friendly pub was voted Bristol CAMRA pub of the year 2006. The beer garden, BBQs and quizzes all add to the essence of the place.

MAGIC BOX
135 Cheltenham Road
Tel: 970 5140
A big old pub converted from the Christadelphian Hall which had once been the Academy Cinema, the Magic Box takes its name from the film about the Bristolian inventor of the cinematograph, William Friese Greene.

PRINCE OF WALES
5 Gloucester Road
Tel: 924 5552
www.powbristol.co.uk
New owner John Gorman (not the ex-City and England football coach) is proud to offer a totally organic experience. The food (which is fantastic), the beer and the wine comes without additives. There is a great outside space too.

PROM MUSIC BAR
26 The Promenade, Gloucester Road
Tel: 942 7319
www.theprom.co.uk
The transformation of the cramped old wine bar into a Mediterranean-flavoured cafe and blues bar has hit the lower end of the Gloucester Road like a ray of sunshine.

Probably the best pub/bar refurbishment in Bristol in recent years, the Prom's capacity is bigger, its menu is bolder and its colour scheme is most definitely brighter. Friendly, relaxed, untouched by the fickle hand of fashion and home to one of the longest-running pop quiz nights on Planet Earth. Easy Mediterranean pavement cafe by day, beatific beat bar by night. Mo' better blues.

RISING SUN
86 Gloucester Road
Tel: 989 2471
Converted from what used to be one of the largest greasy chicken 'n' chip emporiums this side of Albuquerque, the name might suggest it's the city's first oriental boozer but sadly there isn't a pint of chow mein in sight. Now a Scream chain bar, this is home to gangs of teenage revellers hell bent on snogging anything that moves come kicking out time.

ROBIN HOOD'S RETREAT
197 Gloucester Road
Tel: 924 7880
The transformation of the Sherwood Forest hangout is complete. Not so long ago the only food you could find in here was the odd discarded crisp. Two smart and expensive looking make-overs later and Gloucester Road has a light and bright pub with a good reputation for its menu and beer selection.

SPORTSMAN
Neville Road
Tel: 942 7525
www.the-sportsman.co.uk
With 12 full-size eight-ball pool tables and four big-screen televisions, the Sportsman can make some sort of claim to live up to its name. Well at a push. For a backstreet neighbourhood pub it's very substantial and much livelier than you'd expect. And it's got another pub, the Annexe, and a restaurant attached to it.

TINTO LOUNGE
344 Gloucester Road
Tel: 942 0526
From the people who brought you the decidedly chilled Lounge cafe bar on North Street, Southville. Just like its south-of-the-river sister, the Tinto Lounge is a new kind of bar that buzzes with the low-decibel hum of the neighbourhood drop-in centre. With none

of the self-conscious branding that defines most new bar ventures, the Tinto Lounge manages to be a uniquely modern experience.

THE WELLINGTON
538 Gloucester Road, Horfield
Tel: 951 3022
Many people will know this as the pub in which to meet before a football or rugby match at the nearby Memorial Stadium. And it's an ideal pre-match venue with its excellent Bath Ales, spacious interior and beer garden. But there's so much more to the Wellington and a return trip on a non-sporting day is recommended when you can enjoy the Horfield Common surroundings, the food and lovely ale at a more sedate pace.

Stokes Croft BS2

ATTIC
1 Stokes Croft
www.fmbristol.co.uk
Attic stands for Alternative Technological Tourist Information Centre and is an ambitious scheme by JJ of the Prince of Wales pub on Gloucester Road (p210) to turn what used to be the goth hangouts the Full Moon and Eclipse into an 'eco-hostel'. Organic food, recycling, and a sculpture park are among the plans. Attic will become a bar, restaurant and international backpackers' hostel. Watch this space, there are exciting things to come.

THE BELL
Hillgrove Street
Tel: 909 6612
The only pub in Bristol that celebrated DJs John Stapleton and Ian Green would have even considered giving up a few hundred Tuesday nights for. The Bell is one of those pubs that doesn't have to try too hard. Possibly the best pub in Bristol.

THE CROFT
117-119 Stokes Croft
Tel: 987 4144
www.the-croft.com
The Croft has assumed the mantle of 'Bristol's most chilled club-bar', and it certainly provides Bristol club culture with a left-sided kick up the arse. It's the bar of choice for the movers and shakers who look like setting the city's next music agenda. The clientele of leftfield musos

and muses expect DJs and live acts playing everything from funk dub to alt. guitar and metal breakbeat disco. The fact that it used to have a club night called Twats' Disco suggests that it doesn't take itself over-seriously.

JUNCTION
51 Stokes Croft
Tel: 942 4470
This used to be the Beaufort Arms, a bleak, single-lightbulb dive favoured by hardcore tramps. Then some bright spark noticed that it was just across the road from the Lakota club and turned it into the pre-club venue it is today. Genius!

Redland BS6

CLYDE ARMS
129 Hampton Road
Tel: 923 7936
Depending on your viewpoint, the Clyde is either a lovely quiet street corner local or one of the most consistently boring pubs in Bristol. Conversation usually revolves around the pub's unique stained-glass windows.

KENSINGTON ARMS
35 Stanley Road
Tel: 942 4394
Easily the best pub in Redland, the Kenny is now using its original name after a brief spell as the Rat & Carrot. It's worth hiking all the way to Redland for, and you don't hear that said too often.

SHAKESPEARE
Lower Redland Road
Tel: 973 3909
A regular sort of pub with a regular sort of clientele using regulation pub tables and regulation pub seating. It's the kind of place to go to on a damp Tuesday evening in February. You know, regular.

Cotham, Kingsdown BS6

THE BELL INN
21 Alfred Place, Kingsdown
Tel: 907 7563
Not to be confused with the Bell in Hillgrove Street, Stokes Croft. Actually, it's a good idea to confuse it, because then you get to go to

Listings

two great pubs. This Bell is more local than its cosmopolitan neighbour and oozes proper pub character.

COTHAM PORTER STORES
15 Cotham Road South, Kingsdown
Tel: 903 0689
www.cothamporterstores.co.uk
At last, a cider pub within stumbling distance of a hospital! The seating, the flooring, the wallpaper and the toilet facilities count for nothing. If you come in here, it's cider you're interested in and nothing but cider (although they do serve beer now). You should have had at least two of each before going to Casualty.

DECO LOUNGE
50 Cotham Hill, Cotham
Tel: 373 2688
The successful Lounge formula is to tweak the basic concept of a continental cafe-bar to suit the particular needs of an area. So Cotham's Lounge is more restaurant than bar. It's a pleasant, split-level affair where you're spoilt for choice whether you want a three-course meal, a quick after work snifter or elevenses and smoothies with the young 'uns.

HARE ON THE HILL
41 Thomas Street North, Kingsdown
Tel: 924 6746
Another excellent no-nonsense Bath Ales pub in the lower Kingsdown/Upper Cheltenham Road area. When the Hillgrove is too crowded, a few steps to the right is all that's needed. You'll find another proper pub which is pretension and prat-free and has a great selection of bar snacks.

HIGHBURY VAULTS
164 St Michael's Hill, Kingsdown
Tel: 973 3203
One of Bristol's most celebrated drinking dens. Complete with its stark wooden flooring and stark wooden seats, the Highbury is always busy and usually full of students. But don't let that put you off. Great beer, great staff, great big garden (now with heaters).

THE HILL
33 Cotham Hill, Cotham
Tel: 973 3793
Once upon a time, this used to be Crockers, a top live music venue and one of the most essential pubs of the 1970s. Then it became an

'Irish' pub, a real good craic, fiddles-R-us. Now it's a Bar Room Bar pizzeria pub, whatever the hell that is. Don't expect authenticity.

HILLGROVE PORTER STORES
53 Hillgrove Street North, Kingsdown
Tel: 907 7267
Laid back and modestly hip boozer that attracts a genuinely varied crowd. From real ale fans to frazzled freaks, ageing hippies to youngsters who want to avoid The Bell at its busiest, the Hillgrove is more popular than ever but it somehow remains one of Kingsdown's best kept secrets.

MICAWBER ALE HOUSE
24 St Michael's Hill, Kingsdown
Tel: 926 4500
Okay, hands up, who among you has been in here or knows somebody who has been in here? Not one of you? That's because this bizarre ornamental box of a pub only exists in Dickensian times, sometimes appearing as a hallucination to drunks on St Michael's Hill.

SCOTCHMAN AND HIS PACK
20 St Michael's Hill, Kingsdown
Tel: 929 1327
The Scotchman and his pack of what? Fags? Condoms? Geese? Who cares, all you need to know is that this is a popular and friendly real ale pub that gets busy without being rammed. It has a roof terrace for summer drinking.

WHITE BEAR
133 St Michael's Hill, Kingsdown
Tel: 929 7265
Dark and insalubrious, the White Bear offers vodka deals and Black Rat cider for two quid. Not a pub for good ales, but you do still get to press a magic button during happy hour (5pm-7.30pm) to see if your drink is going to be full price, 10% off, or free. Hence its popularity with locals and students.

Montpelier BS2/BS6

BEAUFORT
21 York Road
Tel: 955 5216
A great place to go if the Cadbury House is heaving and you don't fancy the fight to get to the bar. No landlord on earth is as unflappable as Garth. Fantastic reggae jukebox.

CADBURY HOUSE
68 Richmond Road
Tel: 924 7874
The place most regularly chosen as the winner of any best pub in Bristol awards and probably quite rightly so. Always rammed to breaking point and driven by a pretty decent jukebox, it's the one thing that stops Montpelier from turning into a giant recycling centre. The Cadbury is a bit of a legend in Bristol.

OLD ENGLAND
43 Bath Buildings
Tel: 924 7870
It doesn't matter how many coats of paint they slap on, the Old E will always be known as the pub where the crusties used to go. If you go upstairs, you can still spot a few hangers-on necking cider. It can be okay in summer, when it's a popular spot to sit outside, even though the setting feels a bit like a car park.

PIPE AND SLIPPERS
118 Cheltenham Road
Tel: 942 7711
www.thepipeandslippers.com
Plush seating and nice wooden tables set the tone. With quality DJs, occasional live music and those yummy Pieminister pies to chomp on. The music in the toilet is REALLY loud like there's another party going on in there, then you step back into the real world and it's back to being background music again. Odd.

STAR AND GARTER
33 Brook Road
Tel: 940 5552
The number of lock-ins that Dutty Ken has hosted at the Star and Garter defy calculation. It seemed his penchant for a late 'un would be his undoing when he was hauled before the beak in 2005, but such was the local support for Ken that, instead of being closed down, he got a legit late licence. Now you can play pool at the Star and Garter until sunrise. A Bristol institution and a strong community pub.

St Werburghs BS2

DUKE OF YORK
2 Jubliee Road
Tel: 941 3677
This real community boozer can be spotted by the grafitti covering the outside. It has a skittle alley, games room, regular dub sessions and a nifty selection of guest ciders.

THE FARM
Hopetown Road
Tel: 944 2384
Unsurprisingly, given it is a neighbour to the city farm, this feels like a country pub in the city. Catering for the hippies and young families of St Werburghs, events are their passion, from fireworks night to New Years Eve.

MINERS' ARMS
136 Mina Road
Tel: 955 6718
Not a miner in sight but St Werburghs' biggest and most central pub isn't ready for forced redundancy just yet. The variety of local residents who drink here choose from a menu that includes cask ales, malt whiskies and decent wines. Good pub.

THE VICTORIA
40 James Street
Tel: 941 3682
Where? Not far from the bridge on the way to IKEA. The face on the sign that hangs outside is supposed to be Victoria Beckham's but it doesn't look anything like her. The pub has been getting a lot of good press for its good atmosphere and fine Sunday lunches.

Old Market BS2

OLD CASTLE GREEN
46 Gloucester Lane
Tel: 300 9140
www.oldcastlegreen.com
Years ago, this used to be a cosy sort of place with a grumpy landlord who kept a nice pint of beer and (bizarrely) cooked the best pub curry you're ever likely to encounter. It's been through loads of guises since then and is most recently a popular lesbian and gay venue with wall-to-wall music videos and a 4am licence on Fridays and Saturdays. (See Gay Bristol, p266)

OLD MARKET TAVERN
29-30 Old Market Street
Tel: 922 6123
www.oldmarkettavern.co.uk
Good homemade food, excellent 6X and a lovely beer garden make this old-fashioned boozer a popular lunchtime and early evening

destination for Old Market office workers and journalists from the *Bristol Evening Post* building. The OMT is also one of the city's leading gay pubs. (See Gay Bristol, p266).

PUNCH BOWL
23 Old Market Street
Tel: 929 4756
There used to be lots of Victorian pubs like the Punch Bowl in Old Market, but many, including the mighty Gin Palace, have fallen by the wayside. The Punch Bowl has a particularly nice tiled front. Inside it's a busy lunchtime pub and cosy in the evenings. There's a large beer garden out back.

PRINTER'S DEVIL
10 Broad Plain
Tel: 926 4290
Small, friendly pub popular with *Evening Post* journos at lunchtime and early evening. The favoured watering hole of the *Post's* famous theatre critic the late David Harrison. Truly a legend in his own lunchtime.

STAG AND HOUNDS
74 Old Market Street
Tel: 929 7048
The 'Slag' as it has been so wittily nicknamed by nearby office dwellers, stands on the site of the 12th-Century Pie Poudre open air courts which were set up to deal with petty crims on market days when Old Market was the site for the market that served Bristol Castle. The Court still existed technically until 1973 because an annual proclamation had been made at the Stag every year inviting all who had business before the court to appear. But after the 1973 proclamation, some killjoy adjourned the court and 500 or more years of tradition was dropped in favour of an underpass.

Easton BS5

BLACK SWAN
438 Stapleton Road
Tel: 939 3334
A very happening cultural centre in the heart of Easton, the Black Swan is a large pub with a huge room at the back hosting firing dance all-nighters, national dub sound systems, local bands and DJs. An important alternative venue, Bristol would be the poorer without the Black Swan.

SUGARLOAF
51 St Mark's Road
Tel: 939 4498
A busy pub on the bustling St Mark's Road. Several pool tables and a good range of real ale and cider. The Sugarloaf can be a bit gloomy indoors, but has an unexpectedly pleasant beer garden out the back. But, be warned, it's covered with 'No spliffs here' signs. There is also regular live music.

South of the river BS3/4

139° NORTH
139 North Street, Bedminster
Tel: 953 1483
This used to be the Spotted Cow, a regular old Bemmy boozer; now it's a trendy-ish bar in a Cadbury House or Farm style. It's possibly just a little too far away from the Tobacco Factory to cash in on the new south of the river chic. It's not easy bringing style to Bedminster.

APPLE TREE
27 Philip Street, Bedminster
Tel: 966 7097
One of Bristol's few remaining working-class cider houses. Dark interior, lino on the floors. Don't spill anyone's cider. A curiosity.

AVON PACKET
185-187 Coronation Road, Southville
Tel: 987 2431
www.avonpacket.com
Named after a passenger steamer from the 1860s, the Packet retains the offbeat character that it shares with many of Bristol's traditional waterside boozers. This is a friendly local with a wide range of beers, good-value home-cooked meals and a bar billiards table. The garden is surprisingly large and has a play area for nippers.

BANCO LOUNGE
107 Wells Road, Totterdown
Tel: 908 6010
The people behind the Lounge success story identified Totterdown as an area that was desperate for their 'community bar' format in 2001, but it took them more than four years to find the right building. They moved into the old Lloyds Bank in July 2006 alongside the Power Station gym. Lots of stripped wood, art deco lights, a big menu and a huge range of

drinks from smoothies to Champagne set the scene. Could Banco Lounge be the catalyst for the regeneration of the Wells Road? It's a tall order, but you never know…

BAR SALT
4-6 North Street, Bedminster
Tel: 953 1446
www.myspace.com/barsalt
In the late 19th Century, the landlord of The Star, as it was then called, kept a tiger in a cage in the bar to drum up trade. Sadly, a pissed regular entered the cage and got eaten. That's the most interesting thing about a pub which went through a series of 're-blandings' from the mid 1990s before adopting the Bar Salt persona. The décor is fairly bright in a stainless steel kind of way and there's a menu of burgers, steaks and light bites. Bar Salt is worth investigating in summer for its courtyard garden. The pool tables are housed in old stables out the back. There's a tidy roster of DJs and live music most evenings and Bar Salt has a late licence at weekends.

BOCABAR
Paintworks, Bath Road
Tel: 971 3377
www.paintworksbristol.co.uk
The Tobacco Factory is so last year – here is its west-side competition, based in the valiantly well-intentioned Paintworks 'creative quarter', whatever that means. This is a massive, airy space with random sofas, wicker chairs and garden furniture dotted about. Brazilian cocktails, unobtrusive music and some fancy lager on draught make this a mecca for media types. Now with a full kitchen, it offers the yummy but too expensive pizzas of its sister venture Bocacina. The trendification of Brislington starts (and ends) here…

CORONATION
18 Dean Lane, Southville
Tel: 940 9044
Delightful boozer. Bristol's only Hop Back Brewery pub has a thriving local crowd, but also attracts beer purists from far and wide in search of the sensational Winter and Summer Lightning, Crop Circle and other hop-laden delights. It specialises in special take-away jugs. What a great idea that is! Friendly and unpretentious, The Corrie does homemade pizzas and hosts one of the best quiz nights in town.

LOUNGE
227 North Street, Southville
Tel: 963 7340
The first of the Lounge chain spreading around Bristol. A good range of beers and wines, nice atmosphere. (See Eating Out Listings, p216).

NEW FOUND OUT
60 Green Street, Totterdown
Tel: 977 7031
Small one-room pub just up the road from the famous Totterdown boozer, The Shakespeare. It's a bit scruffy, but does a decent pint of Bass. When The Shakey gets packed, nip down here for a quieter pint.

THE SHAKESPEARE
1 Henry Street, Totterdown
Tel: 907 8818
www.theshakey.co.uk
The Shakespeare has been around since 1870. Once the home of Mad Ern and his less chaotic partner Sane Joan, the Shakespeare used to be the most peculiar pub in Bristol. Ern is long gone, yet The Shakey has retained some of his character and the DJ den he built in the middle of the pub. It's a loud, smoky pub with good beer, organic Sunday lunches and is the centre of a vibrant local scene. You'll either love it, or wonder what the fuss is about.

TOBACCO FACTORY
Raleigh Road, Southville
Tel: 902 0060
www.tobaccofactory.com
The bar that' is responsible for changing the face of South Bristol. (See Eating Out, p216 and BS3, p30).

THE WINDMILL
14 Windmill Hill, Bedminster
Tel: 963 5440
www.thewindmillbristol.com
The trendy young types of South Bristol have been crying out for a spot like this for ages. Run by the Pipe and Slippers (see p213) crowd, they have worked out exactly what their fashionably-tousled crowd want: Pieminister pies, tapas, groovy music, organic lagers, good wines, a courtyard and a non-smoking area that doubles up as a crèche. It can sometimes get a bit noisy downstairs – which is the kids' fault, not the adults – though it is a very welcome addition to the, frankly, dull pub scene around these parts.

Listings **Eating Out**

A couple of years back, *Sunday Times* food critic AA Gill described Bristol as 'a place where a tin of Heinz tomato soup passes for sophisticated grub'. Does he have a point? No, of course he doesn't. Some of you might say that AA Gill was a pompous, selectively educated tosser who wouldn't recognise a perceptive piece of cultural analysis if it came up to him and pissed in his gaspacho.

Bristol might not have the range of celebrity-endorsed eateries that London now boasts, but who wants to book a table six months in advance just so they can sit within chewing distance of Neil Morrisey anyway? Bristol's eating out scene has undergone a similar explosion to the one that lifted London out of its pie-and-mash past but on a much smaller scale. We've seen the arrival of the aloof post-modern dining experience with restaurants such as Riverstation and Severnshed but nothing with a pretentiousness rating of, say, The Ivy.

What the city has now that it didn't have before is more choice. It's easy to find not only French, Indian and Italian cuisine but North African, Portuguese and Japanese these days. And if AA Gill thinks this amounts to the culinary equivalent of a tin of Heinz tomato soup, then he's clearly not familiar with the concept of a whole wide world of food.

Harbourside, Centre BS1

ARBI 'N' TAP
The Corinne Marin, Narrow Quay
www.arbintap.co.uk
Arbi 'n' Tap started life as a coffee bar and boutique but has extended its culinary repertoire to include a full-on Mediterranean-influenced evening menu.

BOCANOVA
90 Colston Street
Tel: 929 1538
The flavour here is very definitely South American. Owner Humberto Benevenuto serves authentic Brazilian fish dishes in an atmosphere that has more to do with the subtle bossanova than the flashy samba.

BORDEAUX QUAY
V Shed, Canons Way
Tel: 906 5550
www.bordeaux-quay.co.uk
This ambitious project, which incorporates a restaurant, brasserie, bar, deli, bakery and cookery school, is the brainchild of Barney Haughton, head honcho of Quartier Vert on Whiteladies Road (see p224). He applies his QV philosophy of locally-sourced produce, but at BQ, Haughton sets his aims higher by introducing zero waste objectives and responsible energy consumption. The food in the restaurant upstairs is exceptional while the bistro downstairs is great for informal (and cheaper) dining. Despite being on the Harbourside alongside a host of dreadful bars, BQ manages to offer both class and relaxation.

BYZANTIUM
2 Portwall Lane
Tel: 922 1883
www.byzantium.co.uk
Byzantium conjures up an exotic cocktail of North African and Middle Eastern cuisine in a warehouse-sized entertainment palace where magicians and belly dancers float between the tables. The 'food lanterns', consisting of six starters, are particularly popular with the regular punters.

CITY CAFE
Temple Way
Tel: 910 2700
www.citycafe.co.uk
This wonderful cafe inside the well-respected City Inn has a great reputation in Bristol. Foodwise, it offers a menu that changes with the seasons as well as a wide range of vegetarian and healthy-eating options. Their wine list is huge too. A great spot. Not your average hotel cafe.

CONRAD AT JAMESONS RESTAURANT
30 Upper Maudlin Street
Tel: 927 6565
www.conradatjamesons.co.uk
One of Bristol's most established restaurants, Jamesons had started to look a little dated until brothers Simon and Conrad Lynton-Jenkins took over a while back. The wallpaper may have changed but the commitment to quality cuisine remains the same.

DYNASTY
16a Thomas Street
Tel: 925 0888
When Wendy Ho decided to open a restaurant in Bristol, she didn't do anything by half measures. She housed Dynasty in a glittering oriental ballroom, flew her head chef in from Hong Kong and laid on an authentic menu so vast it takes at least 15 minutes to read. In 2006, *The Observer* voted Dynasty as one of the top five Chinese restaurants in the UK. And very well-deserved too.

EL PUERTO
57 Prince Streeet
Tel: 925 6014
www.el-puerto.co.uk
Boasting the biggest and most authentic tapas selection in town, El Puerto also has regular Flamenco nights.

FIREHOUSE ROTISSERIE
Anchor Square
Tel: 915 7323
www.firehouserotisserie.co.uk
Chef and owner Richard Fenton spent many years in Hollywood catering for the likes of Burt Bacharach, Tina Turner and, er, Midge Ure. It's no surprise, then, that the Bristol version of the Bath eatery does the best spit-roasted chicken in the city.

5 LEGENDARY LATE-NIGHT TAKE-AWAYS

1. RITA'S
94 Stokes Croft
Tel: 924 9119
You haven't lived until you've stumbled into Rita's at 2am and ordered a huge portion of chips which you spill on the floor all the way home, just like Hansel and Gretel out on the piss.

2. FALAFEL KING
The Blue Van, St Augustine's Parade
You should be able to find him somewhere near the Neptune statue at the Centre. This is tasty, filling and, most remarkably of all, pretty healthy stuff. The Falafel King is the forward-thinking stomach's alternative to grim burgers and fries. So you won't feel quite as bad in the morning.

3. SLIX FAST FOODS
89-91 Stokes Croft
Tel: 924 8743
This place used to be the coolest burger bar in town. It was somewhere to hang out and look tough and put tomato ketchup on your burger in an aggressive manner after Lakota. How sad is that?

4. TRIANGLE KEBAB HOUSE
3-4 Triangle South
Tel: 927 3097
Perfectly situated on the Triangle, this kebab house is an old favourite if you're in the city centre a little worse for wear and the only thing that will hit the spot is a kebab. If you like your supper to drip down your chin and all over your shirt, this could be just the place for you.

5. CENTRE SPREAD
3-4 St Augustine's Parade
Tel: 929 3712
It's feeding time at the zoo and every Trev, Dave, Maxine and Sharon from miles around comes in here. 'Ere, are you looking at my chips? Outside. Now!' and 'I ain't got no friggin' relish!' are just two of the regular phrases you may hear used. Not exactly a classy joint but it does the job!

Eating out

Listings

FUCHSIA
Nelson House, Nelson Street
Tel: 945 0505
www.fuchsia-bristol.com
Re-opened in 2006 under the ownership of
George Lai, this is a classy joint which seems at
odds with its Broadmead surroundings. Offers
classic menu of regional Chinese dishes.

GLASS BOAT
Welsh Back
Tel: 929 0704
www.glassboat.co.uk
Floating restaurant whose novelty value wore
off about 100 years ago but whose menu
continues to attract high praise from most
quarters. If you come here, remember that
people on glass boats shouldn't spit olive pips.

GOLDBRICK HOUSE
69 Park Street
Tel: 945 1950
www.goldbrickhouse.co.uk
Cafe, Champagne and cocktail bar and
restaurant. (See Pubs and Bars, p200).

LA GROTTA
7 Union Street
Tel: 929 0466
Forget about deep pan, stuffed crust, ham and
pineapple and all those other abominations,
if you want real pizza, say 'buon giorno' to
Alfonso and Anita. This place is as Italian as a
Franco Baresi tackle. But much friendlier.

IL BOTTELLINO
22 Bond Street
Tel: 926 8054
Excellent family-run pasta house and
pizzeria offering impossibly cheap lunchtime

alternatives to the soggy sandwich and the
stale hamburger. Pity it overlooks a dual
carriageway. In 2006, they opened another
branch in the old police station in Bedminster.

KATHMANDU
Colston Tower, Colston Street
Tel: 929 4455
When Paul McGann heard that his favourite
Indian and Nepalese take-away was to become
a restaurant, he was only too happy to be
the guest of honour on the opening night.
Importing their own spices from Nepal, this is
authentic and truly enlightening.

MATAZI
13 Small Street
Tel: 927 7937
Quality Lebanese and North African restaurant
in a vaulted cellar. Good selection of Lebanese
wine, prices are reasonable and the lunchtime
buffet is of belly-busting proportions.

MUD DOCK CYCLEWORKS & CAFE
The Grove
Tel: 934 9734
www.mud-dock.co.uk
When the Mud Dock first opened, the owners
admitted that 'the details of setting up the
cafe were minor in comparison to issues such
as which pumps and inner tubes to order'.
Ten years and several awards later, this easy
Mediterranean oddball is a testament to the
value of not trying too hard. The food can be
pricey but generally worth it.

NEW WORLD
Frogmore Street
Tel: 929 3288
www.newworldgroup.co.uk

Vegetarian and vegan Bristol

Although there are very few completely
vegetarian (and even fewer vegan)
restaurants, cafes and takeaways in Bristol,
most places do have decent options for the
vegetarian and there is, nowadays, plenty on
offer for vegans too.

The city's dedicated veggie places
include Cafe Maitreya in Easton, One
Stop Thali Cafe in Montpelier, Tiffins on St
Michael's Hill, Riverside Garden Centre Cafe
in Ashton, Kebele Cafe (vegan) in Easton

and Cafe Kino (vegan) in Stokes Croft. The
wonderful Royce Rolls in St Nick's Market
doesn't sell meat but does use fish in its
lovely rolls and bagels.

We've highlighted in the listings text
other places which particularly cater for
the veggie palate, but if you want an in-
depth guide, there's an excellent *Vegan
Guide to Bristol* which adopts an admirably
broadminded approach to the subject.
The guide is in print and online. For more
information please visit:
www.veganbristol.makessense.co.uk

If a combination of an all-you-can-eat Chinese buffet and karaoke constitutes your ideal night out, look no further.

OBENTO
60 Baldwin Street
Tel: 929 7392
Japanese restaurant that specialises in Bento boxes (a sort of Japanese lunch box) as well as sushi, noodles and more. It also offers a lunchtime express menu which has proved popular with the locals.

OLD INDIA
34 St Nicholas Street
Tel: 922 1136
www.oldindia.co.uk
Set in the Victorian splendour of Bristol's former stock exchange, Old India is worth a visit simply for the surroundings. But this place isn't just about location, it has one of the most innovative selections of contemporary and traditional Indian fare in town.

OLIVE SHED
Princes Wharf
Tel: 929 1960
www.therealolivecompany.co.uk
This instantly popular place typifies the bold new spirit of Bristol's restaurant renaissance. Offering fine views of the harbourside, the Olive Shed sighs with the aroma of the deepest Mediterranean flavours.

OVER THE MOON
117 St George's Road, College Green
Tel: 927 2653
76 Victoria Street, Redcliffe
Tel: 922 6688
Robert Anderson and Nicki Brown are chuffed to bits, pleased as punch. In short, they are over the moon. Their Redcliffe restaurant was so popular, they opened another. A sign above the door says: 'The management reserves the right to refuse admission to anyone with a miserable disposition.'

RISTORANTE DA RENATO
19 King Street
Tel: 929 8291
The sister restaurant of the much-loved La Taverna (see below) opposite, this is an altogether quieter affair offering genuine Italian fare in a warm, cosy atmosphere right in the heart of buzzing King Street.

RIVERSTATION
The Grove
Tel: 914 4434
www.riverstation.co.uk
When Riverstation arrived in December 1997, Bristol had never had a diner quite this sophisticated before. And while the sleek glacial edges may be a little blunter these days, it's still the most modern European diner anywhere in Bristol. If you don't want to eat, you can just go for a waterside drink.

SAN CARLO
44 Corn Street
Tel: 922 6586
www.sancarlo.co.uk
This is a huge, hectic and, at times, horrendous modern eatery complete with vast and very impressive menu and authentic sneering Italian waiters. It is best to avoid Friday and Saturday nights if you like to be able to hear yourself chew.

SEVERNSHED
The Grove
Tel: 925 1212
www.severnshed.co.uk
Housed in one of Isambard Kingdom Brunel's boathouses, this is home to Europe's only floating bar, a 360-degree rotating miracle on hydraulics. Its cocktails are top notch, and the three-hour weeknight 'happy hour' is a stroke of beautiful benevolence. The balcony overlooks the harbour, and you can get excellent modern European food.

SPYGLASS
Welsh Back
Tel: 927 2800
www.spyglassbristol.co.uk
With one half on the water and the other on dry land, Spyglass is a big hit in the summer. This is al fresco eating at its most appealing, with the simple barbecue and grill menu given added spice by the dream location.

RENATO'S LA TAVERNA DELL'ARTISTA
33 King Street
Tel: 929 7712
This pizzeria and bar is the more lively alternative to its sister restaurant Renato's (see above) across the road. Being next door to the Old Vic, it is no surprise that the walls are hung with autographed pictures of actors.

Eating out

Listings

Clifton, Hotwells BS8

BRIDGE CAFE
Avon Gorge Hotel, Sion Hill, Clifton
Tel: 973 8955
www.thebridgecafe.co.uk
With spectacular view of Clifton Suspension Bridge, you can enjoy a classy meal chosen from an interesting menu offering more than just the usual – smoked trout and Champagne risotto anyone? You can even order your own roast prior to your visit.

BRUNEL WINE BAR
38 The Mall, Clifton
Tel: 973 4443
A friendly local wine bar that's worth checking out for the interesting range of tapas. Ideal starting point for a night out in the Village.

CHI CHINESE CUISINE
21 Regent Street, Clifton
Tel: 907 7840
www.chi-chinese.co.uk
Specialising in Pekinese and Cantonese cuisine, Chi offers an extensive selection of dishes, including such favourites as aromatic Peking duck or stir-fried squid with ginger and spring onions. Be prepared for a very friendly welcome from the proprietors, the Lau family.

CLIFTON SAUSAGE
7-9 Portland Street, Clifton
Tel: 973 1192
www.cliftonsausage.co.uk
This used to be the much-loved family-run Greek restaurant Bouboulinas, now it's a non-smoking eatery specialising in English regional dishes such as beer-battered haddock, boiled Cotswold ham with parsley sauce, griddled Cornish scallops and toad in the hole cooked with your own choice of quality sausage.

CREATE CAFE
Smeaton Road, Cumberland Basin
Tel: 903 1201
Off the beaten track, but usually busy with workers and visitors to the Create Centre. The breakfasts are substantial and there are daily lunchtime specials as well as the standard cafe fare. All tea and coffee and many ingredients are fairtrade. They also offer good veggie options too.

LA DEMI LUNE
118 Hotwell Road
Tel: 927 7112
www.spring-gardens.co.uk
This used to be the Spring Gardens pub, which has always had an excellent reputation for food, but they have ditched the pub idea to focus on the food. You could be mistaken for thinking this is still a pub, as the bar stands proud in the centre of the room, along with regulation pub dog and morose regulars. But around it now sits an elegant restaurant, with the garden offering sheltered al fresco dining.

DUSK
St George's Road, College Green
Tel: 925 1115
www.dusk-bristol.com
Although it's best-known for its steaks (24oz T-bone anyone?), this modern and stylish eaterie also does a lunchtime express menu, famous Sunday roasts and fresh fish.

FISHERS RESTAURANT
35 Princess Victoria Street, Clifton
Tel: 974 7044
www.fishers-restaurant.com
There is no sign of diminishing European fish stocks here. The appropriately-named Fishers has been so busy, they were forced to create additional seating upstairs. Sink your harpoon into shark, barracuda or skate.

FREDDIES
40-44 St Paul's Road, Clifton
Tel: 973 4214
Languishing underneath the Westbourne Hotel, Freddies is a laid-back bistro given real elegance by its cosy alcoves and a stunning subterranean garden.

HERMANOS
55 Queens Road, Clifton
Tel: 929 4323
Just when you thought Bristol was saying no more to tapas, along comes a southern European bar offering light Greek, Spanish and Italian finger-foods. Sound familiar? Fear not, it's authentically executed and offers soups, salads and Pieminister pies too.

HOWARDS
1a-2a Avon Crescent, Hotwells
Tel: 926 2921
www.howardsrestaurant.co.uk

Howards was run for more than 25 years by Chris Howard and became one of Bristol's most select diners. The Jamesons took over in 2003 and have maintained the quality as well as introducing a daytime bistro menu.

KRISHNA'S INN
4 Byron Place, Triangle South, Clifton
Tel: 927 6864
www.mcdosa.com
Top-quality south Indian restaurant with a particularly good veggie and vegan selection.

LOCKSIDE
1 Brunel Lock Road, Cumberland Basin
Tel: 925 5800
www.lockside.net
The peculiar pre-fab building on stilts tucked underneath a flyover used to be a famous greasy spoon and was the location for Sid's Cafe in *Only Fools and Horses*. But since 2004, it has become one of Bristol's most pleasant family eateries. Perhaps in recognition of its transport caff roots, Lockside is open from 7am on weekdays (8am Sat, 9am Sunday) so it's ideal as a dockside breakfast location and equally appealing for candlelit dinners. Informal, relaxed and friendly.

MA PROVENCE
2 Upper Byron Place, Clifton
Tel: 926 8314
Another Bristol success story. Despite being hidden up a sidestreet just off the Triangle, it's almost impossible to get a table here without booking in advance. Blame the superb home-cooked French cuisine.

NEW EMPEROR COURT
Portland Street, Clifton
Tel: 973 1522
www.newemperorcourtrestaurant.co.uk
Award-winning chef Thanh Que Vien has been serving up high-quality Peking, Szechuan and Cantonese food in Clifton Village for longer than he cares to remember. A simple, authentic Chinese restaurant.

PEARL OF SRI LANKA
3a Regent Street, Clifton
Tel: 973 9937
www.pearlofsrilanka.com
With an interesting menu, this Sri Lankan restaurant comes highly recommended by the locals. A surprising amount of veggie options.

TOP 5 GREASY SPOONS

1. YORK CAFE
1 York Place, Clifton.
Tel: 923 9656
An eclectic mix of truckers, trendies and students have flocked here for generations to down the legendary hangover-curing monster breakfasts. The last time *Naked Bristol* visited the York Cafe, you could get a Budget Breakfast for just 99p. The cafe was an undertakers' shop until 1926 when it became the York Restaurant. It has been in its present form since about 1969. This is the best greasy spoon in Bristol and anyone who tells you otherwise is an imposter, a charlatan and a fool. Belching is forgiven.

2. THE FRIARY
2 Cotham Hill
Tel: 973 3664
One of Bristol's longest-established cafes that thrives on its uniquely friendly atmosphere. The long benches mean you inevitably have to eat one of their famous breakfasts with someone you've never met before. An interesting start to the day.

3. BRUNEL BUTTERY
Wapping Wharf, Harbourside
Tel: 929 1696
This dockside snackbar is home to the best bacon butty in Bristol. Sit outside and enjoy one on a Sunday morning. Mind the gulls!

4. METRO
218 Gloucester Road, Bishopston
Tel: 924 9736
If this is part of a new breed of 21st-Century greasy spoons then fans of buckled cutlery and brown sauce stains are in trouble: you're not even allowed to smoke. Even outside. Beware false prophets wielding bacon sarnies.

5. GREG'S CAFE
141 Wells Road
Tel: 977 6639
Proper transport caff that opens early and closes by about 3.30pm. There's a big menu of breakfasts and lunches with a daily specials board. The homemade pies are recommended. No frills, no-nonsense.

Eating out

Listings

PIZZA EXPRESS
31 Berkeley Square, Clifton
Tel: 926 0300
35 Corn Street
Tel: 930 0239
2 Regent Street, Clifton
Tel: 974 4259
www.pizzaexpress.co.uk
Long-established pizza chain that hit the headlines a while back when they reduced the size of their pizzas after floating on the stock exchange. Size issues apart, they are still streets ahead of the other big non-Italian pizza houses. Numerous local musicians have earned a crust in the Berkeley Square branch.

PIZZA PROVENÇALE
29 Regent Street, Clifton
Tel: 974 1175
www.pizzaprovencale.co.uk
Not exactly authentic Italian but still an excellent pizza house. Decked out with wooden seating and wooden tables, the place has the feel of one of those farmhouse restaurants you accidentally wander into on holiday. Pizzas, pastas and pancakes.

PRIMROSE CAFE
1 Boyces Avenue, Clifton
Tel: 946 6577
Hidden away in a quiet corner of Clifton, the Primrose is an organic cafe by day and in the evening it transforms into an intimate candlelit BYO diner. Excellent breakfasts while Cornish fish is the speciality in the evening.

RACKS
St Paul's Road, Clifton
Tel: 974 1626
www.racks-bristol.co.uk
Long-established Bristol favourite with a large terrace. A popular student choice for a spot of tucker before a night on The Strip.

RUCOLA
59 Apsley Road, Clifton
Tel: 973 4892
It might only be an avocado stone's throw from the main drag but tapas and mezze emporium Rucola operates on a far more serene level than the rest of the busy Whiteladies Road. That said, the clean lines of the stripped wooden floor and the sharp chrome seating make breakfast, lunch and dinner a thoroughly modern affair.

SANDS
95 Queens Road, Clifton
Tel: 973 9734
www.sandsrestaurant.co.uk
Sands is one of Bristol's most remarkable restaurants. When owner Raad Hassan took over in 2001, he set out to provide the complete Lebanese eating experience. As you walk in, you feel as if you've swapped continents; dim smoky lighting reveals a cavernous tomb-like cave complete with stone floor and rounded sandy walls. The food is spicy and often unfamiliar; the post-meal bongs do not have any dope in them.

SIAM HARBOURSIDE THAI RESTAURANT
129 Hotwell Road
Tel: 330 6476
www.siam-thai.co.uk
Big on choice and bigger on service; from crab claws to chicken satay, duck curry to smoked fish, the Siam has added a much-needed promise of the exotic to the Hotwells menu.

SS GREAT BRITAIN CAFE
Great Western Dockyard, Gasferry Road
Tel: 926 0680
www.ssgreatbritain.org
Snacks, paninis and baked potatoes may not be at the cutting edge of Bristol's gastro scene, but the pleasant Harbourside location is the main attraction here.

WALRUS AND CARPENTER
1 Regent Street, Clifton
Tel: 974 3793
www.thewallybath.co.uk
Following the success of this Bath institution, this popular family business has expanded into Bristol. This is identical, in look and menu, to the Bath version, but I suppose, if it ain't broke, don't fix it.

Blackboy Hill, Whiteladies Road BS8

BANGKOK HOUSE
70 Whiteladies Road
Tel: 973 0409
For 30 years, this was the House of Wong but, in 2005, it shifted the emphasis from Chinese to Thai food. Good vegetarian selection.

BOOP CAFE
16 Lower Redland Road
Tel: 973 7372
Tucked away off Whiteladies Road, this small cafe and sandwich shop asks more questions than it answers about why it celebrates Betty Boop. But if you want to wake up with Betty, this is just the place for tea, toast and a modest fried breakfast.

BUDOKAN
Clifton Down, Whiteladies Road
Tel: 949 3030
31 Colston Street
Tel: 914 1488
www.budokan.co.uk
Christopher Wicks, the guy behind Bell's Diner and One30 has taken over at Budokan. Things are basically the same – eating noodles on communal benches – but with Wicks behind the wheel, I bet the food will be one hell of a lot nicer. Budokan specialises in the peasant food of Japan, Thailand, Malaysia, Indonesia and Singapore.

CAFE COSMOPOLITAN
147 Whiteladies Road
Coffee, juice and paninis aplenty. Outside seating adds the European dimension.

CLIFTON TANDOORI
211 Whiteladies Road
Tel: 973 2491
This is one popular Indian restaurant and take-away. Being one of the closest eateries to the halls of residence across the Downs, it caters for a regular student clientele. The benefit is is that it offers sensible prices to match and 10% NUS discount.

COLLEYS SUPPER ROOMS
193 Whiteladies Road
Tel: 973 0646
www.colleyssupperrooms.co.uk
One of the most unforgettable dining experiences in town. A meal here is based on an Edwardian dinner party theme, so there's just one sitting per evening with everyone turning up at the same time. The meal starts with a selection of hors d'oeuvres followed by soup and a choice of two entrees (such as roast tomatoes with asparagus and grilled goats cheese or chicken thighs). Then there's sorbet to clear the palate before you get stuck into the main course, which is typically a

choice of roast leg of pork, pan fried calf's liver, poached cod or oyster mushroom wontons with sticky rice in ginger and coriander broth. Puddings are then paraded around the room and after you've eaten them, you're offered some cheese. Tremendous value at around £28 for the lot, or £16 for a 'lite' lunch version.

DEASON'S
43 Whiteladies Road
Tel: 973 6230
www.deasons.co.uk
This used to be legendary Bristol drummer Dave Francolini's parents' place. It was classy then and it's classy now, with chef Jason Deason combining the classical and the experimental in a menu that changes with the seasons. *Good Food Guide* recommended.

FISHWORKS
128 Whiteladies Road
Tel: 974 4433
www.fishworks.co.uk
Following on the success of chef Mitchell Tonks' original Bath restaurant, this emulates the winning, if wallet-busting, formula of the freshest fish, finely cooked. If students get taken to Fishworks by visiting parents, they know there's still cash in the family kitty. If they are treated to a take-away fish supper from the more modest Fishers (p220) up the road, the folks are probably brassic. The taramasalata at Fishworks comes highly recommended.

OCEAN CAFE
185 Whiteladies Road
Tel: 946 9825
www.ocean-cafe.co.uk
Estate agent takes over building next door when Caribbean restaurant closes and opens tapas bar to great critical acclaim. There's gotta be a gag in there somewhere. The Ocean Cafe is small, but relaxed, and serves an authentic range of tapas although the portions are a bit small. Food ranges from breakfast snacks to whole roast suckling pig for parties of six or more (order in advance). Still no gag. Damn!

PLANET PIZZA
83 Whiteladies Road
Tel: 907 7112
www.planetpizza.co.uk
Small, brightly-coloured pizza joint where the front-of-house terrace makes it an ideal people-watching place in summer. And yes,

Eating out

the pizzas are named after the planets. They have a sister restaurant in Gloucester Road.

QUARTIER VERT
85 Whiteladies Road
Tel: 973 4482
www.quartiervert.co.uk
Previously known as Rocinantes, this is a pioneer of local organic produce. A bakery, catering service and cookery school complete the service. Eat out on the terrace, in a light and airy ground floor or a mellow upstairs dining room. They have even cooked for Prince Charles at Highgrove, don't you know. In 2006, owner Barney Haughton opened a adventurous new venture on the Harbourside called Bordeaux Quay (p216).

RAJPOOT
52 Upper Belgrave Road, Clifton
Tel: 973 3515
www.rajpootrestaurant.co.uk
Elegant Indian restaurant with courtyard set over two levels in the basement of a Georgian townhouse facing the Downs. The Rajpoot is rated by many as being among the finest Indian restaurants in town and is in a fabulous location. Prices are reasonable, there's a good choice of fish, vegetarian and vegan dishes.

RENATO'S NUMERO UNO
203 Whiteladies Road
Tel: 974 4484
Like the current Italian football team numero uno, Gigi Buffon, Renato's is an easily loveable keeper of the faith. Owner Renato Fucci has spent 11 years at the top of Whiteladies Road and his commitment to authentic Italian food at reasonable prices has been unwavering.

PICTURE HOUSE
44 Whiteladies Road
Tel: 973 9302
www.whiteladiespicturehouse.com
Nothing typifies the changes on Whiteladies Road more than the Picture House. It was once called the Dog & Duck and was the anonymous sort of place you drifted into by mistake. Since 2004, it's been the ultra swish Picture House where you can enjoy first-rate food in tapas-sized portions. There's a strong local flavour to the menu and the Barrow Gurney Aberdeen Angus with all the trimmings is among the city's most famous Sunday lunches.

TOP DRAWER CAFE AT MASKREYS
62-64 Whiteladies Road
Tel: 973 8401
It's worth climbing the many stairs through one of Whiteladies Road's poshest furniture shops to discover this cafe on the top floor. The food (served 11.30am-3.30pm) is pleasant light lunch fayre, but it's the small roof terrace that makes the Top Drawer a joy. The best high-level, al fresco experience on Whiteladies Road. And free from the Saturday crowds, which can't be bad!

ZIO'S
96a Whiteladies Road
Tel: 923 8105
Distancing themselves from the legions of American-owned fake Italian pizzerias, Zio's attempts to bring the spirit of the old country onto the high street. This means authentic pizza, pasta and seafood, and waiters who sound like Roberto Benigni.

Park St, Triangle BS1/8

BEIJING BISTRO
72 Park Street
Tel: 908 5468
This plush, carefully-lit, two-level noodle bar has gained a reputation to match its polished surfaces. And with all dishes costing about six quid a pop, you won't break the bank.

BOSTON TEA PARTY
75 Park Street
Tel: 929 8601
This is a great space. Two floors (one with sofas) and a garden out back. A bit on the pricey side for a toastie and often packed with posh students at lunchtime but the toasted sandwiches are good. This is great place to have a coffee and read a book out of peak hours when the students should be in class.

BROWNS
38 Queens Road
Tel: 930 4777
www.browns-restaurants.com
It's easy to feel lost in this cavernous former student refectory. In most respects, Browns typifies the multi-national chain restaurant experience. It's either cold, empty and hollow, or hot, packed and shallow.

CHILLIS TANDOORI
39 Park Street
Tel: 949 9884
Chillis is not your average Park Street joint. Not many places on Bristol's most elegant hill offer Indian, Pakistani and Bangladeshi cuisine at prices that make it affordable to students.

FOLK HOUSE CAFE BAR
40a Park Street
Tel: 908 5035
www.bristolfolkhouse.co.uk
The Folk House cafe has always held a special place in the affections of many Bristolians. The lovely walled garden offers rare inner city calm just off Park Street and was recommended in a *Guardian* 'Urban Oases' feature in 2005. The cafe, though pleasant, was limited in its range, but then the Liz Haughton Cooking Company arrived in 2006. Liz is part of Bristol's Haughton Food Dynasty along with brothers Phil (Better Food Company) and Barney (Quartier Vert, p224 and Bordeaux Quay, 216). Liz has introduced an organic and fairtrade menu at a reasonable price. Good veggie options.

LA TASCA
1 Clifton Heights, Triangle West
Tel: 925 9933
www.latasca.co.uk
There were 53 La Tasca restaurants in the UK by the summer of 2006, so the formula of tapas, paella, wine and beer is obviously a winner. There's the option of 'tapas to go' too.

OPPO
72 Park Street (entrance on Park St Ave)
Tel: 929 7766
www.oppoharmonicfusion.co.uk
With its entrance off the main drag, this music cafe offers a quiet alternative to other bustling Park Street cafes. Sofas, good coffee and a great people-watching view of the busy street below. It is just a shame their sandwiches aren't quite up to scratch.

THREE
9 Park Street
Tel: 930 4561
www.barthree.com
A bar, a restaurant and a place to dance whose hyper-coloured glass dome looks as if its been transported from the set of *Close Encounters of the Third Kind*. Members and two guests must make prior arrangements to be allowed into

TOP 5 FISH'N'CHIPS

1. ARGUS FISH BAR
114 West Street, Bedminster
Tel: 966 4850
An outstanding corner chippy that serves up consistently excellent chips and fresh fish cooked in a secret batter recipe that has been in the family for generations. It's one of only four fish 'n' chip shops in Bristol to have a Seafish Friers Quality Award. The others are the Clocktower, Farrows on the Kingsway and the Frying Machine in Bradley Stoke. The Argus is a hidden gem in the not-so-lovely Bemster High Street.

2. PELLEGRINO'S FISH BAR
19 Christmas Street
Tel: 927 3580
Florio and Roberto Pellegrino have won a number of awards for the quality of their fish and chips and they are well deserved. The aroma of freshly fried fish that drifts up Christmas Steps is irresistible.

3. KELLAWAY FISH BAR
4 Kellaway Avenue
Tel: 944 5220
Nominated in a *Guardian* online poll to find the best chip shop in Britain. Famed for its haddock and its light, crispy batter. Many North Bristolians rate this the best chippy in town. Those in South Bristol would beg to differ...

4. MAGNET FISH BAR
55 Dean Lane, Bedminster
Tel: 963 6444
Jim Singarda's famous chippy is a one-time winner of the *Evening Post*'s Best Bristol Chippy award. The secret of the Magnet's success is apparently the beef dripping that everything is fried in. Not really recommended for vegetarians.

5. RENDEZVOUS
9 Denmark Street
Tel: 929 8683
Conveniently placed next to the Bunch of Grapes, Rendezvous is renowned for both its cod and its curry sauce. Some adventurous diners have been known to combine the two.

Eating out

the ludicrously-named 'Perrier Jouet Lounge' where, presumably, they just might rub shoulders with someone like that mysterious ambassador fella off the chocolate ads.

WOODES CAFE
18 Park Street
Tel: 926 4041
Freshly-made homemade sandwiches for a couple of quid and good bacon butties before 11am. Proper choices – none of this 'skinny lattecino' rubbish – like a cup or a mug? Milk or cream? Red or brown sauce? White or brown bread? How refreshing.

Gloucester Road, Stokes Croft BS7

232 BISTRO
232 Gloucester Road
Tel: 924 9736
Relaxed, stylish cafe-bar and gallery that welcomes children. Serves a decent breakfast till noon and then moves into more exotic territory with tapas and the likes of crispy duck on carrot and ginger pikelets or Shetland mussels with ginger, lemongrass, chilli and coconut oil. There's a nice heated courtyard garden out the back which boasts a fully cushioned-up Balinese daybed for serious loungers. A place to take it easy.

AMICI
239 Cheltenham Road
Tel: 924 5879
It may be vast and have a sign that looks like it's been taken from the set of *Blake's 7*, but Amici likes to go beyond the typical Italian restaurant experience. Legend has it that Milan-born owner Carlo Dall'Occo once ran a cabaret in Moscow.

BISTRO LA BARRIQUE
225 Gloucester Road
Tel: 944 5500
Formerly called Picasso's, this substantial and airy bar-restaurant really comes to life in the summer when the large terrace lends Gloucester Road the air of a Parisian boulevard. The food is fantastic and there are millions of wines by the glass. Make sure you ask for a terrace table in the summer months as it gets mighty hot inside.

BLUE LAGOON
20 Gloucester Road
Tel: 942 7471
Sounding more like a shampoo from the mid 1980s than a coffee bar, Blue Lagoon is actually more sussed than its name suggests. Instead of becoming the latest volunteer to jump on the growing pile of sofa-strewn Gloucester Road bars, it offers a stripped down sandwich and coffee alternative in a more frivolous setting.

CAFE KINO
3 Ninetree Hill
Tel: 924 9200
www.cafe-kino.com
Vegan cafe where Nanny's House used to be. Check out the Edwardian dining rooms downstairs if it's busy 'up top'.

CAFE UNLIMITED
209 Gloucester Road
Tel: 904 8523
It's worth seeking out this excellent fairtrade cafe, especially if you've got hungry kids in tow. Downstairs there are comfy sofas, toys and books for the young-uns, work by local artists on the walls and plenty of papers and magazines. The food is GM free, fairtrade where possible and very reasonably priced. This is one of those rare places where adults and children can feel equally at home.

CASA MEXICANA
Zetland Road
Tel: 924 3901
www.casamexicana.co.uk
This place was the first Mexican restaurant in Bristol, and is now 17 years old. It has prospered largely because of the commitment of the owners Kevin and Lesley Duff. Even the national press have got down with their Mexican way.

COFFEE #1
157 Gloucester Road
Tel: 942 9909
33 Princess Victoria Street
Tel: 923 8021
Genuine coffee attracts all kinds of locals, passers-by, pushchair mums, groups of friends who all seem to come in, drink their coffee and leave, just like continentals. Lunchtime offers paninis and that kind of thing, well it's a small place and simplicity is the key.

DELMONICO
217 Gloucester Road
Tel: 944 5673
www.delmonico.co.uk
If you are prepared to ignore the possibility that Delmonico is too upmarket for Gloucester Road, you will discover one of the most stylish restaurants in the city, serving a 'fusion' menu of meat, fish and veggie dishes.

EZO
6 The Promenade, Gloucester Road
Tel: 944 2005
One of Bristol's few Turkish restaurants, Ezo offers a selection of mezze, kebabs and fish. There' is a particularly good choice for vegetarians, both from the mezze and the main menu.

FUNG'S
330 Gloucester Road
Tel: 923 2020
No-nonsense Chinese eat in and take-away. Boasts a huge menu and friendly cafe atmosphere. Everything is freshly cooked and there's a wide (if tofu-heavy) selection of veggie dishes. Does a nice cuppa green tea.

THE GANGES
368 Gloucester Road
Tel: 924 5234
With the identity of Indian food being diluted more every day, it's reassuring to know that there are a few places that remain faithful to the glorious cuisine of the sub-continent.

HALO
141 Gloucester Road
Tel: 944 2504
www.halobristol.co.uk
Another welcome addition to the increasingly cosmopolitan Glossy Road, Halo mixes easy English and Meditarrean food into a laid-back drinking atmosphere and manages to make you feel like you've got all the time in the world. A picture postcard garden makes Halo even more irresistible in summer.

KALABASH
120 Cheltenham Road
Tel: 330 9991
www.kalabash.org
This West African restaurant is one of the few places in Bristol where you'll find whole chargrilled tilapila (it's a yummy dish) on the

menu. Goat pepper soup and chicken gizzards are among the more unusual choices, there's also a reasonable selection of vegetarian dishes (and plenty more to chose from if you eat fish) and a well-stocked bar that includes palm wine and bottled African beers.

MACKIES BAR
84 Stokes Croft
Tel: 924 9995
After spending many years as The Bank – the least inviting pub on Stokes Croft – this place finally got a makeover and added a touch of class to the scraggy end of the Gloucester Road eating mile.

OH! CALCUTTA
216 Cheltenham Road
Tel: 924 0458
www.ohcalcutta.co.uk
There are no booths or flock wallpaper at Oh! Calcutta. This popular, contemporary Indian diner is bright, open plan and has an equally modern take on the food. The old favourites are there, but you'll also find a good selection of fish curries and vegetarian dishes.

PIEMINISTER
24 Stokes Croft
Tel: 942 9500
www.pieminister.co.uk
Jon Simon and Tristan Hogg started Bristol-based Pieminister back in 2002. They have gone national, with their delicious pies appearing in delis and pubs all over the country. They do a heap of veggie pies too.

PLANTATION
221-223 Cheltenham Road
Tel: 907 7932
www.plantationrestaurant.biz
Founded by Beverley Forbes in 2003, Plantation is one of the city's leading Caribbean restaurants with a menu that particularly respects Beverley's Jamaican family roots. Good for vegetarians and vegans.

LA RUCA
89 Gloucester Road
Tel: 944 6810
La Ruca may sound like something that large French men do when they play Le Rugby, but in fact, it's a light and pleasant first-floor cafe over the wholefood shop of the same name. There's a Latin American twist to many of

the dishes and a big emphasis on fairtrade ingredients. They offer a good vegetarian and vegan selection.

SHEESH MAHAL
13a Gloucester Road
Tel: 942 2942
When you walk through the doors of the Sheesh, you enter a time warp that takes you back to Bradford in 1975. East is most definitely East in this place. Booths, net curtains and the colours purple and green figure strongly.

Redland, Cotham, Kingsdown BS6

A COZINHA
40 Alfred Place, Kingsdown
Tel: 944 3060
Bristol's leading Portuguese restaurant is an intimate little hideaway far from the munching crowd. The simple, authentic food, prepared in front of you in the open kitchen, is traditional fare with seafood at its heart.

AHMED'S CURRY CAFE
1e Chandos Road, Redland
Tel: 946 6466
A new concept in Indian food, Ahmed's is a curry cafe that offers a full range of top-quality curries at knockdown prices – they even have a happy hour where you can pick up a curry with rice and a naan bread for a bargain price.

ANTHEM
27 St Michael's Hill
Tel: 929 2834
The colourful Anthem sign is stapled onto a wonky looking 17th-Century building on the steepest bit of St Michael's Hill. Its menu is equally eccentric. One moment it's Cajun, the next it's Thai. A much-loved oddity.

BLUEJUICE
39 Cotham Hill
Tel: 973 4800
Funky, oasis-like juice bar at the heart of Cotham Hill with a great sunken terrace out front. Its exotic juices and smoothies (South American Acai berry anyone?) are sure to boost your vitamin levels, as are its vegan wraps and salads.

LA CAMPAGNOLA
9 Zetland Road, Redland
Tel: 924 8372
The only restaurant in Bristol to take its name from a make of racing bike gears, this is one of only a handful of authentic Italian pizzerias in town. You won't find any stuffed crusts in here, Mr Inglese.

JUNIPER
21 Cotham Road South
Tel: 942 1744
www.juniperrestaurant.co.uk
One of Bristol's best-known neighbourhood restaurants, Juniper is testament to the vision of owner Nick Kleiner. The à la carte menu offers mostly modern and traditional British and European fare, such as roast lamb or homemade bread and butter pudding.

HAVANA COFFEE
37a Cotham Hill
Tel: 973 3020
www.havanacoffee.net
Why is it that it's always Che Guevara and not Fidel Castro that hangs from the walls of cafes like this? If you are happy having a coffee instead of a revolution then this South American-themed bubble offers Spanish dishes, fairtrade coffees and a Latin-jazz soundtrack. Hardly Havana but more glamorous than Cotham. Now on Welsh Back and in North Street, Bedminster, South Bristol.

MOREISH
6 Chandos Road, Redland
Tel: 970 6078
www.moreishrestaurant.co.uk
In yet another change on Chandos Road, Moreish now replaces Okra. The first solo project of Tim Moores, Moreish occupies a prime corner spot right in the middle of Chandos Road. Cafe by day and restaurant by night, it offers the best of both worlds. Inside it is all wooden tables and floor boards and piles of cakes on plates, while outside, the terrace offers a sunny spot on this quiet road. It's an unpretentious spot, offering good food.

ST MICHAEL'S CAFE
145 St Michael's Hill
Tel: 907 7804
Appearances really can be deceptive. More than a greasy spoon with a moth-eaten frontage, St Michael's Cafe's is distinctly cool.

Packing bags of bohemian charm, you'll discover an outsized jukebox, walls dotted with Hendrix and Bowie pictures, and a nice little garden. On a sunny day, the journey from the garden back into the cafe's dark bowels is marvellously disorientating. The green haze that assails your eyes as you stumble back up the stairs is one of the best legal highs in town.

ZORBAS
7 Cotham Hill
Tel: 973 1469
Genuine Greek restaurants are a rarity in Bristol and Zorbas is as close as you can get to a traditional taverna without hopping on a plane to Athens. Sophisticated it ain't, but if you want to wash down a kebab or two with a few shots of ouzo, this is the place to come.

Montpelier, St Paul's, Easton BS2, BS5

BELL'S DINER
1 York Road, Montpelier
Tel: 924 0357
www.bellsdiner.co.uk
A popular and long-established half-hidden favourite located in an ex-cornershop at the bottom of York Road, Bell's offers the perfect blend of fine contemporary cuisine in an informal setting. 'Eat, drink, da bells, da bells,' as their press ad almost says.

THE BRISTOLIAN
2 Picton Street, Montpelier
This is the place where the Montpelier counter-culture gathers for breakfast, a roll-up and a cup of tea. There's nothing too fancy about the Bristolian in its latest guise but the Turkish breakfast is definitely a winner. The toilets have been decorated by Ghostboy and his work has drawn somewhat unflattering, but highly amusing, comments on the walls.

CAFE MAITREYA
89 St Mark's Road, Easton
Tel: 951 0100
www.cafemaitreya.co.uk
Because it's situated right at the heart of the busy St Mark's Road, it's no surprise to find Cafe Maitreya more like a chill-out zone than a hectic diner. The veggie and vegan menu always uses seasonal produce.

CASBAH CAFE
96 St Mark's Road, Easton
Tel: 939 8804
www.lacasbah.co.uk
Tagines, couscous and all things Moroccan are on offer at this popular restaurant. The lamb tagine comes particularly recommended as does the couscous with seven vegetables. Downstairs there's a Moroccan bazaar selling hand-made merchandise.

ONE30
130 Cheltenham Road
Tel: 944 2442
If anything points to the gentrification of Stokes Croft, it was the arrival of the One30 bar and restaurant in 2003 with its shabby-chic style. The menu is a tasty mix of flavours from Europe and Asia with dishes such as Provençale fish soup, red onion and goat's cheese tart, skewered salmon with Asian spices, pak choi and noodles and rib-eye steak. Local artists exhibit their work here too.

ONE STOP THALI
12 York Road, Montpelier
Tel: 942 6687
www.onestopthali.co.uk
From humble beginnings, this rulebook-ripping adventure into the heart of Asian cuisine has grown into something of a nationwide phenomenon. And they make it look so easy. Their secret? Fresh, tasty, home-cooked exotica served on steel plates at reasonable prices. Join their tiffin club.

TEOH'S
28 Lower Ashley Road
Tel: 907 1191
Teoh's has managed to thrive despite being located half way between the busy St Paul's junction and the M32. No-one does Malaysian and Thai food so cheaply. Crispy duck, chicken satay and beef rendang we know. But what on earth is Penang fried ho fun? There's now a Teoh's in Southville too.

South of the river BS3/4

AL'S TIKKA GRILL
33 Ashton Road
Tel: 953 5950
BYO curry bistro near the Bristol City ground that is a South Bristol institution. This is a

Listings

great greasy spoon by day and a BYO Indian restaurant and take-away in the evenings. They now have a Hot and Spicy version in North Street too (966 9008).

ASILAH
Wells Road
Tel: 07816 202827
Belly dancing and flamenco guitar evenings are just two of the regular attractions for diners at this neighbourly Moroccan eaterie. There's a wide ranging menu of soups, fish, tagines and couscous dishes with a reasonable veggie selection. It's BYO so you're not going to break the bank. If you want a laugh, ask the owner, Bridget, about the night she hired an Egyptian male belly dancer.

BOCACINA
184c Wells Road
www.bocacina.co.uk
From the people behind Bocanova (p216) and Bocabar (p215), Bocacina is a neighbourhood cafe and pizza place with a small selection of deli stuff. Cafe by day and fancy pizza joint (including take-away) by night.

CURRY HOUSE
Bath Road, Brislington
Tel: 977 9090
Refurbished in 2003, the Curry House is a young and stylish restaurant which has very quickly built up an excellent reputation. It also does take-aways, but take a book and be prepared for a wait: this place always gets busy. I guess that means it's good!

GLASNOST
1 William Street, Totterdown
Tel: 927 0938
This famous community diner has been lording it over South Bristol since 1994. There was a change of ownership in 2005, but it seems that the quality of the menu and the famous friendly atmosphere has remained unchanged. Years ago, the restaurant went through a bizarre cafe-with-launderette phase. The combination of powder and chowder didn't wash.

LOUNGE
227 North Street, Southville
Tel: 963 7340
107 Wells Road, Totterdown
Tel: 908 6010

From the people who run Byzantium, Lounge is one of the new breed of Bristol bars-cum-restaurants. The atmosphere is pleasant without being too trendy and the range of food is good, most of it for under £7. In 2006, the Totterdown branch on Wells Road opened offering Totterdown locals somewhere central to drink and get a bite to eat.

TEOH'S
278 North Street, Southville
Tel: 902 1122
Next door to the Tobacco Factory, this is the second Teoh's to open. Excellent Malaysian and Thai food with some dishes you surely won't recognise.

TOBACCO FACTORY
Raleigh Road, Southville
Tel: 902 0060
www.tobaccofactory.com
Extensive menu ranging from Mediterranean nibbles to full-on Sunday roasts. Service can be a bit slow, so beware if you're in a rush.

QUBA ICE
220 North Street, Southville
Tel: 963 9222
www.qubaice.co.uk
A lively restaurant-bar that specialises in Caribbean food. The mixed platter is good and vegetarians are well catered for. There's outside pavement seating and a garden.

RIVERSIDE GARDEN CENTRE CAFE
Clift House Road, Ashton
Tel: 966 7535
www.riversidegardencentre.com
Completely veggie menu which includes as many organic, fairtrade and locally sourced ingredients as possible. Everything is made on the premises. A lovely spot to eat outside and there's a small play area for the nippers.

WINDMILL HILL CITY FARM CAFE
City Farm, Philip Street, Bedminster
Tel: 963 3252
www.windmillhillcityfarm.org.uk
Famous for its hearty meat and veggie breakfasts, they also do a full lunch menu, cakes and snacks. The courtyard garden is a joy in the summer. The farm is an great place to bring the kids too (see Children's Bristol, p182).

BRISTOL'S TOP TAKE-AWAYS

A TEAM OF 15 TAKE-AWAY CONNOISSEURS NOMINATED THEIR FAVOURITE SPOTS...

AHMED'S CURRY CAFE
1e Chandos Road, Redland
Tel: 946 6466
The best curry take out ever! Also a nice but cramped restaurant.

AL'S TIKKA GRILL
33 Ashton Road, Southville
Tel: 985 3016
Still the best after all these years.

BELLA PIZZA
361 Bath Road
Tel: 300 9966
Among the best in town. If you want globe artichokes and parmesan shavings, look elsewhere. This is a genuine pizza experience.

BRISTOL SAUSAGE SHOP
St Nicholas Market
Tel: 747 8302
Speciality sausages in either sandwich form or a take-away. Always a queue. The best.

CIAO BURGERS
207a Gloucester Road
Tel: 942 6228
Why would you go to McDonalds or Burger King when you can come here? Garlic, chilli, American style. And thin fries to go.

CHARCOAL GRILL
236 Gloucester Road
Tel: 942 8888
Don't be fooled by the unassuming facade, this place serves the finest kebabs in Bristol.

FALAFEL KING
The Centre
The best veggie take-away option in town.

KATHMANDU
Colston Tower, Colston Street
Tel: 929 4455
The Kancha Kukhura Special (Tandoori chicken cooked in Nepalese spices) is the most popular dish according to a customer poll. The veg and fish dishes are also fantastic.

LA CUISINE
392 Gloucester Road
Tel: 907 6534
Exotic name disguises a ludicrously wide-ranging menu with excellent kebabs.

LA RUCA
89 Gloucester Road
Tel: 944 6810
The veggie chimichanga with guacamole or falafels is brilliant.

MAGIC ROLL
3 Queens Row, Triangle South
Tel: 9221435
Seriously gorgeous food. From homemade muesli and hot porridge to fantastic wraps.

MELA
19 York Road, Montpelier
Tel: 924 9272
The thalis are great value and if you fancy a pint in The Beaufort next door, they'll come and get you when the curry is ready. What a nice bunch.

ROYCE ROLLS
St Nicholas Market
Homemade bread bagels, pasties and more. Lots of veggie stuff.

SUEYS
264 Gloucester Road
Tel: 9839133/4
Authentic Chinese, Cantonese and Thai take-aways and home deliveries that pride themselves on being very low in MSG.

TAVEIRA
13 Cannon Street, Bedminster
Tel: 963 7676
Great value Lebanese take-away that uses lots of fresh herbs and spices.

Listings **Shopping**

A
lthough Bristol can't claim to have anywhere near the clout of London, or the nook-and-cranny appeal of its near-neighbour Bath, it does register an above-average score as a post-globalisation retail centre. Okay, the Gloucester Road isn't quite Portobello Road, and Broadmead is even further away from Knightsbridge, but we do have two enormous shopping super-centres.

Despite being Broadmead-with-a-roof, and less beggars, The Mall at Cribbs Causeway is extremely popular. A case of never mind the quality, or the variety, just feel the width? Of course. But that's not Bristol's fault, it's Britain's. The city has managed to hang onto a decent number of independent shops but has lost just as many to the ruthlessness of 'the market'.

There are, for now anyway, some alternatives to Mall life. We won't bother telling you about Gap, Top Man, HMV, Next and their kind because you know more than you need to about them already. This guide tries to get under the skin of Bristol's retail experience and tell you what's good and what's bad. We will point you in the direction of the most cutting-edge record shops, the most radical second-hand stockists, the best places to pick up contemporary home design and the whereabouts of the most essential bookstores. Go forth, spend money – support your local shop.

Fashion

BEAST
224 Cheltenham Road
Tel: 942 8200
St Nicholas Market
Tel: 927 9535
Beast is so much more than a cool clothes shop, it's a worldwide cultural ambassador for Bristol. But Beast doesn't spread the word about the city through fancy websites and multi-million pound marketing campaigns, it uses T-shirts bearing Bristolian phrases such as 'ark at ee', 'gert lush', 'theyz me daps mind', 'Mint innit' and 'cheers drive' which are proudly borne on chests around the world. The Bristolian community in Sydney is particularly fond of them. Lucy Wheeler and Andy Keith-Smith produced their first Bristol T-shirt ('gert lush') at the beginning of 2004 and, by the summer of 2006, had almost 30 in the range. 'We love Bristol, we're very proud of it,' says Lucy. 'The T-shirts convey a positive image of Bristol using phrases we used when we were kids and which you still hear in the city today.'

BISHOPSTON TRADING COMPANY
193 Gloucester Road
Tel: 924 5598
www.bishopstontrading.co.uk
Fairtrade is all well and good in principle, but surely no-one in their right mind can expect us to wear clothes made out of hemp? Well, not quite. This fairtrade workers' co-operative was set up in 1985 to create employment in the South Indian village of K.V.Kuppam and offers simple but quality clothing for all – babies through to adults.

BS8
34 Park Street
Tel: 930 4836
A whole arcade displaying the work of young Bristol designers in addition to all manner of other left-of-centre club chic. Split over three levels, it's the ideal place to visit if you want something new to throw on that evening. You can pick up anything from skimpy throw-a-way tops and cool hats to elegant evening wear and *Sopranos* T-shirts. This is a shopping haven for those who like a rummage.

COOSHTI
57 Park Street
Tel: 929 0850
Other than John Anthony, this is Bristol's only credible designer store. You'll find names such as Duffer of St George, Replay, Hope & Glory, Firetrap and Red or Dead scattered through every section.

DNA
24 Park Street
Tel: 934 9173
What began as a warehouse full of irresponsible 1960s shirts is now packed with mostly trendy stuff for girls. DNA also stocks more hippest ashtrays, postcards and bags than anywhere in town.

FUNKTION ROOM
Clifton Down Shopping Centre,
Whiteladies Road
Tel: 973 8007
Clifton Arcade, Boyces Avenue
Tel: 973 0000
Offering a classy selection of clothes, bags, soap, jewellery, homeware and more, all at reasonable prices. The policy for all their products appears to be 'make it shiny or make it retro'. Funktion Room is much loved by young girls in their early teens and also their mums. The Funktion Room at Clifton Down could possibly be the smallest shop anywhere in Bristol.

H&M
Odeon Building, Union Street
Tel: 945 1870
www.hm.com
Yet more Swede's doing it far better than anyone else on the High Street. Born in 1947, H&M has scattered the concept of high fashion at low prices all over the world with a whopping 2,000 stores in 22 countries. H&M are without a doubt the out-and-out market leader on the nation's homogenised shopping arena. With one eye permanently fixed on the catwalks, H&M somehow manage to produce far more interesting and fashionable men's, women's and kid's clobber than their limited budget should really allow. No wonder the UK's hippest youngsters have been gravitating to the store in growing numbers over recent years. All of a sudden, going out and spending £80 on a pair of jeans makes you look like a complete twat.

RETAIL HEAVEN: THREE CLASSIC SHOPS

1. 20TH CENTURY FLICKS
3 Richmond Terrace
Tel: 974 2570
www.20thcenturyflicks.co.uk
If only all video shops were made this way. It's not just that there are 10,000 titles to choose from, nor that every single conceivable genre of film is covered. What makes movie buffs really fall in love with 20th Century Flicks is the fact that the staff really know and care about films. They'll offer advice, discuss scripts, give on-the-spot reviews, suggest possible alternatives and come out with comments such as: 'It's the best sci-fi thriller of the mid 1980s' when you least expect it. You don't get that in Blockbuster. Do you?

2. REPSYCHO
85 Gloucester Road
Tel: 983 0007
Andy Minter knows a decent pair of whacked-out 1972 men's slacks when he sees them. His long-standing second-hand clothing emporium on Gloucester Road has everything you could want. Authentic clobber is what it's all about but you'll also find T-shirts bearing brand legends like Moog. Apparently, Linter trawls car boot sales as well as Europe's clothes markets to find his stock. Upstairs is full of moulded nu-plastic furniture. Downstairs is Prime Cuts, a 1960s pysch-beat and soul record shop (see p239).

3. BRISTOL SWEET MART
80 St Mark's Road
Tel: 951 2257
www.sweetmart.co.uk
A bit of a legend, not just in Easton, not just in Bristol, but all over the world. Take a few minutes to wander around the shop and you'll realise that their success is built on two equally vital factors: organisation and love. Lots of wondrous food stuffs you've never heard of from right across the known universe. This is the place to go for fresh herbs and it also sells Hobbs House bread from the Chipping Sodbury master bakers.

Shopping

Listings

JIGSAW
80 Park Street
Tel: 926 5775
www.jigsaw-online.com
One of the classiest and most enduring women's fashion shops, Jigsaw has made the art of easy understatement its own and has always managed to look completely unruffled by the frequent blasts of air that pass for this week's latest trend.

JOHN ANTHONY
108 Broadmead
Tel 922 0799
www.john-anthony.com
The labels in John Anthony read like Armani, Cerruti and Versace and the price tags scream quality. If you're looking for some high-income townie kiddie clobber, this is the place.

KAREN MILLEN
68 Queens Road
Tel: 2264085
www.karenmillen.com
Sleek, slinky and sexy designs for fashion conscious foxes and ultra-modern minxes, Karen Millen is one of the last remaining independent boutiques and this allows these ladies to operate on a higher, more timeless level while still appealing to all ages.

LAURA ASHLEY
62 Queens Road
Tel: 0871 223 1325
www.lauraashley.co.uk
Why anyone wants to dress up like Charlotte Bronte and Helena Bonham Carter is a mystery to members of the opposite sex. Quaint, twee and about as sexy as rounders.

MISS SELFRIDGE
86-88 Broadmead
Tel: 923 0385
www.missselfridge.co.uk
If Andy Warhol could have designed a girl's clothes shop for the 21st Century, he would have come up with Miss Selfridge. The clothes are throwaway, disposable and irresistible for teenage girls in a fashion statement mood.

PINK SODA
59 Gloucester Road
Tel: 942 0420
Be careful out there girls: there's some really quite adventurous independent design happening in Pink Soda. They have cute 1950s dress stylings and socks with fingers and so much more. This is wobbly hippie chic at its best. It looks like Pink Soda are just not afraid to love all our pasts.

SEVEN 7
60 Park Row
Tel: 929 8898
Designer T-shirts, vintage and import trainers, jewellery and accessories, as well as exhibitions and artwork.

WESTWORLD RETAIL CORP
37 Park Street
Tel: 925 3823
In an age dominated by the dreary fashion conservatism, Westworld is the last outpost of UK street fashion. Selling baggy jeans and T-shirts with 'Bench' written on the front of them.

Shoes

CARA
26 Park Street
Tel: 925 7495
www.carashoes.co.uk
Elegant, timeless femininity from one of the more interesting shoe and boot stockists in Bristol. The designs can be traditional, stylish, even quirky and the atmosphere unhurried.

HANDMADE SHOE COMPANY
64 Colston Street
Tel: 921 4247
Handmade shoes that look like they've been designed by druids who live near a rainbow. Another gloriously stylistic offering bought to you by the people who gave us sandals.

KBK SHOES
203 Cheltenham Road
Tel: 924 3707
Boots. Made for walking. For nearly 100 years, this place has sold nothing that doesn't come with an air sole underneath. One of the largest stockists of Dr Marten shoes and boots in Britain, the staff have Masters Degrees in DM Studies and attract shoe fanatics from all over.

SOLETRADER
8 Broadmead Gallery
Tel: 929 1122
www.soletrader.co.uk

With the choice in men's shoes melting away in the last few years, Soletrader has established itself as the only shop for hundreds of miles who actually stock some half-decent footwear.

WORKSHOP
1-2 Perry Road, Park Row
Tel: 922 1566
www.wonderfulworkshop.com
Limited edition trainers for the skate and hip-hop generation. Also, check out the regular exhibitions they host from Bristol's cutting-edge street artists.

Second-hand clothing

BILLIE JEAN
208 Gloucester Road
Tel: 944 5353
If you laid out all the velvet they stock in Billie Jean, it would cover an area approximately the size of Kent. Are they expecting a bulk order of smoking jackets from the ghost of Oscar Wilde or something?

MARCUSS STORES
177-181 Hotwell Road
Tel: 929 7427
They made a mint when Echo & The Bunnymen made it fashionable to go out looking as if you were on a military manoeuvre. They cashed in on the 1990s trend for combats. And now they're doing a roaring trade in gas masks for paranoid people.

NAFF CLOTHING
13 Cotham Hill, Cotham
Tel: 973 7458
'This place is the perfect antidote to bland, high street clothes stores,' says a friend. Perhaps, but there are rather too many hippie sacks and horribly pleated 1980s jackets among the more interesting stuff.

REPSYCHO
85 Gloucester Road
Tel: 983 0007
(See Retail Heaven, p233).

SOBEY'S
13 Gloucester Road
Tel: 942 6688
And finally, after rummaging through 179 charity shops on Gloucester Road, you

eventually stumble into a second-hand store that knows its Dwight Yoakam collar from its post-modern T-shirt-with-a-slogan. Look out for the 'Flax Bourten' T-shirts.

UNCLE SAM'S
54a Park Street
Tel: 929 8404
Considering that 1950s Americana hasn't been fashionable since, ooh, 1984, Uncle Sam's has done well to still be open after all these years. It specialises in T-shirts, shirts, jackets, jeans and huge amounts of leather.

Books

AREA 51
143 Gloucester Road
Tel: 942 4655
www.area51online.co.uk
Abandon any hope of ever meeting girls all ye who enter here. As its name suggests, this is the sort of place that attracts blokes who fantasise about being trapped inside a UFO with the ginger half of the *X-Files*. Comics, cult movies, *Star Wars* posters and cyber-nonsense.

ARNOLFINI BOOK SHOP
16 Narrow Quay
Tel: 917 2304
This outstanding specialist arts bookshop also stocks magazines on art, design, literature and film as well as posters, cards and gift wrap.

BISHOPSTON BOOKS
259 Gloucester Road
Tel: 944 53 03
www.antiqbook.com
A proper second-hand bookshop with shelves creaking under the weight of words.

BOOKS FOR AMNESTY
103 Gloucester Road
Tel: 942 2969
www.booksforamnestybristol.org.uk
This superb little shop stocks a vast array of second-hand novels and academia and is the kind of place where it's easy to lose an hour.

THE BOOK CUPBOARD
361 Gloucester Road
Tel: 942 4447
Best bookshop on the top bit of the Gloucester Road. Yes. Okay, it's the only bookshop on the

Shopping

Listings

top bit of the Gloucester Road. They rudely refused to stock the first edition of *The Naked Guide to Bristol* because we forgot to include them in the bookshop section even though the author only lives 50 yards away from the shop. Sorry! This time we've included them, but we're buggered if we're going to supply them with any books. Hah!

BORDERS
48-56 Queens Road
Tel: 922 6959
www.bordersstores.com
And so the giant, double-decaf cappuccino of home leisure stores rolls into town and sends the word-selling locals scurrying into their dust jackets for cover. Low prices all round. Unsurprisingly popular with Bristol's huge student population.

BLACKWELL
89 Park Street
Tel: 927 6602
www.blackwell.co.uk
This is one serious bookshop. Occupying several floors on the top of Park Street, Blackwell's is a sprawling testament to the written word in all its forms.

CLIFTON BOOKSHOP
84 Whiteladies Road
Tel: 983 8989
www.cliftonbookshop.co.uk
Very friendly and well-stocked bookseller that has a particularly good range of local books, and a children's section.

DURDHAM DOWN BOOKSHOP
39 North View, Westbury Park
Tel: 973 9095
There's an old-fashioned decency about the shops on North View, typified by this charming bookshop with helpful staff. Let's hope it doesn't go the same way as some other recent losses in the area.

FORBIDDEN PLANET
Units 4&5 Clifton Heights, Triangle West,
Tel: 929 7767
You are greeted with an avalanche of sci-fi themed Americana as soon as you walk through the door. Nothing but cult comics, cult magazines, cult videos, cult novels, cult memorabilia. It is cult shopping at its finest. For the geeks among us.

STANFORDS
29 Corn Street
Tel: 929 9966
www.stanfords.co.uk
You can lose yourself in a world of travel adventure just by looking at the maps in Stanfords. This specialist travel bookshop has a staggering collection of books, globes, atlases and travel paraphernalia. The staff know what the hell they are talking about too. Which makes a change from many other bookshops.

WATERSTONES
College Green
Tel: 925 0511
Galleries, Broadmead
Tel: 925 2274
Cribbs Causeway
Tel: 950 9813
University
Tel: 925 4297
www.waterstones.co.uk
Sizeable mainstream bookstore that lays out all the latest fiction titles with their covers facing upwards. It also stocks a vast array of travel, history and art books in the more traditional upright position.

Video shops

20TH CENTURY FLICKS
3 Richmond Terrace, Clifton
Tel: 974 2570
www.20thcenturyflicks.co.uk
(See Retail Heaven, p233)

CHOICES VIDEO
294-296 Whiteladies Road and elsewhere around town
Tel: 973 1587
The following is a conversation that recently took place in Choices Video store. Customer: 'Excuse me, do you stock *The Player*?' Shop manager: 'Is that the old one?' Customer: 'Er, um, yes I suppose it is, if you insist.' Shop manager: 'No we ain't got it.'

HOLLYWOOD NITES
449 Gloucester Road
Tel: 951 0510
Useful it may be but Tinseltown it certainly isn't. This top-end-of-Gloucester-Road film shop sells hundreds of old titles that you wouldn't find anywhere else.

Cheap shops

THE POUND STORE
334 Gloucester Road, Horfield
Tel: 942 0147
Don't make the same mistake I did in here when I picked up something and turned to the assistant and asked 'How much is this, please?' 'Everything in here is a quid'. 'Everything'. 'Yes'. Even the 24-piece solid silver cutlery set.

RAJANI SUPERSTORE
Maggs Lane, Speedwell
Tel: 958 6448
If Aladdin had the most out-there suppliers in the world, his cave would still look half-empty when compared with this place. Spread over two jam-packed floors in a litter-strewn Fishponds business park, Ranjanis stock a kaleidoscopic array of products, from the familiar to the never seen in your life before. Luggage, mirrors, kitchenware, three-foot high red Indian ornaments, electrical goods, toys, towering dead-eyed china dolls, bins, blah-blah-blah.

TK MAXX
The Galleries, Broadmead
Tel: 930 4404
www.tkmaxx.com
Tempts you inside with the promise of cheap designer clothing. If you have a few hours spare, you might actually find some.

WILKINSON
15 Union Street, Broadmead
Tel: 929 1667
www.wilko.co.uk
Very much a belt-and-braces type of hardware store, Wilko's is big on functionality and even bigger on low prices. Comments like: 'Surely dishwasher powder ought to be more expensive than that!' and 'Remarkable! Just £1.14 for a mop and bucket!' are common.

Interiors

BRISTOL GUILD
68-70 Park Street
Tel: 926 5548
www.bristolguild.co.uk
Basically, this is pottery's way of telling you you've got too much money. The Guild sells a huge range of ornaments, gadgets, jewellery, kitchenware, toys and arty stuff for middle-class tastes.

DUSK TIL DAWN
188 Cheltenham Road
Tel: 944 2388
As its name suggests, this store sells a full range of contemporary beds and equally original furniture. Mass produced it isn't.

FIRED EARTH
65a Whiteladies Road
Tel: 973 7400
www.firedearth.co.uk
If you've been to B&Q and didn't like any of their tiles or paint colours, Fired Earth could be your saviour. They offer a huge range of off-beat tiles and shades of paint that you won't find anywhere else.

HABITAT
Beacon House, Queens Road
Tel: 973 7012
www.habitat.net
The arrival of IKEA brought some serious competition for Terence Conran's trailblazing store, but it remains popular and you don't have to queue up on the M32 for ages.

IKEA
Eastgate Shopping Centre, East Gate Rd, Eastville, Bristol.
Tel: 0845 355 2264
www.ikea.com
Anyone who moans about IKEA is not seeing the flat-packed wood for the self-assembly trees. The multi-storied, aggressively modernist, persistently cheap Scandinavian superstore is not so much a furniture retailer as a utopian revolutionary of interior design. So what if they have clogged up a little stretch of the M32, it was never the most picturesque of places anyhow. What IKEA have done is make good taste in furniture design accessible to all. Sofas with angles, bathroom cabinets for the price of a Terence Conran soap dish and coolish retro lamps for under £2? What more do you want!

IOTA
83 Gloucester Road
Tel: 924 4911
A real rarity in these days of the homogenised high street, IOTA actually trades on its quirky

Shopping

originality. Owner Meibh O'Conner Morse stocks products she likes and this makes for an eclectic mix of 1950s lunchboxes, retro clocks, sleek kitchen utensils and some great post-modern vases.

KITCHENS
167 Whiteladies Road
Tel: 973 9614
A huge, hangar-sized store devoted entirely to, you guessed it, kitchens. From Le Creuset saucepans to giant wooden chopping boards, they have everything and more for cooks who mean business.

SOFA MAGIC
121 Coldharbour Road
Tel: 924 8282
www.sofamagic.co.uk
If you're going to spend a large part of your life sitting on something, you really ought to sit on something that won't give way at the first sign of your fat auntie Rene's arse. Sofa Magic make made-to-measure settees that fit your lifestyle.

Specialist shops

50:50
16 Park Row
Tel: 914 7783
www.5050store.com
The spirit of Dogtown and the Z-Boys lives on here. 'Skateboarder owned and operated' reads the shop slogan and this total commitment to four-wheeled radicalism means the hipper of Bristol's teenagers come here before heading off down to College Green.

BIRDS OF BALDWIN STREET
35 Baldwin Street
Tel: 927 3676
Nothing is more idiotic than laisse-faire capitalism on the high street and the UK is the biggest idiot in all of Europe. Here's why: If you want a packet of cigarettes in France, you have to go to a compact little independent shop called a tabac. You cant get fags anywhere else. Result? Small businesses are allowed to flourish, profits shared across the board, everyone is happy. Not here. By the year 2015, there could be just one shop left and its name will be Tesco. Do something, act now, vote with your lungs, get down to Bird's and shop like you used to. This must be one of the city's

last surviving specialist shops. 20 Chesterfield s'il vous plait.

BRISTOL TICKET SHOP
12 The Arcade, Broadmead
Tel: 0870 4444 400
www.bristolticketshop.co.uk
An excellent little ticket seller in Broadmead that covers just about every event in the area and beyond.

CHRISTMAS STEPS COSTUME HIRE AND JOKE SHOP
47 Colston Street
Tel: 926 4703
They've been selling silly moustaches and crazy wigs at the top of Christmas Steps for over 50 years and now stock more than 2,000 fancy dress costumes on three floors. Do people really still hold fancy dress parties?

CORKS OF COTHAM
54 Cotham Hill
Tel: 973 1620
www.corksof.com
One of a rare breed of independent off-licenses on the high street, Corks is driven by a passion for wine and providing unusual specialities such as French Grey Goose vodka.

FOCUS ON THE PAST
25 Waterloo Street, Clifton
Tel: 973 8080
An eclectic range of antique goodies over two well-stocked floors. Make sure you have an hour or two spare for browsing.

KITESTORE
39a Cotham Hill
Tel: 974 5010
www.kitestore.co.uk
Who'd have thought that anyone could make a decent living out of owning a shop selling kites. Martin and Avril Baker have. But when they opened one of the UK's only specialist kite stores, they surely did it for the love of standing in the wind with a plastic bag on the end of a piece of 60-foot string. One day they'll fly away, you know.

LA MAISON DU ZIGOU DAM
336 Gloucester Road
Tel: 944 2111
This fairtrade shop is run by Cameroonians and specialises in clothes, art, books, music and

videos from Central Africa. It's also the base for the Zigou Dam dance group which works mainly with schools and covers everything from traditional to contemporary African dance and hip-hop.

MEMORIES
St Nicholas Market
Tel: 977 5488
Memories is a treasure trove of a stall. It stocks a remarkable selection of pictures of old Bristol, from the Centre to little local parks. Lots of the pictures are from family collections, so you can turn up some really unusual snaps of familys in excellent olde outfits. Most of the prints are a fiver, which is a total bargain.

NEAL'S YARD REMEDIES
126 Whiteladies Road
Tel: 946 6034
www.nealsyardremedies.com
Winner of many awards for its natural health and beauty products, Neal's Yard also has therapy rooms and runs lectures and courses. 'We believe real health is generated from inside,' they say.

RICHER SOUNDS
143 Whiteladies Road
Tel: 973 4397
www.richersounds.com
Forget about those hi-fi centres up at the Mall, there's only one place to go when you want to update your sound system. You'll have to queue but the deals are well worth it.

SEVEN GENERATIONS
10-12 Picton Street, Montpelier
Tel: 0845 330 3934
www.sevengenerations.co.uk
Fantastic green/eco shop with an intriguing selection of goods and an excellent selection of niche books you'll struggle to find anywhere else in Bristol. Sure, you can get all your household natural cleaning refills and eco-friendly paint here and an ever-expanding range of green stuff, but where else could you also buy a press to make fire logs out of newspaper, a book on how to make your own cider and a pack of reusable nappies?

TANGY GIFTS
286 Stapleton Road
Tel: 951 2202
www.tangygifts.co.uk

This is, um, like, Bristol's Head Shop, yeah? They've got skins, bongs, pipes, seeds, tins, scales, books, funky cards, hats and, um, some other stuff about blow and that.

Music shops

THE BRISTOL MUSIC SHOP
30 College Green
Tel: 929 0390
If you want to buy a brass or woodwind instrument, then this is the place to go. Centrally located right on College Green, you'll find lots of students and teens and other wannabe musicians searching out their favourite guitar tabs.

DRUM BANK MUSIC
203 Gloucester Road
Tel: 975 5366
www.drumbankmusic.co.uk
Bang, crash, wallop, thump, clatter, crack, boom, etc. It's amazing that this shop devoted mainly to percussion is still standing considering the sonic battering it gets.

FOPP
43-45 Park Street
Tel: 987 9700
99 Whiteladies Road
www.fopp.co.uk
Stepping into Fopp is a Bermuda triangle experience. You intend to pick up one album and, before you know it, four hours have disappeared and you approach the counter looking like a contestant who's just done well on an alt. culture version of *The Generation Game*. Everything you meant to buy when it came out but never got around to it, and most of it under a tenner.

MICKLEBURGH
1-9 Stokes Croft
Tel: 924 4158
www.mickleburgh.co.uk
Sprawling, elegant musical instrument stockist whose range of pianos, guitars, keyboards, drums and amps are spread sparsely over a vast floor space. If Stan Getz was a Bristolian, he'd probably shop here.

PRIME CUTS
85 Gloucester Road
Tel: 983 0007

Shopping

Prime Cuts resides below the RePsycho second-hand clothes shop (p233) and deals purely in second-hand vinyl including a great selection of rare and imported music. Check out the second-hand videos, most of which you've never heard of, and some of which are worth buying on comedy value alone.

ROOTED RECORDS
9 Gloucester Road
Tel: 907 4372
www.rootedrecords.co.uk
Friendly staff and a cool atmosphere makes Rooted Records a pleasant place to buy music. A favourite for DJs, they stock a good range of drum 'n' bass, hip-hop and breaks, alongside other genres including jazz, latin, downbeat, electro, and electronica. Competitive prices.

SAUNDERS RECORDERS
205 Whiteladies Road
Tel: 973 5149
www.saundrecs.co.uk
A staggering selection of recorders on offer from a shop that has been at the centre of the Bristol recorder scene since the 1970s.

Art

ART WAREHOUSE & FRAMING FACTORY
Wapping Wharf
Tel: 929 8089
www.artwarehouse.co.uk
This Harbourside home to a large, yet often unusual, selection of sculptures, cards, original work and limited edition prints, is a refreshingly odd establishment.

BRISTOL BLUE GLASS
Unit 2, Kenn Court, South Bristol Business Park, Roman Farm Road
Tel: 964 9070
Bristol has been the home of blue glassware for almost 400 years and the industry is still thriving in the city today. The distinctive blue colour is apparently created by adding cobalt oxide to the molten glass.

CRAFT WORKS
355-357 Gloucester Road
Tel: 942 1644
Well-established craft shop with a wide range of materials. Also does picture framing.

CREATIVITY
7-9 Worrall Road
Tel: 973 1710
Well-stocked, friendly arts and crafts store for grown-ups and children. Great place to browse – or ask the helpful staff if you're in a hurry.

FRAMERS' WORKSHOP
269 Gloucester Road
Tel: 944 6355
Whether it's Matisse or your kids' potato prints, art needs a frame almost as much as frames need art. This busy, independently-owned shop has every style and material for frames your walls can handle.

HAROLD HOCKEY
170-174 Whiteladies Road
Tel: 973 5988
Stationery and artists' materials specialists based in a wonderfully sprawling shop. Whether you want a pencil sharpener or a Winsor & Newton Bristol easel, this is the place to come.

Food suppliers

ASHTON FRUIT SHOP
269 North Street, Southville
Tel: 966 6838
A strong emphasis on local and seasonal fruit and veg and a good organic selection. Probably the best place in Bristol to get Seville Oranges for marmalade-making in February.

BETTER FOOD COMPANY
Bristol Proving House, Sevier Street
Tel: 935 1725
www.betterfood.co.uk
Phil Haughton's organic supermarket is the ragamuffin cousin of Clifton's uber-posh Fresh & Wild (p242). Situated on a roundabout on the Montpelier, St Paul's, St Werburghs borders, BFC brings locally produced, organic food to the inner city. Much of the veg is sourced from Phil's Barley Wood Walled Garden in Wrington.

BOB WHERLOCK BUTCHERS
250 North Street, Southville
Tel: 966 3593
There's usually a queue outside this traditional butchers on Saturday mornings. Famous for its home-made sausages and Mendip lamb.

BOBO DELI
74 Colston Street
Tel: 929 1076
www.bobodeli.co.uk
Specialists in pan-Asian food with a mighty selection of ingredients from mainland China, Japan, South Korea, Thailand and Malaysia.

THE BREAD STORE
45 Gloucester Road
Tel: 9421 654
Whisper it gently, but a growing number of 'bread heads' reckon this place is even better than Herbert's and Hobbs House. There's a huge selection of speciality breads alongside the standards.

BRISTOL SAUSAGE SHOP
Glass Arcade, St Nicholas Market
Tel: 07817 478302
www.bristolsausageshop.co.uk
Boasting more than 20 sorts of sausage all made from locally-sourced produce where possible, this is heaven for banger lovers. Remember, never prick a Bristol sausage. The natural casings are designed to keep the yummy flavours in, so they take a bit longer to cook and need to rest for a few minutes before scoffing.

BRISTOL SWEET MART
80 St Marks Road, Easton
Tel: 951 2257
www.sweetmart.co.uk
Kassam Ismail Majothi arrived penniless as a refugee from Uganda in 1972 and founded the Sweet Mart in 1978. Since then, it has become the major supplier of ethnic foods, spices and more in the south west. Sweet Mart is at the centre of the regeneration of St Mark's Road which is one of the most interesting shopping streets in Bristol. Wandering around this wonderful shop is a great experience, one that inspires you to explore new flavours.

CAKE ETC
Tel: 914 0749/07929 221802
francinefood@aol.com
Specialist supplier of cakes and bakes including a variety of gluten-free creations for all occasions. Francine Russell's chocolate brownie and glitter birthday cake is stunning and the spiced pumpkin cake is beyond compare. Cake etc is a regular at the Slow Food Market.

CHANDOS DELI
121 Whiteladies Road
Tel: 970 6565
6 Princess Victoria Street
Tel: 974 3275
97 Henleaze Road
Tel: 9074391
39 Queens Road
Tel: 925 9911
Bristol Uni Sports Centre, Tyndall Avenue
www.chandosdeli.com
Chandos Deli was established in back in 1992 and is now expanding rapidly around Bristol and Bath. Chandos offers a fabulous range of cheese, breads, cooked meats, wines and great selection of take-away sandwiches if you fancy something different for lunch. The helpful staff are really knowledgeable and you won't go far wrong if you follow their recommendations. The Princess Victoria Street branch in Clifton also offers a superb selection of fresh fish.

CHARLES SAUNDERS
Albert Road, St Philips
Tel: 971 5454
www.charles-saunders.com
You can buy anything from live lobsters to frozen Spotted Dick at Charles Saunders. The wholesaler is a major supplier of fresh fish to the South West catering trade and also has a staggering range of frozen meals which it supplies to restaurants. The choice of fresh fish is easily the biggest you'll find anywhere in the whole of Bristol and, although Charles Saunders is mainly a wholesale business, members of the public can also buy directly from the St Philip's premises as long as they spend a minimum of £20. We think it is well worth the spend.

EARTHBOUND
8 Abbotsford Road, Cotham
Tel: 904 2260
There was such an enthusiastic review of Earthbound on the *Vegan Guide to Bristol* website that we thought we'd reprint a bit of it. Here it is: 'Rammed full of the best quality organic fruit and veg, with fresh deliveries daily. Great selection of hummus including San Amvrosia and Natural Vitality, plus smoothies, juices, hemp oil and a first rate selection of vegan chocolate, as well as the Sikelia range of exotic Sicilian pestos.' Earthbound is a must-visit experience if you value your food.

Shopping

Listings

ESSENTIAL TRADING CO-OPERATIVE
Unit 3, Lodge Causeway Trading Estate, Fishponds
Tel: 958 3550
www.essential-trading.coop
Essential is an organic and ethical wholesale food co-operative which carries more than 6,000 product lines. Apart from supplying the retail and catering trade, you can also buy direct if you join or form a food co-operative.

FISHWORKS
128 Whiteladies Road
Tel: 974 4433
www.fishworks.co.uk
Mitchell Tonks pioneered his concept of a 'fishmongers with tables' with his Bath restaurant and the Bristol one follows the same formula. The quality of the fish (much of it line-caught) is excellent.

FOOD FOR ALL
Hartcliffe Food Co-op, Gatehouse Centre, Hareclive Road, Hartcliffe
Tel: 946 5285
www.hheag.org.uk
Run by the Hartcliffe Health and Environmental Action Group (HHEAG), Food For All is a workers' co-op selling a wide range of Essential Trading products and vegetables brought by bike trailer from Hartcliffe Community Market Gardens. Free-range eggs, meat, bread and more. Anyone can shop at Food for All but they offer a 10% discount for co-op members.

FRESH & WILD
85 Queen's Road
Tel: 910.5930
www.freshandwild.com
The Clifton outlet was Fresh & Wild's first store outside London. Although there's a huge range of top-quality food, drink and other products, Fresh & Wild thrives on its exclusive reputation – this is organic food as a lifestyle statement. And you certainly need quite an affluent lifestyle if you want to do your weekly shop here.

GERT LUSH CHEESE COMPANY
Glass Arcade, St Nicholas Market
www.gertlushcheese.co.uk
Speciality cheese from small producers. Also has a stall at the Slow Food Market.

HARVEST
11 Gloucester Road
Tel: 942 5997
www.harvest-bristol.coop
Harvest is the retail outlet of the Essential Trading Co-operative (above) and, as such, is one of the longest established wholefood co-ops in the west. The philosophy here is to support ethical, organic, vegan, vegetarian and fairtrade products so there's a huge range of carefully-selected produce. There's a small deli counter too selling yummy quiche, wraps and spicy things.

HERBERTS
Wellington Avenue, Montpelier
Tel: 924 7713
www.herbertsbakery.co.uk
The Herbert family has been baking excellent bread in Bristol since the 1960s. Don't leave Montpelier without a loaf or two.

HOBBS HOUSE BAKERY
39 High Street, Chipping Sodbury
Tel: 01454 317525
www.hobbshousebakery.co.uk
Although they are based in Chipping Sodbury, Hobbs House bread is available at selected outlets throughout Bristol including Chandos Deli, Bristol Sweet Mart and Fresh & Wild. Check the website for a full list of outlets.

KALAHARI MOON
The Covered Market, St Nicholas Market
Tel: 07886 887 523
www.kalaharimoon.co.uk
South African food and drink specialists. What exactly is sliced biltong?

KIN YIP HON
16a St Thomas Street, St Thomas
Tel: 929 9098
Next to the Dynasty Chinese restaurant (see Eating Out Listings, p217), the sprawling Kin Yip Hon is a treasure trove of fresh, frozen and tinned ingredients from fish to dim sum and fresh oriental vegetables.

LA RUCA
83 Gloucester Road
Tel: 944 6810
Well-stocked wholefood shop run by a Chilean family with many fairtrade products. There's always a good selection of well-made deli snacks on offer.

Shopping

LICATA'S

36 Picton Street
Tel: 924 7725
332 Gloucester Road
Tel: 924 7718
www.licata.co.uk
Brilliant Italian deli and grocery shop run by
what seems to be several generations of the
same family. Licata's has been in Picton Street
for as long as anyone can remember. The
quality of the food and drink is excellent.

LINCE

18 Filton Road, Horfield
Tel: 377 9712
Deli and cafe full of Portuguese ingredients.

LUNA ROSSA

Covered Market, St Nick's Market
927 6897
Don't make the mistake of asking if they sell
pasta. By the time Peppe Coppola has listed
the 150 fresh and dried varieties on offer,
you'll have missed your dinner. This is a
fantastic Italian deli and a must for coffee
lovers. 'Life is like coffee. If you make good
coffee, you have a good life,' says Peppe.

MASALA

North Street, Bedminster
Tel: 963 6062
www.masala.uk.com
Naomi from Masala was planning to move
over the road opposite Bar Salt at the time
of writing, so check the website for any new
contact details. Masala stocks a selection of
organic veg and wholefoods plus household
and fairtrade products and a tasty selection of
Middle Eastern deli snacks.

PAK BUTCHERS

4 Roman Road
Tel: 951 8057
www.pakbutchers.co.uk
Abdul Malik started out at Pak as a work
experience youngster in 1990. He now runs
the show and has built the business into the
South West's main supplier of Halal meat and
poultry. Pak also sells fish.

PAPADELI

84 Alma Road
Tel: 973 6569
www.papadeli.co.uk
'If it's delicious and handmade, we sell it', is the

LOCAL BEER PRODUCERS

1. BRISTOL BEER FACTORY
www.bristolbeerfactory.co.uk
George Ferguson, architect of Tobacco
Factory fame and champion of independent
businesses in Bristol, bought the old
brewery in Ashton in 2004. He teamed up
with production manager Simon Bartlett
and head brewer Chris Thurgeson to
resume making beer on the site where
Thomas Baynton originally started brewing
in 1840. In 2006, the Brunale Milk Stout
(brewed to celebrate the 200th anniversary
of Brunel's birth) was named Overall Winner
from the 100-plus ales at the CAMRA Bristol
Beer Festival. Other brews include Red, No.
7, Sunrise and Gold which are available at
an ever-growing number of pubs in the city.

2. BATH ALES
www.bathales.com
Formed in 1995 and based in Warmley
between Bath and Bristol, Bath Ales are
as well-liked for their pubs as they are for
the beers. There's no such thing as a bad
Bath Ales pub, y'see. The Hare on the Hill
in Kingsdown, The Wellington on Horfield
Common, The Bridge in St Thomas and The
Merchants Arms in Hotwells were the four
Bath Ales boozers in Bristol at the time of
writing with the promise of more to come.
There are six Bath Ales brews and not a drop
of lager in sight.

3. ZERODEGREES
www.zerodegrees.co.uk
The first branch of Zerodegrees opened in
August 2000 in Blackheath in South East
London. Obviously a success becuase they
opened the Bristol version back in 2004. The
distinctive Black Lager, Wheat Ale, Pilsner
and Pale Ale are all brewed on-site at the
microbrewery. For the health conscious
among you, you will be pleased to hear
that Zerodegrees don't sterile filter their
beer. This basically means that all their
beer is unpasteurised, free of additives and
colouring, which can't be bad. Sat on two
floors on Colston Street, Zerodegrees is also
a good Italian-style restaurant.

Shopping

Listings

philosophy at Papadeli. This well-stocked deli and cafe has an excellent selection of take-away food and you can order hampers online or over the phone.

RADFORD MILL FARM SHOP
41 Picton Street
Tel: 942 6644
On the site of the old One Planet shop, this community-based wholefood shop has a good selection of fruit and veg, tinned and dried organic food, plus deli counter and cafe.

REAL OLIVE COMPANY
Princess Wharf, Harbourside
Tel: 925 1762
www.therealolivecompany.co.uk
Built on the philosophy that 'a day without olives is like a day without sunshine' the Real Olive Company deli is a celebration of Mediterranean food. There's an impressive range of grilled vegetables, speciality stuffed olives, peppers, cheeses, vinegars and much more. The stuffed vine leaves are tops. Attached is the great Olive Shed restaurant (see Eating Out Listings, p219) which offers excellent food and view over the Harbourside.

RED SQUARE
Wells Road, Knowle, West Street, Old Market, Fishponds Road, Fishponds
Eastern European foodstore with loads of dried fish and cooked meats. There's a big range of tinned and pickled vegetables and incredibly sweet cakes and biscuits.

REG THE VEG
6 Boyces Avenue, Clifton
Tel: 07890152628
Excellent vegetable shop on this popular cul-de-sac in Clifton, opposite the Primrose Cafe. Scotch bonnets on the counter is a good sign of a quality greengrocer.

SCOOPAWAY
113 Gloucester Road
Tel: 987 2199
There aren't many shops that require the customers to help themselves by employing that well-known gathering action, the scoop. Here you'll find yourself diving into a range of organic and fairtrade options and saving all that packaging and marketing money through your exertions.

SHEEPDROVE ORGANIC BUTCHERS
3 Lower Redland Road
Tel: 973 4643
www.sheepdrove.com
The only completely organic butcher in Bristol. The meat is sourced from Peter and Juliet Kindersley's Sheepdrove organic farm in Berkshire, the shop also sells organic honey, wine, flour and more.

SOUTHVILLE DELI
262 North Street
Tel: 966 4507
www.southvilledeli.com
Friendly neighbourhood deli and café specialising in organic, fairtrade and locally produced food and wine.

STONEGROUND
5 The Mall
Tel: 974 1260
There's a good range of organic, healthfood and fairtrade produce at Stoneground and a modest deli selection plus some interesting alcohol choices. The quiche is lovely.

T&P MURRAY BUTCHERS
153 Gloucester Road
Tel: 942 4025
This well-established butchers is a good source of organic and free range meat. There's also a host of salami, preserves pickles and cheeses in the deli. The sausages, including The Bishopston, are made on site. There's often a pavement barbecue on which the aforementioned sausages sizzle.

TASTE SEAFOOD & DELICATESSEN
Lakeside, Barrow Gurney
Tel: 01275 474586
www.taste.gb.com
Situated towards Bristol Airport, Taste specialises in British seafood and locally-reared organic meat and game as well as the deli regulars. It can be particularly good for wild food and is the only place we've heard of that sometimes sells squirrel.

TEOHS
28-34 Lower Ashley Road
Tel: 902 1122
Pretty much all the ingredients and accessories you need to create a far-eastern feast are

available at Teohs. The staff are always happy to give recipe advice.

TONY'S CARIBBEAN FOOD
128 Grosvenor Road
Tel: 941 4266
If you need a matokie and some cho-cho to go with your sweet yam and ackee, you need look no further.

TOVEYS
198-200 Stapleton Road
Tel: 951 0987
www.toveys.co.uk
It's often an experience visiting Toveys seafood shop which was established in Bristol in 1935. It's a lively, bustling place full of banter, wisecracks and lots of fish, as fresh as it comes. The staff are knowledgeable and will help you decide what you want. Toveys also stocks a wide range of frozen food. Make sure you ask for your fish to be descaled, watching the descaler in action is worth the trip alone. Just don't forget to take a ticket or you'll just never get served.

VALLEY SMOKEHOUSE
Elton Farm, Dundry
Tel: 0870 747 0850
www.valleysmokehouse.com
A traditional smokehouse specialising in poultry, ducks, cheese, fish, meat, garlic and more. The trout is locally caught and if you phone up, you can arrange to take your own food to be smoked. There's also a great delicatessen on site.

VIVA OLIVA
30 Oxford Street, Totterdown
Tel: 07967 202625
Mediterranean deli in the heart of Totterdown which sells a wholesome selection of olives, tapenade, stuffed vine leaves, breads and lots more.

WAI YEE HONG SUPERMARKET
4 Station Road, Montpelier
Tel: 942 8629
Big selection of Chinese ingredients with a good fruit and veg section.

WILD OATS NATURAL FOODS
9-11 Lower Redland Road
Tel: 973 1967
www.woats.co.uk

Wild Oats has a huge selection of natural foods from organic breads to chilled and frozen foods, organic wines and beers and lots of deli fodder. There's also a big range of food supplements, skin care products, herbs, homoeopathic remedies and aromatherapy. It's run by people who are passionate about food and can provide a wide range of advice on everything from Feldenkrais technique to Japanese cookery and oriental medicine.

WINDMILL HILL CITY FARM SHOP
Philip Street, Bedminster
Tel: 963 3252
www.windmillhillcityfarm.org.uk
There's every possibility that you've seen the bacon you buy here before – when it was in the pig sty with the brothers and sisters you've already eaten. If that puts you off eating meat (the shop also sells lamb, beef, chicken and occasionally goat), the bantam, hen, duck and goose eggs are collected daily from the farmyard and they sometimes have their own goats' milk. For vegans, there is a great selection of organic vegetables from the extensive farm allotments.

Shopping

Listings **Culture**

One long-established theatre, a couple of very credible art schools, the highest concentration of patient Plasticine botherers in the UK and an unusually high percentage of hippies and post-hippies all add up to give Bristol an arty, creative public image. Compared to, say, Leicester or Carlisle, Bristol is like San Francisco c.1968.

True, improvisational theatre has never really taken off in Knowle West or Stockwood but you shouldn't have too much trouble finding a freely expressive amateur dramatic society in Montpelier or St Werburghs. Someone, somewhere

in the city, is always pursuing art for art's sake. It could be a beat poetry evening at the Cube, a South West scriptwriters work-in-progress play at the Macready Rooms, an electrical installation art at the Arnolfini or an afternoon of 13th-Century embroidery instruction at the Folk House.

Of course, if we used the broad definition of the word 'culture' here, we'd have to include karaoke nights in Kingswood, illegal car rallies at the Showcase Cinema and hen night city centre pub crawls; all are valid cultural happenings. But to make things simpler, this is where you'll find a selection of art, theatre, cinema and animation offerings.

Art Galleries

3D GALLERY
13 Perry Road, Park Row
Tel: 929 1363
Contemporary ceramics, sculpture, jewellery, painting, abstract and figurative art.

ARNOLFINI
Narrow Quay
Tel: 929 9191
www.arnolfini.org.uk
One of only a handful of Arts Council-funded galleries in the country, the Arnolfini is host to the most contemporary and most challenging national and international artists around. It reopened in September 2005 after massive re-development and expansion.

BRISTOL CITY MUSEUM AND ART GALLERY
Queens Road
Tel: 922 3571
From Old Masters to contemporary fine, applied and oriental art, the old museum may be a bit dustier than your average showroom but it's still a great place to walk around for an

hour or two. And it's free to get in. Check out the old maps of Bristol on the balcony on the first floor. Fascinating.

CREATE CENTRE
Smeaton Road
Tel: 925 0505
www.bristol-city.gov.uk/create
You just can't miss the size of this thing. It is one of those huge red buildings out near the Cumberland Basin. It has a few levels, usually hosting community projects and exhibitions over three rooms.

CUBE GALLERY
12 Perry Road
Tel: 377 1470
www.cube-gallery.co.uk
Since 2002, the Cube Gallery have been promoting work by established artists from the local area. They have moved to bigger premises so things are obviously going well.

FUSION GALLERY
17 Christmas Steps
Tel: 927 3002
www.fusion-gallery.co.uk
Nicely placed on Christmas Steps, this gallery

provides affordable art. Their 'guest wall' is a great way for highlighting new artists.

GINGER GALLERY
84 Hotwell Road
Tel: 929 2527
Paintings, etchings, sculpture, ceramics, jewellery, photography, ceramics. Form is clearly no barrier for this Hotwells gallery.

GRANT BRADLEY GALLERY
1 St Peter's Court, Bedminster Parade
Tel: 963 7673
www.grantbradleygallery.co.uk
This pleasant, uncluttered gallery space with mezzanine has set itself the challenge of bringing culture to Bedminster. The Gallery is dedicated to the memory of Peter Bradley, Rev Gregory Grant's former business partner and co-founder of the The Grant Bradley Charitable Trust. The mission statement aims include: to promote the values and ideals of The Kingdom of God through art and education; to promote dialogue and understanding of different cultures and religious beliefs through the appreciation of art; to promote education through art for people of all ages; to be a centre for cultural exchange of art and ideas; to bring world-class art to local communities and to promote the work of local artists.

HERE GALLERY
108 Stokes Croft
Tel: 942 2222
www.thingsfromhere.co.uk
The gallery opened back in 2003, originally to house an 'From The West Coast To The West Country' exhibition. A bunch of brave and enthusiastic souls then fought to keep the gallery open. What you have now is an exciting gallery, showcasing local and international artists. There is also a quirky little shop selling anything from underground art to wonderful hand-made clothing.

IL BORDELLO
Welsh Back
Tel: 925 3500
www.ilbordello.co.uk
If the idea of a members-only media bar in Bristol conjures up images of local TV news presenters Peter Rowell and Dave Garmston sitting at a table bouncing irrelevant news items off each other, fear not. Art, poetry, music and silent film are on the agenda on

board the boat moored at the bottom of the famous King Street. Bordello once made national headlines for its AWOL (Alcohol Without Liquid) alcohol vaporiser.

INNOCENT FINE ART
7a Boyce's Avenue, Clifton
Tel: 973 2614
www.innocentfineart.co.uk
Specialises in contemporary artists from the South West with particular emphasis on the Cornish School. The gallery includes paintings, ceramics, sculpture and glassware.

OFF-CENTRE GALLERY
13 Cotswold Road, Windmill Hill
Tel: 987 2647
Contemporary international art from as far afield as Japan, Russia and the Ukraine. Be warned, it is only open by arrangement, day or evening. But well worth the trek.

ROYAL WEST OF ENGLAND ACADEMY
Queens Road, Clifton
Tel: 973 5129
www.rwa.org.uk
Much-respected old school of art that seamlessly embraces classic art and the modern age with exhibits such as Jacqueline Pennel's multi-media installations.

SOMA
Clifton Arcade, 1a Boyces Avenue
Tel: 973 9838
www.somagallery.co.uk
Soma is a gallery space and shop which opened in swanky Clifton Village in 2004. Showcasing artists from the UK with a focus on those from Bristol and the South West.

SPIKE ISLAND
133 Cumberland Road
Tel: 929 2266
www.spikeisland.org.uk
One of the production companies run by Stephen Williams, Charles Mills and Terry Brain. Current projects include TV pilots *Universally Challenged, The Pudding* and *Slimin' Sniffin' Snorks*. They are also producing a Europe-wide Coca-Cola ad campaign. Spike Island is currently undergoing a £2.25 million refurbishment, and is closed to the public until early 2007. Meanwhile, off-site events and exhibitions will take place during 2006.

Culture

Listings

STEPS GALLERY
15 Christmas Steps
Tel: 930 4137
www.stepsgallery.co.uk
A vibrant gallery which features established artists as well as the new talent from the South West. Built c.1630, the building which houses the gallery is worth the trip.

WATERSHED MEDIA CENTRE
1 Canons Road
Tel: 927 5100
www.watershed.co.uk
Still the city's most versatile art space, it offers contemporary photography exhibitions, cinemas, darkrooms, media events and multimedia exhibits.

Theatre

ALBANY CENTRE
Shaftesbury Avenue, Montpelier
Tel: 954 2154
New-age fringe venue with an emphasis on ethnic, political and feminist shows.

BRISTOL OLD VIC
King Street
Tel: 987 7877
www.bristol-old-vic.co.uk
The Theatre Royal was built in 1766 and has been home to the Bristol Old Vic since 1946.

HIPPODROME
St Augustines Parade,
Box Office: 0870 6077500
www.bristol-hippodrome.co.uk
Vast 2,000-seater theatre that has been a fixture in the city centre for a very long time. Specialises in often quite well-known musicals and pantomimes.

REDGRAVE THEATRE
8 Percival Road, Clifton
Tel: 315 7601
As soon as Sir Michael Redgrave declared it open in 1966, this theatre established itself as one of the most desirable venues in town.

SHOW OF STRENGTH THEATRE
74 Chessel Street, Bedminster
Tel: 902 0235
www.showofstrength.org.uk
Professional theatre company based in South Bristol who specialise in putting on undiscovered plays from lesser-known writers.

TOBACCO FACTORY
Raleigh Road, Southville
Tel: 902 0344
www.tobaccofactory.com
Happening new stage space and bar that has revitalised what was once a dark and dingy corner of South Bristol. The drama ranges from the Shakespearean to the experimental.

QEH THEATRE
Jacobs Wells Road
Box Office: 930 3082
www.qehtheatre.com
Vibrant venue that showcases a wide-ranging programme of theatrical happenings.

WICKHAM THEATRE
University of Bristol, Woodland Road
Bookings: 987 7877
This is the stage for the Bristol University Drama Department. Most productions are put on by students and are usually of an extremely high standard.

Cinemas

ARNOLFINI
Narrow Quay
Tel: 917 2300
www.arnolfini.org.uk
Much-needed, no-apologies, art house cinema specialising in the latest European releases and re-runs of American classics.

CINEWORLD
Hengrove Park
Tel: 0871 220 8000
www.cineworld.co.uk
Enormous out-of-town 14-screener multiplex complete with comfortable seats, totally overpriced refreshments and all the latest crap Hollywood blockbusters. Oh, they do a kids show on a Saturday morning too.

CUBE CINEMA
4 Princess Row, Kingsdown
Tel: 907 4190
www.cubecinema.com
This is easily the most vibrant, challenging, non-funded counter-cultural art and media alternative in the West.

IMAX THEATRE, AT-BRISTOL
Harbourside
Tel: 0845 3451235
www.at-bristol.org.uk/IMAX
Because the Imax screen is 21 metres wide and 15 metres tall, it makes you feel like you are actually there. Shame about the standard of films though.

MY VUE
The Venue, Cribbs Causeway & Aspects Leisure Park, Longwell Green
Tel: 08712 240 240
www.myvue.com
These out-of-town-in-the-middle-of-nowhere multiplexes has 12 screens, digital stereo surround sound and premiere size screens. You'll also find a couple of inauthentic multi-national eateries here.

ODEON
Union Street, Broadmead
Tel: 0871 22 44 007
www.odeon.co.uk
Fading, pre-multiplex city centre picture house that runs a handful of major releases.

ORPHEUS HENLEAZE
Northumbria Drive, Henleaze
Tel: 0845 1662381
Admirable three-screen independent that runs the most popular films for longer than anybody else does.

SHOWCASE CINEMA
Bath Road, Avon Meads
Tel: 0871 220 1000
www.showcasecinemas.co.uk
This is the sort of place that puts the big into big screen. The complex has 1,500 car parking spaces, 14 screens and no less than 3,600 reclining armchair seats.

WATERSHED
Cannons Road, Bristol
Tel: 927 5100
www.watershed.co.uk
Two screens offer intelligently selected left-of-centre mainstream, arthouse and retrospective seasons. You can almost overlook the uncomfortable seats and lack of popcorn. They also offer interesting talks and meetings and, of course, the cool Watershed bar where you can have a pint by the water before your film.

BRISTOL ARENA

There are two things that Bristol seems to have a mental block about – building a big swimming pool and a decent concert arena. Every so often the great Bristol public poses the question: why not build a stadium that Rovers, City and Bristol Rugby can share, use it as a concert venue and chuck in a swimming pool while you're about it? Such suggestions are met with a mildly confused expression by the city authorities who carry on blithely giving bits of planning permission for the Memorial Stadium and Ashton Gate, talking about redeveloping the Colston Hall and closing the occasional neighbourhood swimming pool.

Against this background, it's hardly surprising that the £100 million Bristol Arena scheme for land between Temple Meads and the Wells Road has not been straightforward. By the summer of 2006, plans had not been submitted and there wasn't a developer on board, yet the completion date for the arena was still officially 2008. Outline plans for the arena, a casino and 10-storey flats that had appeared in the local press were met with a wave of hostility by local residents appalled at the lack of ambition. They showed a 500-space car park for the 10,500-capacity arena, poor public transport links and confused pedestrian, car and cycle access.

Yet there is general agreement that Bristol needs an arena. The city has missed out on the touring bands and other events that are too big for the Colston Hall so our friends across the bridge in Newport and Cardiff have taken the Bristol pound by providing such facilities.

At the time of writing, the arena development was completely unclear and there was growing concern among local residents that the promised consultation had failed to materialise.

■ **Bristol Arena Concern:**
www.bristolarenaconcern.org.uk
■ **Totterdown Residents Environmental and Social Association (TRESA):**
www.tresa.org.uk
■ **Temple Quarter:**
www.templequarter.com

Culture

ASHTON COURT FESTIVAL

BRISTOL'S BIGGEST AND BEST WEEKEND OFFERS LOCAL TALENT THE CHANCE TO GET SEEN

If there is one event that really defines Bristol culture, it is the ever-popular Ashton Court Festival, the biggest gathering of its type in the world. The reason that the organisers can be sure of that claim is that there really isn't anything else like Ashton Court anywhere outside Bristol.

Although there has been a small entry charge since 2002, for most of its history since the first festival in 1974, Ashton Court has been free. Thousands of musicians, artists, stage builders, sound engineers and volunteers of all shapes, sizes and ages have given their services free of charge to make sure that, against all odds, the two-day festival goes ahead every July.

In recent years, the festival has attracted headline acts such as Portishead back in 1997, Robert Plant in 2003 and Simple Minds and Dreadzone in 2006. But big headline bands are not what Ashton Court is really about – one of the reasons why Ashton Court is so different from the piles of other festivals around the country. The aim is straightforward: to provide a stage for local talent across a wide range of musical and artistic disciplines. In most years, the festival has achieved that in the face of apathy (at best) and hostility (at worst) from the local authorities.

The first festival was organised by a character called Royce Creasey, who still lives in Easton. He's a remarkable person: a former RAF technician, Formula One pit mechanic, motorcycle journalist, printer and a motorcycle designer of rare vision. The idea of a free festival in the grounds of the Ashton Court Estate was suggested to Royce by a young New Zealand couple who had heard of his formidable reputation for 'getting things done'. Royce took over the project with a vision for a bandstand in the park based on his experiences at the Hell's Angels festivals in Windsor Great Park. He cajoled and persuaded the local authorities to let him and his self-styled Hippy Deviant mates organise the event. At all times,

Creasey worked on the principle that: 'Life is a confidence trick. If you've got the confidence, you can pull the trick.'

In 1974, the first Ashton Court Festival was held over four weekends and the stage was a back of a lorry; Fred Wedlock was among the performers as were a band called Pussy Spasm. Since then most of the musicians mentioned in this book (see Bristol Beat, p140) have performed at Ashton Court at some time or another.

The festival has grown since its early days and nowadays, the festival attracts more 100,000 people over the two days. Sadly it is no longer free and the running costs are enormous. Certainly Royce Creasey feels that it's is no longer true to its roots: 'Free festivals are about being free, not free entry,' he has said. Certainly Ashton Court has now become a huge commercial event, but if you scratch the surface you will always find that beneath all the rules, regulations and huge budget, there is still a dedicated group of Bristol people working for nothing to create a showcase for local talent. Why do they do it? Because they want to.

Contact Ashton Court Festival
- Tel: 904 2275
- 1 Ninetree Hill, Stokes Croft
- www.ashtoncourtfestival.com
- info@ashtoncourtfestival.com

How to get there
A special festival bus service (costing around £2) usually runs from the Colston Hall, from the bottom of Blackboy Hill and from opposite the old ABC cinema on Whiteladies Road. The website offers maps and directions for any which way you may choose to arrive.

Tickets
You can just turn up and pay on the day but you can save yourself a few quid by getting hold of discounted advance tickets too – usually from Bristol Ticket Shop and the Colston Hall.

Culture

Culture

Listings **Local Media**

Television, film, newspapers, magazines, books, radio, Internet. PR, advertising, marketing, design, video production. Bristol is now home to a multi-faceted array of media companies all jostling for so-called 'creative' space. The unprecedented growth of this sector has done much to raise the overall quality of the output with many organisations operating on a national, not just local level. But for every adventurous new art scene web mag, there is a dreary and irrelevant parochial yawn that passes for a free newspaper. You'll find both good and bad media here. We've concentrated on media that the public knows, as a list of creative digital communications agencies in Bristol would need a phone directory of its own. If you do produce a bi-monthly pamphlet on red squirrel activity in the Withywood area, we must apologise for missing you out.

Television

BBC WEST
www.bbc.co.uk/pointswest
'Hello and welcome to Pointless West.' The flagship show of the Bristol arm of the BBC's nationwide network suffers from an extreme case of 'local media syndrome'. It's cosy, superficial, its presenters wink at you from their sofa, the weatherman tells you about primary school fayres he is opening in lovely Minchinhampton.

ITV WEST
www.itvregions.com/west
This undistinguished lump of Brislington concrete is the commercial wing of the local television experience. It has been the perfect place to pump out an endless stream of toe-curlingly embarrassing programmes over the years, most of them fronted by the world's unfunniest man, Jon Monie. Every single leisure-type HTV show has been appalling but *Trip in the Cosmic Buggy* must be the worst.

ENDEMOL WEST
www.endemoluk.com
Based in a not-so-hip Bath Road industrial estate, this is the South West branch of the company that brought you *Big Brother*, *The Games*, and, somewhat surprisingly, BBC2's *Restoration*. Endemol employs up to 800 people in London, Bristol and Glasgow and is part of the international Endemol Group; a worldwide network of production companies spanning 22 countries. Endemol is owned by Spanish telecoms and media giant Telefonica – the largest provider of telecom and internet services in the Spanish and Portuguese language world with more than 62 million customers. Keep an eye open for adverts in the local press and you could end up in the studio audience for Noel Edmonds' *Deal Or No Deal* show which is filmed in Bristol.

Animation

AARDMAN ANIMATIONS
www.aardman.com
Can anyone smell burning plasticine? Well Morph and his cohorts may have starred in an impromptu version of the *Towering Inferno* when Aarman's St Phillip's warehouse burned down in 2005 but not even a charred cast of thousands has stopped Nick Park's ever-expanding animation empire from swelling ever wider.

BOLEX BROTHERS
www.bolexbrothers.co.uk
Perverse pixel-warping short film terrorists who debuted with the grotesque *Secret Adventures of Tom Thumb* in 1993. Deformed infants, ravenous insects and a hatful of surreal obsessions have been their themes ever since. David Cronenberg surely approves.

LICORICE FILM
www.licoricefilm.com
Even without seeing her frankly remarkable Mavis Riley/William Burrough's impersonations, *The Simpson's* creator Matt Groening described Hazel Grain as a 'funny filmmaking genius'. Now Bristol animation's first lady has gathered all her brilliantly warped shorts under the Licorice banner. Licorice? Tis the devils string.

Radio

BBC RADIO BRISTOL
www.bbc.co.uk/bristol
If it's funny stories about making tea in Fishponds you're after, don't touch that dial. Hosted by John Turner and a few other blokes who sound like John Turner, this is radio circa 1961; yokel, pedestrian, coming live from flower shows in Melksham. To be fair Radio Bristol has a strong sense of community and John Turner's phone-ins are occasionally priceless. Is Steve Yabsley serious or as surrealist as Geof Twentyman's moustache? Keith Warmington is good as well. Actually, we listen to it quite a lot.

VIBE FM
www.vibe101.co.uk
Previously known as Galaxy 101, this is the sort of commercial pop radio station that listeners who don't like music tune into. In other words, it's wall-to-wall R 'n' B, hip-hop lite and other assorted 'urban' tuneage. Basically shite, in other words.

STAR FM
www.starbristol.co.uk
Why is it that some radio stations just can't let go of the 1980s? It was, lest we forget, the poorest musical decade of the latter half of the 20th Century. The Thompson Twins? OMD? Howard Jones? Ooooohhh Vienna.

BURST
www.burstradio.org.uk
Bristol University's official radio station is a lively mix of national and local news bulletins, special reports, arts and sports and a music policy that is just about on the right side of decent... most of the time. We agree that it is fantastic idea for the university to have its own station, but James Blunt? Come on guys! Are you for real?

TYPICAL POINTS WEST NEWS STORIES

....

1. WESTLAND HELICOPTERS
If a nut is done up too tight or a rotary blade out of synch, they wheel out Malcolm Frith for a 17-minute piece-to-camera lead story. Even the helicopters fall asleep.

2. BRIDGWATER CARNIVAL
Every year *Points West* descend on masse to the Bridgwater carnival. From the building of the floats, to the odd light bulb crisis, costume dilemmas to music selection, every aspect of this oh-so-thrilling 4-mile-an-hour drive-by is covered. The by far more interesting Ashton Court Festival, on the other hand, barely gets a mention.

3. CAKES
If the bakery is closed for good, what are they going to do with all the cakes? Don't worry, Chris 'hello' Vacher and friends will save the day by donating all the pastry excess to a charitable organisation of their choice. That's a lead story if ever I saw one!

4. THE RED ARROWS
For what feels like 3,000 years, *Points West* has covered the bloody Red Arrow's whenever and wherever they've been in flight. Listen, the Red Arrows were crap in 1973, they are worse than soddin' balloons. Every year it's the same: 'Oh look balloons', 'oh look the Red Arrows'. Enough is enough.

5. CONCORDE
Remembering it. Coming over all sad about its demise. Falling out over the museum version of it. *Points West* loves Concorde so much, it made a video of its life story. More than a thousand pensioners cued for two days to get their hands on a copy.

6. WHATEVER IS IN THE EVENING POST
Save yourself the cost of buying an evening paper, put your feet up with a cup of tea and have that nice Chris Vacher read it out to you. Sometimes 'newsgathering' on local television news seems to involve nipping down the newsagents.

Media

Listings

GWR
www.gwrfmbristol.co.uk
Home to Bush and Troy, black thunder jeeps, late-night love and oodles of other tacky promotional stuff you thought had died with Smashy 'n' Nicey. 'We've vetoed manufactured bands,' they shout before lining up the new Lee Ryan single.

THE HUB
www.uwesu.net/thehub
UWE's much hipper take on the official uni radio station is based in Bower Ashton and encourages student involvement at every turn. 'Hey, we are always on the look out for new DJs to put more funk in our trunk!!' enthuses the website, embarrassingly. Right, where is that gaffer tape?

GRAND THEFT AUDIO
www.grandtheftaudio.co.uk
A free, 24-hour urban internet radio station that plays hip-hop, drum 'n' bass, garage and breakbeat. They also provide an opportunity for producers and DJs to get themselves heard out there where it matters.

PASSION 106.2
Playing predominantly roots reggae, ragga, dub, jungle and breaks, Passion FM is probably the most listened to pirate radio station in town. The DJs at Passion have to pay subs, which upsets a fair few of them! The naff local adverts that clog up the airwaves are so bad – picture cheesy digital voiceover effect complete with Bristolian accent – they become part of the entertainment.

Newspapers, Magazines & Websites

EVENING POST
www.epost.co.uk
Okay, so it's half way between the *Daily Mail* and the *Yorkshire Post* but you have to admit it improved a hell of a lot under the editorship of Mike Lowe, even though sales fell dramatically. Then owners Northcliffe announced they were selling off all their regional papers and wanted 37 redundancies in Bristol. According to insiders, bullying and backstabbing became a way of life at the *Post* and *Press* as some people who wanted redundancy were refused it and

some who wanted to stay put were shown the door. Mike Lowe and his deputy Stan 'The Man' Szecowka left when Mike Norton was appointed as managing editor of the *Post* and *Western Daily Press*. With morale at the *Post* said to be the lowest ever, it's hardly surprising that the quality of the paper declined rapidly during the blood-letting. In the mid 1980s, the circulation was about 110,000 a day. Sales at the beginning of 2006 had plummeted to 56,000.

WESTERN DAILY PRESS
www.westpress.co.uk
As the *Evening Post* zooms off into the future in its slinky new multi-sectioned shoes, the *Western Daily Press* puts some coal on the fire and prepares to chug around the station for a while. The WDP is the rural morning paper covering the whole of the South West from the Cotswolds to Dorset. It's an old fashioned Tory workhorse, traditionally staffed by former Fleet Street hacks. Despite it's *Daily Mail* tendencies, it's a well produced paper and seems to know its readership far better than the *Post*. Circulation, though falling, is relatively stable with sales of about 47,000 per day.

VENUE
www.venue.co.uk
Without doubt, the finest regional listings magazine in the country. *Venue* began as a kind of *City Limits* for Bristol under the visionary stewardship of the relentlessly single-minded Dave Higgett and the idiosyncratically entrepreneurial Dougal Templeton. It is now owned by Northcliffe but is still the only magazine to buy if you want to know what is going on in Bristol.

ORIGIN PUBLISHING
www.originpublishing.co.uk
A Future Publishing off-shoot (and now part of BBC Worldwide), Origin snatched all the hairdressing, sewing and fishing titles and relocated to a 1970s tower block near The Bierkeller. Doesn't sound very glamorous does it? But having an annual turnover of £21m proves there's gold in dull hobby magazines.

DECODE
www.decodemagazine.com
In an age when even the good guys are dancing with the devil, *Decode* magazine is a divine inspiration. Produced every couple of

months by a committed and passionate team working for no monetary benefits, *Decode* is a thoughtful, stylish, cutting-edge title that takes an informed stance of music, art, films, theatre, exhibitions and writing and then takes the temperature of the city's current cultural state of play.

TRADE-IT
www.trade-it.co.uk
Published every Wednesday, Friday and Sunday, *Trade-It* is a free ads publication covering Bristol, Bath, Swindon, Gloucester, and the surrounding areas, offering 50,000 ads in categories ranging from computers to holiday homes. The Free to Collector section always contains some very weird stuff. Half-a-tonne of pebbledash for nothing? Now, that's a bargain.

THE SPARK
www.thespark.co.uk
What does *The Spark* tell us about Bristol? Well, it's the only city in the country that can sustain a free 33,000 circulation quarterly newspaper devoted to alternative therapy, psychotherapy, counselling and healing. Editor John Dawson founded *The Spark* in 1993 and since then it has become the focus for the alternative community in the South West. It's based on the free newspaper principle of advertising paying the wages and production costs and is eagerly awaited every quarter by those with an interest in the content and those who enjoy a look at the alternative world. It's easy to poke fun at *The Spark*, and they are not beyond a touch of self-deprecation, but how can you disagree with a mission statement that begins: 'Our aim is to keep you in touch with locally-based creative solutions for a changing world and to help you get the best out of life.'

POUT
www.poutmagazine.co.uk
Expensively shiny free mini-mag that covers fashion, clubbing, food, health and beauty and property with lots of glossy colour photos and some very ordinary advertorial writing. They aren't going to change the world but they might just change their shoes.

PORN MAGAZINE
www.myspace.com/pornmagazine
Street-talking music and culture freebie riddled with phrases like 'drop a fattie' and 'big ups'. But underneath all the Nathan Barley twanging there are genuine attempts to make sense of it all. The rights and wrongs of Jeep beats are laid bare, an enthusiastic analysis of consensus politics covers three pages and chavs get the piss ripped out of them in 10 easy stages.

BRISTOL REVIEW
www.bristolreview.com
It's difficult to imagine the scene at the birth of this particular magazine. 'Right, we'll sell about 40-odd pages of adverts and fill in the remaining half-a-dozen with some shabby first-person 'reviews' of a few pubs, restaurants and clubs. Any questions?' It is not a guide to the city. It isn't really a magazine.

BRISTOL REVIEW OF BOOKS
www.bristolbooksandpublishers.co.uk
An ambitious team of independent Bristol publishers have put their competitiveness to one side and banded together to produce this rather good quarterly magazine about Bristol's publishing heritage.

BRISTLE
www.bristle.org.uk
An anarcho, non-aligned, alternative quarterly magazine for the West Country with a think-global, act-local, direct-action agenda. Produced by the Kebele Kulture Projekt, *Bristle* highlights local issues and injustices as well as taking a broader view of national and international issues. There's everything from the 'Buses not Bosses' local transport campaign to in-depth articles on Nicaragua. The book, music and film reviews are well chosen and enlightening and there's a good contact list of local campaigning groups.

BRISTOL INDYMEDIA
www.bristolindymedia.org
This is an essential source of alternative news and views plus details of local protests, demos and campaigns as well as national and international issues. The site is updated daily and has a policy of not editing comments and views unless they are malicious. There is a huge archive of Bristol's non-aligned political activity and good links to subvertising sites and more. This is one of the few sources of information in Bristol and around that isn't controlled by that giant Northcliffe.

Media

Listings **Nights Out**

Mention Bristol to anyone north of Cheltenham or south of Bath and it won't be long before their eyes widen and they start banging on about the city's club scene. The thing is, it's all true: Bristol is a clubbing city. Anything that's happened in the last two or three decades has happened within earshot of a bruising rhythm and a throbbing bass. Punk rock came and had reggae at its side. Some of us even spent Live Aid in a St Paul's blues club. We began going to the Dugout a few times a week, absorbing reggae, disco and early hip-hop beats. It was in and around independent black clubs like this that the hybrid Bristol sound was born.

Although you never felt the hand of history on your shoulder in the Dugout, it was easily the most vibrant club the city has ever seen. You shuffled along the corridor, pushed your entrance fee under the glass into the hand of the always unfazed Max or Chips, stumbled down a flight of stairs and felt your shoes stick to whatever the substance was that covered the dance floor.

So, is there any room for places like the Dugout these days? Well, one of the last remaining 'alternative' club venues, Easton Community Centre, is no more. The free party scene seems to have run out of hiding places too. But all is not lost to the crazy gods of pointless noise. Fiddlers, the Blue Mountain, the Black Swan, E Shed, the Dojo Lounge and the Thekla aren't afraid of stepping over the boundary ropes and monthly happenings like Blowpop, Espionage and Payback help keep some swagger in the famous Bristol groove. Tomorrow, by the way, probably belongs to Native, the radical rock revolution at The Croft and the warped electroclash mayhem of Metal Disko. Try dancing to that in a pair of sensible shoes!

ANSON ROOMS
Queens Road, Clifton
Tel: 954 5800
This cavernous room on the first floor of the bleak 1960s-built Student Union building is the largest standing venue in Bristol. The Anson Rooms sadly suffers from a stupidly restricted guestlist policy, too many idiot door staff in rugby shirts and the atmosphere of a school assembly hall.

ARC BAR
27 Broad Street
Tel: 922 6456
It strayed away from its avant-garde roots and lost its intimacy when it expanded. A great idea that's gone a bit wrong. Let's hope they remember what made it such a good bar in the first place.

BIERKELLER
All Saints Lane, The Pithay
Tel: 926 8514
Without doubt, Bristol's most miserable live venue. Dingy and unfriendly, this oompah house is characterised by Newcastle Brown Ale, people playing pool while the band is on and flooded toilets. They only book around one decent band every two years.

BLUE MOUNTAIN CLUB
2 Stokes Croft
Tel: 942 0341
The Blue Mountain might not be as famous as it thinks it is, but it is one of the more challenging sonic spaces around. Bleeding-edge party-of-the-moment is Metal Disko, a knees-up for 'disko punks, popkids, supermodels and futurists'.

BRISTOL ACADEMY
Frogmore Street
Tel: 0970 771 2000
www.bristol-academy.co.uk
The best thing about the Academy is that it's home to the excellent Blowpop DJs. Other than that, it's a soulless, functional venue for big names when they visit Bristol, as well as other live music and club nights.

BROWNSTONE BAR
13-15 King Street
Tel: 927 2277
Townie, plush bar and home to the Housework 'dirty, funky house' DJs.

CLUB CASTRO
72-73 Old Market
Tel: 922 0774
Seriously gay, nosebleed-inducing, hard house, high-nrg and trance club best known for its very late nights and, with Sundaze, its willingness to party on a Sunday.

COLSTON HALL
Colston Street
Tel: 922 3686
www.colstonhall.org
Gene Pitney, Status Quo, the Polish National Symphony Orchestra, the Chippendales, Sing-A-Long-A-Abba... if you were being cruel you could describe the Colston Hall's booking policy as 'anything as long as it's crap'. But let's not forget that The Clash played here once. Massive Attack refuse to play here because of the association with slave trader Edward Colston. In January 2006, Bristol City Council approved a £20 million redevelopment of this part of Bristol history.

COOLER
4 Park Street
Tel: 945 0999
Bristol's old indie clubs never die, they just take their copies of James' *Sit Down* around town. Cooler is a rubbish name for a dance club, let alone an alternative one, and is a long way from being progressive, but the reports have been good. Mr Rotten sneers from the Cum flyposters and that is never a bad thing.

COSIES
34 Portland Square, St Paul's
Tel: 942 4110
Hidden away in a stylish Georgian square best known for parking and prostitution, Cosies is a mild-mannered wine bar for office workers by day and a furious miss-mash of leftfield electro beats in the evening.

THE CROFT,
117 Stokes Croft
Tel: 903 0796
www.the-croft.com
An institution in Bristol. Nobody has a music policy quite as switched on as The Croft's. Anticipating the death of the dreary dance scene, they have grabbed the approaching new dawn of diversity with both hands and mix dub, mangled electro synthcore and radical alt. rock nights.

DOJO LOUNGE
12-16 Park Row
Tel: 925 1177
Owned by former England fast bowler Syd Lawrence, Dojo has the knack of being one of the most relaxed, as well as one of most ambitious, clubs in Bristol. The weekend nights are all about the hip-hop favourites Slosh and Payback.

BAJA CLUB
Cannons Road, Harbourside
Tel: 922 0330
www.bajabristol.com
Super-club on the Harbourside, usually full of hen and stag nights. Complete with seven bars, podiums, and glitter balls. What more could you ask for?

FIDDLERS
Willway Street, Bedminster
Tel: 987 3403
Tucked away down a sidestreet off a sidestreet south of the river, this unlikely family-owned success story has carved out a niche for itself by offering mainly earthy blues and roots with a raw live appeal. Simply finding the place is a bit of an adventure.

FLEECE AND FIRKIN
12 St Thomas Street, St Thomas
Tel: 945 0996
Not too long ago, The Fleece was Bristol's foremost gig venue but keeps reverting to counterfeit Stones, pretend Blondies and several Whole Lotta Led Zeps to fill the week, while very average soul covers get the Blues Brothers parties going at weekends.

Nights out

Listings

THE HATCHET
27 Frogmore Street
Tel: 929 4118
The upstairs bar at 'Bristol's oldest pub' has been home to many a rock night over the years. Altamont started up in the summer of 2006 promising to deliver a varied selection from The Stones, to The Smiths and the Pixies. Let's hope they deliver.

LA ROCCA
Triangle South
Tel: 926 0924
With its original disco seating and groovy circular wall holes, La Rocca can be a cool place when the music is right. Sadly, inconsistency is the tune you're most likely to hear.

LAKOTA
6 Upper York Street, St Paul's
Tel: 942 6208
The once mighty Lakota was pulling punters from all over when the rest of Bristol's upstart club venues were empty warehouses. Lakota's status may have faded but it still comes up with the occasional surprise.

LUNA
15 Richmond Terrace, Clifton
Tel: 973 0986
This used to be the Alexandra Club, one of Bristol's oldest nitespots which had been around since the days when clubs were populated solely by blokes over the age of 30 in flared, white three-piece hi-waister suits. Luna is a far more upmarket venue and has gained a reputation for being the in-place for the trendy and chic Clifton crowd who are lured in by the cocktails, table service and private members bar.

LIZARD LOUNGE
66 Queens Road
Tel: 949 7778
Caters for students in the good old fashioned pissed-off-their-heads-dancing-to-*Club-Tropicana* sense of the word. Cocktail nights, salsa nights, mad-for-it nights, pints £1.50 on Tuesday nights. This is student heaven right on the Triangle.

THE LOUISIANA
Wapping Road
Tel: 926 5978
It might be the size of an average toilet and have a curb instead of a proper stage, but this hasn't stopped the Louisiana from pulling in some of the biggest names on the indie scene over the years. It has always been and still is one of the coolest gig venues in town. Let's just pray that the owners Schillacis don't book the Polyphonic Spree.

MBARGO
38-40 Triangle West
Tel: 925 3256
Reinforcing the Triangle's reputation for being a touch more sophisticated than the clubs 'down the hill', Mbargo boasts a decent wine list, cocktails and imported beer.

MR WOLF'S
33 St Stephens Street
Tel: 927 3221
www.mrwolfs.com
A very chilled out little bar in the centre of town where you can get a lovely bowl of noodles. At its best, it acts as a lively pre- or post-club bar. On the downside, the live music can dominate, so unless you really want to see the band, it's best to come early or late.

CONCERT HALLS

ST GEORGE'S
Great George Street, off Park Street
(0845 40 24 001)
www.stgeorgesbristol.co.uk
From Lloyd Cole to the London Fortepiano Trio, Shostakovich's Piano Sonata No 1 to I Don't Want To Go To Chelsea, St George's is a venue that suits them all. Built in 1823 by Sir Robert Smirke, it is known nationwide for its quite exceptional acoustics. In terms of sound quality, this is one of the UK's most highly rated concert halls, it offers the sort of up-close-and-personal sonic intimacy that even ambient perfectionist Brian Eno himself would approve of.

COLSTON HALL
www.bristol-city.gov.uk
Bristol City Council has approved the exciting £20 million scheme to transform Colston Hall into one of the UK's leading performance centres for the creation and enjoyment of all styles of music.

NATIVE
15 Small Street
Tel: 930 4217
Native has taken over from Level as the really cool city centre club. This intimate venue has a great sound system and brings in top DJs.

OCEANA
South Buildings, Canons Road
Tel: 927 9203
www.oceanaclubs.com
This is the most super of super-clubs in Bristol (and we mean super in size, not quality). Its slogan brags five bars, two nightclubs and dining in one destination. It sounds like a meat market to us. And you have to wear proper shoes to get in.

PANACHE
The Pithay, All Saints Street
Tel: 0845 241 7185
Panache rose from the ashes of McClusky's. It bills itself as an 'exclusive' club but at 2am I doubt it's that exclusive anymore. As well as the usual DJs etc, they are big in to events, from boys taking their clothes off to gigs.

POLISH CLUB
50 St Paul's Road, Clifton
Tel: 973 6244
Okay, so it's not really a club in the traditional sense of the word and is generally a private party and members-only establishment. But anywhere that hangs a photo of the legendary 1982 Polish World Cup side behind the bar deserves to get a mention. And it is the most fantastically friendly club in Bristol.

PO NA NA
67 Queens Road
Tel: 925 6225
www.ponana.com
Po Na Na's subterranean halls are famously popular with students. Removed from the melee of the town clubs, it's a classy joint with a music policy that includes classic Motown, funk and disco.

THE PROM
The Promenade, Gloucester Road
Tel: 942 7319
The transformation of the old wine bar into a Mediterranean-flavoured cafe-blues bar has been like a breath of sunshine for the lower Gloucester Road area. Friendly, not bothered by fashion and home to the longest-running Tuesday night pop quiz on Planet Earth.

THEKLA
The Grove, Harbourside
Tel: 929 3301
Bristol's legendary floating nightclub has always been the choice of clubbers who don't really like going to clubs. Downstairs is suitably dark and dingy so that regulars like Espionage and Fruity Antics can thrive.

TIMBUK2
22 Small Street
Underground arches rock to breaks, house, electronica and drum 'n' bass.

WEDGIES
48 Park Street
www.wedgies.co.uk
The Wedge... The Big Wedge... Wedgies... Whatever you want to call it, this is Bristol's greatest and cheesiest student club night. With sports teams, members, VIP cards (apparently you have to strip on a podium to get one), this is more than just a club night, it's a way of life. Best get hammered before you go in. Not the place to enter sober!

Nights out

Listings **Sport**

Bristol is the biggest regional city in England not to have a football team in the top two divisions. Think about it. Liverpool, Manchester, Sheffield, Leeds, Birmingham, Newcastle, Southampton, Coventry, Portsmouth, Bolton, Blackburn, Ipswich, Norwich, Reading and Wigan are all famous for having top flight football in recent years. The last time a Bristol team was in the top division was when City were in Division One between 1976 and 1980. And after getting relegated, they fell straight through the divisions in successive seasons before landing bankrupt at the bottom of Division Four with one almighty thump.

Bristol is simply not a football town, though Rovers and City are among the best supported teams in the lower divisions and the rivalry between the fans is unsurprisingly bitter.

There are probably deep sociological reasons why Bristol football is crap, but the reason you'll hear trotted out is that it's because rugby and cricket are the dominant sports. Sadly, this theory is bollocks. Although egg chasing is a popular West Country pastime, Bristol Rugby Club have suffered poor fortunes since the advent of professionalism while Gloucestershire County Cricket Club is hardly among the modern game's pacesetters, though the standard of both professional rugby and cricket in Bristol is far higher than that of the football.

Besides, have you ever heard anyone argue that football in Manchester has suffered because of the success of Lancashire CC or Sale Rugby Union?

Professional Sport

BRISTOL ROVERS
Memorial Stadium, Filton Avenue, Horfield
Tel: 909 6648
www.bristolrovers.premiumtv.co.uk

BRISTOL CITY
Ashton Gate, Ashton
Tel: 963 0630
www.bcfc.co.uk

GLOUCESTERSHIRE CC
County Ground, Neville Road, Bishopston
Tel: 910 8000
www.gloscricket.co.uk

BRISTOL RUGBY CLUB
Memorial Stadium, Filton Avenue, Horfield
Tel: 0871 208 2234
www.bristolrugby.co.uk

Sports Centres

DAVID LLOYD CLUB
Ashton Road, Nr Long Ashton
Tel: 953 1010
www.davidlloydleisure.co.uk

EASTON LEISURE CENTRE
Thrissell Street, Easton
Tel: 955 8840
Gym: 903 8000

HENBURY LEISURE CENTRE
Avonmouth Way, Henbury
Tel: 353 2555
Gym: 353 2554

HORFIELD LEISURE CENTRE
Dorian Road, Horfield
Tel: 903 1643
Gym: 353 2540

KINGSDOWN SPORTS CENTRE
Portland Street, Kingsdown
Tel: 942 6582
Gym: 903 1637

KINGSWOOD LEISURE CENTRE
Church Road, Staple Hill
Tel: 01454 865701

ST PAUL'S COMMUNITY SPORTS ACADEMY
Newfoundland Road, St Paul's
Tel: 377 3405
Gym: 377 3405

WHITCHURCH SPORTS CENTRE
Bamfield, Whitchurch
Tel: 01275 833 911

Swimming Pools

BISHOPSWORTH
Whitchurch Lane, Bishopsworth
Tel: 903 1600

BRISTOL SOUTH
Dean Lane, Bedminster
Tel: 966 3131

EASTON
Thrissell Street
Tel: 955 8840

HENBURY
Avonmouth Way, Henbury
Tel: 353 2555

HENLEAZE SWIMMING CLUB
Henleaze Lake, Lake Road, Henleaze
www.bristolhenleazesc.org.uk
This is a fabulous members-only lake with high diving boards. This is a perfect spot for a day out in the summer. Get signed in by a member if you want to try it out. Sadly, the waiting list for membership is about two year's long, but worth putting your name down for.

HORFIELD
Dorian Road, Horfield
Tel: 903 1643

JUBILEE POOL
Jubilee Road, Knowle
Tel: 903 1607

SHIREHAMPTON
Park Road, Shirehampton
Tel: 982 2627

SPEEDWELL
Whitefield Road, Speedwell
Tel: 967 4778

Other Sports

CLIMBING
Undercover Rock, Bristol Climbing Centre, St Werburghs Church, Mina Road
Tel: 941 3489
www.bristolclimbingcentre.com
Learn how not to get stuck halfway up the Avon Gorge. Bristol Climbing Centre is a ludicrously popular place with both kids and adults. There is a 12-metre high wall with pillar, fins, overhangs and arches, and a bouldering area. Undercover Rock runs a whole host of courses, works with children from local schools and also offers corporate 'team dynamics' stuff, all based around climbing.

ATHLETICS
Bristol and West Athletics Club
www.bristolandwestac.org.uk
Holds regular training sessions at the Whitchurch and Filton track as well as hill training all around Bristol and training runs at Ashton Court. The club competes in a number of national competitions at all levels.

FENCING
Bristol Fencing Club
www.bristolfencingclub.com
Long-established fencing club based at Redland High School. Organises the Bristol Fencing Open annual event and runs coaching sessions for adults and juniors.

TENNIS
Bristol Lawn Tennis & Squash Club
Redland Green, Redland
Tel: 973 1139
www.bltsc.co.uk
Bristol used to be the last UK grass court tournament before Wimbledon, so loads of top players visited Bristol for the Lambert & Butler Championship. The pre-Wimbledon week has long since gone, but the club remains a top regional tennis centre.

Sport

Listings **Events**

January

BRISTOL ACOUSTIC MUSIC FESTIVAL
www.bristolfolkhouse.co.uk
Not so much unplugged as plugless at the Folk House on Park Street. Usually held mid January.

SLAPSTICK SILENT COMEDY FILM FESTIVAL
www.slapstick.org.uk
Laurel and Hardy, Harold Lloyd, Charlie Chaplin and Buster Keaton blowout based at the Watershed. Usually third weekend in January.

March

FAIRTRADE FORTNIGHT
www.bristolfairtradenetwork.org.uk
Bristol is an active fairtrade city so watch out for promotions, exhibitions, speakers, films and other events for two weeks in mid March.

BRISTOL BEER FESTIVAL
www.camrabristol.org.uk
Now settled into a long-term venue at the Brunel Passenger Shed at Temple Meads station, the Bristol Beer Festival is usually held on the last weekend in March. At the last count it features more than 125 real ales and about 40 ciders. Shame you can't try them all. Or can you? Tickets go on sale in December and are often all gone in a couple of weeks.

May

JACK IN THE GREEN
home.freeuk.net/bristoljack
Pagan frivolity featuring a procession of musicians and dancers dawdling behind Jack from the Harbourside to Horfield Common in a celebration of summer. Expect Morris dancers. Held on the first Saturday in May.

REDLAND FAIR
www.rcas.org.uk
A village fete affair on Redland Green with loads of stalls which has been going since the mid 1970s. So busy you have to push your way through the crowds of teenagers trying to look cool by the coconut shies and cake stands. Surreal fun.

JAMAICA STREET STUDIOS OPEN DAY
www.jamaicastreetartists.co.uk
This Stokes Croft studio with a big reputation throws open its doors in early May.

ECO DAY
www.bristol-city.gov.uk/create
Alternative homes and gardens day at the Create Centre. About 50 stalls ranging from solar energy to recycled stationery, plus talks and events. Usually held mid May.

SOUTH BANK ARTS AND PERFORMANCE TRAIL
www.southbank-bristol.co.uk
Nose around people's houses and look at some art at the same time. Usually held on the third weekend in May.

BATH FRINGE FESTIVAL
www.bathfringe.co.uk
The best event in Bath includes theatre, music, art and kids' events plus the famous Bedlam Street Fair. Usually held the last week of May and the first week of June.

BATH INTERNATIONAL MUSIC FESTIVAL
www.bathmusicfest.org.uk
The opening night is one of the biggest events in Bath with fireworks, music, performance and much merrymaking. Usually held at the end of May and beginning of June.

CHEESE ROLLING
www.cheese-rolling.co.uk
In a tradition that dates back to the 1700s, country folk congregate at Coopers Hill near Brockworth between Cheltenham and Stroud and chase a bloody great big Double Gloucester down the hill. The event takes place on the Whit Bank Holiday Monday.

June

BRISTOL FESTIVAL OF NATURE
www.festivalofnature.org
Centred around the At-Bristol complex, the festival is organised by the Bristol Natural History Consortium and features talks, walks, animal encounters, cookery, real food, green markets, books, art and much more. A great day out for all the family. Usually the first weekend in June.

NATURAL LIVING SHOW
www.naturalhealthshows.co.uk
Alternative therapy, crystals, healing weekend with talks, workshops and performances in the L Shed and Harbourside. First weekend in June.

BRISTOL BIKE FEST
www.bristolbikefest.com
Increasingly popular bike racing event at Ashton Court. Second weekend in June.

ARCHITECTURE WEEK
www.architectureweek.co.uk
Bristol usually comes up with an impressive range of lectures, tours and other events in National Architecture Week in late June

VENN FESTIVAL
www.vennfestival.com
Modern music festival based in Stokes Croft, but which spreads out to venues across the city at the beginning of June.

BRISTOL VEGAN FAYRE
www.yaoh.co.uk
The world's biggest vegan event usually takes place around the L-Shed at Princes Wharf on the second weekend of June.

REFUGEE WEEK BIG FUN DAY
www.refugee-action.org.uk
Free festival of dance, music, art and food in Queen Square celebrating the contribution to Bristol's community of asylum seekers and refugees. Usually the third Sunday of June and the start of a week of special events.

BRISTOL'S BIGGEST BIKE RIDE
www.bristol-city.gov.uk
Thousands of Bristol cyclists set off from town on a mass cycle ride on a variety of routes. Usually the last Sunday in June.

ST WERBURGHS ART TRAIL
www.stwerburghs.org
Using venues as diverse as the allotments and the climbing centre in Mina Road, SWAT has settled on a late June appearance.

RAT RACE ADVENTURE
www.ratraceadventure.com
A fun urban adventure in which teams of three race on bike, foot, kayak, rope and various other forms of transport. It all happens sometime in late June.

July

ST PAUL'S CARNIVAL
www.bristolurban.org.uk
Legendary street fun in the multi-cultural heart of Bristol. Floats, PA battles, lots of food, drink and nocturnal liveliness. First Saturday of July.

SIKH MELA
www.visitbristol.co.uk
Mela is Punjabi for 'festival'. This one is held in Eastville Park on the first weekend in July and showcases the art, music, culture and food of the city's South Asian community.

PRIDDY FOLK FESTIVAL
www.priddyfolk.org
Mendip folk festival usually held early July.

ST WERBURGHS CITY FARM SUMMER FAIR
www.stwerburghs.org
Music, craft workshops, carnival procession. Big fun. Usually early July.

FROME FESTIVAL
www.fromefestival.co.uk
More than 150 events spread over 10 days in mid July in the artiest town in Somerset.

LAWRENCE WESTON CARNIVAL
www.visitbristol.co.uk
Circus-themed community carnival out in Lawrence Weston in mid July.

LOCKLEAZE FESTIVAL
www.visitbristol.co.uk
Carnival procession, stalls, dance performances centred around Gainsborough Square. Usually in mid July.

Events

Listings

SOUTHMEAD CELEBRATION
www.visitbristol.co.uk
Community carnival, usually held mid July.

ASHTON COURT FESTIVAL
www.ashtoncourtfestival.com
The best event in the Bristol calendar featuring bands, kids events, fairground rides and stalls. Held on the third weekend in July.

BRISTOL HARBOUR FESTIVAL
www.bristol-city.gov.uk/harbourfestival
By day, a chance to explore a host of exotic boats, including tall-ships and naval gunboats, plus stacks of music, markets and performance in Queen Square. By night, a nautically-inspired booze-up with lots of fantastic fireworks. Last weekend in July.

August

AMNESTY INTERNATIONAL GARDEN PARTY
A wonderful and rare opportunity to explore the grounds of Goldney House, one of Bristol's best preserved 18th-Century houses, famous for its grotto. Usually held on the first Sunday in August. Hope for sun!

BRISTOL CHILDREN'S FESTIVAL
www.childrensworldcharity.org
Four days of fun for the nippers up on the Downs. Usually early August.

BRISTOL BALLOON FIESTA
www.bristolfiesta.co.uk
If the tacky cynicism of the funfair and the squawkings of the wannabe 'pop' acts don't appeal, go instead to the Avon Gorge Hotel's patio bar and watch Europe's finest hot-air balloons drift majestically by. Mid August at the Ashton Court Estate

BRISTOL FLOWER SHOW
www.bathandwest.com
Bloomin' great! As the *Evening Post* often reports. Mid August on the Downs.

BRISTOL MARDI GRAS
www.bristolmardigras.org
Gay and lesbian festival that seems to have settled on a mid-August date. All the activities are based down at the Harbourside.

LONDON LESBIAN AND GAY FILM FESTIVAL
www.llgff.org.uk
The tour showcasing the best of lesbian and gay film-making usually pitches up in Bristol in the middle of August at the Watershed and across the water in the Arnolfini.

BRISTOL JAZZ FESTIVAL
www.bristoljazzsoc.co.uk
Whether a stage between the Old Duke and Llandoger Trow in King's Street constitutes a festival is debatable. But let's not be mean spirited. This is a fun event held over the August bank holiday.

September

SOIL ASSOCIATION ORGANIC FOOD FESTIVAL
www.soilassociation.org
This is a huge Harbourside celebration of all things organic and green organised by the Bristol-based Soil Association. The event is so big and popular, it even has it's own Fringe Festival where you might find the likes of the Vienna Vegetable Orchestra. It is usually held the first weekend in September.

INTERNATIONAL FESTIVAL OF KITES
www.kite-festival.org
Huge variety of specialist kites and paraphernalia on display in the sublime kite-flying environment that is Ashton Court. First weekend in September.

DOORS OPEN DAY
www.bristoldoorsopenday.org
Popular event in which the finer private, closed and inaccessible buildings and spaces of Bristol are opened to the public in early September.

STREETS ALIVE
www.streetsalive.net
Cars are kicked off Corn Street and surrounding roads for the Streets Alive annual party. This is a great opportunity to enjoy the centre of Bristol without its usual traffic for a whole day. Lounges, music, join-in art, children's acts and all sorts of entertainment are all part of the attraction. Streets Alive is usually held on the third Saturday in September.

Events

BRISTOL POETRY FESTIVAL
www.poetrycan.co.uk
Couplets, ballads, rhymes, blank verse, conceits, elegies, enjambment and maybe even some iambic pentameter. You'll find it all at this 10-day festival which is usually held around mid September.

BRISTOL HALF MARATHON
www.bristolhalfmarathon.com
13-mile jog which is sometimes sponsored by BUPA but which costs the NHS a fortune in ferrying out-of-breath, blistered people to hospital and treating them. Mid-September.

BRISTOL HARMONICA FESTIVAL
www.bristolfolkhouse.co.uk
Cupped hands and blowing at the Folk House in Park Street usually sometime around the end of September.

October

ROYAL WEST OF ENGLAND ACADEMY
www.rwa.org.uk
There are exhibitions here all year, but one of the highlights is the annual Autumn Exhibition between October and December when more than 600 works of painting, printmaking, sculpture and architecture are selected by open submission.

WILDSCREEN
www.wildscreenfestival.org
Annual filmfest for the wildlife media industry usually starts mid October.

BRISTOL CAJUN AND ZYDECO FESTIVAL
www.bristolcajunfestival.com
A weekend of Louisiana-style music, dance, food and drink at the Folk House. Started in 2004 and seems to have selected a late October regular date.

MIVART OPEN STUDIOS
www.mivartartists.co.uk
This great studio space in a Victorian factory building in Easton is home to a wide rage of artists and performers who usually open their doors for public edification sometime around mid October.

November

FIREWORKS FIESTA
www.fireworksfiesta.co.uk
Huge charity bonfire and rocketfest held on the Downs.

ENCOUNTERS SHORT FILM FESTIVAL
www.encounters-festival.org.uk
Showcases the best in UK and international short filmmaking. Cool scene for aspiring industry types, schmoozers and blaggers. Held at the Watershed usually towards the end of November.

FRONT ROOM ART TRAIL, TOTTERDOWN
www.frontroom.org.uk
Go and look at art in people's front rooms, in their cellars, in their kitchens and even in the pub. Usually the third weekend in November.

NORTH BRISTOL ART TRAIL
www.northbristolartists.co.uk
Big art trail that takes in the entire length of the Gloucester Road from Montpelier to Horfield. Last weekend in November.

December

CREATE CHRISTMAS FAYRE
www.visitbristol.co.uk
Ecological Christmas gifts that won't cost the earth (geddit). Very popular. Come early to avoid the rush. Usually during second weekend in December.

CAROL SINGING AT BRISTOL ZOO
www.bristolzoo.org.uk
It's something of a tradition for many Bristolians to stand round the bonfire, cupping some mulled wine and singing along with gusto to Good King Wenceslas and the rest.

MARSHFIELD MUMMERS
This ancient mystery play is performed on Boxing Day (unless it's a Sunday) by Marshfield villagers wearing costumes made from torn up newspaper. There's carol singing at 10.30am before the Mummers perform the play four times at different points in the village and then adjourn to the Catherine wheel.

Events

Listings **Gay Bristol**

P art of the problem with Bristol's somewhat provincial gay and lesbian scene is that it is cleft in two. The main areas – one centred around Old Market and the other around Frogmore Street – are on opposite sides of the city centre, which means that if you want to do a Saturday night pub crawl taking in all that this great city has to offer, then you are forced to witness the drunken primal soup of humanity which is the Centre after 7pm on a weekend. All I can suggest is that you keep your eyes down and your legs moving and try not to get caught up in an overwhelming gaggle of Vicky Pollard-type character dressed as nurses. Unless that's your kind of thing, of course.

What you will find in either area couldn't exactly be described as the cutting edge of gay culture, but rather a bunch of samey bars and clubs churning out camp house re-mixes of 1970s classics. However, Bristol's scene offers more a first impression suggests. Once you get below the surface, you'll find a friendly and comfortable atmosphere. Many do their hard partying in London and, as a result, the scene has a laid-back 'at home for the weekend' feel. Bristol itself is a liberal-minded place and many mainstream places are 'gay friendly'. The Watershed media centre and its modern art counterpart, the Arnolfini, both have a good selection of queer-themed art, film and dance. **Mark Fletcher**

Pubs & Bars

BAR ORCHID
49-51 West Street
Tel: 373 8109
www.barorchid.co.uk
Another of Bristol's gay bars which has been stripped down and glammed up with cheap veneer. Wireless internet access, food and coffee make this a multi-purpose place. Near the club formerly known as 'Just Winns' which was still under refurbishment as we went to press but rumour has it that the new owners are going to 'show Vibes and the Queen Shilling how it is done'. Handbags at dawn!

ELDON HOUSE
6 Lower Clifton Hill
Formerly gay-owned and still 'gay friendly', this miniature locals pub is somewhat out of the way. It is noteworthy for being one of the few places which gay people visit which also sells real (Bath) ale. With good food and a selection of organic beverages, it is a nice spot for some

lunch and a quiet pint. Don't expect to find it full of mincing queens.

THE ELEPHANT
20 St Nicholas Street
Tel: 925 2820
The Elephant is one of Bristol's longest running gay pubs. Popular with men and women, The Elephant was taken over by new management in 2006 who have installed a free jukebox with a broad selection of tunes. It looks promising – hopefully they will inject some new life into the old girl!

THE GRIFFIN
41 Colston Street
Tel: 930 0444
Relaxed, friendly and unpretentious, The Griffin is one of Bristol's most established gay pubs. The building is over an old slave cellar with tunnels to the docks, but the opportunity has been missed to establish a fetish club down there. As the *Naked Guide* went to press, the owners were busy refurbishing the upstairs area into a lounge bar.

Gay

OLD CASTLE GREEN
46 Gloucester Lane, Old Market
Tel: 330 9140
www.oldcastlegreen.com
Small, friendly pub with wireless internet access, music videos and accommodation.

THE OLD MARKET TAVERN
29 Old Market Street
Tel: 922 6123
www.oldmarkettavern.co.uk
This gay-friendly pub attracts office workers for lunch during the day, but a largely gay crowd from 7pm. It is popular with bears and bikers but extremely friendly to everyone, the OMT has a traditional pub feel with good, honestly priced pub food and a big beer garden out back to enjoy it in.

THE PINEAPPLE
37 St George's Road
Tel: 907 1162
www.pineapplepub.co.uk
This is a large, friendly, comfortable pub with a lively atmosphere. Near Vibes and the Queen Shilling, this is a good place to meet up on a night out, as well as a good spot for a quieter Sunday afternoon pint. Visit the Pineapple website for details of the events and cabaret on offer there, of which there is usually quite a good selection.

PRAGUE
53 Old Market Street
Recently stripped down and tarted up, this venue used to be Bristol's only lesbian bar. It is now a cafe-bar with a free jukebox.

Clubs

CASTROS
72-73 Old Market Street
Tel: 922 07744
www.clubcastro.net
More serious, harder clubbing than Vibes and the Shilling, Castros attracts a varied crowd including straight boys and girls.

CLUB 46
46 West Street, Old Market
Tel: 914 0049
A mixed group of punters frequent Club 46, including TVs, TSs and their admirers. It is located next to a straight pole-dancing club.

TOP 5 ALTERNATIVE GAY DATES

1. MISS QUEEN SHILLING
How about surprising your loved one by singing them a power ballad while wearing fishnets? Held in November, the Miss Queen Shilling amateur drag contest is a raucous affair. Why not throw on a face and get down there?

2. A NIGHT AT THE MOVIES
The Watershed and, more recently, the Arnolfini host films from the London Lesbian and Gay Film Festival which goes on tour around the country in August each year. Follow up the show by a visit to the Watershed bar. Last time I was in there on a Saturday night, it seemed to be some kind of unofficial gay dating night with fresh-faced young same-sex couples on every table. Visit www.llgff.org.uk for more information on the Film Festival.

3. BRISTOL BEAR FIESTA
The Old Market Tavern plays host to an annual weekend-long gathering of Bristol's bears in June. It's a full weekend of barbecue, beer and man breasts. The atmosphere is both friendly and laid back, so if you like your boys to be real men, get your tush into some ill-fitting jeans and join the picnic.

4. THE BIG ONE
Bristol's registry office (0117 903 8888) offers civil partnerships for those who wish to make the ultimate date with their loved one. Follow up the big event with some fine dining at the Hotel du Vin, or perhas a pint down The Elephant – whichever takes your fancy.

5. BRISTOL GAY FETISH PRIDE
Bristol's attempts to get a pride parade or Mardi Gras festival off the ground are always a bit poor. Why not try Bristol Gay Fetish Pride and show your loved one off on a lead? Events include Mr Pierced and a World Dog Show! I've never been myself... I can't think why not.

Gay

Listings

Let's hope punters don't get the two confused or everyone will be in for a surprise.

CLUB WONKY
Zanzibar Rooms, St Nicholas Street
www.clubwonky.com
This is Bristol's answer to Pop Stars – a monthly club night which sells itself as 'for all homos who hate house, trance or technic'. DJ Madam Bernie plays an eclectic alternative selection of both indie and pop. It is well worth a visit if you have grown bored of everything else Bristol has to offer.

LAKOTA
6 Upper York Street
Tel: 942 6208
Lakota has long been listed as 'gay friendly' but it is quite off the circuit and doesn't really pull in a large gay crowd. Still, it is nice to know they care and it might be worth a visit if you are sick of cheesy house and you fancy dancing to some serious techno.

QUEEN SHILLING
9 Frogmore Street
Tel: 926 4342
www.queenshilling.com
One of Bristol's favourite clubs, this is clubbing served with a large slice of cheese. It can often be heaving at the weekend with a friendly mixed crowd.

VIBES
3 Frog Lane, Frogmore Street
Tel: 934 9076
The décor is a little B&Q, however, it remains a really lively place to party. Popular with a young crowd, it doesn't get quite as busy as its better-established neighbour, the Queen Shilling, but it is still pretty damn chocka on a Saturday night.

Shops

CLONE ZONE
45 Colston Street
Tel: 929 7666
www.clonezone.co.uk
Everything a gay man could need – if everything you need is poppers, porn and comedy postcards, that is.

THE COTTAGE
19 West Street, Old Market
Gay sauna. ID required for membership.

Contacts

BRISTOL LESBIAN AND GAY SWITCHBOARD
Tel: 942 0842
www.bristolblags.org.uk
This organisation provides information and support to Bristol's gay, lesbian, bisexual, transgender and transvestite community. The lines are usually open Monday, Wednesday and Thursday from 8pm to 10pm. They are always looking for volunteers to help out if you have some time to spare.

FREEDOM YOUTH
Tel: 337 3677
www.freedomyouth.co.uk
A youth group based in the centre of Bristol, for lesbian, gay and bisexual young people, and those questioning their sexuality aged between 13 and 25.

GAY WEST
Tel: 0870 811 1990
www.gaywest.org.uk
Well-established social and support group for lesbian, gay and bisexual people in the South West, especially for those who find all of the shenanigans listed above a bit too much!

QUEER BRISTOL
www.queerbristol.co.uk
Some of Bristol's smaller bars change hands as often as lady Di changed her outfit. Check out the latest news on Bristol's queer website. The site also offers forums, personal ads and general information about the growing gay scene in Bristol.

TERRENCE HIGGINS TRUST WEST
Aled Richards Centre, 8-10 West Street, Old Market
Tel: 955 1000
The South West base for this well-known national charity. It offers support and advice for people living with AIDS and HIV. This proactive charity does a great deal of outreach and education work within Bristol's gay community.

Gay

Bristol at-a-glance

Get to know Bristol with a quick guide to language, population and some other useful stuff

A note on the lingo

Don't be alarmed the first time you encounter somebody talking in a broad Bristolian accent. The speaker will not harm you. Probably. As with all accents, there are subtle variations across the city, the most obvious one being between a Gloucestershire accent (North and East of the city) and a Somerset burr (South Bristol).

The main linguistic features of the great Bristolian accent include:
The post-vocalic 'R': Pronouncing the R where it occurs after a vowel as in CaRt, PaRty, alaRm, neveR. Asder (ASDA)
The add-on 'er': Most commonly heard in lover (love), slider (playground slide).
Rising intonation: When a statement is made to sound like a question.
The Bristol 'L': Adding an L to the end of words that end in an unstressed vowel as in Australial (Australia), ideal (idea) and areal (area). Also sometimes heard in the middle of words as in drawling (drawing).

For years, speaking in a Bristolian accent was regarded as a sign of simplicity. Indeed, there have been several stories over the years of Bristol footballers having to leave teams from outside Bristol because they or their partners and families got the piss taken out of their accent so badly. But, all that has changed, thankfully. The three main champions of the Bristolian accent are football manager Ian Holloway, *Little Britain*'s Vicky Pollard character and clothing shop Beast, whose Bristolian T-shirts are spreading the word across the world.

Five phrases...
In Bristolian

❶ **Cheers drive**
Thank you bus driver for a safe and pleasant journey.

❷ **Gert lush**
Absolutely wonderful.

❸ **Awright me babber/lover**
Hello.

❹ **Ark at ee**
Listen or look at that.

❺ **Where's ee to?**
Do you by chance know the whereabouts of…?

Flower of Bristol

The Scarlet Lychnis (Lychnis Chalcedonica) or Nonsuch has been associated with Bristol since the Middle Ages when it was known as the Flower of Bristowe. It is thought the flower is native to the Middle East and was imported to Bristol by sea traders, or possibly by returning crusaders. The association of the flower with the city is recognised by Bristol University in the choice of its distinctive colour for academic hoods.

Coat of Arms

Until 1569, the Bristol Coat of Arms was only the shield. The coat of arms with the unicorns and crest was granted to Bristol in 1569 by the College of Arms. The background to the shield is red with a golden ship sailing on blue waves out of a silver castle which stands on a green mound – all signifying Bristol's huge importance as a major port.

Above the shield is a silver helmet, a red wreath and two crossed arms holding a green serpent and golden scales representing wisdom and justice. The unicorns are a symbol of extreme courage, virtue and strength. The motto translates as: 'By virtue and industry'.

Bristol figures

393,400 Bristol population – 2004 estimate

188,200 Males	193,500 Females
80,100 0-17 years	79,900 18-29
166,000 30-64	55,600 65 and over

8.2% are from black or ethnic minority groups

33% of households are single-person

Fallen Comrades

Our tribute to places we liked that have departed since the publication of the first edition of *The Naked Guide to Bristol*.

☀ **The Albert Inn, Bedminster;** The Old Fox, Easton; **The Gin Palace, Old Market;** Hand of God stencil on Totterdown Bridge; **Mixu The Chicken, Totterdown;** Bristol Books, Stokes Croft; **Replay Records, Park Street and Bedminster;** House of Darts, Gloucester Road; **Soup Etc, Hotwells;** The view over Bristol from Park Row blotted out by the Zerodegrees bar; **Eat The Beat, St Nick's Market;** Alterior Clothing, Park Street; **Greenleaf Bookshop, Colston Avenue;** Smiles, Colston Avenue; **Level, Park Row;** Imperial Music, Park Street; **Last floodlight from Eastville Stadium, Eastville;** Bristol North Baths, Gloucester Road; **Old Possums Wine Bar, Redland;** The Bristolian paper.

Phew! it's gone

☀ It took six months to demolish, but Tollgate House has gone. The huge horrendous tower block at the bottom of the M32 was a grim welcome sign for Bristol. It must have been a strong sense of irony that persuaded the Department of the Environment to move into such a monstrous blot on the landscape. Tollgate House was dismantled to make way for the new Broadmead development, surely what replaces it can not be any worse. Can it?

Bibliography

Bibliography

Bristol Books and Publishers
A consortium of most of the city's book publishers who produce local and national titles. To find out more information, please visit their website at www.bristolbooksandpublishers.co.uk. Bristol Books and Publishers also produce a quarterly magazine called *Bristol Review of Books* which you can pick up free of charge in local libraries and book shops.

Beastly Bristol
Julian Lea-Jones
Redcliffe Press, £6.95
ISBN: 1904537529

The Bristol Treasure Island Trail
Long John Silver Trust
Broadcast Books, £4.95
ISBN: 1874092591

A Dictionary of Bristle
Harry Stoke and Vinny Green
Broadcast Books, £5.95
ISBN: 1874092605

Secret Underground Bristol
Sally Watson
Broadcast Books, £14.95
ISBN: 1874092958

**The Street Names of Bristol:
Their Meanings and Origins**
Veronica Smith
Broadcast Books, £11.95
ISBN: 1874092907

Let's Have Coffee: The Tao of Ian Holloway
Alex Murphy
Toilet Books, £4.50
ISBN: 0954417798

Bristol Beyond the Bridge
Michael Manson
Past and Present Press, £8.95
ISBN: 0953208222

**The Titch Hikers' Guide:
Bristol for Families**
Edited by Lindsey Potter
Freedom Guides, £9.99
ISBN: 0953464849

**The Freedom Guide:
Bristol for Young People**
Edited by Lindsey Potter
Freedom Guides, £9.99
ISBN: 0953464857

Children's Bristol
Edited by John Sansom
Redcliffe Press, £8.50
ISBN: 1904537227

Pevsner Architectural Guide to Bristol
Andrew Foyle
Yale University Press, £9.99
ISBN: 0300104421

**From Gothic to Romantic:
Thomas Chatterton's Bristol**
Alistair Heys
Redcliffe Press, £14.95
ISBN: 1904537200

Wall and Piece
Banksy
Century, £20
ISBN: 1844137864

**Bristle: Political Street Expression in
Bristol and the South West**
Edited by Bristle
www.bristle.org.uk, £5

Webliography

www.britishpubguide.com
Regularly updated section on Bristol pubs.

www.hotwells.freeserve.co.uk
Jezza's guide to Bristol is stacked with all manner of local links. It's also a portal to several excellent and informative sites about Hotwells and the city docks.

Bibliography

www.members.lycos.co.uk/brisray/
The best Bristol site ever. Ray has left Bristol now and lives in Indiana, USA. But he's still updating this enormous historical site. It's not only the most comprehensive website about Bristol but the humour and choice of subject matter make it the most genuine.

www.cems.uwe.ac.uk/~rstephen/ livingeaston
The Living Easton pages don't seem to have been updated since 2004, but the archive contains some great research material and is particularly strong on the social and industrial history of Easton.

www.longjohnsilvertrust.co.uk
Support the campaign to introduce a Treasure Island Trail around Bristol's dockside and erect a statue of Long John Silver. We reckon a collossus straddling the floating harbour outside the Industrial Museum would be fine and dandy. Yo-Ho-Ho!

www.beast-clothing.com
Amuse yourself by clicking on the T-shirt slogans for an example of the vernacular.

www.churchcrawler.co.uk
Remarkable site detailing every church in Bristol, usually with a detailed description. Random example: 'St Clement's was a large church on the corner of Houlton Street and Newfoundland Road. The foundation stone was laid on 24 May 1854 and the church was opened in 1855.

www.bristol-city.gov.uk/twinning
For people to get an idea of what international activity goes on in Bristol and the important historical role Bristol has played in promoting world peace, reconciliation and development.

www.camrabristol.org.uk
Beer.

www.venue.co.uk
Venue magazine's web presence is a useful source of listings and reviews. Some decent jokes as well.

www.thecoronationtap.com
More than just a pub website, the Corrie Tap has interesting local links and a regularly updated news section.

www.ashtoncourtfestival.com
Find out how to get involved with Bristol's community festival.

www.cubecinema.com
Details of forthcoming events, of course, but also a massive archive and links to loads of artists who have appeared at Bristol's premier alternative film and performance venue. Check out the Cube Cola section. It's a hoot.

www.lookingatbuildings.org.uk
Pevsner architectural guide online.

www.sweetmart.co.uk
Try the recipes section on the Sweet Mart site.

www.visitbristol.co.uk
Allegedly the all-encompassing Bristol online city guide under the Destination Bristol banner. The idea is that you can plan your trip to Bristol online, from booking a hotel or reserving a restaurant table to reading a city guide. At the time of writing, the concept was still more impressive than the reality.

www.pictturesonwalls.com
The best place to buy Banksy prints. There are loads of other featured artists with a particularly strong Bristol presence from the likes of 3D, Sickboy and Nick Walker.

www.thatbebristle.co.uk
Hilarious spoof of the Northcliffe thisisbristol website. Sadly, the site's creators Vinny Green and Harry Stoke stopped updating it in 2005 but it's still worth dipping into the archive for a giggle.

www.letthemhang.co.uk
Bristol-based version of pictures on walls. A collection of limited edition, hand-screened prints from renowned contemporary graphic artists and designers, street artists and illustrators. Sells the likes of Mr Jago, Sickboy and Will Barras.

LINK TO THE NAKED GUIDE WEBSITE

If you want a reciprocal link between **www.nakedguides.co.uk** and your site, email us through our website.

Index

Index

PROPER BRIZZLE BEERS ME BABBER!

Translation: "Quality Bristol brewed real ales, my friend!"

St Nicholas Market
Corn Street • Bristol

St Nicholas Market - *The best of Bristol's independent retailers are found here in the heart of the Old City. Browse a fantastic selection of products, have a bite to eat and enjoy a friendly and relaxed atmosphere. Shopping at its best.*

Monday – Saturday: 9.30am – 5.00pm

Farmers Market
Every Wednesday on Corn Street 9.30am – 2.30pm

Slow Food Market
1st Sunday of the month, Corn Street 10.00am – 3.00pm

Nails Market
Friday and Saturday, Corn Street 10.00am – 5.00pm

 Something for everyone.

CAFE BAR AL FRESCO DINING LIVE
MUSIC THEATRE COMEDY SUNDAY
MARKETS CREATIVE WORKSPACE
STUDIOS FOR HIRE LIVING SPACE
FILM VENUE ANIMATION STUDIOS
SCIENCE CAFE EXHIBITION SPACE

SOUTH BRISTOL'S
INDEPENDENT
REVOLUTION!

WWW.TOBACCOFACTORY.COM